ALL
MY
HOPE
III

LOREN L. JOHNSON

WESTBOW
PRESS®
A DIVISION OF THOMAS NELSON
& ZONDERVAN

WestBow Press books may be ordered through booksellers or by contacting:

WestBow Press
A Division of Thomas Nelson & Zondervan
1663 Liberty Drive
Bloomington, IN 47403
www.westbowpress.com
844-714-3454

cover and interior images credit: Loren L. Johnson

ISBN: 979-8-3850-2014-0 (sc)
ISBN: 979-8-3850-2015-7 (e)

Library of Congress Control Number: 2024905462

Print information available on the last page.

WestBow Press rev. date: 04/17/2024

REFERENCES

All Scriptures in this book are of the New King James Version. Nelson Thomas studied Bible, and all others will be posted. Copyright 1982 used by Permission. Attention: Bible rights and permissions; P. O. Box 141000 Nashville, TN 37214-1000 All rights reserved

These Scriptures are taken from the (KJV); the Expositors New Testament Counselor's Edition (Modified by Jimmy Swaggart for easier reading.) Commentary by (JSM) Jimmy Swaggart Ministries and translated out of the Original Greek. Copyright 2005,2008. Jimmy Swaggart Ministries P O Box 262550 Baton Rouge, Louisiana 70826-2550 (225)768-7000 Website:www.jsm.orgE-Mail: info@jsm.org

Quotes from the book: "He did it all for you ". pg.39(1) (KCM) Kenneth Copeland Ministry Kenneth & Gloria Copeland's book p.45,46,48,49,66,67,70,80,81. "Reprinted with permission from Kenneth Copeland Ministries".

Source: S. Covington, D. Griffin and R. Dauer. "Helping Men Recover" A program for treating addiction (with a special edition for the Criminal Justice System). San Francisco, CA—Jossey-Bass,2011, rev.2022.

P.P. ——Paraphrasing

Gideon Bible——Forward pages, of the different languages of John 3:16 KJV; and my Heritage; Ch.7 p.33.

NKJV -ref. Commentary: pages 1603;1707;2009;1779;1898;1899 2006;1538;1810;1350.

These are the people most mentioned in my dreams, in this book in no particular order: Matthew Mc Conaughe, Jean Erassarret Sr., Rosie O'Donnell, Sally Fields, Kirk Douglas, Michael Douglas, Robert Downy Jr., Tom Cruise, Sam Steward Sr., Jackie Gleason, John Goodman, Ken Jeong, Michael Landon, Dutch Toews, Robert Duvall, Sylvester Stallion, Kelsey Grammer, Jim Cary, Howard Garlinger, Robert Conrad, Clint Howard, Ron Howard, Robert De Niro, Kathy Bates, Elvis Presley, Arnold Schwarzenegger, Anthony Hopkins, Al Odermann (coworker), Gary and Lorenz Johnson (my brother and Dad) and other family members and friends, Clint Eastwood, Elizabeth Taylor, Richard Burton, Alex Baldwin, Cher Bono, Leonardo Di Caprio, Kate Winslow, Carol Burnett, Nicole M., Bruce Willis, Ed Harris, Sibble Shepherd, and Robert Pastorelli. These names are living, or they have passed on to the next plane of existence. All real people were on my mind and heart to pray for. And note that these Dreams are purely fictional events.

The Merriam-Webster Dictionary Copyright 2016.

Strongs Concordance; Hebrew- Aramaic Greek Translation. The New Strong's Expanded Exhaustive Concordance. Copyright 2001.

Decisions Magazine: After the prayer with God, it says to contact the Evangelist Association. By online: Peace with God.net (English)&(Spanish) PazConDios.net: With free Sign-up weekly E-mail devotional at: billygraham.org/subscription personal discipleship coach @knowJesus.net and ConociendoaJes'us.net. Or write: Christian Guidance Dept. Billy Graham Evangelistic Assoc. 1-Billy Graham Parkway Charlotte, NC 28201-0001 USA E-mail us: help@bgea.org. (US) info@bgea.ca. (Canada) Call us: Toll-free Monday-Friday 8:30 am to 9 pm Saturday 10:30 am to7pm Eastern Time at: (877)247-242 (BGEA) Billy Graham Evangelistic Association.

"Beware! The Lies of Satan" By Pastor Frederick K.C. Price—Founder - Crenshaw Christian Center-Faith-dome—7901 S. Vermont Avenue Los Angeles, Ca. 90044 www.crenshawchristiancenter.netmailing address: PO Box. 90000 Los Angeles, Ca. 90009 Chapter 6 "Lie"— "Thank God for Everything no matter what"

Billy Graham Evangelistic Association—Decision Magazine Junes Addition 2021 by Franklin Graham—story p.4,5. Titled: "Hope in an age of lawlessness"

A book: "Think Better-Live Better" By Joel Osteen; Senior Pastor of Lakewood Church Houston TX-(Victory begins in the mind) E-mail: JoelOsteen.com Hachette Book Group.

And the last chapter of: All My Hope III was written from memory, from the only dream that I dreamt on the outside years ago, from the mid- 1990s to 2000 and when it happened, it was as though I was watching a movie that I haven't seen before, and I retained 90-95% of it. And I immediately wrote it down. I typed it out on the computer back then like a movie script. I even sent a letter to Bruce Willis up in Idaho. But it came back. That's Ok.

Joyce Meyer Ministries-World Missions: Hand of Hope-Book Marker, with a message of hope, that God Loves You. That Joyce Meyer Ministries as well as others mentioned in this book are there to help you and pray for you. To bring you to Christ Jesus, our Lord, and or help build you up in the faith.

And lastly with quotes from my Dad Lorenz G. Johnson; In fond memories of him. Born 1922-2020. Who came to know the lord before his passing, and to whom do I dedicate this series of books too?

"Commentary of the book"

Original date 6-14-21 by Raymundo M. III. I asked Raymundo overall; What he thought about: 'All My Hope III; and were there any inspirational stories in it that touched him, or he could relate to? Were you encouraged or edified by this book?

"He answered, 'It had a good message of prayer, and God's Holy message within the Scriptures, Words, and Jesus. There are better stories and events that come from the book of Revelation, which makes that exciting! Also, strong, respectful, and comfortable stories about what one likes when it comes to the Holy Bible! I was encouraged and edified by this book with a lot of blessings, Amen!'"

TABLE OF CONTENTS

CHAPTER 1

'FORWARD'

p.1 Hello There, as we continue the Journey. This is the third in a series, for your enjoyment and mine. I pray that you will be blessed, and encouraged, as we go through this adventure together. God is for you, not against you. (Jeremiah 29:11) V11) "For I know the thoughts that I think toward you, says the Lord, thought of peace and not of evil, to give you a future and hope. "(Acts 24:15) V15) "I have hope in God, which they also accept, that there will be a resurrection of the dead, both of the just and the unjust."

(Romans 5:1,2)

V1) "Therefore, having been justified by faith, we have peace with God through our Lord Jesus Christ, V2) through whom also we have access by faith to this grace in which we stand, and rejoice in the hope of the glory of God."

(Romans 5:5,8,9)

V5) "Now hope does not disappoint, because the love of God has been poured out in our hearts by the Holy Spirit who was given." V8) "But God demonstrates His own Love toward us, in that while we were still sinners, Christ died for us. V9) Much more then, having now been justified by His blood, we shall be saved from wrath through Him."

This book, and as well, the other two. I give God the glory for the work done on it. This series of books is a Testimony of my life, and the experiences I have had. People, places, and events that I went through. Dreams that I have shared. The family that is on my mind and heart, and also the people, God wanted me to pray for, actors, comedians, and performers.

"GOD CAN"

Every Sunday my bunkie and I encouraged each other with a message and a song. We got our packages that weekend. R&R came to the Gym to distribute the packages. Praise God. Thanks be to God. God can! My bunkie gave testimony of fixing a lady's car. And he knows nothing about car engines or fixing, he says. He stopped on the side of the road behind her. His son recognized the lady as one of his teachers. So, he stopped to see what he could do. To give them a ride or something? The teacher and her child, and the two kids in my bunkies vehicle; Nicole kept saying, look at the engine to get it going. But he kept telling them I don't know anything about engines. But, God can! So, at their persistence, he said a little prayer; 'Father, I know I can't do this, but you can help me with it' So, he had her open the hood latch. And he looked, not knowing what he was looking at. But for something that may be out of place? The only thing he saw was this wire laying down by itself. We'll spark plug wires don't usually fall out, but this one did. He put it back on and became the Hero. But he gives the whole credit to God. Amen. God can! The verses he gave me that go along with this are: (Ps. 107:19-21; Mal. 4:2; Ps. 103:2-8; Matt.19:26). (Whatever we need, God Can; according to His will, do anything we need him to do). He is able, He loves you. Ask, and it will be given unto you. Sometimes we ask for the wrong reasons, and we ask, and it is amiss, meaning that, you may spend it on your pleasures. Your fleshly lusts. If we seek God first. You will be surprised what God will bless with? So (Matt. 7:7-11) says: V7) "Ask, and it will be given to you; p.5 Seek, and you will find; knock, and it will be opened to you. V8) For everyone who asks receives, and he who seeks finds, and to him who knocks, it will be opened. V9) Or what man is there among you who if his son asks for bread, will give him a stone? V10) Or if he asks for a fish, will he give him a serpent? V11) If you then, being evil, know how to give good gifts to your children, how much more will your Father who is in heaven give good things to those who ask Him!" Let's get on with the study; (Ps. 107:19-21) NKJV V19) "Then they cried out to the Lord in their trouble, And He saved them of their distresses. V20) "He sent His word and healed them and delivered them from their destruction. V21) "Oh, that men would give thanks to the lord for His goodness, And His wonderful works to the children of men!" My comment at the end of verse nineteen is that God saved them out of their distress. Oh, give thanks to the Lord our God, He is good! And His mercy endures forever. Amen. Whom God has redeemed from the hand of the enemy. In verse twenty, God sent His Word (Son) and delivered them, (His Word is the beginning and the end, He is the God of the Old Testament as well as the New), and verse twenty-one; If we could just recognize God's hand in things and give God the glory. Oh, that men would give thanks to the Lord for His goodness. As we continue with: (Mal. 4:2) V2) "But to you who fear My name The Sun of Righteousness shall arise with healing in His wings; And you shall go out and grow fat like stall-fed calves." In my bunkies message, he had someone in mind with this Scripture, of an Inmate and his mother sick in the hospital. And God can heal, regardless of what the Doctor says is happening. Not to say doctors are bad; no, they are great, but God is greater. God Can.

(Ps. 103:2-8) V2) Bless the Lord, O my soul, and forget not all His benefits, V3) Who forgives all your iniquities, who heals all your diseases, V4) Who redeems your life from destruction, who crowns you with loving-kindness and tender mercies, V5) Who satisfies your mouth with good things, so that your youth is renewed like the eagles. V6) The lord executes righteousness and justice for all who are oppressed. V7) He made known His ways to Moses, His acts to the children of Israel. V8) The lord is merciful and gracious, slow to anger, and abounding in mercy. In verses two through six, the word reminds us not to forget God, and all his benefits. Who forgives all our iniquities, and heals our diseases? He redeems us and blesses us with good food to eat. And restore strength to our bodies. And God uplifts the downtrodden and those who are oppressed. God can. And in (Matt. 19:26) Nothing is too hard for God. V26) says:

"But Jesus looked at them and said to them, 'With men, this is impossible but with God all things are possible.'" God Can.

"MYSTERY"

This is the topic that kept coming up this week. So, with prayer and pursuing this message of this mystery. This first part is going to be in Colossians in the fourth chapter, verses two to six, in the king James version of Jimmy Swaggart's ministry commentary version, out of the original Greek. (Colo. 4:2-6) and (Eph. 6:18-20).

V2) "Continue in prayer (prayer should be a habit with every believer), And watch in the same (Don't let the habit of prayer be broken) with Thanksgiving (most prayer should be made up of thanksgiving); V3) Withal praying also for us, that God would open unto us a door of utterance (reminds us that even though the spread of the Gospel is under divine direction [Acts 16:7], it is also subject to Satanic hindrance [I-Thess. 2:18], to speak the Mystery of Christ (concerns that which had been previously hidden, but now has been made fully know -The Cross and what it means), for which I am also in bonds (refers to Paul's imprisonment in Rome): V4) That I may make it manifest (preach Christ), as I ought to speak (manifest Christ as Christ ought to be manifested). V5) Walk in wisdom toward them who are without (refers to ordering one behavior), redeeming the time (make wise and sacred use of every opportunity to present Christ). V6) Let your speech be always with Grace (gracious and pleasant), seasoned with salt ("salt" represents the incorruptible word of God), that you may know how you ought to answer every man (as it regards Christ)."

And then (Eph.6:18-20)

V18) Praying always with all prayer and supplication in the Spirit (an incessant pleading until the prayer is answered) [Luke 18:1-8], and watching thereunto (being sensitive to what the Holy Spirit desires) with all perseverance (don't stop) and supplication (petitions and requests) for all Saints (saints praying for other saints); V19) And for me (pray for me), that utterance may be given unto me (pray that the Lord would anoint him to preach and teach), that I may open my mouth boldly (refers to being fearless and confident in the presentation of the Gospel), to make known the Mystery of the Gospel (to properly preach and teach the New Covenant, which is the story of the Cross), V20) For which I am an Ambassador (for Christ) in bonds (a prisoner): that therein I may speak boldly, as I ought to speak (that he would not allow the persecution to stop him from preaching as he should preach)."

(Corinthians 2:6-8)

V6) "However, we speak wisdom among those who are mature, yet not the wisdom of this age, nor of the rulers of this age, who are coming to nothing. V7) But we speak the wisdom of God in a mystery, the hidden wisdom which God ordained before the ages for our glory, which none of the rulers of this age knew; from had they known, they would not have crucified the Lord of glory."

(Corinthians 2:10-16)

V10) "But God has revealed them to us through his Spirit. For the Spirit Searches all things, yes, the deep things of God. V11) For what man knows the things of a man except for the spirit of the man which is in him? Even so, no one knows the things of God except the Spirit of God. V12) Now we have received, not the spirits of the world, but the spirit who is from God, that we might know the things that have been freely given to us by God. V13) These things we also speak, not in the words which man's wisdom teaches but which the Holy Spirit teaches, comparing spiritual things with spiritual. V14) But the natural man does not receive the things of the Spirit of God, for they are foolishness to him; nor can he know them because they are spiritually discerned. V15) But he who is spiritual judges all things, yet he is rightly judged by no one. V16) For who he has known the man of the Lord that he may instruct Him? But we have the mind of Christ."

Loren L. Johnson

(Mark 4:11, 12)

V11) And He (Jesus) said to them (Disciples), To you it has been given to know the mystery of the kingdom of God; but to those who are outside all things come in parables, V12) so that seeing they may see and not perceive, and hearing they may hear and not understand; lest they should turn, (turn away -Greek to repent) And their sins are forgiven them.'"

(Ephesians 1:7-10) V7) "In Him, we have redemption through His blood, the forgiveness of sins, according to the riches of His grace (Is Christ and him crucified) V8) which He made to abound toward us in all wisdom and prudence; V9) Having made known to us the mystery of his will, according to his good pleasure which he purposed in himself, V10) That in the dispensation of the fullness of the times he might gather together in one all things in Christ, both of which are in heaven and which are on earth; in Him."

(Romans 11:25)

"For I do not desire, brethren, that you should be ignorant of this mystery, lest you should be wise in your own opinion, that blindness in the part has happened to Israel until the fullness of the Gentiles has come in." Verse twenty-six talks about all of Israel will be saved, and Salvation was just for Israel. But, after the Cross and the Victory of Jesus destroyed sin and death by dying on the Cross, as an atonement or payment for sin and Death, and destroying the works of the Devil. And not only saving the Jews, but also the Gentiles, and all who would believe in Him. In His death, burial, and resurrection; where God the father raised Jesus Christ from the grave on the third day, according to the Scriptures. And is seated at the right hand of God in the heavens. And believing therein by faith; that we are made righteous by that repenting to God, for our sins and receiving Jesus Christ by faith; we have Salvation, and receive the promise of God, the Holy Spirit as a down payment. And waiting for Jesus Christ's glorious coming, that we who believe have eternal life with Him.

'The purpose of the Mystery'

6

(Ephesians 3:8, 9, 12, 13)

Paul is speaking:

V8)" To me, who am less than the least of all the Saints, this Grace was given, that I should preach among the Gentiles the unsearchable riches of Christ, V9) and to make all see what is the fellowship of the mystery, which is from the beginning of the ages has been hidden in God who created all things through Jesus Christ; V12) In whom we have the boldness and access with confidence through faith in Him. V13) Therefore I ask that you do not lose heart at my tribulations for you, which is your glory." Next: This is where we should thank God and be appreciative of God's amazing Grace. How he allowed this mystery to be fulfilled?

(Ephesians 3:16-21)

V16) ...that He would grant you, according to the riches of His glory, to be strengthened with might through His Spirit in the inner man, V17) that Christ may dwell in your hearts through faith; that you, being rooted and grounded in love, V18) may be able to comprehend with all the saints what is the width and the length and the depth and the height V19) to know the love of Christ which passes knowledge; that you may be filled with all the fullness of God, V20) Now to Him who can do exceedingly abundantly above all that we ask or think, according to the power that works in us, V21) to Him the glory in the church by Christ Jesus to all generations, forever and ever. Amen.

CHAPTER 2

'MOVING DREAM'

I was at a business, with this young man, and he is moving, and he's boxing up, cleaning up, organizing, and desks, here and there. He had musical equipment or something, about to fall one way, all perched on other things. So, I moved it, and it falls down the other way. He said that's OK. He had this music box, and I picked it up. He said I could have it. You just have to have it cleaned out well for the dust. It was like time speeded up. And more was done. And we were in the street of the business complex shopping center outside now. I walked around the corner and saw them with their tractors leveling the dirt. To get ready for asphalt. Time was speeding again. Then I woke up.

"J&K LETTER"

I hope this letter finds all of you in the greatest of spirits, as well as our Lord's favor, and that you are healthy and blessed by the Lord. Don't you just hate it when we get cut off in the phone call, I was hesitant to talk about what I was going to do? Because I couldn't tell you everything of when I get out about my plan, in one or two minutes. Besides I can't do anything without God. I need to correct myself, God willing he allows me the safety network job. Finish writing the second book and get both published. God willing, I have, 'Johnson's homes', a home flipping business, or a small catering business, a box van breakfast business, with room for expansion. Or work at air one radio in some manner, and help with the counseling lines, with my schooling at Harvest Bible University and my bachelor's degree. My counseling certificate, and the Holy Spirit, God willing, He allows me this grace. And I also have an idea for an office supply product. I had been praying about going to other prisons, and the Holy Spirit impressed upon me, that CVSP or Chuckawalla is where I need to go. I don't know why? And I thought I was done there. But I guess I'm not. So, there is still something I need to learn there. (As it happens, I was endorsed to CVSP again, but that was during C0VID-19, and they cut our endorsements, and we all went to Corcoran State Prison. When Mc Farland private prison closed.) Before I get back to Bakersfield, God willing have a special dinner, for me and my family and friends, when the time is right, at Woolgrowers and God willing there will be a place for me to go. I am hoping for a New Hope mission through Harvest Bible University in Wasco, CA. And 10-15 minutes away is AIR-1 Radio, which is in Shafter, CA. I told my brother about getting a fixer-up motorcycle and roadster style and that I would pay him back when I get out. And that way I would have some cheap transportation to go to work in. Signed: LJ

'1ST EX-WIFE DREAM'

My first ex-wife is not married anymore, and we are alone on her double bed, with a canopy. As we are sitting on the side of the bed together. (But, in real life, she is married now.) She is fiddling with these twinkling lights that are there above us. (You know the tiny Christmas lights you would put on a Christmas tree). We were looking at each other and kissed a bit. And then we are on the other section of the bed, and we were dressed. And I gave a deeper kiss to her. And she looked at me funny, and I don't know if she was saying in her body language, I am not interested anymore or I am not sure if we should take this any further. The End (First of all, it is better to verbally communicate with each other, then guess, or miscommunicate with body language).

CHAPTER 3

'Cutie Pie Dream'

My Cellie was talking about old girlfriends, and how they were what he calls, cutie pies. So, Monday night I dreamt about a cutie pie, and I'd seen her before. But don't know where? Except in another dream. In this dream, I am in a two-story house filled with people. In the one room I was in, a man was completely drunk, and wanted to fight. And was using some kind of club or piece of metal, but also ready to pass out any second. I am trying to keep him at bay, and (meaning keep pushing him back away from me), keep him in the middle of the room where he doesn't hurt anyone. And then he passes out, and I grabbed him, so he doesn't fall hard. (The only bad part people were encouraging his bad behavior, and when he asked for a bigger piece of metal, they were trying to get one.) So, in the hallway at the first door to the right, went up to the second floor. And a husband-and-wife couple was helping to hand down this huge piece of metal with arms on it. (It looks like one of those old lamps from the 60s and 70s, a pole with lamps on it, and a spring to hold it to the ceiling). So, he hands it to me from the upstairs balcony, down. Then I see her, I've seen her before. Long dark hair, deep dark shiny pretty eyes. Very nicely dressed and all pristine. With a nice smile. And I wake up.

Loren L. Johnson

'LIVE LONG & PROSPER'

This is one of the messages that my Cellie gave me on a Saturday (Sabbath day). We switched our message day to Saturday with one song. Instead of the three songs Sunday. We added our praise songs to the lord for He is worthy of all praise, honor, and glory. Amen. This message he gave was to live long and prosper. And here are the verses for this study: (Deut.30:19; John 11:25,26; Jere. 29:11; III-John v2; Nehemiah 2:20; Ps. 1:1-3) Let's start with the first one.

(Deut.30:19)

V19) "I called heaven and earth as witnesses today against you, that I have set before your life and death, blessings and cursing; therefore choose life, that both you and your descendants may live;" My take on this scripture is when you read the verses before it and after; God commanded us to ..." love the Lord your God, to walk in His ways, and to keep His commandments, His statutes, and His judgments, that you may live and multiply; and the Lord your God will bless you in the land which you go to possess." Then verse 17 gives a rebuke not to turn away from God, and serve idol gods, even worship them. (Putting them first before God) He says you will perish. Verse 18 emphasizes today. (Meaning, today, is the day of Salvation; today, if you harden not your heart. And today, you turn to the living God.) For you are not promised tomorrow. Turn from sin, and old ways. Put God first in all things. Walk in his ways, and he will bless you in the land which you go to possess.

Reference (NKJV)

V19) ...' heaven and earth as witnesses': all the creation witnessed Moses's instructions, his challenge to the Israelites to love and obey God, and the people's response (in 32:1). Choose... that both you and your descendants May live: The present generations choice would determine the direction of future generations. "(End quote) There is another verse about prolonging your day here on earth. And that is honoring your father and mother. Amen. (Ex.20:12) And (Matt.15:4).

(John 11:25,26)

V25) "Jesus said to her, 'I am the resurrection and the life. He who believes in Me, though he may die, he shall live. V26) And Whoever lives and believes in me shall never die, do you believe this?'" Not only can we live longer on earth, but as well in heaven. If we believe in Jesus for salvation. We will live long and prosper. If we are abiding in Him and obey His Word; walk in His Spirit and His will. We will prosper. We will also suffer for His name's sake. While we are here on earth. (James 1:4) "But let patience have its perfect work, that you may be perfect and complete, lacking nothing."

Reference NKJV (John 11:25-27)

Christ is 'the resurrection' For those who believe and are physically dead He is 'the life' for those who believe and have not yet died. When Jesus asked Martha if she believed, she responded with words similar to the ones John used to describe the purpose of his book (20:31). To have eternal life, a person must place his or her faith in Jesus, who is 'the Christ, the son of God,' who came into the world to bring eternal life to those who believe. (end quote)

Let's go on to the next one :(Jeremiah 29:11)

V11) "For I know the thoughts that I think toward you, says the Lord, thoughts of peace and not of evil, to give you a future and a hope." God wants to give you a future and hope; he wants you to live long and prosper. Like our forefathers in Job, Abraham, Isaac, and Jacob, Noah, and the gospel of John.

You prisoners of hope… Christ in you, the hope of glory… Jesus Christ, our hope; … And… You, a reason for the hope; … Who has this hope in him?…and this…hope does not disappoint.

The three greatest things we have in the Bible are found in: (I-Corinthian 13:13).

V13) "And now abide faith, hope, love, these three; but the greatest of these is love."

We have faith in Christ Jesus our Lord for salvation in his finished work on the cross, and nothing we must do for that free gift of salvation by the grace of God. And we are redeemed by his shed blood on the cross. We have the hope of the resurrection of life eternal in the heavens. And last; and most importantly. We have His love, for God is love. If we are in Christ, and Christ is in us by the Holy Spirit. We will exhibit His Spirit; and will produce fruit in us, and show others that we are His, by are love.

(John 13:35)

V35)" By this, all will know that you are my disciples if you have love for one another."

(III John v2)

V2) "Beloved, I pray that you may prosper in all things and be in health, just as your soul prospers."

John is praying a blessing over his friend and colleague in the Lord. That Gaius who John is writing that he physically and spiritually be well. To live long and prosper.

(Nehemiah 2:20)

V20) So I answered them, and said to them, "The God of heaven himself will prosper us; therefore, we his servants will arise and build, but you have no heritage or right or Memorial in Jerusalem." ....

Reference NKJV 2:20

Nehemiah ignored his opponent's accusations that he was rebelling against the king. He asserted that God was involved in what he was doing. Nehemiah 's motive was not rebellion against the king, but submission to God. 'You have no heritage': Nehemiah indicated that Samaritans and foreign people had no place in Jerusalem (see Ezra 4:3) end quote.

And last Scripture used for this study is: (Ps.1:1-3)

V1)" Blessed is the man who walks not in the council of the ungodly, nor stands in the path of the sinners, nor sits in the seat of the scornful;

V2) But his delight is in the law of the Lord, and in his law, he meditates day and night.

V3) He shall be like a tree planted by the rivers of water, that brings forth its fruit in its season, whose leaf also shall not wither 'And whatever he does shall prosper.'"

This last line is not guaranteed to us. But it can be, when we are walking in God's righteousness, and His faith, and yielding to His will. And that righteous person is always useful and productive to the Lord. Live long and prosper. the end

'DINGHY DREAM'

I was by this stream that was moving along pretty rapidly. Looking up to the mouth of where it was coming from. So, I walked around to the other side of the river and up to the top where the water was coming from. I met my sister Carrie up there and she said, 'do you want to go on a boat ride? 'And I said, 'yes.' So, each of us had our own little boat 'dinghy'. She said, 'the lake is really low, you have to go to the left.' I said 'OK', and off we went to this pond area. We paddled toward the flowing river going out. She went first, and I was about to climb over her in my boat going too fast. So, I steered to the left of her and missed her. Then the water turned into torrents of water flowing and whirling around to miss her. Then turned around to try again, and then I woke up.

CHAPTER 4

'CARPEDIEM'

(Which means to seize the day)

And don't leave God out of it. Sing-Praise/ Talk about God/ What Ever You Do, do it with all your might. Do something good, or talk about something. Do it for the glory of God.

(Ecclesiastes 9:10)

V10) "Whatever your hand finds to do, do it with your might; for there is no work or device or knowledge or wisdom in the grave where you are going."

(Matthew 6:30,33)

V30) "Now if God so clothes the grass of the field, which today is, and tomorrow is thrown into the oven, will he not much more clothe you, O you of little faith?"

V33 "Seek first the kingdom of God and His righteousness and all else will be added unto you."

Loren L. Johnson

(Proverbs 27:1)

V1) "Do not boast about tomorrow, for you do not know what a day may bring forth." We can only say we have this day. Amen!

(Ps. 90:10-12)

V10 "The days of our lives are seventy years; and if by reason of strength they are eighty years, yet their boast is only labor and sorrow; for it is soon cut off, and we fly away."

V11) "Who knows the power of Your anger? For as the fear of You so is Your wrath.

V12) "So teach us to number our days, that we may gain a heart of wisdom."

Live every day, as it is your last; seize the day, or make the most of it. 'Carpediem'. Amen.

(Ps.118:24)

"This is the day the lord has made; we will rejoice and be glad in it."

Rejoice today and now, because you have today. Ask the question, to yourself; what can I do, for the glory of God? Today?

(Ecclesiastes 12:13,14)

V13) "Let us hear the conclusion of the whole matter: Fear God and keep His commandments, For this is man's all, V14) "For God will bring every work into judgment, including every secret thing, Whether good or evil." Fear God, keep His Commandment, this is your whole duty.

'AMAZING GRACE'

Today, God, granted me Grace to the Christian service, and prayer circle. We have an upper-tier and a lower-tier day room. And I got permission, in the beginning, to come out, and even later with different CO's, I was blessed. My Cellie (Bruce), leads the 8:10 pm; which lasts 20 minutes before going in. And he was already out there being a porter. And that's also why I have the open door. Since then, we changed the time, to 7:40 PM, because the day room is over at 8 PM now. Last call of the night to be out except for medical and porters. Phone calls were done at 8:30 PM. Bruce calls his ministry, 'Amazing Grace Ministry'. And a person named Beto; gave scripture, to tell us who we are and that our families are covered in the power of the blood of Christ. That will protect us from all harm. (Coronavirus). Faith in His word, and His blood of redemption. 'Praise God'.

The song Sal was playing on his guitar, with Beto, was:

"Hallelujah"

(Is Hebrew, and in English means "Praise the Lord "). I was accompanying Sal in song, to the Lord.

Beto gave numerous Scriptures: 'El Poder De La Sangre De Jesucristo' A.P. 12:10-11. (Rev.); Exo. 12:3,7,13 (Ex.); Mt. 26:28 un pacto (Matt.); Rom. 5:9 Justification (Rom.); EFE 2:13 Cerca De Dios (Eph.); Col. 1:20 Paz Con Dios. (Col.); I-Juan 1:7 Nos Limpia De Pescado (I-John); A.P. 5:9. Redimidos. (Rev.); Heb. 9:12-14 Limpia La Conciencia (Hebrew).

(Rev. 12:10, 11)

V10) "Then I heard a loud voice saying in heaven, 'Now salvation, and strength, and the kingdom of our God, and the power of His Christ have come, for the accuser of our brethren, who accused them before our God Day and night, has been cast down."

V11) "And they overcame him by the blood of the lamb and by the word of their testimony, and they did not love their lives to the death."

(As a little side note)

When I was in C-SAT-F for almost a year. The same prison Robert Downey Jr. was in, possibly the same yard too, 'F' yard. Anyway, he was before me, and I heard he is the one responsible for donating some glue down commercial carpeting. Most of it was still there in 2016 and 17 and really cut the sound down in the day room. It was being vacuumed every day. So, thank you, for that Mr. Downey.

Also, there were a couple of Christian groups that got together and blessed us with an X-Fest. For entertainment, bicyclers were doing tricks and backflips on a ramp. English and Spanish Christian music were playing. And Testimony's of God 's deliverance, and salvation. There was a woman there who gave me a word from the Spirit of God. And a scripture (Revelation 12:11) "And they (the saints of God) overcame him (the devil) (Satan GK) Diabolos -Strongs #4567) (The word Diabolos signifies a slanderer, one who accuses another.) Hence the name in v10)' the accuser of our brethren'... by the blood of the Lamb (Faith in Christ Jesus our Savior, who was the Lamb of God; the Innocent sinless lamb sacrificed on the cross and shed His blood for humanity; To appease the wrath to come by paying the penalty for sin and death; A debt no one could pay but Him.) and by the word of their testimony,....(By the word of God of sinners professing Christ Jesus as Lord and Savior by faith, and Jesus' finish work on the cross; His ...death, burial, and resurrection, and three days later as God the Father, raised Jesus Christ, (the Son of God) from the grave on the third day according to the Scriptures; and to the sinner who became a saint by his or her belief in Christ Jesus to receive the gift of salvation by Faith, and the Indwelling Holy Spirit, and that faith, in turn, made the believer righteous in Christ, by His Grace from the Almighty God.), and they did not love their lives to the death." (There will be saints of God, dying for their faith in Christ Jesus; back in the day of Jesus' time, the present, and in the future, and as the book of Revelation reveals.)

(Ex. 12:3,7,13)

V3) "Speak to all the congregation of Israel, saying: On the 10th of this month every man shall take for himself a lamb, according to the house of his father, a lamb for a household."

V7) "And they shall take some of the blood and put it on the two door posts and on the lintel of the houses where they eat it."

V13) "Now The blood shall be a sign for you on the houses where you are. And when I see the blood, I will pass over you; and the plague shall not be on you to destroy you when I strike the land of Egypt."

(He is saying, we can apply that faith in Christ Jesus, and the power of His blood now; just as the shadow of that was done, back in the Old Testimony.)

(Matthew 26:28)

V28)" For this is my blood of the new covenant, which is shed for many for the remission of sins."

(In this verse, Jesus is referring to His blood shed on the cross, and using the cup of wine, to represent that which was to take place shortly. This is at the last supper.)

(Romans 5:9)

V9)" Much more then, having now been justified by His blood, we shall be saved from wrath through Him." (If we are blood-bought, children of the faith promise; Holy Ghost filled? We are resting in Christ's work of redemption on the Cross. We are walking in faith now and on the day of Jesus Christ's return. Where all will be fulfilled. And the Complete (Jesus) will be here to take us home. And do not fear or be dismayed.)

(Ephesians 2:13)

V13)" But now in Christ Jesus you who once were far off have been brought near by the blood of Christ."

(Our sins separated us from God, but the blood of Christ brought us near to God the Father. For the veil has been lifted. And we can boldly go to the throne of grace. And receive comfort.)

(Colossians 1:19,20)
'Reconciled in Christ'

V19)" For it pleased the Father that in him all the fullness should dwell, V20)" and by Him to reconcile all things to Himself, by Him, whether things on earth or things in heaven, having made peace through the...

blood of His cross." (V14) Reiterated V20) ..." in whom we have redemption through His Blood, the forgiveness of sins.")

(1-John 1:7)

V7)" But if we walk in the light as He is in the light, we have fellowship with one another, and the blood of Jesus Christ His Son cleanses us from all sin."

(If we keep in step with the Holy Spirit and that light shines through us. And faith and trust in our Savior, His blood cleanses us from all unrighteousness.)

(Revelation 5:9)

V9)" And they sang a new song, saying: You are worthy to take the scroll, and to open its seal; For you were Slain, and have redeemed us to God by Your blood out of every tribe and tongue and people and Nation, ...

(Only Jesus is worthy of opening the seals. As V3) says: V3)" And no one in heaven or on the earth or under the earth was able to open the scroll or to look at it.") And lastly, let's look at (Heb. 9:12-14);

V12)" Not with the blood of goats and calves, but with His own blood he entered the most holy place once for all, having obtained eternal redemption."

V13)" For If the blood of bulls and goats and the ashes of a heifer, sprinkling the unclean, sanctifies for the purifying of the flesh, …

V14)" How much more shall the blood of Christ, who through the eternal Spirit offered Himself without spot to God, cleanse your conscience from dead works to serve the living God?" (Amen).

'TODDLER DREAM'

The dream starts out me measuring a job for new flooring. I am in this big room, about 33'x 100'. (When you are considering carpet for a room; carpet normally comes on a roll 12 feet wide. For this room, I would consider spending a little extra on carpeting and have less carpet seams to deal with, or potential problems down the road. So, I would order three 100-foot cuts, (which is 133 1/3 yards each cut) plus, 2 square yards. Which is 18"x 12'-because the last part of the role is where potential damage can occur, from the forklift Stinger or folds or the cardboard paper pole crease from the factory; when the carpet is still warm on the roll. That crease does not come out easy. (The best way is steam clean) (Your thinking, why do I have to clean my carpet, it's brand new?) Most of the time, it's not that bad. Sometimes, it looks like a carpet cross-seam, when in fact, it isn't. And not to be too exact or net, as we call it in the business, but to add a couple of inches to each cut. (For un-squareness: carpet, rooms, cuts, etc.) And the carpet may come a couple of inches short, on their end. Not only that, but the carpet or pad as it is cooling, it shrinks as it contracts.) Since this is what I use to do, I'm giving you an example:

3-Carpet Cuts of: 12'x100'-133 1/3 yards each + 12'x1'6"- 2yds. +12'x 0'9"-1yd. = 12'x 302'3" = 403 sq. yds. W/ 2-100' Long seams and 1-3' cross seam for the tree. (The tree is in the Dream).

(This is what we call figuring a job by cuts, with a width of 12' wide.) (The other method used by some salesman in the carpet selling business, is a formula of length times width, and divide by nine. Then add 5 to 10% to that amount. This also depends on your room sizes too for fills and waste.)

Now back to the dream, I'm walking, and for the most part, the room is empty. But I'm walking from the long end to the other end. And I see what looks like a tree trunk going up to the ceiling. It's probably about 1 foot or 12 inches in diameter. And I'm thinking to myself, we'll, all I need to do, is to put another cross seam in where I cut the carpet at the tree. And thinking, it isn't unusual to see a tree inside a big building? And keep going. I get to the end wall, and there are kids, lined up. Little one and a half to two years old toddlers lined up, balancing themselves with the wall. One, I was thinking maybe was my new grand baby? And one was like a little android with a wheel on the bottom of his feet. There was about a 1/2 dozen kids there. Why? Woke up. (Maybe because I laid carpet in a DAY-CARE before, and maybe because I'm going to be a grand pa, and maybe I saw on TV, kids with these fancy tennis shoes with wheels on the bottom of them.)

CHAPTER 5

'3-SONG SUN.'

Bruce and I every Sunday now, we sing three songs each to the Lord, "acapella". This Sunday was no different. My selection to honor and praise God was: (The # in the song book.)

Song 1 - #62   'We Exalt Thee'

For Thou, O Lord, Art High Above all the earth Thou art exalted far above All gods. For Thou, O Lord, Art High Above all the earth Thou art exalted far above All gods. And We Exalt Thee, We Exalt Thee We Exalt Thee, Oh—Oh Lord And, we Exalt Thee, We Exalt Thee We Exalt Thee, Oh—Oh Lord.

Song 2 #67   'I Love You, Lord'

I Love You, Lord, and I lift my voice to Worship You O my soul, rejoice!

Take Joy, my King, in what You hear, let it be a sweet, sweet, sound in Your ear.

Song 3 # 0   'He Is Lord'

He is Lord, He is Lord, He has risen from the dead, and He is Lord!

Every knee shall bow, every tongue will confess,

That Jesus Christ is Lord.

'GLEASON / GOODMAN'

I saw John Goodman on a hospital construction job. Second floor, or above floor, with an aluminum square beam trusses to hold the floor up. I was checking out a section, to put something in. And I opened the floor up, and there was about 1 foot to one and a half feet in between floors, and no insulation? It was a cream-colored piece of thin plastic as a ceiling in the floor below. (Suspended ceiling) I said, 'That's all you have in between floors? John says, 'yeah, and to keep it down' (meaning don't talk too loudly. 'Not only that they were using inferior metal from around the corner, at a local supply store.' (The street we were on in real life, is where I got my flooring supplies, and that area is all commercial buildings. There could have been a metal supply store near there, but there was no retirement hospital there.) So, I'm looking for what I need, and to go to the supply store in walking distance. And Jackie Gleason is a workman like me walking over too, to the supply store. He is a really nice guy, he seemed like just one of the guys. As we walked along chatting. Then I woke up.

'NO – BREAKFAST'

This is the first time, since I've been down, no breakfast; and the same for my Cellie. Usually if there isn't going to be a main breakfast or dinner meal, they would give you two sack lunches. But not today. My Cellie said, 'Even San Quentin will feed you up there; you may get beat-up, but you may feel full and satisfied.'

CHAPTER 6

'BE GRATEFUL'

One of my Cellie's messages, at our prayer circle nights. (Ps.105:1-5); (Ps. 34:1-3); (Ps.26:7); (Ps.92:1-4); (Luke 17:12-19).

Let's start with (Ps.105:1-5)

V1)" Oh, thanks to the lord! Call upon His name; Make Known His deeds among the peoples! V2)" Sing to Him, sing psalms to Him; Talk of all his wondrous works! V3)" Glory in His holy name; Let the hearts of those rejoice who seek the Lord! V4)" Seek the Lord and His strength; Seek His face evermore! V5)" Remember His marvelous works which He has done, His wonders, and the judgments of His mouth, O seed of Abraham His servant, you children of Jacob, His chosen ones!"

Next is: (Ps. 34:1-3)

V1)" I will bless the Lord at all times; His praise shall continually be in my mouth. V2) My soul shall make its boast in the Lord; The humble shall hear of it and be glad. V3)" Oh, magnify the Lord with me, and let us exalt His name together."

(Ps.26:7)

V7)" That I may proclaim with the voice of Thanksgiving, and tell of all Your wondrous works."

'Praise God'

(Ps.92:1-4) A Psalm. A Song

...for the Sabbath Day.

V1)" It is good to give thanks to the Lord, and to sing praises to Your name, O most High;

V2)" To declare Your lovingkindness in the morning, and Your faithfulness every night.

V3)" On an instrument of ten strings, on the lute, and on the harp, with harmonious sound.

V4)" For you, Lord, have made me glad through your work; I will triumph in the works of your hands."

And lastly (Luke 17:12-19)

V12)" Then as He entered a certain village, there met him ten men who were lepers, who stood a far off. V13)" And they lifted up their voices and said, 'Jesus, master, have mercy on us!'" V14)" So when He saw them, He said to them, 'Go, show yourselves to the priests.' And so it was that as they went, (That was an example of walking in faith) they were cleansed. V15)" And one of them, when he saw that he was healed, returned, and with a loud voice glorified God, V16)" and fell down on his face at His feet, giving Him thanks. And he was a Samaritan. V17)" So Jesus answered and said, 'were there not ten cleansed? But where are the nine?' V18)" Were there not any found who returned to give glory to God except this foreigner V19)" And He said to him, 'A rise, go your way. ('Your faith has made you well.'") ....

These men had faith, that God could heal them, but nine out of 10, wasn't as grateful as they could have been. I know, I would be a happy camper, if God healed me from leprosy.

God did in fact heal me of what the doctor calls chronic sinusitis and sleep apnea. Chronic: (means it happens often). And sinusitis: (was for me, a virus of the sinus' that went to a bacterial sinus and lung infection, that I used antibiotics every 3 to 4 months). That was in the early 1980s, I was working, laying carpet in this motel / house on Flower Street, In Bakersfield. And the Manager prayed for me, and I didn't have it anymore after that. I received my healing by faith in Christ Jesus. (The mighty healer). Then he said, 'do you want to speak in tongues?' I said, something like 'yes, if it has anything to do with, more of God, I want it.' I was a new Christian then, and I asked him, 'how do I receive it?' He said, 'just raise your hands and start praising God. And thank Him for the gift.' So, I did, and my mouth was moving more than when I do it alone. Angelic words to God that I didn't understand, but God does.

(1-Cor. 14:1,2) 'Praise the Lord'

V1)" pursue love, and desire Spiritual gifts, but especially that you may prophesy. (There are two kinds of prophecy, one forecasts the future, and the other is to preach the word of God.) V2)" For he who speaks in a tongue does not speak to men but to God, for no one Understands him; however, in the spirit he speaks mysteries."

And the second healing was in prison. In 2015-16-time frame. I was diagnosed with a milder case of sleep apnea, in a San Diego hospital. And Sleep Apnea:(Generally people overweight, but not the rule; there's snoring on your back, and times when you stop breathing, wake up, and gasp for air in a panic.) Which I had before coming into prison, and with that extra weight of 225 pounds. Also, it caused high blood pressure. And I was ordered a B-Pap Machine which is a mask for your nose only; and a C-Pap is both for your mouth and nose. But I never used it. Before leaving Chuckawalla, two brothers prayed with me for healing, and I received that healing, before I went to C-SAT-F prison in Corcoran, CA. Then before leaving C-SAT-F, to a private prison, GSMCCF in McFarland, California. I gave the machine to the doctor, and told him; 'I don't need it, and Jesus healed me of that.' 'I have not used it at all, and don't have any symptoms. 'PP

So, concluding Bruce's message in a nutshell was: It's a good thing to praise the Lord; It's a blessing to sing and play musical instruments. And we should be grateful for the little, or a lot. Paul said, I can be content in all things, with food or no food just be grateful. Amen. PP

'REPO DREAM'

This Is a dream of my van getting stolen, or repo-ed. But, the good news, by the end of the dream, I was given back a used van to drive to work, from my friend who made the deal and bought the van. With sales slip and title in hand. (Which we use-to call a pink slip.) And of course, I would pay my friend back for doing that service for me, to keep me working. I would look at this as a blessing from God. The old van disappeared, but God provided a new used one for me to drive. Even though in the dream it seems that I hadn't driven it in a while, I was a little rusty. Not to be in a hurry; look where I was going; yielding to the other drivers; keep checking my mirrors....

I was in the downtown traffic, I got out for some reason, and someone else got in. Then it was gone? So, I was in this parking lot now looking for vans to buy. Then lastly getting a van in an upscale neighborhood. Buying it, driving it out of the driveway. Then scraping mirrors, and turning around in a 'Y' intersection. Then I woke up.

'CONSTR. DREAM'

I was in a big commercial building under construction. Sam Stewart was there checking out the floor work. What was done, and what else needs to be done? In what looks like a kitchen and bar counter. It was the end of the day, and I was tired, but I needed to put this cement patch down, to fill-in these huge cracks and valleys. So, they could dry overnight to be ready to lay more vinyl product tomorrow. Other- wise it would waste a day waiting on patch to dry properly. So, I went up the stairs to the second floor looking for the patch, and I found some; plus, some pails of glue (adhesive). So, I was bringing the buckets down. The floor is wide open, with no walls yet. You can even look out to the sky. But there is another floor above me also. As I was leaving upstairs, In my work gear. There was a group of people together in a circle for something. (In real life that was probably representing our prayer circle in our Dorm, 3B03). (about 10-12 people)

I seem to know them all. I got what I needed and headed back down, with my hands full. I wanted to acknowledge to say I was there. But I couldn't wave, and they called to me before I hit the stairs. So, I stopped and curtsied. Ha, Ha, they said, 'very funny.' (then I woke up)

CHAPTER 7

'TOM DREAM'

The dream starts off with Tom Cruise, was there, near this thing that, I thought was a dream catcher. Except, it was too big and shaped differently. It was more like a funnel of string or rope. Like you would catch water in a container. But, instead of plastic for it, that would roll off easier and develop condensation, from the heat of the sun. It was a rope-shaped netting, like a fishing net. Cone shaped. (Then, it came to me; It was like that movie he did in the desert, with the M-6 Secret Agent lady from England. He had to dive into a funnel of water and go into the underwater computer storage, swap out the computer -card, and open the drain. But he went unconscious, and the English Secret agent did it for him.)

'MY HERITAGE'

I am going to show you what (John 3:16) says in my own two languages which I am first 3/4 Swedish, and 1/4 Norwegian. And two more, in Finnish and English. My grandparents came from a Swedish village in Finland, called Vasa. My grandpa could speak Swedish, Finnish, and English.

Swedish:

Ty sa' 'a'lskade Gud v'a'rlder, att han utgav sin enf'o'dde Son, p'a det

att var och en som tror p'a honom skall icke f'o'rga's, utan hava evigt liv.

Norwegian:

For sa' har Gudelsket verden at han gav sin Sonn, den enba'rne,

forat hver den som tror pa' ham, ikke skal fortapes, men ha evig liv.

Finnish:

Sill'a' niin on Jumala maailmaa rakastanut, ett'a' h'a'n antoi ainok-

aisen Poikansa, ettel yksik'a''a'n, joka h'a'neen uskoo, hukkuisi, vaan

h'a'nell'a' olisi iankaikkinen el'a'm'a'.

English:

(John 3:16)

V16)" For god so loved the world that he gave his only begotten son, that
whoever believes in him should not perish but have everlasting life."

'MAYOR DREAM'

I had a dream, I was working in the mayor's home, laying carpeting in
this small town. And there was a half dozen older ladies who were the
sponsors of this old house. They all had something special in the history
individually in this small community. I didn't see this man personally, but
heard a lot about him, and mostly positive. And I assume he was passed,
if he has caretakers of his home. One of the ladies there mentioned, she
or her relative, was present when the first railroad car came to town. As I

am going in and out of my vehicle for tools and supplies. I get a call from a plumber wanting to do a job for me and has a special on sewer cleaning. I said, ('I don't have the time right now, but thank you and hung up.')

The ladies are all sitting outside waiting patiently to be done. As some of the furniture is sitting outside too. There was the lady from across the street who came over and walked right up the steps into the living room. (Which looked like an office now.) I said, 'Can I help you?,' And she said, 'Oh, so this is the Mayor's house?,' I Replied, 'Yes', she said, 'I have looked at it for years, but I have never came inside.' Then, she turned in the doorway and asked the ladies a question. 'Who was running the 'General Store', 100-200 years ago?' (I didn't get to hear the answer. I had woken-up.)

CHAPTER 8

'KICK-IN' BACK DREAM'

In this dream I was in the back of my RV, and it has a big window toward the back. I was relaxing when a car pulled up behind me and the guy gets out and asks me, 'where is Berkeley Street?' I was in an unfamiliar city, on the side of the road, taking a breather from driving. But I always have resources for the road. A physical map, a G.P.S. device, and possibly a prepared Street guide to my location(s). And before I told the guy for directions, I was remembering in the previous dream, that I was on foot downtown walking and I happen to be on Berkeley Street, as I looked up at the street sign. But it also turns into third Street.

(In real life I couldn't tell you where that street was? Maybe San Francisco California. But about the RV, I use to have one, and be prepared with maps and GPS.

'BARN DREAM'

I had a dream about a Church barn. No, we didn't hold Church Service in the barn. A community church owned or rented this barn. To hold auctions in. It was a regular barn. I assume with barn stuff inside because the doors were shut. You know, farm tools and little animals, or maybe horses. But, if it was used for auctions, I would say it was cleaned out, and

37

chairs brought in, and a podium put in. Possibly electrical, with lighting and a microphone and an amp / with speakers.

Now, the reason I said it was possibly rented. It is the fact, that there were half a dozen large barns on that dirt street, all connected together. And it was out in the country, meaning the dirt road it was on. (As I read on in my notes, as I scribble down in the middle of the night.) I see, we are suppose to set up for an auction. My guess, lights, cooler, chairs, check microphone and general cleaning.

'MULTI-TASK DREAM'

I was dreaming of one job, and one place. Thinking and concentrating on the task at hand for this company. Then I get a call for a different car company job. That I promised the week before to deliver the car that day. (Well, I guess I stretched myself thin, and forgot about the obligation for the second job.) So, I said, to the customer, 'I will get back with you.' (Meaning right away.) Then, I left that job to go check on the second one. (I didn't say I would definitely have your car tonight.) (Because I don't know if the garage is still open now?) As I am leaving at 8:30 PM, and giving an excuse, and that I'll be back shortly. I'm getting on the phone to the garage as I am sitting in my vehicle. And calling to find out the status, and they are closed. So, I called back to the customer and told him the garage is closed now, and I said, 'Sorry for any Inconvenience, and in the morning; first thing. I'll bring it to you, as long as the garage has no Further problems. I'll call you in the morning at 7 AM.

CHAPTER 9

'JESUS RETURN?

This is another brother at amazing Grace ministry; and his name is Jose, and this is his title and scripture; but he briefly got into it, because of time. So, we will look into it a little closer. The Scripture are:

How? I Thess. 4:13-18; I Cor. 15:50-58; Hope? Rom. 8:18-25; I John 2:28-29; 3:1-3; Where/How? Acts 1:11-12; Zech. 14:4-5; Ps. 118:22-29; Mark 11:1-2; 7-10; Matt. 23:39; Luke 19:37-40; I Thess.4:17; Rev. 22:17,20,21.

(His message was Rev.21:1-27) Maranatha (COME) "LORD JESUS"

Let's write these out to see what the Word of God says: (I Thess. 4:13-18)

V13)" But I do not want you to be ignorant, brethren, concerning those who have (fallen asleep), lest you sorrow as others who have no hope.

V14) For if we believe that Jesus died and rose again, even so God will bring with Him those who sleep in Jesus.

V15) For this we say to you by the word of the Lord that we who are alive and remain until the (coming) of the lord will by no means proceed (go before) those who are asleep.

V16) For the Lord himself will descend from heaven with a shout, with the voice of an archangel, and with the Trump of God. And the dead in Christ will rise first.

V17) Then we who are alive and remain shall be caught up together with them in the clouds to meet the Lord in the air. And thus, we shall always be with the Lord. V18) therefore comfort one another with these words."

The first words in parentheses talks about (falling asleep); This is a metaphor for dying. These Old Testament believers, (and had a great faith) believe in the resurrection from the dead at His second coming.

V14– (God will bring with Him those who sleep in Jesus). We know Moses and Elijah at the transfiguration knew the Lord more intimately. And was already translated. V16– (And the dead in Christ will rise first). The Old Testament faith, had to wait till the resurrection of the dead. At the Lord's coming. Depending on their measure of faith in the Messiah to come. V15–The (coming) of the Lord: The word (coming): in the Strongs Concordance #3952 the Greek word parousia literally means "presence". The word was commonly used in the New Testament times to describe the visitation of royalty or some other important person. Thus, that Word signals no ordinary (coming).

(II Corinthians 5:8) ref.

(The presence of the Lord). We have confidence of the resurrection and the presence of the Lord. The New Testament believers, as walking in faith; "We are confident, yes, well pleased rather to be absent from the body and to be present with the lord." In the twinkling of an eye, we will be changed to Immortality.

(I. Cor. 15:50-58). How?

V50)" Now this I say, brethren, that flesh and blood cannot inherit the kingdom of God; nor does corruption inherit incorruption. V51) behold, I tell you a mystery; we shall not all sleep, but we shall all be changed V52) in a moment, in the twinkling of an eye, at the last trumpet. For the trumpet will sound, and the dead will be raised incorruptible, and we shall be changed. V53) For this corruptible must put on incorruptible, and this mortal must put on immortality. V54) So when this corruptible has put on incorruptible, and this mortal has put on immortality, then shall be brought to pass the saying that is written: "Death is swallowed up in victory." V55)" O Death, where is your sting? O Hades, (hell) where is your victory?" V56)" The (sting of death is sin, and the strength of sin is the law.) V57) but thanks be to God, who gives us the victory through our Lord Jesus Christ. V58) Therefore, my beloved brethren, be steadfast, immovable, always abounding in the work of the Lord, knowing that your labor is not in vain in the Lord." In verse 56); So, (The sting of death is sin, and the strength of sin is the law.) In The New Testament, we are not bound by the law anymore, we are under grace. Jesus, himself, fulfill the law. As the perfect Son of Man and became the perfect sacrifice for mankind. That paid the penalty of the law. That price of His shed blood on the cross at Calvary. Paid the ransom for sin and death. That's why there is no more sting, for the believers in Christ Jesus (The Son of God) by faith.

(Romans 8:18-25). Hope?

V18)" For I consider that the sufferings of this present time are not worthy to be compared with the glory which shall be revealed in us. V19) For the earnest expectation of the creation eagerly waits for the revealing of the sons of God. V20) For the creation was subjected to futility (useless), not willingly, but because of Him who subjected it in hope; V21) because the creation itself also will be delivered from the bondage of corruption into the glorious liberty of the children of God. V22) For we know that the whole creation groans and labors with birth pains together until now. V23) Not only that, but we also who have the first fruits of the Spirit, even we ourselves grown within ourselves, eagerly waiting for the adoption the redemption of our body. V24) For we were saved in this Hope, but hope that is seen is not hope; for why does one still hope for what he sees? V25) But if we hope for what we do not see, we eagerly wait for it with perseverance." Let's take the word futility in V20) Ref. NKJV says: Futility, which means "vanity, emptiness" refers to the curse on creation (see Gen.3:17-19).

V17) Then to Adam He said, "because you have heeded the voice of your wife, and have eaten from the tree of which I commanded you, saying, "you shall not eat of it": Cursed is the ground for your sake; In toil you shall eat of it All the days of your life, V18) Both thorns and thistles it shall bring forth for you, and you shall eat the herb of the field. V19) In the sweat of your face you shall eat bread till you return to the ground. For out of it you were taken; For dust you are, and to dust you shall return."

Let's look at Romans 8:20 again; V20)" For the creation was subjected to futility",…(Let's stop there, creation useless, vain, and empty. It wasn't getting better, it was going downhill with no hope)…"not willing," (That the creation was not willing to yield to its Creator) " but because of Him…" (because of Jesus Christ and his mercy, compassion, and grace.)…"who subjected it in hope;" (He, having the Authority and control, wanted His creation to survive, and devised a plan and hope to redeem His creation.) (Through the Father, the Son, and the Holy Spirit.) And the Mystery was revealed to Mankind in Jesus' day. That he was the that hope Himself, to make humanity right. He became the propitiation for mankind. The Lamb of God who takes away the sins of the world. His mission was to die on the cross. It was 'Christ and Him crucified.' Amen.

Let's look at V21) again, "Because the creation itself also will be delivered from the bondage of corruption into the glorious liberty (freedom) of the children of God. "Ref. NKJV Rom. 8:21: Creation awaits the coming glory because it also will be delivered the bondage of corruption further describes the futility of verse 20. Nature is a slave to decay and death because of sin. (End quote)

We our saved, with this hope and our redemption draws near; to be delivered from this mortal tent, and into our glorified bodies to be with our Lord. Amen.

(1- John 2:28-29; 3:1-3)

V28)" And now, little children, abide in Him, that when He appears, we may have confidence and not be ashamed before Him at His coming. V29)

If you know that He is righteous, you know that everyone who practices righteousness is born of Him."

(1- John 3:1-3)

V1)" Behold what manner of love the father has bestowed on us, that we should be called children of God! Therefore, the world does not know us, because it did not know Him. V2) Beloved now we are children of God; and it has not yet been revealed what we shall be, but we know that when He is revealed, we shall be like Him, for we shall see Him as He is. And everyone who has this hope in Him purifies himself, just as He is pure."

Ref. (NKJV) 3:1 (Behold what manner of Love): John stands in amazement of God 's love. But the greater amazement and appreciation is for the fact that God 's love is expressed to human beings, that Christians are included in His family. God loves all believers, the week as well as the strong. John describes Jesus on the night of His betrayal as 'having loved His own who were in the world', and writes that, 'He loved them to the end '(John 13:1) God's love is in stark contrast to the love of the world. The world loves those who love them, while God loves even those who disobey him.

3:2 (Be like Him): though we do not know all the specifics of our future existence, we do know that we will have a body like Christ (see Phil.3:21). Believers will put on immortality and become free from the sin nature that presently plagues us.

3:3 (Everyone who has the hope): of seeing Christ and being like Him(v2) realizes that Christ is morally pure. This realization helps a person pursue purity even more. (end quote)

(Acts 1:11-12) Where/How?

(Two men in white apparel) V11) .... who also said, "Men of Galilee, why do you stand gazing up into heaven? This same Jesus, who was taken up from you into heaven, will so come in like manner as you saw Him go into heaven." V12) Then they return to Jerusalem from the Mount called Olivet, which is near Jerusalem, a Sabbath day's journey.

As we see from these verses, that Jesus ascended from the Mount called Olivet, and the two men who stood in white apparel (2-Angels) said, 'Jesus will return in like manner.' This answers the question where, and how is in v9) ...He was taken up, and a cloud received Him out of their sight." And now what is a Sabbath day journey? Ref. (NKJV)

"A Sabbath day's journey"

(1:12) referred to the distance a Jew could travel on the Sabbath (Saturday) without breaking the law. This distance was usually reckoned to be about "2000 Cubits" (About 1000 yards 10 football fields long) because of the distance between the ark of the covenant and the rest of the Israelite camp in the wilderness (Joshua 3:4).

The idea was that every person within the camp or city would be close enough to the center of worship to take part in the services without having to travel such a great distance that the Sabbath became a harried (worry or harass) and busy day. This law, although noble in intent, was soon abused by a strict legalism. In the New Testament, Jesus often clashed with the Pharisees because of their blind legalism over observance of the Sabbath (Matt. 12:1-9). (end quote)

(Zech. 14:4-5)

'The Day of the Lord'

V4)" And in that day his feet will stand on the mount of olives, which faces Jerusalem on the east, And the mount of olives shall be split in two, from east to the west, making a very large valley; Half of the mountain shall move toward the north and half of it toward the south. V5) then you shall flee through My mountain valley, For the Mountain Valley shall reach to Azal. Yes, you shall flee as you fled from the earthquake in the days of Uzziah king of Judah. Thus, the Lord my God will come, And all the saints with You."

Here again we see where, and now, Jesus we care for the Israelites. The Jewish people of modern day. At Jesus second coming.

(Ps. 118:22-29)

V22)" The stone which the builders rejected Has become the chief cornerstone (Jesus) V23) This was the Lord's doing; It is marvelous in our eyes. V24) This is the day the lord has made; we will rejoice and be glad in it. V25) Save now, I pray, O Lord; O Lord, I pray, send now prosperity. V26) Blessed is he who comes in the name of the Lord! We have blessed you from the house of the Lord. V27) God is the Lord, and he has given us light; Bind the sacrifice with cords to the horns of the altar. V28) You are my God, and I will praise you; You are my God, I will exalt You. V29) Oh, give thanks to the lord, for He is good! For His mercy endures forever."

(Mark 11:1-2;7-10)

V1)" Now when they drew near Jerusalem, to Bethphage and Bethany, at the Mount of Olives, He sent two of His disciples; V2) and He said to them, "Go into the village opposite you; and as soon as you have entered it you will find a colt tied, on which no one has sat. Loose it and bring it." V7)" Then they brought the colt to Jesus and threw their clothes on it, and He sat on it. V8) And many spread their clothes on the road, and others cut down leafy branches from the trees and spread them on the road. V9) Then those who went before and those who followed cried out, saying: "Hosanna! 'Blessed is He who comes in the name of the Lord!' V10) Blessed is the kingdom of our father David that comes in the name of the Lord! Hosanna in the highest!"

This is the prophetic entry of King Jesus entering Jerusalem. And the citizens singing (Ps. 118:25,26); And Jesus riding a lowly donkey. (Zech. 9:9)

'The Coming King'

V9)" Rejoice greatly, O daughter of Zion! Shout, O daughter of Jerusalem! Behold, your king is coming to you; He is just and having salvation, lowly and riding on a donkey, a colt, the foal of a donkey."

(Matt.23:39)

V39) ...." or I say to you, you shall see Me no more till you say, 'Blessed is he who comes in the name of the Lord!'"

(Luke 19:37-40)

V37) Then, as He was now drawing near the descent of the mount of olives, the whole multitude of the disciples began to rejoice and praise God with a loud voice for all the mighty works they had seen, V38) saying: "'Blessed is the King who comes in the name of the Lord!' Peace in the heaven and glory in the highest.' V39) And some of the Pharisees called to him from the crowd, 'Teacher, rebuke Your disciples.' "V40) But He answered and said to them, 'I tell you that if these should keep silent, the stones would immediately cry out.'"

(I Thess. 4:17)

V17)" Then we who are alive and remain shall be caught up together with them in the clouds to meet the Lord in the air. And thus, we shall always be with the Lord."

(Rev. 22:17,20,21)

V17)" And the Spirit and the bride say, 'Come!' And let him who hears say, 'Come!' And let him who thirst come. Whoever desires, let him take the water of life freely." V20) "He who testifies to these things says, 'Surely I am coming quickly.' Amen. Even so, come, Lord Jesus! V21) The Grace of our Lord Jesus Christ be with you all. Amen."

His message was: (Rev.21:1-27)

When God restores all things and completes the revelation of the Bible. Chapter 21 is all about God making all things new. A new heaven and a new earth. And a new holy city, a new Jerusalem. We need to continue our faith in Christ till the end. And when he comes to receive His bride, the Church and take us Home. To a place He has provided for us. Our father has many mansions. We need to be overcomers, as in verse seven.

V7)" He who overcomes shall inherit all things, and I will be his God, and he shall be My son."

'BOSS DREAM'

I was working in this house coordinating with all these bosses, and we were working on two houses at the same time. And they seem interconnected, but they're not. It's just that the fence isn't put in yet, and you can just walk through the other home. Because I was walking with one boss and explaining what we are going to do. But it is more like the bosses and I are a team. And my 1st ex-wife was there, and we walked through on the right house. And she came out on the left home's driveway. I said, goodbye to the one boss, as we are walking up the sidewalk to the other. I said, 'I need to check the logbook, on this vehicle, and say goodbye to my ex-wife. Who was watching and listening, and taking it all in. She was very quiet. And was about to tell me something, when the cell doors popped unexpectedly, for chow, and woke me up. So, I jumped up to receive the food. In the mornings, we have been getting cell-fed. Because of 3-602's down the way, that missed breakfast a few times. But, at dinner, we go and get it. I would call this dorm, the old man dorm. I would say at least half, if not more are over 50 years old. We have some in their 70's. So, those men down the way, we're sleeping through breakfast chow. So, everyone gets fed now.

'KIRK & SALLY DREAM'

I had a brief dream, very vivid of Sally Fields on a set, being interviewed. She always looked cute and adorable. She was more mature in this dream. She had short salt and pepper hair color. She was talking, and then stopped, paused like she was honoring someone, with a moment of silence. Then another flash of a picture of an older great movie star (Kirk Douglas). Except the picture, he is young. And I am sure it was him; and not his son, (Michael Douglas). Everyone could use a little prayer. The Lord revealed to me through the Holy Spirit, that he wanted me to pray for these individuals and others. These people just happen to be famous. It is not uncommon for a believer in Jesus Christ (The Son of God for Salvation by faith in Him and His finished work on the Cross at Calvary). To pray for other people. Not only do I pray for you, but Jesus Christ prays for you too, and the Holy Spirit also intercedes for you too.

CHAPTER 10

'RV AUNT DREAM'

I was at my Aunt Niama's on the floor, just hanging out, they were both there watching TV in the den. And I got up and said, 'goodbye', and went out the front door, back to my RV. And the front had some pretty bushes and flowers.

But before this, it seemed I was along the side of the road sleeping. But not permanent. But, wasn't comfortable. So, anyway I traveled what seemed across the street and started setting up my bed again, near the sidewalk where I was just at. Except The RV is right behind me, and was going to go back in there. But, as I started getting back in what seemed the hard way, backwards and in the dark. I realized, I don't have my wallet and so I ran across the street.

Back to my aunt and Uncle John's house where I thought my wallet fell out while watching TV together. And I walked right in and started looking around. And my aunt comes in, and ask me, 'what happened?' And I said, 'I lost my wallet, and reached for my pocket and it wasn't there? I reached back again, and it was there all along. So, I left there and started back, and this time I locked the door and left as she is helping me close it.

As I hurry back to where I was at the RV. She ran out, behind me and ran across the grass. And I am using the front sidewalk to the house. And we met up in about the same place and I see her running across the grass. And I was about to kiddingly tell her, you look just like my Aunt Niama, and then asked her, 'What are you doing out here? I thought you two were going to bed?' But I woke up first.

'GARAGE/CHAPEL DREAM'

I was driving down this alley to go to this car garage to put my van in for repairs. This auto garage was very small, and cars were all over. But I saw a place to park or basically back into the parking spot with my van. I really didn't want to wait, I preferred to drop it off at a later time.

So, the dream shifts a little when I go in; I am at a church chapel, with about 10 long pews on each side. I sat up near the front to the left. As I am waiting in there. I see other people waiting too, except they're like waiting for something to happen. The people there are inmates with uniforms on, all spaced out from each other because of the coronavirus, I Imagine.

The two old gentlemen stepped up. One big guy with his hair all messed up and started the show And one nicely dressed man in a suit, slender in size, and sat down at what looks like a grand piano. He started playing some Christian music, and I liked that.

And halfway through, he stops and says a few words. There were just a couple of us clapping at his performance. I looked back, and see a guy sleeping six rows back, and it looks like he's laying down, and breathing this giant party favor. As he is breathing it in and out. And then I woke up.

'SUPERHERO DREAM'

There were these two gangs. A small army, and this big, organized gang. I imagine there was a challenge made, because we are headed for this big fight with pistols, automatic rifles, bazookas, and flamethrowers, and handheld missile launchers.

But we never got that far, let me back up a little. It started when this small gang went over to the rival gang's mansion. They must have taken out the guards. Because, they were in this six-car garage, and all the cars were out somewhere? It was dark in there, with one bad guy, against three that came out of the house. One had a head, but no body? Then the big guy drop kicked the head and took out the other two in the dark, with a little light coming through the door. The head was talking to them before this, saying, 'What are you doing here? Shine that light over here.' That's about the time he gets the dropkick in the head and hits the wall.

Back at the confrontation, each of the two gangs were about 50 to 75 yards or 150 to 200 feet away from each other. There was a building way off to the left, and to the right was open fields, literally acres of just dirt. Except these rock planters, there was 3 to 4 rock planters spaced about 10 to 15 feet apart, in a diamond shaped. The rocks and cement planters are about 2 1/2 feet high filled with dirt and a shade tree in each. It was about 10 to 12 feet square, and it made it great for gun fire cover. They had them as well. I was first there and got behind the planter in the front. And there was a big convoy behind me. Even a big 18-wheel tanker full of fuel. That didn't sound so good if it blows up? It's too far for a flame thrower anyway, it doesn't need to be there. Then I am firing away with a semi-automatic pistol, shooting at rocks and metal. And two magazines later; was like being out at the range shooting with targets too far away.

(Like my coworker and I did on a job up in the mountains on private property, and permission. We set up some targets and fired at them. We mainly fired at cans and bottles, but we didn't hit much; it was too far.)

Besides that, in the dream, I brought a pistol to an automatic rifle and grenade launcher fight. Automatic rifle firing coming my way, then a bazooka missile went right behind me, and hit the planter behind me. And exploded with rocks flying everywhere. I fell back, I'm not prepared for this kind of battle. (Besides in real life, I am not a gang member or unlawfully out on the street; just a flooring contractor, with a work-related injury and using alcohol and ice packs for nerve pain and got out of control.)

Meanwhile at the garage where the confrontation started. There were rollup doors to this garage. And one was partially open. And this Asian guy, who had superpowers came down and did the splits, and went under the door. This yellow energy was flowing out of his legs and arms to fly. He goes in and sees the damage and goes out. And there was someone else there, just like him, flying too. (I imagine they were going to fly out to where we were and stop the whole fight before it gets too bad.) Then I woke up. P.S. (Later I recognized who the Asian guy was, it was Ken Jeong).

CHAPTER 11

'THE MOUNT'

(KJV)(JSM) With commentary:

'Jimmy Swaggart Ministry'

This is the sermon on the mount; Jesus'-most poetic words ever expressed. And with the commentary help explain to the average layman, The expression, more of Jesus' perfect intent. By the Greek Translation.

My Sister said that Jesus' words were most important, and even gave me a book of just Jesus's words alone. But we also must make complete sentences with that, and the occasions of what was being said. —Let's start reading Matthew chapter 5 through seven. Amen. (Black letters are fill words; purple is commentary; and red is Jesus 's words.)

(Matthew 5:1-48; 6:1-34; 7:1-29)

5:1) And seeing the multitudes, He went up into a mountain (unknown, but probably was a small mountain near the Sea of Galilee; two sermons, both delivered on mountains, opened and closed the Lord's public Ministry; the last was upon Olivet near Jerusalem [Matthew chapter 24]): and when He was set, (He sat down in order to teach, which was the custom at that time), His Disciples came unto Him (referring not to the 12, but to any and all who closely followed him at that time): V2) And He opened his Mouth (signifying a carefully thought-out Message of purpose and will), and taught them, saying, (begins the greatest moment of spiritual and Scriptural instruction that had ever been given in the history of mankind), V3) Blessed (happy) are the poor in spirit (conscious of moral poverty): for theirs is the Kingdom of Heaven (the moral characteristics of the citizens of the Kingdom of the heavens; and so it is apparent that the New Birth is an absolute necessity for entrance into that Kingdom [John 3:3]; this Kingdom is now present spiritually, but not yet physically). V4) Blessed are they who mourn (grieved because of personal sinfulness): for they shall be comforted (What the Holy Spirit will do for those who properly evaluate their spiritual poverty). V5) Blessed are the meek (the opposite of the self-righteous; the first two Beatitudes guarantee the "meekness") for they shall inherit the earth (speak of the coming Kingdom Age, when the "Kingdom of Heaven" will be brought down to Earth, when the Saint's will rule, with Christ as its Supreme Lord). V6) Blessed are they which do hunger and thirst (intense desire) after Righteousness (God 's Righteousness, imputed by Christ, upon Faith in His Finished Work): for they shall be filled (but first of all must be truly empty of all self-worth). V7) Blessed are the merciful (shows itself in action which goes beyond the thought): for they shall obtain mercy (to obtain mercy from God, we must show mercy to others). V8) Blessed are the pure in heart (those who have received a new moral nature in regeneration): for they shall see God (will see Him manifest Himself in one's life). V9) Blessed are the peacemakers (pertains to peace with God, which comes with Salvation, and all who proclaim such are called "peacemakers") for they shall be called the Children of God (expresses the "peacemaker" and the one who has received the "peace"). V10) Blessed are they which are persecuted for Righteousness' sake (means that those who operate from the realm of self-righteousness will persecute those who trust in God's "Righteousness"): for theirs is the Kingdom of Heaven (having God's Righteousness, which is solely in Christ, such have the Kingdom of Heaven). ...

V11) Blessed are you, when men shall revile you, and persecute you, and shall say all manner of evil against you falsely, for My sake (only Christ could say, "For My sake," for He is God; there is an offense to the Cross [Galatians 5:11]). V12) Rejoice(the present inner result of one who is "blessed"), and be exceedingly glad (self-righteousness persecuting Righteousness is the guarantee of the possession of Righteousness, and the occasion for great joy): for great is your reward in Heaven (meaning it will not necessarily come while on Earth): for so persecuted they the Prophets which were before you (presents the fact that "God's Way" will bring "persecution," severely so, at times by both the world and the Church). V13) You are the salt (preservative) of the Earth: but if the salt has lost his flavor, wherewith shall it be salted? it is henceforth good for nothing, but to be cast out, and be in to be trodden under foot of men ("Salt" is a type of the Word of God; the professing Believer who no longer holds to the Word is of no use to God or man). V14) You are the Light of the world (we are a reflector of the Light which comes from Christ). A city that is set on a hill cannot be hid (proper light will not, and in fact, cannot be hid). V15) Neither do men light a candle, and put it under a bushel, but on a candlestick (the light is not to be hid); and it gives light unto all who are in the house (that is the purpose of the light). V16) Let your light so shine before men, that they may see your good works (proper Faith will always produce proper works, but proper works will never produce proper Faith), and glorify your Father which is in Heaven (proper works will glorify our Heavenly Father, while improper works glorify man). V17) Think not that I am come to destroy the Law (this was the law of Moses), or the Prophets (the predictions of the Prophets of the Old Testament): I am not come to destroy, but to fulfill (Jesus fulfilled the law by meeting it's just demands with a perfect life, and satisfying its curse by dying on the Cross. [Gal.3:13]). V18) For verily I say unto you (proclaim the ultimate authority!), Till heaven and earth pass (means to be changed, or pass from one condition to another, which will take place in the coming Perfect Age [Rev. Ch. 21-22], one jot (smallest letter in the Hebrew alphabet) or one tittle (a minute ornamental finish to ancient Hebrew letters) shall in no wise pass from the Law, till all be fulfilled(the Law was meant to be fulfilled in Christ, and was in fact, totally fulfilled by Christ, in His Life, Death, and Resurrection, with A New Testament or New Covenant being brought about [Acts 15:5-29; Rom.10:4; II Cor. 3:6-15; Gal. 3:19-25; 4:21-31; 5:1-5,18; Eph.2:15; Col.2:14-17]). V19) Whosoever therefore shall break one of these least Commandments, and shall teach men so, he shall be called the least in the Kingdom of Heaven (those who are disloyal to the authority of the Word of God shall be judged; "He shall be called the least, " means that he will not be in the Kingdom at all): but who-soever shall do and teach them, the same shall be called great in the Kingdom of Heaven (the Lord sets the Bible as the Standard of all Righteousness, and He recognizes no other). V20) For I say unto you, that except your righteousness shall exceed the righteousness of the Scribes and Pharisees (which was self-righteousness), you shall in no case enter that into the Kingdom of Heaven (the absolute necessity of the New Birth is declared here as imperative in every case). V21) You have heard that it was said by them of all time (referring back to the Law of Moses), Thou shall not kill (should have been translated, You shall not murder); and whosoever shall kill (murder) shall be in danger of the judgment (Ex. 20:13; Lev. 24:21; Num., Chpt.35; Deut. 5:17; 19:12); V22) But I say unto you (Christ gives the true interpretation of the Bible, with in fact, the Bible and Christ, in essence, being one and the same), That whosoever is angry with his brother without a cause (places unjust anger in the same category as murder, i.e., "springs from an evil heart") shall be in danger of the judgment (certain of judgment): and whosoever shall say to his brother, Raca (the words "Raca" and "thou fool" were Hebrew expressions of murderous anger), shall be in danger of the Council (Sanhedrin): but whosoever shall say, Thou fool, shall be in danger of hell fire (men may beat justice in a human court of law, but will never do such in God's Court of Law).

V23) Therefore if you bring your gift to the Altar (referring to the Brazen Alter as used in the offering of Sacrifices in the Law of Moses), and there remember that your brother has ought against you (is meant to describe our relationship with our fellow man); V24) Leave there your gift before the Alter (the intimidation is that the Lord will not accept our "gift" unless we do all within our power to make things right with the offended party), and go your way(make every effort to bring about reconciliation, if at all possible); first be reconciled to your brother, and then come and offer your gift (worship will not be accepted by the Lord, if we have wronged our brother, and have not done all within our power to make amends). V25) Agree with your adversary quickly, while you are in the way with him (if we offend our brother and do not make amends, the Lord becomes our adversary, or opponent, which places one in a serious situation indeed); lest at any time the adversary deliver you to the judge, and the judge deliver you to the officer, and you be cast into prison (regarding a Believer who offends a fellow Christian, and will not make amends, God becomes that person's Adversary, and thereby is Judge instead of his Savior, and thereby, spiritually speaking, puts such a person in a spiritual prison). V26) Verily I say unto you (the absolute solemnity of this statement), You shall by no means come out thence (come out of this spiritual prison), till you have paid the uttermost farther (the Lord's method of teaching was symbolic and figurative; if the Believer doesn't make amends with his fellow man who he has wronged, he will suffer one reverse after the other; God will see to it). V27) You have heard that it was said by them of old time (the Mosaic Law), You shall not commit adultery (the Seventh Commandment [Ex. 20:14]). V28) But I say unto you (the phrase does not deny the Law of Moses, but rather takes it to its conclusion, which could only be done by Christ; the Old Covenant pointed the way to the New Covenant, which came with Christ), That whosoever looks on a woman to lust after her(to look with intense sexual desire) has committed adultery with her already in his heart (the Lord addresses the root of sin, which is an evil heart; the Cross is the only answer). V29) And if your right eye offend you, pluck it out, and cast it from you (as stated, the Lord's method of teaching was symbolic and figurative): for it is profitable for you that one of your members should perish, and not that your whole body should be cast into Hell (the Lord does not intend for His statement to be taken literally, as He has already explained that the offence is not in the "eye "or "hand, " but, instead, the heart!; in effect, a blind man can lust). V30) And if your right hand offend you, cut it off, and cast it from you: for it is profitable for you that one of your members should perish, and not that your whole body should be cast into Hell (showing the fact that if such action is not stopped, the person will lose their soul; as stated, the Cross is the only means by which evil passions can be subdued [Rom. 6:3-5, 11, 14]). V31) It has been said, (Deut.24:1-4), Whosoever shall put away his wife (refers to divorce proceedings), let him give her a writing of divorcement (the Jews had perverted the Law, greatly weakening the sanctity of marriage): V32) But I say unto you (the Lord now gives the true meaning of the Law), That whosoever shall put away his wife (divorce her), saving for the cause of fornication (cohabiting with others, thereby breaking the marriage vows), causes her to commit adultery (if she marries someone else, but the intimation is that the fault is not hers): and whosoever shall marry her who is divorced commits adultery (the man who marries the woman who is divorced unscripturally, even though it's not her fault, commits adultery as well; we should learn here the sanctity of marriage, with divorce and remarriage allowed only on the grounds of fornication and spiritual desertion [I Cor. 7:10-11]). V33) Again, you have heard that it has been said by them of old time (such phraseology means that the Word of God had been twisted to mean something it did not say), You shall not forswear yourself, but shall perform unto the Lord your oaths (Vss. 33-37 have to do with the Third Commandment, "You shall not take the Name of the Lord your God in vain" [Ex. 20:7]):

V34) But I say unto you (proclaiming the true meaning of the Law), Swear not at all; neither by Heaven; for it is God's Throne (this has nothing to do with profanity, but rather a flippantly using God's Name): V35) Nor by the earth; for it is His footstool: neither by Jerusalem; for it is the city of the great King (not only must the Name of God not be flippantly used, but as well, His Creation is off limits also). V36) Neither shall you swear by your head, because you cannot make one hair white or black (man is God's highest creation). V37) But let your communication be (verbal communication with others), Yes, yes; No, no: for whatsoever is more than these cones of evil (the followers of Christ must stand out by their truthfulness, honesty, and integrity; subterfuge and doubletalk are out). V38) You have heard that it has been said, an eye for an eye, and a tooth for a tooth ([Ex. 21:24; Lev. 24:20; Deut. 19:21]; the letter of the Law was that which God would carry out in His Own way [Mat. 7:2] man was not to resort to such, even as Jesus will now say): V39) But I say unto you, that you resist not evil (do not reward evil with evil): but whosoever shall smite you on the right cheek, turn to him the other also (once again, the language is figurative, for the Lord when smitten on the cheek [Jn. 18:22-23] did not turn the other cheek but with dignity rebuked the assailant). V40) And if any man will sue you at the law, and take away your coat, let him have your cloak also (this does not refer to righteous action, which is something necessary, but rather to a contentious spirit, which demands one's rights, down to the minute detail). V41) And whosoever shall compel you to go a mile, go with him two (the entirety of the idea has to do with the heart of man, not so much his outward actions, but which most surely would guide his actions accordingly). V42) Give to him who asks of you, and from him who would borrow of you turn not you away (this pertains to those truly in need, and not those who are lazy and will not work [II Thess. 3:10]). V43) You have heard that it has been said, you shall love your neighbor, and hate your enemy (once again, Christ is correcting the perversion of Scripture; the "hating of the enemy "probably derived from Deuteronomy 7:1-6; but nowhere in that Passage does it say to hate the enemy; while we are to hate the sin, we are not to hate the sinner [John 3:16]). V44) But I say unto you, love your enemies, bless them who curse you, do good to them who hate you, and pray for them which despitefully use you, and persecute you... (the actions of the enemies of goodness and of righteousness are to be "hated" with a holy hatred; but personal hatred is to be met by love); V45) That you may be the Children of your Father which is in Heaven: for He makes His sun to rise on the evil and on the good, and sends rain on the just and on the unjust (we are to imitate our Heavenly Father). V46) For if you love them which love you, what reward have you? do not even the publicans the same? (Only those who have the true Love of God in their hearts can love those who do not love them.) V47) And if you salute your brethren only, what do you more than others? do not even the publicans so? (If our love is of no greater definition than that of the world, then our claims are empty.) V48) Be you therefore perfect, even as your father which is in Heaven is perfect (Jesus is not teaching sinless perfection, for the Bible does not teach such; He is teaching that are imitation of our Heavenly Father must be as a perfect as possible; the Holy Spirit Alone can help us do these things, which He does according to our Faith in Christ and the Cross [Romans 8:1-2,11]).

Chapter 6:1-34

V1) Take heed (a serious matter) that you do not your alms (Righteousness) before men, to be seen of them (what is the reason for our giving?): otherwise, you have no reward of your Father which is in Heaven. V2)

Therefore when you do your alms (in this case, giving, and portrays the necessity of giving), do not sound a trumpet before you (do not make a show), as the hypocrites do in the Synagogue and in the streets, that they may have glory of men (be seen of men). Verily I say unto you, they have their reward (God will not reward such, whether on Earth or in Heaven). V3) But when you do alms (Righteousness, and once again, proclaims the necessity of giving), let not your left hand know what your right hand does (not meant to be taken literally, but rather to point to the intent of the heart): V4) That your alms may be in secret (simply means that from the heart it is done as unto the Lord, and not for the praise of men): and your Father (Heavenly Father) which sees in secret Himself shall reward you openly (both on Earth and when you get to Heaven). V5) And when you pray (the necessity of prayer), you shall not be as the hypocrites are: for they love to pray standing in the Synagogues and in the corners of the streets, that they may be seen of men (they do it for show). Verily I say unto you, they have their reward (meaning that there will be no reward from God in any capacity). V6) But you (sincere Believer), when you pray, enter into your closet, and when you have shut your door, pray to your Father which is in secret; and your Father which sees in secret shall reward you openly (the word "closet" is not to be taken literally, but means that our praying must not be done for show; if we make God's interests our own, we are assured that He will make our interest His Own). V7) But when you pray, use not vain repetitions, as the heathen do (repeating certain phrases over and over, even hundreds of times): for they think that they shall be heard for their much speaking (they will not be heard by God). V8) Be not you therefore like unto them: for your Father (Heavenly Father) knows what things you have need of, before you ask Him (He is omniscient, meaning that He knows all things, past, present, and future). V9) After this manner therefore pray you (is meant to be in total contrast to the heathen practice; as well, it is to be prayed in full confidence, that the Heavenly Father will hear and answer according to His Will): Our Father (our prayer should be directed toward our Heavenly Father, and not Christ or the Holy Spirit) Who is in Heaven, Hallowed be Your Name (we reverence His Name). V10) Your kingdom come (this will definitely happen at the Second Coming), Your Will be done in earth, as it is in Heaven (the Will of God is all-important; it will be carried out on Earth, beginning with the Kingdom Age). V11) Give us this day our daily bread (we are to look to the Lord for sustenance, both natural and spiritual). V12) And forgive us our debts, as we forgive our debtors (the word "debts" here refers to "trespasses" and "sins"; His forgiveness on our part is predicated on our forgiving others). V13) And lead (because of self-confidence) us not into temptation (help us not to be led into testing—the idea is, in my self-confidence, which stems from the flesh and not the Spirit, please do not allow me to be led into temptation, for I will surely fail!), but deliver us (the trap is more powerful than man can handle; only God can deliver; He does so through the Power of the Holy Spirit, according to our Faith in Christ and the Cross [Rom.8:1-2,11]) from evil (the Evil One, Satan himself): For Yours is the kingdom (this Earth belongs to the Lord and not Satan; he is an usurper), and the power (God has the Power to deliver, which He does, as stated, through the Cross), and the glory (the Glory belongs to God, and not Satan), forever (none of this will ever change). Amen (this Word expresses a solemn ratification; in the Mind of God, the defeat and destruction of Satan and, therefore, all evil in the world, is a foregone conclusion). V14) For if you forgive men (it must be the God kind of forgiveness) their trespasses (large sins), your Heavenly Father will also forgive you (forgiveness rest totally on the Atoning Work of Christ; it is an act of sheer Grace): …

V15) But if you forgive not men their trespasses, neither will your Father forgive your trespasses (if we want God to forgive us, we must at the same time forgive others; if not, His forgiveness for us is withheld; consequently, such a person is in jeopardy of losing their soul). V16) Moreover when you fast (no set time), be not, as the hypocrites, of a sad countenance: for they disfigure their faces, that they may appear unto men too fast. Verily I say unto you, they have their reward (so much in the religious realm falls into this category; it is done for "show" whether it be fasting or giving, etc.; the Lord will never reward such). V17) But you (referring to those who are truly God's Children), when you fast, anoint your head, and wash your face (the "anointing" and the "washing" were actually symbols of joy; this was the opposite of the sad countenance); V18) That you appear not unto men to fast (there is to be no appearance of fasting), but unto your Father (Heavenly Father) which is in secret; and your Father, which sees in secret, shall reward (bless) you openly (the implication is God was not the "Father" of the Pharisees, and will not be the "Father" of any who follow in their train). V19) Lay not up for yourselves treasures upon earth (everything on the Earth is temporal), where moth and rust does corrupt, and where thieves break through and steal (if the eye be set upon treasures on Earth, the life and character of the Believer will be shrouded in moral darkness): V20) But lay up for yourselves treasures in Heaven, where neither moth nor rust does corrupt, and where thieves do not break through nor steal: V21) For where your treasure is, there will your heart be also (a man's aim determines his character; if that aim be not simple and Heavenward but earthward and double, all the faculties and principles of his nature will become a mass of darkness; it is impossible to give a divided allegiance). V22) The light of the body is the eye (a figure of speech; He is, in effect, saying that the light of the soul is the spirit): if therefore your eye be single (the spirit of man should have but one purpose, and that is to Glorify God), your whole body shall be full of Light (the spirit of man is single in its devotion to God [meaning not divided then all the soul will be full of light). V23) But if your eye be evil, your whole body shall be full of darkness (if the spirit be evil, the entirety of the soul will be full of darkness). If therefore the light that is in you be darkness (the light is not acted upon, but rather perverted), how great is that darkness (the latter state is worse than if there had been no light at all)! V24) No man can serve two masters: for either he will hate the one, and love the other; or else he will hold to the one, and despise the other. You cannot serve God and mammon (this is flat out, stated as, an impossibility; it is total devotion to God, or ultimately it will be total devotion to the world; the word, "mammon" is derived from the Babylonian" Mimma," which means "anything at all"). Therefore, I say unto you, take no thought for your life, what you shall eat, or what you shall drink; nor yet for your body, what you shall put on (don't worry about these things). Is not the life more than meat, and the body than raiment? (Life is more than things, and the physical body is more than the clothes we wear.) V26) Behold the fowls of the air: for they sow not, neither do they reap, nor gather into barns; yet your Heavenly Father feeds them. Are you not much better than they? (The fowls of the air are a smaller part of God 's great Creation. If the Lord has provided for them, most assuredly, He has provided for His Children.)

V27) Which of you by taking thought (worrying and fretting) can add one cubit unto his stature? (Whatever is going to happen cannot be stopped by worry; and if it doesn't happen, there is nothing to worry about. For His Children, the Lord always fills in the bottom line.) V28) And why do you take thought (worry) for (about) raiment (clothes)? Consider the lilies of the field, how they grow; they toil not, neither do they spin (the man grows the flaw [toil] the woman weaves it [spins]; the statement is meant to proclaim the fact that the beauty of the lily has nothing to do with its effort, but is given completely by the Creator): V29) And yet I say unto you, That even Solomon in all his glory was not arrayed like one of these (it is said that the lilies of Israel had brilliant coloring, and especially the purple and white Huleh Lily found in Nazareth). ...

V30) Wherefore, if (since) God so clothed the grass of the field (is meant to portray God 's guarantee), which today is, and tomorrow is cast into the oven (portrays how inconsequential is this part of His Creation, and yet, how much care He expends on it), shall He not much more clothe you, O you of little faith? (We are told here the reason for our lack; it is "little faith"; because God is Faithful, He can be trusted fully to completely carry out His commitments to us in Christ [I Cor. 1:9; 10:13; II Cor. 1:18; I Thess. 5:24; II Thess. 3:3; etc..].) V31) Therefore take no thought (don't worry), saying, what shall we eat? or, what shall we drink? or, Wherewithal shall we be clothed (The Greek Text actually means that even one anxious thought is forbidden. Such shows a distrust of the Lord.) V32) (For after all these things do the Gentiles seek:) (Gentiles had no part in God's Covenant with Israel; consequently, they had no part in God's economy, and, basically, had to fend for themselves) for your Heavenly Father knows that you have need of all these things (the phrase is meant to express the contrast between those who do not know the Lord and those who do; if we live for Him, ever seeking His Will, we have the guarantee of His Word, which He will provide for us; is God's Word good enough? I think it is!). V33) But seek you first the Kingdom of God, and His Righteousness (this gives the "condition" for God 's Blessing; His interests are to be "first"); and all these things shall be added unto you (this is the "guarantee" of God's Provision). V34) Take therefore no thought for the morrow (don't worry about the future): for the morrow shall take thought for the things of itself (this is meant to refer back to Verse 27). Sufficient unto the day is the evil thereof (this means that we should handle daily difficulties in Faith, and have Faith, for the future that the present difficulties will not grow into larger ones; we have God's assurance that they won't, that is, if we will sufficiently believe Him).

Chapter 7

V1) Judge not, that you be not judged (this statement by Christ harks back to Verses 25 through 34 of the previous Chapter; the idea is, God may permit poverty to test His Child, but fellow Believers are not to err, as Job's friends did, and believe the trial to be a judgment for secret sin; as well, the word, "judging, "as used here, covers every aspect of dealing with our fellowman). V2) For with what judgment you judge, you shall be judged (whatever motive we ascribe to others, such motive will ultimately be ascribed to us); and with what measure you mete, it shall be measured to you again (a double emphasis is given here in order to proclaim the seriousness of the Words of our Lord; when we judge others, we are judging ourselves). V3) And why do you behold the boat that is in your brothers i.e., the believer is not to be looking for fault or wrongdoing in the lives of fellow believers, but consider not the beam that is in your own eye? We have plenty in our own lives which need eliminating, without looking for faults and others. The "mote" and "beam" are contrast! The constant judging of others portrays the fact that we are much worse off than the one we are judging.) V4) Or how will you say to your brother, let me pull out the mote out of your eye (the seriousness of setting ourselves up as Judge, jury, and executioner); and, behold, a beam is in your own eye? (Once again draws attention to the fact the person doing the judging is in far worse spiritual condition than the one being judged.) V5) You hypocrite (aptly describes such a person), first cast out the beam out of your own eye; and then you shall see clearly to cast out the mote out of your brother's eye (the very fact that we do not address ourselves, but rather others, portrays the truth that our personal situation is worse; when we properly analyze ourselves, then, and only then, can we "see clearly"; this is speaking of character assassination and not the correction of doctrine).

V6) Give not that which is holy unto the dogs, neither cast you your pearls before swine (there may be problems in the Church, as Verses one through five proclaim, but still, the Church is never to reach out into the world, i.e., "dogs," for help in order to solve its internal disputes), lest they trample them under their feet, and turn again in rend you (no help will be coming from the world, but rather destruction.; We are to take our problems to the Lord, obeying His Word, concerning disputes [Mat. 18:15-17]). V7) Ask, and it shall be given you (if we ask for wisdom as it regards the settling of disputes, or for anything, it shall be given); seek, and you shall find (the answer may not be forthcoming immediately; therefore, we should "seek" to know the reason why); knock, and it shall be opened unto you (we must make sure that it is His door on which we are knocking; if it is, it definitely will be opened to us): V8) For everyone who asks receives; and he who seeks finds; and to him who knocks it shall be opened (assumes that the person's heart is sincere before the Lord). V9) Or what man is there of you, whom it if his son ask bread, will he give him a stone? (Even a human being will not do such, much less God!) V10) Or If he asks a fish, will he give him a serpent? (If, in fact, what we are asking for is not God's Will, and would turn out to be a "stone," or "serpent," He will guard us from receiving such, and during the time of waiting and consecration, will show us what we truly need.) V11) If you then, being evil (refers to parents sometimes giving their children things which are not good for them, as well as things which are good), know how to give good gifts unto your children, how much more shall your Father which is in Heaven give good things to them who ask Him? (The Lord gives only good things.) V12) Therefore all things whatsoever you would that men should do to you, do you even so to them; for this is the Law and the Prophets (this rule does not authorize capricious benevolent action, but only what is reasonable and morally helpful, and controlled by Divine imitation [Mat. 5:48]; this principle of action and mode of life is, in fact, the sum of all Bible teaching). V13) Enter you in at the strait gate (this is the Door, who is Jesus [Jn. 10:1]): for wide is the gate, and broad is the way, that leads to destruction, and many there will be which go in there at (proclaims the fact of many and varied religions of the world, which our false, and lead to eternal hellfire): V14) Because strait is the gate, and narrow is the way, which leads unto life, and few there be that find it (every contrite heart earnestly desires to be among the "few"; the requirements are greater than most are willing to accept). V15) Beware of false prophets, who come to you in sheep 's clothing, but inwardly they are ravening wolves ("beware of false prophets" is said in the sternest of measures! there will be and are false prophets, and are some of Satan 's greatest weapons). V16) You shall know them by their fruits (this is the test as given by Christ as it regards identification of false prophets and false apostles). Do men gather grapes of thorns, or figs of thistles? (It is impossible for false doctrine, generated by false prophets, to bring forth good fruit.) V17) Even so every good tree brings forth good fruit; but a corrupt tree brings forth evil fruit (the good fruit is Christlikeness, while the evil fruit is self-likeness). V18) A good tree cannot bring forth evil fruit, neither can a corrupt tree bring forth good fruit (the "good tree" is the Cross, while the "corrupt tree" pertains to all of that which is other than the Cross). V19) Every tree that brings not forth good fruit is hewn down, and cast into the fire (judgment will ultimately come on all so-called gospel other than the Cross [Rom. 1:18]). V20) Wherefore by their fruits you shall know them (the acid test). V21) Not everyone who says unto Me, Lord, Lord, shall enter into the Kingdom of Heaven (the repetition of the word "Lord" expresses astonishment, as if to say: "Are we to be disowned? "); but he who does the Will of My Father which is in Heaven (what is the Will of the Father? Verse 23 tells us). V22) Many will say to Me in that day, Lord, Lord, have we not Prophesied in Your Name? and in Your Name have cast out devils? and in Your Name done many wonderful works? (These things are not the criteria, but rather Faith in Christ and what Christ has done for us at the Cross [Eph. 2:8-9, 13-18]. (The Word of God alone is to be the judge of doctrine.) ...

V23) And then will I profess unto them, I never knew you (again, we say, the criteria alone is Christ and Him Crucified [I Cor. 1:23]): depart from Me, you who work iniquity (we have access to God only through Christ, and access to Christ only through the Cross, and access to the Cross only through a denial of self [Lk. 9:23]; any other Message is Judged by God as "iniquity," and cannot be a part of Christ [I Cor. 1:17]). V24) Therefore whosoever hears these sayings of Mine, and does them, I will liken him unto a wise man, who built his house upon a rock (the "Rock" is Christ Jesus, and the Foundation is the Cross [Galatians 1:8-9]): V25) And the rain descended, and the floods came, and the winds blew, and beat upon that house; and it fell not: for it was founded upon a rock (the Foundation of our belief system must be Christ and Him Crucified [Gal. 6:14]). V26) And everyone who hears these sayings of Mine, and does them not, shall be likened unto a foolish man, who built his house upon the sand (but for the foundation, this house looked the same as the house that was built upon the rock): V27) And the rain descended, and the floods came, and the winds blew, and beat upon that house; and it fell: and great was the fall of it (while the sun shines, both houses look good; but, when adversity comes and come it shall, Faith, which is alone in Christ and Him Crucified will stand [I Cor. 1:18]). V28) And it came to pass, when Jesus had ended these sayings (ended the Sermon on the Mount) the people were astonished at His Doctrine (this Message proclaimed the True intent of the Law of Moses, and, above all, laid the Foundation for the New Covenant): V29) For He taught them as one having authority (refers to Divine Authority, which He had by the Power of the Holy Spirit; this Sermon and that of Luke, Chapter 6 are probably one and the same; the Holy Spirit here lays the emphasis on the heart, while in Luke, emphasis is laid on actions produced by the heart; consequently, the distinction between "standing" and "state" is apparent), and not as the Scribes (those who claimed to be expert in the Law of Moses).

As you can see this is all of Jesus speaking from chapter 5:3 to 7:27. It is a Holy Spirit Powered speech. From the Son of God, with All Authority. Jesus is the fulfillment of the Old Testament, to the New Testament, and His New Covenant. He is the New Covenant for all mankind. (Gal. 6:14) ;(I Cor. 2:2)....'except Jesus Christ and Him Crucified'.

CHAPTER 12

'THE HILL DREAM'

There was a line of cars and trucks a mile long. We all were on a military base. There was this long, straight, slanted road, up into the base. And a guard shack with a chain-link fence on each side, and a gate for coming in and going. And today was free pancake day. I was inching my way up to the entrance. And I even got out and parked my van down the road. I am walking up the hill in a double shirt (in real life I was wearing two, a shirt and a sweatshirt) and a long terry cloth robe. (Which in real life I was not wearing) Then the guy at the shack announces over the loudspeaker in my dream. (everyone goes back in your cells we are done, we are having a meeting, that is everyone including porters) (this happened in real life) (we had pancakes, and I went back to sleep).

Everyone turns around and heads down the hill. And I am walking back maybe a quarter mile, to my vehicle. And as I am walking which seems tiresomely; then my robe opens, showing my underwear. Then I noticed some people walking up in the middle of the road? So, I closed my robe quickly. It was a good thing; these men were filming. One man carrying a professional TV camera, and one guy next to him walking at his side. Looking straight at the guard shack. I said, 'Good morning', but they just kept moving forward. And didn't pay attention to me. (In real life, we recently were getting cell fed and free pancakes were coming to our cell door, and yes, sometimes by CO's. Who sometimes said, 'Good morning', and some didn't. They are the ones keeping their eyes on us like a camera, always watching). So, I kept walking, and then I see, two or three trucks, and I'm going, 'where is my van?' I walked a little more, 'oh there it is', a Dodge, dark gray maxi cargo van, a three-quarter ton. (Even though, I beefed it up to one-and-a-half-ton suspension in real life). I woke-up.

'MORAL DREAM'

I was at a guy's house, and he turned on his sprinklers to make a physical point about a moral issue, to wash away filth of this person or the situation; and people were complaining. But I was all for him. And he made his point in the yard. So, I was leaving his house on the driveway side. I saw where the sprinkler shut-off was, and I shut it off for him. It was flooding. (Like Noah's day) And he had a big dog, he was friendly enough, and sniffing under my arms and tickled me. Then a second dog shows up and did the same. They look intimidating, but gentle. (Like angels, but they are not, they are dogs). I went to the front of the house of the owner. This white-haired old man said, 'Turn the sprinklers on again; the TV crew is here'. (He's looks and appears to be a mature man of wisdom) This Man had a huge sign in His lawn saying. 'Don't wash it under the rug. But wash the filth away', As the letters, are literally running down His is yard to the gutter. There is a slight slant to the yard. So, I went to the backyard again, and turned the water back on. To make His point to the Media. (Woke up)

'JOB DREAM'

I was in this front building, of this ranch. It was a gym. And the owner was renting the room for exercising. They had openings for an instructor, and caretaker of the ground. It was a minimum wage kind of job. And I thought it wouldn't be too bad. But pretty low pay. (Even though, in real life, while in high school; as a summer job as a sophomore or junior; welcomed any kind of pay, and I worked at 'Jack La Lanes gym and health spa'. For a month or two and was a helper for a fence builder.)

Then the owner comes and asked me to come in the backyard (which was basically the front yard of this big estate) which was a huge grass area with many acres. And a fence corral made of wood. We walked a bit, and he asked about me to do this job? He showed me a fence post that needed to be reset, leveled and cemented in. I said, 'I can do that'. I also said, 'This is a bigger job of maintenance and would require more money to take care of all of this. Someone was working on the post, but it was only half done. I was thinking about my first impression with this man, and how I looked and responded to his questions. I was evaluating myself. And (I woke up).

CHAPTER 13

'AL DREAM'

I was over at my friend and co-worker's dad's house. (In real life, Al told me he was a minister, and that he pasted years ago) And one other son was there, or like a son, (I don't know in real life he has a brother? but it also could be a spiritual son, like Paul and Timothy in the Bible) He was resting in his bed. The person that was at his bed side was comforting him. He didn't seem to be ill? But I don't know? They seem to know me as Al's friend and wasn't bothered that I was in his master bedroom. And there was a reason I was there too. I was supposed to ask if I could get the spelling game, that Al got out earlier, but it was up near the top of the bed. It seemed OK. This was a big house, and a large back yard, when I came in earlier through the back door. (In real life, I've never been there, but Al's home is big and has a large back yard).

'RECEPTION DREAM'

I was outside, behind a big Facility in the open, with crowds of people all around. And I brought my sister to this one church. She was younger, and nicely dressed. In her 20's or 30's years old. And twelve of the bridesmaids her own age was their too. It was a huge party in the back yard, for possibly a reception. Everyone was dancing and happy, but I seemed to be pushed here and then there. (I woke-up)

'MESSAGE/ LEVI'

When Jesus called Matthew, his name was Levi. (Matthew 9:9) V9) "As Jesus passed on from there, He saw a man named Matthew sitting at the tax office. (That was a fancy name for a tollbooth set up alongside a Highway [a road] to levy taxes on merchandise transported on that road) (Which we do the same thing today, as truckers go through weight stations and pay from state to state that they go through) In (Matt. 10:1-4) it lists the 12-Apostles, that were called and sent to bring a message of hope and deliverance. In verse three, and specifically mentions Levi, as Matthew; V3) .... Philip and Bartholomew; Thomas and Matthew the tax collector; In (Luke 5:27) (Jesus, was out and about and had just healed a paralytic man. V27) After these things He went out and saw at tax collector named Levi, sitting at the Tax Office. And He said to him, "follow me". V28) So He left all, rose up, and followed Him.) (That is amazing itself that he dropped everything and follow Jesus. In V28 says he left all, he left all the tax money there? Or he left his job to someone else? There was probably more than one person sitting there. As Matthew left all, he probably told his partner I resign and to tell Herod Antipas as well. He was the man in charge of Jesus day. Also, it was a great honor to be chosen of, by A Spiritual teacher, or master of the Jewish religion of that time.) In verse 29) V29) [Then Levi (Matthew) gave Him a great feast in his own house. And there were a great number of tax collectors and others who sat down with them. V30) And their scribes and Pharisees complained against His disciples, saying, "why do you eat and drink with tax collectors and sinners?" V31) Jesus answered and said to them, "Those who are well have no need of a physician, but those who are sick. V32) I have not come to call the righteous, but sinners, to repentance."] (NKJV)(Ref.) (Luke 5:32) Jesus' mission was to call sinners to repentance. Upon His ascension, Jesus commissioned His disciples to the same task (24:47,) see also (3:3,8,13:1-5;15:7-10,16:30; 17:3,4; Acts 26:20) In this passage, repentance is pictured as a patient who recognizes that illness is present and that only Jesus, the Great Physician, can treat it. A humble approach to God for Spiritual healing is the essence of repentance. (end quote)

CHAPTER 14

'REPENTANCE'

I can relate of a humble approach and recognize a need of Spiritual healing. I am in a self-help class, done in my cell, and corresponding back-and-forth to the instructor. The class here at CSP is called 'Helping Men Recover'. In one of the lessons give, it was said; that my primary role: 'lost child' that I determined, that best fits me; one of four; mine being number three and being the third living child of my siblings. Showed all the negative and positive aspects that remarkably was like me. As the workbook laid-out. When I came into prison, I had a lot of the negative list. Like, low self-esteem, distorted self-image, including lonely, isolated, sad, depressed, fantasize, inactive, and indecisive. Quote: Question number 3A), What are one or two things that you can do immediately that will lessen the negative impact that this has on your life? "(end quote)

One, was to repent of my sins, and behavior, get on my knees, and turn toward God. Second, get back into church; praise the Lord, and thank God for restoring me back in a right relationship. I have to say one thing, God restored me, forgave me, and got me back in a right relationship back with Him. I repented of my sins, and confessed of my fallen state or backsliding condition, but not unto Salvation again. I was saved in my early 20's. And coming in, was my disobedience, drunkenness, and abuse of alcohol, due to a neck injury and became an addict or alcoholic. And subsequently, committing a crime in my deplorable condition. My negative aspects were contributed mostly by my alcohol abuse.

Now that God has healed and restored me. I can be again, what was on the positive list: Quote:

Creative; Imaginative; Well-developed skills; With manual Dexterity; Well read; Good listener, observer.

Spiritually, Resourceful; Can work independently; Non-conformist; Enjoys solitude. (end quote)

(This is out a special Edition for use in the Criminal Justice System by: Stephanie S. Covington, Dan Griffin, and Rick Dauer.)

'SCOTT & SELMA DREAM'

I was riding along down the sidewalk, on a hoverboard, that you sit on. It had a pole and a seat to sit on, and handlebars, with a jet propulsion. (In real life I had a battery powered scooter, was like that I described) This board had a top speed of about 3 to 5 mph; and practically walking speed, and barely made it up the steps to get to the level of the High School grounds.

The gate was open, so I cut across their yard, during recess. I was supposed to go around, I think? But I putted along, and no one bothered me. There were teachers, and administrators out there too. They didn't say anything either. I was headed for the new building with the storage of different supplies. There were stacks, and stacks everywhere. Only things I recognize was, toilet boxes, and coffee mugs as I drive right up to this opened doorway. A large opening, to a big building. It didn't even have a sidewalk around it yet, or driveway entrance for the big door opening? I headed for this rock next to the slab of concrete. And popped up into the building. And two people were standing there talking. Having a slight heated argument. One looked like Scott Glenn in his middle years, as I would see him in his cowboy movies and other dramatic roles. And a woman named Salma Hayek; very nice and pretty, who was throwing some coffee cups as she is upset about something. But she is throwing them in jest (joke playing). Like some of her roles where she gets her dandruff up. But she is really playing with Scott. And doesn't really mean it. (I am not sure what all this is for, but we are all working together; maybe we were organizing a distributing center from donations?) That's the end of the Dream.

'DIN. -B-DREAM'

There was a family dinner, downtown and friends and relatives were there, but it wasn't like before. It was different. (In real life, God willing, I wanted to host a dinner for my family and friends when I get out.) We were all coming from different directions; some kids running up the alley. It's not the best of neighborhoods, and they didn't want to linger in the alley too long either. Then the dream jumps to a house environment, with relatives here and there. With Brenda my first ex-wife (or baby's mama), and she was caring for two girls, one about five years old, and the other about 9 to 10 years old. We had some communication, and we talked, but we weren't together. A mutual bond for each other. (Then I woke up)

CHAPTER 15

'BRUCE & I'

This is Scripture in a form of a letter, that I used on Saturday, November 7, 2020. To instruct, and rebuke, and encourage a brother in the Lord. With references at the end. "Wait on the Lord: be of good courage, and He shall strengthen thine heart." "God is our refuge and strength, a very present help in trouble." "As I was with Moses, so will be with thee: I will not fail thee, nor forsake thee. Be strong and of a good courage." "Why art thou cast down, O my soul? And why art thou disquieted with in me? Hope thou in God." "I called upon the Lord in distress: the Lord answered me and set me in a large place." "For we walk by faith, not by sight." "[Cast] down imaginations, and every high thing that exalteth itself against the knowledge of God, and [bring] into captivity every thought to the obedience of Christ."

"Be careful for nothing; but in everything by prayer and supplication with Thanksgiving let your requests be made known unto God. And the peace of God, which passeth all understanding, shall keep your hearts and minds through Christ Jesus." "Let us hold fast the profession of our faith without wavering; (for He is faithful that promised)." "Cast not away therefore your confidence, which hath great recompence of reward. For ye have need of patience, that, after ye have done the will of God, ye might receive the promise." "[Cast] all your care upon Him; for He careth for you." "My God shall supply all your need according to his riches in glory by Christ Jesus."

"Wait on the Lord, and keep his way, and He shall exalt thee to inherit the land." "He shall be like a tree planted by the rivers of water, that bringeth forth his fruit in his season; his leaf also shall not wither; and whatsoever he doeth shall prosper." "Let them shout for joy, and be glad, that favour my righteous cause; yea, let them say continually, let the Lord be magnified, which has pleasure in the prosperity of his servant." "Give, and it shall be given unto you; good measure, press down, and shaken together, and running over, shall men give into your bosom. For with the same measure that you mete withal it shall be measured to you again." "I have showed you all things, how that so laboring ye ought to support the weak, and to remember the words of the Lord Jesus, how he said, … It is more blessed to give than to receive." "If ye forgive men their trespasses; your Heavenly Father will also forgive you: But if ye forgive not men their trespasses, neither will your Father forgive your trespasses." "Then came Peter to Him, and said, Lord, how oft shall my brother sin against me, and I forgive him? till seven times? Jesus saith unto him, I say not unto thee, Until seven times: but, until 70×7." "Be ye kind one to another, tenderhearted, forgiving one another, even as God for Christ's sake hath forgiven you." "Be strong and of good courage; be not afraid, neither be thou dismayed; for the Lord thy God is with thee whithersoever thou goest." "Neither be ye sorry; for the joy of the Lord is your strength." "Be glad in the Lord, and rejoice, ye righteous: and shout for joy, all ye that are upright in heart." "Teach me thy way, O Lord, and lead me in a plain path, because of mine enemies." "I will instruct thee and teach thee in the way which thou shall go: I will guide thee with mine eye." "Commit thy way unto the Lord; trust also in Him; and he shall bring it to pass." "The steps of a good man are ordered by the Lord." "He led them on safely, so that they feared not." "Trust in the Lord with all thine heart; and lean not unto thine own understanding. In all thy ways acknowledge him, and he shall direct thy paths." "I can do all things through Christ which strengtheneth me." "I will never leave thee, nor forsake thee. So that we may boldly say, the Lord is my helper, and I will not fear what man shall do unto me." "Cast all your cares upon Him; for He careth for you." "My presence shall go with thee, and I will give thee rest." (KJV)…

(KJV)(JSM) Reference Scripture:

(I Pet.5:7)(Ex.33:14)(Phil.4:13)(Heb.13:5-6)(Ps.27:4)(Heb.10:23) (Acts
20:35)(Ps.37:23)(Ps.46:1)   (Heb.10:35,36)(Matt.6:14,15)(Ps.78:53)
(Josh.1:5,6)(Eph.4:32)(Prov.3:5,6)(Ps.42:11)(Phil.4:19)(Josh.1:9) (Jere.33:3)
(Ps.118:5)(Ps.37:34)(Ps.32:11)(Mark 11:24) (II Cor.5:7)(Ps.1:3)(Ps.27:11)
(Lk.10:19) (II Cor.10:5)(Ps.35:27)(Ps.32:8)(Rom.8:31)(Phil.4:6-7)(Lk.6:38)
(Ps.37:5)(Matt.18:21-22).

'MICHAEL DREAM'

I was dreaming I was playing golf with someone. He and I went from
hole to hole. On one fairway, I looked over to my right, and there was this
young man, slender wearing blue jeans overalls and a red plaid shirt. He
runs over the hill, as he is following a ball, and before it stops, he's almost
trying to stop the ball at a certain point. He wanted to take a picture of all
of that, with this big old-time camera. (Which really isn't, he said, "this is
my first new digital camera".)

And I'm thinking to myself, he's not supposed to stop the ball in golf,
but I looked closer, and it is a baseball. And where it stopped was a grassy
knoll, (that's another whole story), and under was dirt if it kept rolling. He
wanted it in the grass and wanted to take a picture of his home run. (Now
awake, I'm thinking two things, how did he race out to the Ball that fast?
And why isn't he running the bases?) (A) Because it is a dream and then
he turned my way, and it was a younger Michael Landon; (Now, when I
awakened, I know Michael was a Spiritual man, and his movie series', he
made with 'Little House on the Prairie'; and 'Highway to Heaven'. But,
if God wants me to pray for them, then I will. As I said before, 'everyone
needs prayer'. And even if they're alive, or if they have passed on now.
You can intercede for that person; you can pray for a person's Salvation,
or sanctification, and or for the Lord to have mercy on their souls/spirit.)

(Later on in the dream, I go back to the clubhouse, and my dad and
grandmother (his mom) were there, so I prayed for them also. My Christian

grandma passed away a long time ago. She was born in 1897. Now my dad, presently as I am writing this, he is 98 years old, and born in 1922. He is fighting pneumonia.) So, back to the dream; there was a girl standing there who must have just walked up. She is coming my way. As she gets closer, it is a girl from High School. She is very cute, long blonde hair, and she wore braces for a while. But she was not wearing them now and her name is Stephanie.

Michael is saying, 'oh, I am out of film'. (But in real life it is a card you put in with a digital camera. Maybe, this is where it came from in my subconscious. —On vacation with my family in the mountains; I told my daughter we'll go on a special drive up to the top of the mountain. And I brought my 35 mm camera, we spent a couple hours, and stopped along the way, and took what I thought was a whole roll of film, and when we got back the camera was empty; even though it said on the counter I was taking a number of pictures? And my daughter is named Stephanie. And I have been recently reading a workbook written by Dr. Stephanie Covington. So, it is no wonder, she showed up in the dream.) So, suddenly Stephanie 's family shows up all around her. And people start popping up behind the grassy knoll behind us. (That's a whole nother story) And starts taking pictures, and says, 'we got your pictures, of Stephanie and her family, and Michael's Landon's special home run baseball, on the ground.' (In real life, to get a home run, you have to run the bases and not after the ball.) (I am not putting him down, he was a smart, bright, and talented man, and I also liked him in Bonanza. I like cowboy movies.) Now, Stephanie in the dream, came over to me and she is putting on clear lip-gloss, and I am on a blanket now. She looks like she wants to use those lips on me. But I woke up. (In real life, we were just friends and nothing more.) The end

'DAD & I DREAM'

Dad and I are working together, laying carpet in this dream. At this little old house, with a separate garage in the alley. We were finishing up for the day. It was about 5:45 PM. This was an empty house also. So, we left the porch lights on as we are leaving, like it appears as if someone is home.

And I guess we are not quite done, because there was a small roll in the garage we haven't brought in yet? But we need to lock up before we go, and I guess we did.

My dad is getting into his old 1978 1/2-ton Ford-150 super cargo van, which he bought brand new in the day. Which could handle a medium size 12-foot-wide carpet or vinyl in between the seats and shut the doors. It was the original pumpkin orange color in the dream. (Later in real life, I bought the van from him, and had it painted dark brown) I had just remembered we needed something to finish the job and I told him I need to go to the supply store before they close at 6 PM. (But, in real life the supply store closes at 5 PM.)

CHAPTER 16

'WED. RECEPT. DREAM'

I have been dreaming of a Wedding Reception dream lately at different persons homes, or they are family reunions? There are family members in these homes, but also people I don't know? Who, all are nicely dressed. Which makes me think it is a reception, then a family reunion. I arrived at this one home, and I was heading for the front door across the grass by the front living room bay window. As I walked by, I see my sister in the kitchen toward the back. She is preparing something, so, I waved to her. And the people in the living room see me, and ask my sister 'Is that one of Eric 's kids?' They said it loud enough I could hear it. I thought to myself in the dream, that was a compliment, they are about 35 years younger, or it was people I didn't know, and they also didn't know me.

Eric is my ex-brother in-law. We always had family gatherings, at Christmas and Thanksgiving, and Family Reunion's with he and his wife and two children. From my 2nd ex-wife.

'PARK DREAM'

I was at an Amusement Park for kids in this dream. And our two children are in it playing, from my 1st ex-wife. At about ages 2 and 5 years old. They were in some kind of a structure.

I said, Hi, to them by waving through this port window. And then they came out. There were other play structures there you could learn about dinosaurs or science. And a bonus to have your parents there. When they came out, I gave both an airplane ride. And swing them around and around. Also, there were two attendants there to be helpful in anyway. The both of them were wearing white, white shirts and pants. (Maybe they were the two guardian angels assigned to them.) Then I woke up.

'FIX-IT DREAM'

This dream is about Howard and my dad. And Howard had a fix-it project. He wants it done and needs a little help with it. I had spent the night at my in-law's house next door to my dad's to wait for them to get back from Cindy's Restaurant where they had coffee and tea every morning together. I am at the house waiting, and they get back, and come to what was my old bedroom. I said, 'We need to get going, to work on that project of yours.' And Howard speaks up and says, 'Oh, that's done'; 'We did that early, before breakfast (coffee & tea). (Howard, is one of those, getter-done kind-a-guys. A real go getter. He is like the Army motto; 'We get more done before 9am, then you do all day.'

Howard is the same age as my dad. Born in 1922. He was also in WWII, but the Navy in the South Pacific conflict. And Dad (Lorenz), was stationed in England as a pilot, in a B-24 plane fighting the Germany's. He was in the Army-Air Corp. They were combined back then. And after the war in 1945, they separated the military services. So, Howard walks out and my dad is taggling behind. He hooks his shirt on some wire off the wall and can't see it very good to get it unstuck. So, I help him with it, and off he goes.) (Wake-up)

(In real life, that exact thing never happened, but similar activities we did do with projects.) End

CHAPTER 17

'ROSIE DREAM'

My friend and I were in line together for something, I don't know? (But that's nothing new for someone who has been in prison) We were from the same dorm together. (In real life, he was a childhood playmate from Elementary, Jr.-High, and High School, and his name is Chris P.) He was upset about something. And he wanted to take it out on someone. And he saw this big guy, and I recognized him from A-2. And so, he wanted to fight him. He wants to hit him for no reason? (There was an incident where a big guy punched this little guy for no reason. He may have had a reason, but to everyone else, and the one who was punched, it was unjustified.) Back to the dream, he wanted to pick a fight and took me to the side. Even Tho, he is twice his size. He starts swinging.

There was a woman in line, I recognized her as Rosie O'Donald. So, I help her to the side, to keep her out of harm's way. And she replies, 'Well, I never?' (In real life, Chris is a peaceable, soft-spoken kind-a-guy. Not an Angry type.) (And Rosie in my dream, is just surprised, no harm done.)

(But what I have learned in AA-12-steps programs is; That in Step 8&9, that you are supposed to make amends. To people you have harmed by your addiction. Mine happens to be Alcohol. I was thinking of my friend in the dream, thinking he is going to have to make amends with him later. And when he does; Even Tho they might not except it. He must try to say, and show he is sincere, and say he is sorry for what he did. As long as it doesn't harm them worst or others, or even himself, to put them in jeopardy.) End

'HIGHWAY DREAM'

We were along the highway where we were in front of their farm property, up to the frontage road. This man and his two sons, maybe 10&12 years old. He was trying to talk to his boys about cutting this strip grass on the top of the berm. A dirt strip with grass on it. He had already done the sides. The guys that usually did this, are not available, and the teenager kids weren't too excited about doing it. So, I spoke up and said, 'I'll do it for $20, and the tools are already out. I had $100, and I wanted to buy something for $120. So, off I went and he pre-paid me. Before I started, and as I was walking; people were coming from somewhere, out of nowhere? End

'WHO ARE YOU'

As a born-again Believer, sin has no dominion over you. It can't dominate you, unless you let it. It must leave you; Satan is a defeated foe—he is not your god. He is your enemy. James 4:7 says if you resist him, he will flee from you. You need to see yourself 'In Christ' and know the reality of it. If you ask some people today, "Are you a son of God?" They'll say, 'Who, me? certainly not!' Are you not a child of God? Then act that way. Based on your faith in God, and His Word. When you ask, 'Are you saved?', I get, 'I don't know? I think so, I use to be?, or they'll say, 'Oh yes, thank God, I'm just an old sinner, saved by grace.' No, you are not! You were a sinner; you got saved by Grace! You can't be both at the same time. You are a new creation in Christ Jesus.

(II Cor. 5:17); "Anyone who belongs to Christ has become a new person. The old life is gone; a new life has begun!" NLT You have been born into the kingdom of his love. Spiritually speaking as far as God is concerned, you are holy, blameless, and beyond reproach. So quit thinking, speaking, and acting like the world. Let go of all those religious 'sin tags. Begin confessing that you are the righteousness of God in Christ. "So now there is no condemnation for those who belong to Christ Jesus. And because you belong to him, the power of the life-giving Spirit has freed you from the power of sin that leads to death. The law of Moses was unable to save us because of the weakness of our sinful nature. So, God did what the law could not do. He sent his own Son in a body like the bodies we sinners have. And in that body God declared an end to sin's control over us by giving his Son as a sacrifice for our sins. He did this so that the just requirement of the law would be fully satisfied for us, who no longer follow our sinful nature but instead follow the Spirit."

(Romans 8:1-4) NLT (ref. from p39)[1]

If you do sin, confess your sins to God, and He is faithful and just and to forgive us our sins and cleanse us from wickedness, so we will have a clean conscience at His coming. (ref. I John 1:9).

CHAPTER 18

'LA VIDA'

Here we have another title from Amazing Grace Ministry @CSP, from Bruce Benson. The title is Spanish; in English, it means: "The Life". We will use the Scripture he had and expand on those verses. Here we go. ——— Gen. 2:7; Ps. 91:16; Job 12:10; John 5:24; John 6:47-51; John 11:25,26; Prov. 3:1,2; Eccl. 12:7.

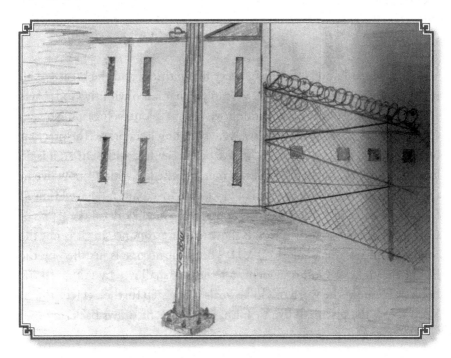

(Genesis 2:7)

"And the Lord God formed man of the dust of the ground and breathed into his nostrils the breath of life; and man became a living being." So, we see, we start off as dust of the ground. And God breath's life into our body. And at the end of our life, dust we shall return. Ref. (Gen. 3:19).

(Ps. 91:16), "With long life I will satisfy him, and show him My Salvation." God wants to give us long life and reveal Himself to us. For He is Salvation. For the Son of God's name means Salvation. As far as having a long life, it is contingent on us. Are we doing what it says in the Word of God, the Bible? Are we following in His Commandment's, and Statues, as He has laid out for us? Sin separates us from God. And continued sin brings death. Are we honoring our father and mother? That can bring us longer life. God is Holy, and He wants His children who believes in Him, to be Holy (set-apart), pure and blameless. Sanctification is a process of ridding your old life, and sin nature, and putting on the new man. For you are a new creation in Christ Jesus. (II Cor. 5:17) "Therefore, if anyone is in Christ, he is a new creation; old things have passed away; behold, all things have become new."

(Job 12:10)

V10) "In whose hand is the life of every living thing, and the breath of all mankind?" Well, from this verse, we can see that it is obviously God. (Acts 17:28) .... for in Him we live and move and have our being, ... Now, as Christians, we are not our own, we were bought with a price. The precious blood of Jesus. (Gal. 2:20) V20) "I have been crucified with Christ; it is no longer I who live, but Christ lives in me; and the life which I now live in the flesh I live by faith in the Son of God, who loved me and gave Himself for me." We live by faith in Christ, and His finished work on the Cross of Calvary. The law was our tutor, to show us our error and sin. It is not the total of who we are? (Gal. 3:11) V11) "But that no one is justified by the law in the sight of God is evident, for the just shall live by faith." In the book of Hebrew, the word of God reveals it one step further. (Heb. 10:38) V38) "Now the just shall live by faith; but if anyone draws back, my soul has no pleasure in him." (I Pet. 4:6) V6) "For this reason the gospel was preached also to those who are dead, that they might be judged according to men in the flesh, but live according to God in the spirit." We were dead in our trespasses and sin, before we came to Christ. He made us alive by His Spirit to eternal life. (Gal. 5:16) so then, V16) "I say then: Walk in the Spirit, and you shall not fulfill the lust of the flesh."

(John 5:24)

V24) "Most assuredly, I say to you, he who hears My word and believes in Him who sent Me has everlasting life, and shall not come into judgment, but has passed from death into life." God does want us to have life, and life more abundantly. The enemy (the Devil) wants to kill, still, and destroy. But God is for you. Living ("Vida") for Him.

(John 6:47-51)

V47) "Most assuredly, I say to you, he who believes in Me has everlasting life. V48) I am the bread of life. V49) Your fathers ate the manna in the wilderness and are dead. This is the bread which comes down from heaven, that one may eat of it and not die. V51) I am the living bread which came down from heaven. If anyone eats of this bread, he will live forever; and the bread that I shall give is My flesh, which I shall give for the life of the world." God, the Father 's Son, did give His life as a ransom for many. His act of love, by dying on The Cross, for the penalty of sin and death. That there was Victory in the Cross. As He rose three days later. Was seen by many witnesses, and He tarried 40 days, then ascended into Heaven. And He will be back to judge the living and the dead. He is the living bread of life; He is also the living water. If we nourish ourselves on His living bread. (His Word), it will pour out of us like living water. For out of the abundance of the heart our mouth speaks. Being full of His Spirit.

(John 11:25-26)

V25) Jesus said to her, "I am the resurrection and the life. He who believes in Me, though he may die, he shall live. V26) And whoever lives and believes in Me shall never die. Do you believe this?" I like her answer. She

first affirmed her faith in Him and calls him Lord, and says, 'Yes Lord'....
She then acknowledges Him as the Anointed One, (The Christ). Then
takes it one step closer, and said, that He is the Son of God, who is to
come into the world. The long-awaited Messiah, the Savior of the World.

V27)" She said to Him, "Yes Lord, I believe that You are the Christ, the
Son of God, who is to come into the world." She is affirming her belief.
Remember when Jesus said, let your yes be yeses and your noes be no,
anything other than that comes from the evil one. Then she called Him
Lord, and when you truly believe Jesus is Lord, that affirmation comes
from the Spirit of God. Then she is affirming what the Old Testament
has revealed to her Jewish faith, in the Word. And she believes in the
resurrection from the dead on the last day, as she claimed in V24) In these
Scriptures, Jesus is talking to Martha, the sister of Mary and Lazarus her
brother. According to the story Jesus tarried (waited) in another town to
make sure Lazarus was in the Tomb (It was a cave) for 4-days, where there
was no question that he was dead. All for the glory of God. So, when Jesus
told Martha, "I am the resurrection and the life" .... He can lay down
His Life and pick it up again. His Father gave Him that ability. And
that Resurrection Power in Him. As in Faith and Authority commanded
Lazarus to come forth. In V43) ...." Now when He had said these things,
he cried with a loud voice," ...Lazarus, come forth!!" He was wrapped in
grave clothes, and He instructed them to lose him from his bonds. "All
Glory Goes to God."

(Prov. 3:1-2)

V1)" My son, do not forget my law, but let your heart keep my
Commandments; V2) For length of days and long life and peace they will
add to you. "(KJV)

Here we see the Scriptures saying keep my Commandments, so obedience
is connected to a longer life.

And lastly, we have (Eccl.12:7).

V7)" Then the dust will return to the earth as it was, and the spirit will return to God who gave it." KJV So, as it started, we are God's children and He gives life to every living creature, and the circle of life (Vida). So, at the end, the dust goes back to the ground (Our body or tent); And our spirit goes back to God, once it came from. End

'BIKE DREAM'

I was on the road somewhere on the edge of town on a dirt highway. Which presently is muddy. There was a convoy of trucks that went by in groups. Fast, and nonstop, and if one spun off the road or one hit some debris, they kept going. They drove really close and fast, and one even went backwards. He was driving an 18-wheeler backwards in formation. It was the single long box trailer, and not two of Course. But still it was unusual to see. Then I find myself at the destination, at the halfway point. Where there was a room full of serious long-tour cyclists. These bicyclers meet a couple of times a month and have this big potluck. At the halfway point, to rest, to talk about whatever. Everyone was really nice, everyone was tall and slender, really fit. This one guy introduced me to this other guy, he said, "You'll be riding with him on your route back". I assume there are multiple starting points, being so many bikers. It looked like about 75 to 100 in two medium size rooms. And one phone. I thought to use the phone, as we are taking turns. To call my second wife, to tell her where I am at, and approximate time home. But I don't have too, no one is there? Besides she didn't like me doing activities without her. (Then I woke up)

'ALL FOR YOU'

There was some important information I read in this book by Kenneth and Gloria Copeland, called 'He did it all for you', from the (KCM). And page 39 is repeated from chapter 17. Starting on page 39), except this is a quote: As a born-again believer, sin has no dominion over you. It can't dominate you. It has to leave you. Satan is a defeated foe-he is not your god. James 4:7 says if you resist him, he will flee from you. You need to see yourself "In

Christ" and know the reality of it. If you ask some people today, "Are you a son of God?" they'll say, "Who, me? Certainly not!" When you ask, "Are you saved?" they'll say, "Oh yes, thank God, I'm just an old sinner, saved by grace. "No, you are not! You were a sinner; you got saved by grace! You can't be both at the same time. You are a new creation in Christ Jesus. You have been born into the kingdom of His love. As far as God is concerned, you are holy, blameless and beyond reproach. So quit thinking, speaking and acting like the world. Let go of all those religious" Sin-tags". Begin confessing that you are the righteousness of God in Christ.

'Your Inheritance'

What does it mean to obtain an inheritance? Acts 20:32 says, "And now, brethren, I commend you to God, and to the word of His grace, which is able to build you up, and to give you an inheritance among all of them which are sanctified." The Word will build you up and give you your inheritance. Page 41) He is in you and you are in Him. His inheritance and your inheritance are one of the same. You are a joint heir with Him. The Apostle Paul prayed that the eyes of our understanding would be enlightened to know the glory of our inheritance in the saints and the exceeding greatness of God's power toward us who believe (Eph.1:18-19). The exceeding greatness of His power. What does His power mean to the believers? Let's read on in Ephesians 1:20-23: Which He wrought in Christ, when He raised Him from the dead, and set Him at his own right hand in the heavenly places, for above all principalities, and power, and might, and dominion, and every name that is named, not only in this world, but also in that which is to come: and hath put all things under His feet, and gave Him to be head over all things to the church, which is His body, the fullness of Him that filleth all in all.

Living in Righteousness

P43] Therefore if any man be in Christ, he is a new creation; old things are passed away; behold, all things are become new. And all things are of God, who hath reconciled us to Himself by Jesus Christ, and hath given to us the ministry of reconciliation; to wit [or to know], that God was in

Christ, reconciling the world unto Himself, not imputing their trespasses unto them; and hath Committed unto us the word of reconciliation... For He [God] hath made Him [Jesus] to be sin for us, Who knew no sin; that we might be made the righteousness of God in Him (II Cor.5:17-21). When you become a new creature, your spirit is completely recreated. Old things are passed away, all things become new, and all things are of God... It is every believer's responsibility to renew his mind with God 's Word, and then use that Word to control his body. Look at Ephesians 4:20-24: P44]" But ye have not so learned Christ; if so, be that ye have heard him, and have been taught by him, as the truth is in Jesus: that ye put off concerning the former conversation the old man, which is corrupt according to the deceitful lust; and be renewed in the spirit of your mind; and that you put on the new man, which after God is created in righteousness and true holiness. The word translated righteousness literally means "to be in right standing". When a person receives Jesus as Lord of his life, he is made righteous. By being brought into right standing with God, every believer is given certain privileges or rights as God's child. "(end quote)

"To be in right standing"

(When I came into prison and repented and confessed my sins as (I John I:9) says for Christians who have gone astray and lost their way, like a lost sheep. (I John I:9) says: V9)" If we confess our sins, He is faithful and just to forgive us our sins and to cleanse us from all unrighteousness."

I felt like the lost son, in the prodigal son story in (Luke 15:11-32) In my drunken state and behavior, that caused disastrous results. Even though I was not conscious of most of the condition I was in. It was no excuse for the consequences that had occurred. I came into prison as a Christian, and repented (means turn away, turn from your old ways and behavior) and I turned toward my risen Savior. On my knees, with a contrite heart. Crying, and asking God to forgive me again. Not unto Salvation, but be in right standing with God, and Ultimately to have a clear conscience before God and my righteousness restored in Christ.) When I read that in the book, it made me think of coming into prison. But, also coming to Christ Jesus in my early 20s. You see when I believed the Word of God and acted in faith and received His eternal gift by God 's amazing Grace. It was not my righteousness, how I receive my salvation. Not any merit, or pious thing. My righteousness came from Jesus Christ dying on the cross, and believing what He did for me. I am now in right standing with God the Father, because the Son of God paid the penalty for sin and death. Jesus became sin on the Cross; the innocent, for the guilty. To atone for the curse of the law. That we may have eternal life with Him. He died once, one sacrifice. Not like the Old Testament, one time every year. (Hebrews 7:27) ..." for this He (Jesus) did once for all when He offered up Himself."

Now, holiness and righteousness are two different things. Holiness is more what we do and how we behave. But Righteousness is who we are, in Christ. The Bible refers us, being "In Christ", "In Him" or "In Whom" 134 times in the Scriptures. That is a lot of blessing from God, that we are identified with. Seek the Word, to see how it could identify with you as a Christian walking in faith. For Holiness we are to renew our minds and body with the word. Just like Christ does for His Bride the Church. (Ephesians 5:26) V26) ..." that He might sanctify and cleanse her with the washing of water by the word,..."

and (Romans 12:1-2) V1)" I beseech you therefore, brethren, by the mercies of God, that you present your bodies a living sacrifice, holy, acceptable to God, which is your reasonable service. V2) And do not be conformed to this world, but be transformed by the renewing of your mind, that you may prove what is that good and acceptable and perfect will of God."

Correct ourselves and walk right before God. (Micah 6:8) V8)" He has shown you, O man, what is good; And what does the Lord require of you. But to do justly, to love mercy, and to walk humbly with your God? "God has promises, and gifts He wants you to have. He gives you one or two, and there are some you have to ask for. By Faith in the Word. (I Cor. 12: 4-11) V4) "There are diversities of gifts; But the same Spirit. V5) There are Differences of ministries, but the same Lord. V6) And there are diversities of Activities, but It is the same God who works all in all. V 7) But the manifestation of the Spirit is given to each one for the profit of all; V8) for to one is given the word of wisdom through the Spirit, to another the word of knowledge through the same Spirit, V9) to another faith by the same Spirit, to another gifts of healings by the same Spirit, V10) to another the working of miracles, to another prophecy, to another discerning of spirits, to another different kinds of tongues, to another the interpretation of tongues. V11) but one and the same spirit works all these things, distributing to each one individually as He wills." It is also as He wills, as He sees fit for you to have. As He needs to exercise it, to uplift the body of Christ, when and how He wills. Now, God has promises, basic to every Christian, to the believers God has chosen; he gives eternal life, His peace that passes all understanding. His joy that the world knows not. God gives hope, and prosperity. These are God's promises... I pray that you may prosper... (3-John 2)&(Ps. 1:3) for the Righteous Believer: V3)"He shall be like a tree planted by the rivers of water, that brings forth its fruit in its season, whose leaf also shall not wither, and whatever he does shall prosper." Let me give you a couple examples of not knowing. You didn't miss, something you didn't know you could have? Until someone shows you. Or you seek for yourself?

1) In prison, all your rights were taken away in court. But, according to the title 15 handbook we are given, to show you what the law is in prison, and what rights you do have. If you don't read it, and know it. You can't use it in your 602 grievances form to benefit your situation. I was in one prison, that was cell living, with a lot of older Inmates (OG's). The CO's may not have announced loud enough, or at all breakfast chow. And even popping doors, didn't wake the sleeping men. So approximately 2 to 3 cells missed walking to get their morning and noon meals, (sack lunch). So, they put in their 602 green forms. And shortly thereafter we got breakfast and lunch delivered to the door. The handbook is for the form, to do it properly and legally.

2)This one is from the book by Kenneth and Gloria Copeland, on page 45 and 46. p45) (2a) ... The same principles apply to you as a child of God. Being a believer (being in Christ Jesus) makes you a citizen of the kingdom of God and entitles you to everything in that kingdom. The Bible is your spiritual "bill of righteousness", outlining all the rights and privileges available to you. Whether or not you partake of your rights is another matter. Ignorance will rob you of the abundant life that is freely available to you.

2b) The best illustration of this is the story of the man who saved for years to be able to buy a boat ticket to America. Once he had saved enough, he bought his ticket and boarded the ship. Since he didn't have any money left for food, he brought along some crackers and cheese. Every evening at meal time, he would look into the dining room at the other passengers enjoying their food, then he would return to his cabin and eat his crackers and cheese. The day the ship docked in in New York Harbor, a steward came to him and said, "Sir, have we offended you in anyway? I noticed that you didn't eat any of your meals in … our dining room." The man answered, "OH, no! You see, I didn't have enough money, for meals so I ate in my room." "Then the steward said, "But sir, your meals were included in the ticket!"

As Christians, we have an abundance of privileges available to us. They were bought and paid for by Jesus at Calvary. But if we don't know it, how can we take advantage of them? Claim the Word for your own and walk in your Inheritance. What's in Christ is about you, you're in him, and he is in you. Walking by faith, and not by sight. That's what it is talking about. Pray, seek, humble yourself, to see what God has for you. (James 5:16) V16) …." The effective, fervent prayer of a righteous man avails much. "(Phil. 2:5,7) V5)" Let this mind be in you which was also in Christ Jesus, who, being in the form of God, did not consider it robbery to be equal with God…. V7) but made Himself of no reputation, taking the form of a bond servant, (Slave) and coming in the likeness of men." You are to think the way Jesus thought. He didn't think it robbery to be equal with God. (We are not God, but we are the sons of God by faith promises of God.) (Ref.) (I Peter 5:6) You have to humble yourself under the mighty hand of God and He will lift you up. And keep in mind you are joint heirs with Christ. Jesus is our example, He became a servant, helping and serving others.

(Romans 8:6-9)

V6)" for to be carnally minded is death, but to be spiritually minded is life in peace. V7) Because the carnal mind is enmity (enemy) against God; for it is not subject to the law of God, nor indeed can be. V8) So then, those who are in the flesh cannot please God. V9) but you are not in the flesh but in the Spirit, (born-again in Christ) if indeed the Spirit of God dwells in you. Now if anyone does not have the Spirit of Christ, he is not His."

Not only do we have our Righteousness in Christ, and an Inheritance, but we are also kings and priests.

*p48 According to Romans 8:29, Jesus is …." the firstborn among many brethren."

Glory to God! Jesus is no longer the only begotten Son of God. Revelation 1:5-6 describes Jesus as "the prince of the kings of the Earth. Unto Him that loved us, and washed us from our sins in his own blood, and has made us kings and priests unto God and His father; to Him be glory and dominion forever and ever." You have been made a king and a priest unto God because of Jesus and the inheritance that he provided for you.

From the book of Acts to the Revelation of John, Jesus is known as the first begotten from the dead. If there is a firstborn, then there has to be a second born, a third born, a fourth born, etc. Every believer is counted as a child of God. We are members of God's family and heirs to all He has. Jesus has made you a king and a priest. He has made you the Righteousness of God in Him. In Him, you are the accepted. In him, you are beloved. You are His chosen and His elect- a Royal priesthood that has been bought with His blood and made His own child " (End quote)

With our Righteousness in Christ, we can boldly come to the Throne of Grace.

I encourage you to read Kenneth and Gloria 's book. "He did it all for you". It is a small 81-page book, but powerful and Spiritual knowledge and input, to show God's love of what Christ did for you on the Cross. And how you can walk in faith, Glorifying God in all you do. Put into practice what God has for you.

Speaking of (KCM), I also thoroughly enjoyed reading "Faith to Faith" a daily reading guide, for 365 days of the year. (end)

CHAPTER 19

'Big Bang Dream'

My dad was on a job, in this old building, he was down in the parking garage. I came to visit him, because I wanted to see him on his job. He was putting these two huge steel I-beams together, that had just been delivered, and the other work trucks were there too. These beams were 2 to 3 feet high and 20 to30 feet long, (which in real life would weigh multiple tons) and he wanted to bolt them together. I helped him to slide one of them in place and interlock them together. I said, 'How are you going to lift those up in place?' And he didn't say anything. (In real life my dad didn't say anything for a week before he died.) I said, goodbye and left, and there were no trucks there, he was by himself alone. (In real life, there was a hospice worker with him at the end, about 4 AM in the morning. And I wanted to be at the funeral, and had a eulogy prepared. I said goodbye from my cell and sent a message through my son to say.) But before I walked out of the building structure. There was a man who was running heavy string or lines throughout the building. I'm thinking that looks like demolition cord for explosives. I guess this building is really old, and it was time for it to go. And it's going out with a big bang. (Now, when I wrote this in real life, and after I was more awake, I realized what this meant. My dad just passed away, and the old building was him. And 'the Big Bang'. Just before going to bed, I was reading a pamphlet on Evolution versus Creation, 'Q's what is the big bang theory? So, that was on my mind, but also at my dad's funeral, he did go out with a bang. He got a Veterans gun salute, and the shell casings and flag went to Gary, my brother. For our dad's military service in the Army air Corps, as a B-24 pilot. I heard it was a good funeral, and all went well. If any funeral is good? The only real good thing that lasting positive, is going to heaven, and being with Jesus the Christ, the Son of the living God forever.)

Back to the dream:

Then I went to this other construction workshop. There were young guys there I talked to. Who said hi to me. He said, 'I thought you were in China, doing missionary work? I said, 'No, not right now.' This was summertime, it was bright and hot. I had my shirt off, and I'd been working out. (In real life I was working out in my cell getting fit.) (Also, there was an outdoor job my buddy John, was going to hook me up with. That too, is on my mind for the future; besides doing mission work. I was presently taking a course from a Christian college called Harvest Bible University.) (I woke up)

'AS THE WORLD TURNS'

These are the 'days of our lives'; as we 'search for tomorrow', and 'all my children'. Our natural occurrences to some few individuals incarcerated. With some ear hustling, even if you're trying or not, it is right outside your door, or next door. There was a man with four baby mamas, and a wife, and a girlfriend, all on the phone constantly. He is a porter, not to work so much, but so he could have access to the phone. Also, when scheduled phone list are posted, he would go and ask, if he can have their phone time too. He is constantly talking, pouring out his life. His mom is a drug addict. His life is a wreck. (The Holy Spirit one day, told me, to give him a gospel track. I believe he is a new believer and has a lot of baggage. And he could receive spiritual information, if he would send for it with the address that was on the back.) To give this man hope for a better future. Right now, he is living with a lot of consequences. But, if he focuses on Jesus, and His finish work on the Cross. And take his burdens to Him.

Jesus will restore him and his military-family. Turn your eyes upon Jesus and yield yourself to Him. Amen. (end)

'DUTCH DREAM'

My dad and I were at this guy's house we use to know back in the day, of laying carpet in the 1960s, 70s and 80s. His name is Dutch, and in this dream, he is married to someone we don't know? He has a new wife, and we were just visiting. We were in the living room talking while Dutch was painting his wall. He was good at multi-tasking, and this wall was huge, and by the time we finished the conversation, he was done. He said, 'We better get going.' And I said, 'We don't want to be late for the meeting.' I have been there once, and it was hard to find. And I needed to stick close with my dad, so when we get there, he won't get lost. Before we went into Dutch's home, dad and I were in the garage talking. He was older now, and was retired, but worked many years together. Now, I am on my own. I'm thinking about changing my job I have been doing floor laying and construction most of my life, but it was time for a change. I could stay in what I've been doing and make a pretty good living. It's hard work, with not many benefits; only unless I make them. I said, I just talked to this guy at the park, downtown about being a priest (minister -Rev.). It pays $46,000 a year, which isn't too bad. More than I was making in the floor business, as a contractor. (But it is all what you put into it. I could have multiple employees and have big contracts and make more than that amount, but more headaches as they say, that's the trade-off.)

(About being a priest,— I was also talking to my Bunkie about chapter 18; 'All for you', about holiness, righteousness, and inheritance, and that we are priests and kings in Christ.)-(Godly men, Saints of God, are supposed to be a Spiritual priestly head of the house -hold.)-(And The reason in my dream, I was dreaming about a park, with buildings nearby, because my buddy John was doing construction work by the park and administration, and juvenile courts area, which he told me recently on the phone.)——— back to the dream- So, anyway, I asked him what he thought. I told him, and the other minister; I wanted to pray about it first. (like Phil. 4:6 says),

And I'll get back with you. To me it looked like a church administration building with two or three floors, instead of a sanctuary. This building, at the corner of this large park. (And my Bunkie and I were talking about a pastor's salary, and tithing, offerings, special offerings, and benevolence fund. [Someone in real need, someone hurt or disadvantaged, a mercy fund]. Just before bed.) I said, it would be a little easier on my body. I said I'll have a few flights of stairs to deal with every day. (In real life, with my second wife, I was used to stairs, in a 2 1/2 story house; no, that doesn't mean half the house is missing, on top? It means, it is three stories with two flights of steps, and a finished attic, with low ceilings on the sides.) end.

CHAPTER 20

'B.R. MINDED'

B.R. Minded means to Become Righteousness—Minded. This is another exert from the book I was reading from Kenneth and Gloria Copeland. And on p.66), was something important of walking In Christ and being righteous because of the faith you have in Christ Jesus and His Love, Mercy, and Grace on the Cross at Calvary.

p.66) quote: Paul said in first Corinthians 15:34, "Awake to righteousness, and sin not." Awake to righteousness, become aware that you have been made the righteousness of God in Jesus Christ, that you have been placed in right- standing with Him through the sacrifice of Jesus at Calvary.

When you do, it will stop the sin in your life. As long as Satan can convince you that you don't have any right to things of God, he can keep you under his thumb and sin will control your life. But when you awake to righteousness, you will realize that Satan is a defeated foe, and the struggle is over. (end quote)

(2nd paragraph p.66) quote:

Awake to righteousness... Become righteous-minded! You have been thoroughly equipped to handle every situation that comes your way. You are to reign in life as a king by Jesus Christ, living in conformity with the

Father. Almighty God, creator of the universe, chose to come down on your level in the form of Jesus Christ, to dwell in your heart by the Holy Spirit, and to give you His righteousness, His ability, and His strength… "greater is He that is in you, than he that is in the world." (I-John 4:4) Praise God! (end quote).

(3rd paragraph p.66) quote: Ephesians 3:20 says He is "able to do exceedingly abundantly above all that we ask or think, according to the power that worketh in us." (end quote)

(p.67) quote: 'He was saying we spend too much time in fleshly things, and almost completely ignoring the power of the Word of God to deliver us from the flesh.' (In Heb. 5:13-14) Tell us, "For every one that useth milk is unskilful in the word of righteousness for he is a babe." He doesn't know how to use the Bible—how to believe it or how to fight Satan with it. Verse 14 says, "But strong meat belongeth to them that are of full age, even those who by reason of use to have their senses exercised to discern both good and evil. "(end quote)

When I had come into prison, I was dealing with a few issues of alcohol, cigarettes, and being overweight. Only by feeding on the Word, and prayer. Turning away from those things that had me bound in my flesh. Then using the Word, I can be an Overcomer in Christ. The Word says, "I can do all things through Christ which strengthen me." KJV (Phil.4:13) When you grow in the word your faith increases. And your walk is more in the Spirit of God. Then you have Victory, with the leadership of the Holy Spirit. In the section with Kenneth portion: He has a three-step formula of success in every area of your life. …

p70). 1) find the will of God in your situation by prayer and meditation in the word. Once you have found the will of God, confer no longer with flesh and blood. Don't ask other people what to do. I may discuss a situation with my wife or my staff, but once we have prayed and I know the will of God, then it doesn't matter with what they think or say about it. Get your job done at all costs. Don't allow anything or anyone to stand in the way of God 's will. (end quote)

Just remember, not to be in self-righteousness. Be humble before God, know who made you righteous before God the Father. That His Son, paid the penalty so you can live. By God 'grace, and mercy. As we walk in that faith, through love.

The last chapter of Kenneth and Gloria 's book. Gloria represents that God is love. And Love works all things. And without love it would be meaningless. She says, "So commit yourself to agape —God's love now."

"And when temptation comes, you'll remember your decision and obey Love." (end quote)

And being conscious of your love walk, "Confess that you are the love of God. Base your confession on first Corinthians 13 four through eight. This God kind of love will begin to influence all you say and do. If someone says something unkind to you, love will say, "That's OK. I am not touchy, fretful or resentful, I take no account of that." And you go free! "For love is truly the only sure secret to our success."

(end quote) p.81). (end)

'LESSON 17'

One of my recovery classes in chapter 17, asked me what my new masculinity as a new person is, on the other side of recovery.

My new masculinity is song and the word of God. Singing is a passion of mine. And mostly in praise to God. He gives me the ability to praise and glorify Him back, through the Holy Spirit.

God gave me a praise song in a Christian Spanish worship service at Golden State MCCF McFarland. And I received chords to the words and rearranged some words and was playing a song on my guitar in two days. And a year and a half later I'm still playing and singing it at CSP (Corcoran state prison).

It is a story of being set-free in prison. Before I am released? God blessed me physically, mentally, Spiritually, and emotionally. To be more explicit. I wrote a statement, as a testimonial before I sing this song. The song is entitled:

"I Am FREE "!

…. This will help express some of my inter-remodeling in my house (metaphor), that I didn't explain in lesson number four. And my exterior I am getting physically fit by exercising and lost 50 pounds and gained back 15 to 20 pounds in muscle.

My testimonial goes something like this: I thank God for the opportunity to serve you. God bless you all in the name of Jesus Christ our Lord. This song was inspired in a Christian Spanish worship service. In prison, the Lord freed me, in my body in my spirit. On the outside: I was bound in sin, sickness in mind, drunkenness, depression, and suicidal. I was bound in weight, I was 50 pounds heavier, with high-blood pressure, sleep apnea, night terrors, and fear. God healed it all. So, Jesus, set me free. Free in worship, free in songs of praise to Him. The Lord loosest my bonds. (Amen)!

'This was my song given to me'

1V

I am free, oh-oh Lord, I am free.
Indeed oh-oh Lord, your all I need.
Holy and Righteous are you Lord.
You are King of all creation.

Chorus:

Glory to you Lord,
Glory to you Lord

2V

Thank you, for Your mercy, and Love!
There's nothing more I can say, except,
Thank you, for sending Your dove!
And showing me Your Way.

Bridge:

Yes Lord, I am free, Oh-Oh Lord,
Yes Lord, I am free, your all I need.
If the Son shall set you free,
You will be free indeed. (2x)

End: Alleluia; Alleluia; Alleluia: (end)

'ROBERT DREAM'

I was in this dream with a buddy of mine, and we went to visit an old gentleman, who ran a shop, (a clerk's window) in this little booth. Selling something, or tickets? We came by and said hello, actually jumped over the counter to get to him and talked; that old gentleman was Robert Duvall. We were telling him; we will be receiving some money soon and our troubles are over. He wasn't sure at first but was all for it. I noticed he forgot to pull his tag off his new pants, so I did it for him. (end) and woke up.

(In real life, I had been watching two state movies over and over. Jack Reacher, and in one of them is Robert Duvall playing an owner of a gun shop, behind the counter. And the gun range, behind the shop.) (And, in real life God willing we will be receiving a stimulus check in the mail and deposit in our trust account.). End chapter 20

CHAPTER 21

'SUPERMARKET DREAM'

The supermarket dream with interpretation:

I was in a supermarket (world) and the store owner (Jesus) organizing and separating and saving all the good merchandise. (The Believers/ The Saints of God /The Wheat / The Sheep). And clearing out the old stock, and deadwood as they say. (The Unbelievers / The Tares or Weeds / The Goats). And getting ready for a New Era, after the COVID-19 pandemic. (Getting close to the end of the age and beginning signs of birth pains). This supermarket went back to old school, and in the back of the store; They put in a huge incinerator, to burn trash; (Hell, for burning the unbelieving will be burned). Woke-up. (End)

(In real life my Bunkie and I were talking about soap operas, actors, and celebrities. The conclusion was, they're just people too. Then we discussed, there are only two kinds of people in the world, Believers and Unbelievers. Faith in Jesus and repentance of sin is key to Salvation. Meaning believe and trust in Jesus Christ and Him Crucified, His death, burial, and resurrection, for eternal life). End

'THE BIG HOUSE DREAM'

I was in this big house, and I was leaving, and my second wife had left some lights on, and I am looking for the right switch, to turn it off. (In real life, my wife and I's house had multiple switches everywhere; the front door had four and four steps over had one; then one step over had three more). Then this large room turned into a mobile home, a Double-wide, and Howard showed up; I was watching his home while he was gone. (In real life, he doesn't live in a mobile-home, but he did sell mobile-homes for a living). And I said, 'I was supposed to meet up with dad, to go to your place and do some work.' (In real life my dad and I worked at his home and his business, called Mac Trailer Sales). (I guess he bought the company from Mac, because Howard was the owner?) I am still messing with switches, and putting everything back the way it is supposed to be. He can get upset sometimes. We went in the backyard, and now it is my dad 's backyard, where I grew-up mostly. Howard found some darts and shot them at a target on the fence and the neighbor came out to help and show him, he has a set too.

(In real life we did have a dart set, and that was my father-in-law 's, that was after I married his daughter, when I was 20, and she was 19). (Also in real life, there are the two houses side-by-side with a grape stake redwood fence in between). But, in the dream there was like a sub-open basement, a pit. That was about 8 to 10 feet deep. (Why? I don't know?) (But, in real life, on our neighbor's side, which was about 1 foot lower than our lot; We'll, when it rained, all the water ended up on their side. And there was only dirt there. So, we called it the mud-pit). In the dream, it was a dry-hole and rectangular in shape about 8 feet wide and 20 feet long. (Which in real life was close to the size of their side of the house excluding the fireplace). (It looked more like an oil change pit, for Auto's; come to think of it. He used to pour his oil change out there, but that was before. When you did your own oil changes, and before the environmental agency said, don't pour your motor oil out on the dirt). In the dream, I am telling people there on this situation, and the background story of how this all came about. (But, in real life I don't know what I was saying?) …

Then Howard said, 'This is where we hid the 16 sticks of dynamite. Under here'., As he pointed to the corner of the lot. He said, 'This is during the construction, they needed to make the hole, between the buildings. (And in real life, they don't use dynamite, but a backhoe and a scoop-tractor, and definitely wouldn't bury dynamite. The 16, I'm thinking came from my girlfriend next-door and her 16th birthday party, who became my wife). End

'3-Musketeers Dream'

My sister and her friend, and I were out and about town. And at a certain time, this one store sells so much percentage of hot-wax (In a honey cone shape). And she needed to use it, and we headed for the place that does it. And our dad was coming out, and he asked, 'What are you doing here?' And my sister said, 'We are here, and I need to use 4 ounces.' And he said, 'Well I only need half of that, but I didn't do it, they have a minimum.' So, he was turned down. But we went back in with the rest of us, into the building. (Then I woke up)

(I was thinking why my dad is there? He was pretty hairy in real life).

CHAPTER 22

'SYLVESTER DREAM'

We are in a castle, and the king likes to play kid games. One right after the other. Stallone and I were on this iron fence. We had to travel on it, and around it, and jump from one to the other. To win the goal of the game. (In the dream we weren't told what we would win. It could just be for the king's enjoyment.) So, we were traveling along the fence line and had to jump to the other section on a gate. I went first and made it. I started going to the other section. And Stallone says, (He said it like Rocky), 'I was with jew-u, you should be here with me, when I jump.' I said, 'OK, and headed back toward him. He completed the task, and onto the next section. Now, we are in the castle's outdoor walkway corridor. The stone walls are 20 to30 feet high. And here, we are supposed to kick this newspaper that is all rolled up. Up to the walk over bridge. And there was only one, so I got back like it was a football, I ran up and sailed it up to the next floor. There was a young man up there who says, 'I got it'. I kicked it right up to him, and he reached out with a baseball glove, and he caught it. But it is not a ball, and he doesn't close the glove, and it falls to the ground. So, we didn't waste time and went to the next thing. (I woke up; the door popped open for morning Chow. Got to go.) (I guess I played the game before and knew what was next in the dream, otherwise Sylvester Stallone could have been in the lead.) end.

'KELSEY DREAM'

I was in a dream with Kelsey Grammer, we had just been somewhere. And he brought to me to this farm. And I seem to be younger, in my teens or early 20s. At first, I walked up with him next to me, he was like a mentor but, then like in the movies, it switches to another camera angle. And I could see myself standing next to him. And he wanted to show me something, and he wasn't scared. Off in the distance, maybe a couple 100 feet. There was these plastic-Paris covered statues of a life size, large elephant and a huge tiger. But, bigger, like in the dinosaur days, except without tusks. And the tiger on the backside moved, it was real. And I ran out into the fields. It was all dirt out there; it saw something moving and went out after it. Then Kelsey kept me there, to show me this thing. I said, 'I don't want to be here, let's go.' He said, 'It's alright.' And we waited on the sidewalk, by the farmhouse. Then this giant cat (Bengal tiger in colors) saw us and ran toward us. Fortunately, it turned into some kind-of, not too bright, blob of an animal. With no horns, (but more like a big water buffalo with long hair.) This animal was friendly. He put me up on his neck, (which was about 6 to 7 feet off the ground.) Then my legs got on his mouth and snout like a lump under my legs, and I didn't like that. I thought he might bite my legs.

(And then I woke- up)

(In real life, I had a pair of thick shorts under my legs. I use them when I go to sleep, to put between my legs when I lay on my side.) end.

'DAUGHTER DREAM'

I was dreaming, I was in a hotel room, it was a long rectangle room. With two big slide glass doors on each side of the room. To a patio, and to a view somewhere? It had two double beds and a bunkbed at the end. I was sleeping in the top-bunk. And I was dreaming, (yes, a dream, in a dream.)

And I was dreaming Howard came to the hotel and he was standing by the bed. He wanted to tell me something, and he was (him-ha-ing around) as they say, I fiddled with my pillow in the second dream; I am working out next to the bunk.

And he puts my pillow down below. And my wife grabs my arm to calm me down. As I am sleeping, as I repeat what Howard says. 'I have a daughter', And I said, 'You have a daughter?', 'Why didn't you say something?'

And I am saying this out loud in my dream, in the hotel, and my wife grabs me and is praying for me; I feel tingly, and I woke up in both dreams. (But in real life, I didn't speak out, at least I don't think so. My Bunkie is still sleeping.) (So, afterward I was praying for this family, for reconciliation and salvation. The only problem is Helen (his wife) passed away years ago when I was young, and Howard passed a few months to a year before me coming to prison). But, with God, all things are possible.

CHAPTER 23

'J & K DREAM'

I was dreaming with my friends, J & K or (John and Kim). We were out in front of my dad 's house. We were throwing a blue racquetball back-and-forth. (That wasn't a problem until you drop it. It bounces pretty good, not as much as a super ball. [A smaller colorful rubber ball]. You could bounce that thing up about 50 feet high, practically out of sight, because it was so small too.) Anyway, the racquetball gets away, and rolls across the street, in between all these people working on a construction project. And Kim goes after it and goes right between where the ball went. She gets it, and says, 'I'm sorry', and throws it back across the street. But it goes to the right, and gets in the gutter, and it is flowing with the water. So, I run down the street and get it out of the gutter and walk back to play again. The next-door neighbors who I didn't know, because it is years later. They were out in the yard cleaning and raking Pine needles. (They had two Pine trees near the property line, on the neighbor's side.) Anyway, when I got back. I wanted to get the water off the ball on the outside, but it also seemed heavy, and slushy inside. Anyway, I slammed the ball on the sidewalk. It only went up about 10 to 15 feet high. And it knocked the water off the outside. Now, I did it again to get the inside. Slam! it went up about 25 feet high and landed in the top of the pine tree, which is also how high the street light pole was too, right next to it. So, I grabbed the tree trunk and started shaking it. But the ball wouldn't come out. So, I did it as hard as I could. The ball finally dropped the only thing was, so did a bunch of Pine needles. (My bad.) They had just cleaned this area. I'm glad I didn't have to climb the tree. Anyway, we continue to play. (I woke up)

(In real life, the blue racquetball doesn't have an air-filler, like big balls. So, there couldn't be water on the inside of the ball, go figure?) (end)

'MY PROSPECTIVE JOURNEY'

This is also from lesson 18 the last in H.M.R. (Helping Men Recovery) at C.S.P. (Corcoran State Prison). H.M.R., is a group study to help men with Addictions. To help them grow from the inside out. To have them take an honest look inside themselves. To be a better man or woman. The original program was designed for women recovery. But was adapted for men and the criminal justice system.

This is an exercise about what positive things you will do six months after getting out of prison, looking back. It's now 6 months after release and, as I look back over the last six months of my life;..... I have multi-jobs and Ministry projects, including, three Christian books being completed. And saved enough money to start a catering-van project. For the homeless, and music Ministry.

Being used in a church or churches for ministry. Also having been a regular for Celebrate Recovery, and God willing buy that time leading or before. Being with my family, in family events helping my children, and enjoying my grandchildren. Who are about 4 & 5 years old now.

Sponsor a dinner for my relatives and friends and tell them what Jesus did for me in prison. How I went down that spiral and came back-up again with God's help, and His Amazing Grace.

And complete a promise I made, to take my kids and grandkids to an Amusement Park (Magic Mt.) end.

'RAMP DREAM'

I was on a job, in a home, a rental, apartment/condo with wood floors. (It could be a modular home. Where there is maybe 2,3, or 4, mobile home units put side-by-side. Connect them together and have factory upgrades of all the walls with sheet rock and plaster. Upgrade flooring materials, and upgrade appliances. Upgrade plumbing fixtures and lighting also. Even the doors in the windows. These modulars are put together, and the outside of the home looks like it is one building. And the ground [dirt] is cut away underneath it so it looks like it's on level ground, like a cement floor, but it isn't. Or, they don't have wheels underneath. And if they're small enough, they could be lifted in place with a crane and set on their foundation, specially designed to accommodate these units.)

Anyway, it was a long walk to where this is, and my van is located in the parking lot. I am assessing what the other owner wants done. There is a level-difference between one unit and the other. (In real life, that should have been the responsibility of the people who set it up, to begin with.) (That is who put these buildings in place, but they are long gone.) And left a 20-foot section about 1 inch higher than the other. That is a lot of fill material. I was hired to fix the difference, or to make a ramp to transition from one level to the other, without much difference when you walk into the room.

Fortunately, the upgrade on the carpet and pad will help hide this difference. Even though they didn't hire me to lay down the carpet and pad. Go figure? (This is a dream)

Having not been told, not knowing exactly what I was there for? (In real life I would assess and estimate materials used and hours taken to accomplish this task.) I always have some supplies for filling cracks, holes, and pooling low areas for patching. And enough to make a couple of doorway ramps. (In real life this would multiply hundreds of pounds worth of materials.) (Which I would have to purchase.) I have two kinds; one is a white powder that you mix with water. It looks like plaster material, that you put on the walls, and I have used it for that before. As long as you use a latex-additive to give it twice the strength from 300-350 pounds per square inch to 600 to 700 pounds per square inch. End it is also used for sticking power, meaning for it to bond to the wall or floor, so it doesn't break-up or fall-off.

The second is a gray-powder, which is a cement base. As I was leaving this complex or property. I was walking next to a swimming pool, with some people (tenets). I said, 'Hello', and they said the same. And they wanted to know my name? There was four people sitting at this round table chatting. I said, 'my name is Loren'. And I repeated it, but one didn't understand, I said, 'it is Loren like Lorne Green, from Bonanza'. They said, who is that? (I said in the dream it is spelled the same, but it isn't). So, I wrote it down for them, they happen to have paper and a pencil handy. Then I walked off to my vehicle. There was a man outside the gate to this facility, saying, 'are you done yet?' And I said, 'I just got there. 'It was mid-morning now, maybe 9-10AM, and he was probably the one who wants to move in. It is obviously not ready yet. When I got out in the parking lot. Which is right next to a train going by. Someone was saying that this is the wrong train for San Diego. They got this passenger train mixed-up, in the wrong town? When I was in this big store, just before arriving to check out this job. They also said inside that we have the wrong train here in San Diego?

(Now, if I was to create a ramp for this in real life, I would use pre-made 3 foot or 4-foot-long wedges about 10 to 12 inches wide as a base. These pre-made wedges of wood or rubber are tapered from 0 inches to 1/4, 3/8, or 1/2, thick. Putting them side to side for the 20 feet. Which the wood ones are 3 foot wide, and it would require seven of them to make 21 feet. ...

And since it is carpet and padding going down. We will not use the expensive cement patch, but still will use the milky-white adhesive to do a good job. The white patch is sufficient to do the job. (And in the dream, it may have looked like it was 1 inch difference in the room at the doorways and along the 20-foot wall.

Most mobile homes use 5/8-inch particleboard. An upgrade would be three-quarter inch thick floor. And even better upgrade would be using plywood). (If it was 1 inch difference, I would be able to see the undercarriage structure and beams of the coach. It was probably more like half inch to 3/4 and maybe one of the mobile homes or modulars had settled or sunk in the mud, on their foundations).

(Let's just say it was three-quarter inch difference with a three-quarter inch plywood upgrade. And the 3-foot wedges are in place, nailed down. Now, I would get an empty 5-gallon bucket, and start making some floor patch with water and the milk-additive. They come in 25-pound sacks of gypsum-patch (like fix-all). And whatever it took 6,8,10,12, bags or more to make a ramp 3 feet to 4 feet out from the ledge of the other floor. To make a gradual descent). (Then I would put a fan blowing on each layer of patch. Until it was to the proper height, with a taper down to 0 inches. The fans I used were, a 19-inch, 20 inch, and 24 inches. It would speed dried the ramp. By taking the moisture out of the patch. Besides these patches I use have a catalyst in them to make them dry quicker. With a chemical reaction to heat-up the product to dry faster. So, the farther you go out with the ramp, the smoother the transition you will have from room to room). End

CHAPTER 24

'AL'S CABIN DREAM'

Al and I are at his family cabin in the mountains. Al had been telling me all about his cabin, and his family was up there for a reunion. He was showing me the town and the sites all around the lake. (In real life I have never seen his cabin.) And it is wintertime and there is snow on the ground, cold, and partly cloudy. He was telling me as we are walking along the road next to the lake. We need to go to these friend's house and motivate them to get out and enjoy themselves. I said, 'yes, for sure'; 'And you guys live up here and don't get out and explore nature?' He said, 'I guess people can get stuck in the everyday mondain routine.' We are now downtown at these stairs to the small shops that sell tourist stuff. He tells me that my second ex-wife was in town, and possibly was with someone. I said, 'That's OK, she said, she wanted to move on.' And not to be reminded of me anymore. Besides our relationship was going downhill anyway, the last few years we were together.

First of all, we had two work schedules different. So, we didn't see each other much. Then it seemed she shut herself down, relationship wise. Sometimes I don't even think she knew it, how much I was shut out, and for how long. We were in two different worlds. It probably started two marriages back, where she married this rich guy. But, because of the ethnic culture it was OK to be a player too. That doesn't fly with her. Maybe that's where she learned to shut herself out. Because she stayed a year after their marriage. For the family's sake that she loved. But the one she married, cheated on her the day of the wedding. Maybe not physically, but of the heart. The next husband went 10 years, but at the end there was no connection, and he was fed up and he left. And for me too. I was fed-up and told her there's no connection. We lead separate lives. I have been depressed about our relationship, and I wanted out. And asked her for $40,000, and I'll be on my way. Which is a low number for what she was worth. But she was trying to get me to stay. And tells me, there is nothing wrong with our relationship. The last husband slept in the other room, and so did I, and he walked out on her. We'll at least I told her what I was going to do. Anyway, Al took me to his friend's home, and we went in the backyard. I looked down at my clothes, and I needed to dress up a little and get my coat. But we went in anyway. As we are standing in the backyard, the kids are playing in the snow coming down. The weird part is, it is like it's on the edge of the storm, that is half the backyard is lightly snowing and cold, and the other side isn't. That's where we were standing, looking at the dividing line in the sky, and some landing on the sidewalk too. I walked out 10 to 15 feet, and it was snowing on me, and it was freezing. (And I woke up.)

(In real life, all the cells and the building we're having heating problems. So, we were freezing. But thank God for shelter over our heads and three meals a day.) (In real life my buddy does have or had a family cabin. But, not next to a lake. The lake in the dream was Shaver Lake. Which my buddy and I were never at, At the same time, except Morro Bay State Park. But, this lake (Shaver), my second ex-wife and I went five years in a row to RV vacation. And it was on the TV news recently here showing the snow in the town. The town of Shaver is about 5500 feet elevation. End

'Dishes Dream'

My dad and I, and my brother Gary, we're in our old house, that we grew up in. I was standing in the den. My brother who was younger in the dream. (But in real life he is my older brother.) So, the setting is like in the 1960s to 70s. He was sitting in a chair next to the phone on the wall with the long curly cord. (Except in real life I never saw my brother sit in that chair, and that chair wasn't there till 1975 when our dad got remarried).

Dad is standing in the kitchen, about 6 to 7 feet away. There is a low cabinet there in between us over the stove. For dishes and the exhaust fan. So, there was an opening in between us about one and a half feet to 2 feet high off the kitchen bar counter. He is doing the dishes, loading the dishwasher. And he is talking to both of us. But, neither one of us is listening. My brother is reading a book. (Which in real life that didn't happen; I don't know how he got through High School). (To be honest I wasn't that much better). And at the same time, I am telling him, there is an opened box of frosted flakes, with Tony the Tiger on the front, and on the counter. And a big trail of ants about 1 inch wide coming from the kitchen, over the stove burners and right in the box. It was one of those giant boxes you get at Costco. (But, in real life, Costco hasn't come to our town yet? Of Bakersfield in the time frame of the dream). Dad, keeps talking, and he's now not listening to me either, or I say it again. 'There's ants on the counter, and in the cereal box.' Then I say it again, and again. So, this time I am moving toward the kitchen, walking around the counter. And telling him one more time, and then just throw the box away myself. He was standing there in the kitchen, and from the den I couldn't see his face. I knew he was there. I was talking to him, and he to us, but we weren't communicating. I moved into the kitchen where he was standing, and he was gone. I don't know why I looked in the dishwasher in the dream, but I did? And of course, he wasn't in there either. He is gone. (In real life, this doesn't take much to figure out in this dream; our dad passed away).

(On Nov. 7, 2020); He was born in Finland in 1922, April 8. So, he was 98 years old. He lived a full life blessed by God, even though he didn't fully acknowledge him until his last five years. I am going to miss him. End

'CANDY BUS. DREAM'

I was working in the family candy business, and there is cakes and sweets given to the employees special every week. I was trying to give them away, so I don't eat them. And Charlotte my cousin was walking by heading for the company office. I said, 'do you want some cakes?' (No, I don't think she did?). She just laughed. (I woke-up)

(In real life, my cousin and her husband Ron had their own business). (And in prison at dinner time or chow as they like to call it, I would give or trade my cake away.) (Trying to keep my weight down to a minimum.) End

CHAPTER 25

'GANGS ALL HERE DREAM'

I was walking with someone up the middle of the street where I grew-up. I had been away, and I had something to do, and couldn't go home yet. Dad would be expecting me later. I was working on a project presently, but I stopped over and said hi, to my stepbrother and his wife, and my stepsister and her husband.

They all were at the Lencioni House at 4117. They were all outside cleaning the house and a car. Simona was vacuuming this big luxurious car with four-doors. (Like the Lencioni's use to have a big Lincoln in real life). And Karen was watching the boys, (that is Greg and Bill) and to see if they're cleaning it alright. The front of the old house was turned into a high gloss shiny brown and white barn door. (In real life, the house was white, with a brown trim. But not high gloss paint. And it didn't look like a barn, but the trim boards symbolized barn beams).

Greg and Bill, instead of being on a ladder, and one was there for them. They decided to perch themselves, holding on the edge of the door frame with their feet and grabbing the edge of the wood with one hand or they would fall. (They were competing who could clean the longest without falling). They were about 5 to 6 feet off the ground. Greg, saw me first as I am walking up on the grass, and said, 'How on earth are you?' They were up on these barn doors, where Karen and Brenda's old room used to be. I said something kiddingly. 'I'm new in town. I am your neighbor'. Bill says something funny, and says, 'welcome, what can we do for you?' 'I was looking to borrow a cup of sugar'. He says, 'oh, do you have any references?' I said, 'the old man next-door will vouch for me'. Bill said, 'that's good enough.'

I am standing with my shirt off, all flexed up. When I went away, I had a big beer-belly. Then Simona comes over and welcomes me, so the (girls), Simona and Karen we do the Basque kisses on both cheeks. And in Greg's freehand, he is holding a 2-foot scrub brush with soap on it. (In real life, I am not sure where the soap had come from?) And in bills freehand he has a garden hose with water mildly running out. And Karen is standing by supervising the whole operation. (Then I woke up). End

'JIM DREAM'

Jim and I were in a living room scene. Or more he was in the scene. And I was just watching him. I say scene, because it was a movie take. Jim Carrey is doing some wackiness coming off this couch. Making all kinds of sounds, belching and farting sounds etc. And saying a couple of lines about,' what I think women were thinking? (In real life I'm mixing up movies in my head, that had to do with a Mel Gibson Movie, which was a pretty funny one too.) Anyway, he says, something about being an insurance salesman. (But it was probably the advertising business. And just getting an idea for a slogan).

Then in the same house, and time, when he says, 'I think there's a change in the weather.'(Which in real life I had just said that late night after watching the news with the weather.) (From cold and foggy, in two or three days to sunny. Today's low 37° in high is 56°.) And now I am leaving for work, in the living room to the entry. It is about 9 AM. My first wife was there and was hugging me, and kissing me before I leave, and couldn't wait till I get home from work, to work on our relationship again. (And I woke-up). End

'CONSTRUCTION/MOTOR DREAM'

I was teaching someone to ride a motorcycle. I wasn't riding with him physically, but more his consciousness. As we were riding, he was a natural, no fear, perfect control and balance. Wheelies, hills, road, different terrain. Going from street, to dirt, and back and forth.

The longer he went, he kept going till we ended up in the mountains. And asked me why I have to keep downshifting, it keeps bogging down? I said because the steeper you go, the lower the gear you have to use.

Now, we were up in the wooded mountains and mountain cabins. And they are scattered all around us. And one was being worked on. It was one of my projects. There was a new foundation being prepared to be poured. With new rough plumbing. That is the new sewer lines. And this even goes down to the basement, and the front 4 x 4 car parking area. Then I (woke-up)

(This reminds me to build my foundation on Christ Jesus. And the other thing it reminds me of; the Holy Spirit working inside of you, teaching and instructing you through the gifts of the Spirit, to be in-line with Him; into the image of God the Father 's Son, Jesus the Christ.) (And as a testimony, the rough plumbing that was mentioned, God restored my colon, after my alcohol abuse.) I have to be steadfast immovable and have a firm foundation. Not to be tossed to and fro with every wind of doctrine. Continue forward with Christ and run the race to the end. (l-Cor.15:58) Jesus is the Author and finisher of my faith. And… 'being confident of this very thing, that He who has begun a good work in you will complete it until the day of Jesus Christ… (Phil. 1:6) …, (Not to be tossed around in life, with all that rough terrain. To be like that motorcycle rider and be a natural from one road to the other. Not losing balance, but staying the course, finishing the race. Gaining the prize.)

(Jesus was focused on his mission to the Cross and Calvary, He didn't waiver, he was steadfast in His ministry. And at the end. He got to say, 'It is finished '[John 19:30].

Ref. (Heb.6:1)— (The Lord was reminding me in the Scriptures of coming into prison and putting behind the old....'foundation of repentance from dead works and of faith toward God.' And be about my Fathers business.) In (Eph.4:14-15)

V14)" .... that we should no longer be children, tossed to and fro and carried about with every wind of doctrine, by the trickery of men, in the cunning craftiness of deceitful plotting, 15) but, speaking the truth in love, may grow up in all things into Him who is the Head—Christ... ", ... And what does (1-Cor. 15:58) say, V58)" Therefore, my beloved brethren, be steadfast, immovable, always abounding in the work of the Lord, knowing that your labor is not in vain in the Lord. " (Jesus is my Rock, He is coming soon.) (II Sam. 22:2-3) V2) And he said:

The Lord is my rock and my fortress and my deliverer;
The God of my strength, in whom I will trust;
My shield and the horn of my salvation,
My stronghold, and my refuge;
My Savior, you save me from violence. Ref. (Matt.7:24-25; 16:18-19) End

CHAPTER 26

'V.W. DREAM'

I was over off Belle Terrace Way, in an old VW bug. And I had someone following me. As we turned onto the main street going east. There was a car coming, but I got by him before he hit me. The bug had a high-performance engine in it. I was showing my friend behind me, that it had a lot of zip to it. When we hit 'H' Street, we made a left or north. And I went a couple of blocks and pulled over to the side of the road. Tim was with me, and we were headed for the skin doctor. He was little then, maybe 6 to 8 years old. The friend caught up with us, and we were all standing next to this general store. I told Tim we don't have to go to the doctor now. He said, 'yes we do, we need to go' and ran off. Past the front door of the store. People were coming and going, I said, 'come back here', and saying things to him like 'he's my son,' which he is, and I wanted people around me to know that. That I wasn't chasing down any kid randomly. He went around to the back and was blocked off. I said, 'OK, we will go to the skin doctor. OK'. And we walked back to the front of the building. ….and (I woke up). End

(In real life Tim doesn't have any skin or complexion problem, but I was experience some in prison on my legs and arms mostly.) End

Loren L. Johnson

'RESCUE DREAM'

The dream starts off with my dad, my grandpa, and I standing together in this big commercial garage building, with four or five large bay doors. They are open and ready for use. There are empty racks in there all around us. And then suddenly a storm happens, and water floods that whole garage. Everything is underwater, and we three are floating to the top of the building. We are almost there, and must decide, perish and drown, or go through the doorway and come out on the outside of the building. And the water is coming in so fast, that the door is hidden, and we are nearing the ceiling. So, we all decided to go through the first bay door, it was smaller than the rest but closer. So, one by one in faith swimming under the water and going through the door and came out on the other side or outside. And right away there was a rescue helicopter above to get us. We are being filled with the wind coming over us, splashing the water. And in a moment, we will be changed from this watery grave to the Savior of this helicopter pilot who happens to be in this dream, Jesus. He is looking down and lowers the sling. My grandpa is having the hardest time of treading water, he being the oldest and the heaviest. So, we helped put the sling on him first. And up he goes. Then the sling comes back down. I am all right in the water, but my dad is struggling a little. So, I put the sling on him. And up he goes. So, one by one we are being pulled up and saved.

And instead of letting down the rope again. He signaled like the small copter is at its weight limit. Jesus said, 'I'll be back for you', and says, 'I Am Coming '. (woke-up).

(To me, there seems to be a lot of obvious interpretation here).

(The first thing is the big commercial building is the world, with all its commerce of buying and selling products. The second thing is the empty racks, that are all around us. They represent the people of the world. Every rack is a person and if the rack is empty, it is not good for anything it is meaningless, and discarded. The world has nothing to offer for eternity in Heaven with our Lord. The world is temporary and short lived and, in the end, leave you empty.)

136

In John 10:9, Jesus is referred to as the door. In John chapter 9 and 10 Jesus is explaining to the Pharisees, and healing a man who was born blind. And also explaining to His disciples who the Good Shepherd is. And the way to eternal life.

(John 10:7-10) says:

V7) Then Jesus said to them again, "Most assuredly, I say to you, I am the door of the sheep. V8) All who ever came before Me are thieves and robbers, but the sheep did not hear them. V9) I am the Door. If anyone enters by Me, he will be saved, and will go in and out and find past year. V10) The thief does not come except to steal, and to kill, and to destroy. I have come that they may have life, and that they may have it more abundantly."

(If there were other doors in the world, which could be 4 or 5, they would be the other major religions of the world.)

Jesus also says in the gospel of John, how He being the Son of God, and the only way to God the Father. In (John 14:6) says: V6) Jesus said to him, "I am the Way, the Truth, and the Life. No one comes to the father except through Me."

Did you know that you have a door in your heart? That Jesus wants to come in and dine with you. A fellowship work through the Holy Spirit. Once we realize our need for God and that comes through repentance and faith in what Jesus did on the Cross of Calvary. That paid for our sins by His own blood. We were lost, even when we didn't know we were lost? For the Bible is true and does not lie.

In (Romans 3:10,23) says:

V10) As it is written: "There is none righteous, no, not one;" ... V23) ..." For all have sinned and fall short of the glory of God", ... There happens to be a solution to the sin problem. That is found in Jesus. If you say you haven't sinned, then you make Him a liar. God would have it that you be hot or cold for God, at least He knows where you stand with Him. If you say I have no need of Him.

(Rev. 3:17,19,20)

V17) "Because you say, 'I am rich, have become wealthy, and have need of nothing '– – 'and do not know that you are wretched, miserable, poor, blind, and naked,"- —spiritually speaking. (When I came into prison, Jesus rebuked and chastened me because He loves me. And I repented of my sinful ways, drunkenness, sexual selfish sins, my unbelief of trust, my destructive thinking, my disobedience and my spiraling depression, and listening to the lies of the enemy.)

V19) "As many as I love, I rebuke and chasten. Therefore, be zealous and repent. V20) Behold I stand at the door and knock. If anyone hears My voice and opens the door, I will come in to him and dine with him, and he with Me."

(And once you become a Christian by faith. Confessing your sins, turning from your sinful ways and turn toward Jesus. Believing and professing Jesus as Lord of your life. Know, that Jesus died for your sins on the Cross, was buried and on the third day rose from the dead according to the Scriptures. And is now seated at the right hand of God the Father in Heavenly places. Not only that, but in verse 21) "To him who overcomes I will grant to sit with Me on My throne, as I also over came and sat down with My Father on His throne."

(So, another thing about the dream, the three people had to make a decision of not perishing and being saved. Physically we may still be in the world, but we were not of the world anymore.)

The next thing the door we were going through was a little smaller than the rest. In (Matthew 7:13-14) says, …. V13) "Enter by the narrow gate; for wide is the gate and broad is the way that leads to destruction, and there are many who go in by it. V14) "Because narrow is the gate and difficult is the way which leads to life, and there are few who find it."

The next thing we did is go under the water and come up in a new save area. As you have surrendered, repented, asked Christ Jesus in your heart and life. You have experienced a born-again life by faith in the Son of God. To show your obedience and resolve as a new Christian. As the Lord Commanded, to be fully submerged in Baptism. As a public display and commitment. An outward sign of an inward commitment. You already received the deposit and the down payment of the Holy Spirit. That example of coming out of the water to be saved. You are connected and recognize Jesus 's Death, Burial, and Resurrection.

And in the dream, each one, one by one, came to the Grace and knowledge of Jesus Christ. They came out of the water, looked up and Jesus is there to rescue you. And where I said the wind was filling in coming over us, splashing the water. The wind is another name for the Holy Spirit. In (John 3:8) …. V8)" The Wind blows where it wishes, and you hear the sound of it, but cannot tell where it comes from and where it goes. So is everyone who is born of the Spirit."

(God's Spirit will witness to your spirit that you are a child of God. The next thing I said was that we will be changed in a moment from one condition to another. That is true. When Jesus comes again, all believers will be changed.)

(I Cor. 15:51-52) "Behold, I tell you a mystery: We shall not all sleep, (die) but we shall all be changed—-V52) in a moment, in the twinkling of an eye, at the last trumpet…"

(From physical bodies, to glorified bodies [which are physical and spiritual bodies]. From corruptible to incorruptible, from mortal, to putting on immortality.)

In the last days, like in Noah's day of the flood; everyone will be eating and drinking and marrying, in all unaware that the Son of Man/Son of God is about to return. Except, it is not with water this time, but fire. And the last statement in the dream, I will come back for you, and I am coming. In the book of Revelations, and the last page of the Bible, Jesus says in (Rev. 22:20), …

V20)" Surely I am coming quickly."

(And for the believers it will be a glorious day of celebration. And to the unbelievers, there will be fire and judgment of destruction.) As in closing remarks for Paul to the Thessalonians, so too I end my interpretation using Scripture as a reference.

In (Thess. 4:13-18) NKJV (Paul comforts the people (disciple's) of Jesus coming.)

V13)" But I do not want you to be ignorant, brethren, concerning those who have fallen asleep, lest you sorrow as others who have no hope. V14) For if we believe that Jesus died and rose again, even so God will bring with Him those who sleep (who have died) in Jesus. V15) For this we say to you by the word of the Lord, that we who are alive and remain until the coming of the lord will by no means precede (go before) those who are asleep. V16) For the Lord Himself will descend from heaven with a shout, with the voice of an archangel, and with the Trump of God. And the dead in Christ will rise first. V17) Then we who are alive and remain shall be caught up together with them in the clouds to meet the Lord in the air. And thus we shall always be with the Lord. V18) Therefore comfort one another with these words." End

'GRAHAM SERMON'

This is a Billy Graham sermon, I was so impressed in how Billy Graham preaches, and teaches, and explains exactly what repentance is and what it is not. That I put it in here as the last message of chapter 26. (This excerpt is coming from a magazine in a November 2020 edition of 'Decision', a publication of the Billy Graham evangelistic Association.)— (on pg.30-33) copyright 1967,1996 [revised 1999] BGEA) Repentance is a biblical word. The Old Testament thunders, "Repent, and turn from all your transgressions, so that iniquity will not be your ruin." (Ezekiel 18:30).

The New Testament also vigorously exhorts men and women to repent. "Unless you repent you will all likewise perish, "said Jesus (Luke 13:3).

"Repent... and be converted, that your sins may be blotted out," said the Apostle Peter (Acts 3:19). "Now [God] commands all men every where to repent," the Apostle Paul said (Acts 17:30).

(The Bible commands it, our wickedness demands it, justice requires it, Christ preached it, and God expects it.) The divine, unalterable edict (order or decree) is still valid: God commands all people everywhere to repent. But this theme proclaimed so emphatically (uttered with emphasis) in the Bible by prophets and apostles is secretly mentioned by contemporary preachers. The clear trumpet blast calling men and women to repentance is conspicuous (attracting attention) for its absence from the modern pulpit. We have preached the dignity of humanity instead of our depravity. We have declared our goodness rather than our wickedness. We have vindicated ourselves rather than confessed our guilt. We have made of ourselves, despite all of our inherent sin and evil, little cherubs of perfection with halos on our heads, harps in our hands and wings on our shoulders. Gone is the mourner's bench; gone are the tear-stained cheeks of godly sorrow for sin; and gone is the joy in Heaven over wanderers returning to the Fathers house. None of us wants to accept blame for our sins. But either the Bible is wrong, or we are wrong. When we look at the fruits of this unrepentant generation, I am convinced that we need to blow a loud blast on the trumpet of Biblical repentance.

What is repentance? We might do well to notice first what it is not. First, repentance is not penance. Penance is the voluntary suffering of punishment for sin and does not necessarily involve a change of character or conduct. People who lie on a bed of spikes or throw themselves headlong on the ground are doing penance, but this act does not mean that their guilt has been absolved.

Second, repentance is not remorse. Judas was remorseful over his sin of betrayal of the Son of God, but his shallow regret led to suicide instead of to God, because remorse is not true repentance.

Third, repentance is not self-condemnation. You may hate yourself for your sinfulness, but self-condemnation only opens wider the wounds of guilt and despair.

We should hate our sins, not ourselves. Hate your faults ways, hate your vain thoughts, hate your evil passions, hate your lying, hate your covetousness, hate your greed, but do not hate yourself. Self-hatred leads to self-destruction, and it is wrong to destroy that which was created in Gods image. Repentance is not self-condemnation. Then what is repentance?

Repentance is not a word of weakness but a word of power in action. It is not a self-effacing (retiring, shy) emotion, but a word of heroic resolve. It is an act that breaks the chains of captive sinners and sets heaven to singing. The Bible says, "There will be more joy in Heaven over one sinner who repents than over ninety-nine just persons who need no repentance "…. (Luke 15:7). There are three elements in genuine repentance. First, there is conviction. You must know what is right before you can know what is wrong. If you get on the wrong road, you will never know it until you have some knowledge of the right road. You stray off the highway, and first you miss the familiar markings, the customary scenery, and then suddenly the conviction strikes you that you have lost your way. There can be no turning back unless first there is a conviction that you are going the wrong way. Spiritual conviction is like that. It is a signpost planted in the heart saying, "Stop, Look, Listen! Danger Ahead!" The Spirit of God, your conscience and your better judgment all join to warn, "Detour! Change! You're on the wrong road!" If you have this conviction, be thankful God is waving the red flag, directing you to a proper path. Before men and women can come to the cross of Christ and have their sins forgiven, they must say be convicting work is done by the Holy Spirit upon the soul. The second element of true repentance is contrition. The Bible says, "The Lord is near to those who have a broken heart, and saves such as have a contrite spirit") …. (Psalm34:18). Contrition, or ("godly sorrow,") as it is called in II Corinthians 7:10, is not a shallow sentiment nor empty emotion. It is a sincere regret over past sins and an earnest desire to walk in a new path of righteousness. Peter, that rugged Man who meant so well and erred so often, when he denied his Lord "went out and wept bitterly" (Matthew 26:75). He was never more lovable nor more admirable than when he stood there alone, apart from the crowd, with his frame trembling as the hot tears of contrition ran down his cheeks. In his heart was a noble resolve to live for the One who would die for him. Brokenness, with its godly sorrow for sin, is the second step toward true repentance. Third, repentance carries with it the idea of changing—Changing your mind, changing your attitude, changing your ways, the Bible says, "For godly sorrow produces repentance leading to Salvation" (II Corinthians 7:10).

If we truly repent, our will is brought into action, and we will make a reversal of direction. And God, seeing that we are in earnest, gives us the gift of eternal life. God has raised Him from the dead. That provides the grounds for our salvation. The Holy Spirit acts upon our dead souls. That is God's first step in convicting. God even helps us to repent. We become so contrite over our sins that we decide to change our way of living. Have you repented? Have you changed? Is your life different from how it used to be? God's commands to repent are not capricious. (A sudden whim or fancy, or inclined to do something impulsively).

It is not that He wants to see people groveling in subjection before Him. In His imperative (expressing a command, request, or encouragement) call for people to repent, He has their welfare and happiness as His motive. "For godly sorrow produces repentance leading to Salvation." Repentance is a necessary step to Salvation. The repentant heart is the one that God can use. Peter repented, and he became a mighty rock in the structure of the church. David repented, and his joy broke forth in the music of the psalms. Jonah repented, and a great city heard the Gospel and turned to God. Jacob repented, and God made him an ancestor of the Messiah, the Savior. Paul repented, and God used him to take the light of the Gospel to a pagan world. I have seen hundreds and thousands of lives changed by the power of Christ. And when men and women have come in sincere repentance and trusting faith, their lives, their families, their businesses ——everything——changes.

Repentance is your part, with God's help. The Bible says in Acts 3:19, "Repent... And be converted, that your sins may be blotted out." When you sincerely repent, God does the converting, and He blots out your sins. If the world ever needed spiritual awakening, it is now. The destiny of nations and individuals has been changed when men and women daring to repent of their sins have Turned to Jesus Christ by faith. Sin has cankered

(A spreading sore that eats into the tissue.) Many Civilizations, and at this moment it threatens to destroy ours. There is Hope, but it is only in God. There is forgiveness, but it can only be found at the foot of the cross, where Christ died for our sins. "Repent therefore and be converted, that your sins may be blotted out, so that times of refreshing may come from the presence of the Lord." This is God's promise in Acts 3:19. Repentance and faith go hand-in-hand, you cannot have saving repentance unless it is accompanied by saving faith in the Lord Jesus Christ. We must receive Christ by faith.

Has there been a moment in your life when you repented of sin and then by faith received the Lord Jesus Christ?

If not, you can today. Your life can be changed. Your sins can be forgiven. You can live a new life. You can have the assurance that if you died at this moment, you would go to Heaven. Will you repent now? Will you receive him as your Savior? End

At the end of the Sermon, at the bottom of the page is a prayer, (which is simply talking to God).

You can pray a prayer like this: "Dear God, I know that I am a sinner. I am sorry for my sin. I want to turn from my sin. Please forgive me. I believe Jesus Christ is Your Son; I believe He died on the Cross for my sin, and You raised Him to life. I want Him to come into my heart and take control of my life. I want to trust Jesus as my Savior and follow Him as my Lord from this day forward. In Jesus' Name, Amen." End

CHAPTER 27

'DILIG/ENDUR/FAITH'

The title of this message is: Diligence/Endurance/Faithfulness. Starting with (Galatians 6:9-10): V9)" And let us not grow weary while doing good, for in due season we shall reap if we do not lose heart. V10) Therefore, as we have opportunity, let us do good to all, especially to those who are of the household of faith. " For it is good to do what is right, and help, to support, to give, to encourage, to build up someone else in the faith, and or just their physical needs. Because what you sow, is what you reap. And God will bless you. Not that you do it, to get something back, but more out of love for one another, And especially to your Spiritual brothers in Christ Jesus. —And that…." I press toward the goal for the prize of the upward call of God in Christ Jesus." (Phil. 3:14) We are running a race with God. Some runners are side-by-side, and others are behind, and some in the front, but ultimately, we are running against ourselves, the world and the devil. Looking for our Heavenly crowns. Amen. (Luke 9:62) But Jesus said to him, "No one, having put his hand to the plow, and looking back, is fit for the Kingdom of God."

Whatever happened in the past, is the past. Move forward with vision and diligence. Amen. (Prov. 13:4) says: "The soul of a lazy man desires and has nothing; But the soul of the diligent shall be made rich." (A person characterized as diligent; the diligent in the dictionary is by steady, earnest, and energetic effort. You could even say, 'Painstaking diligence').

And to be a man of Abraham's faithfulness, to believe and trust in God even when Abraham couldn't see the final result or how God was going to accomplish it. Abraham believed God, and it was accounted to him for righteousness as (Rom.4:20-22). V20)" he did not waiver at the promise of God through unbelief, but was strengthened in faith, giving glory to God, V21) and being fully convinced that what He had promised He was also able to perform. V22) And therefore it was accounted to him for righteousness."

(In v20 glory: Glorifying God means declaring who God is. Abraham, by his faith, acknowledged that God was faithful and powerful enough to keep His promise). So, every Christian needs diligence and endurance, with the faithfulness like Abraham. Amen.

'Radio Dream'

I was in the street next to the sidewalk. And was about to cross a busy road at a crosswalk. With the hustle and bustle of people all around with no masks or COVID-19. I was waiting for the light, with my shirt off all flexed-up. (It must have been summertime). And this woman, Ms. Hightower. (In real life Hightower is an Inmate name, called frequently on the speaker for something). I heard them calling out to her across the street. She said, she likes me and thought I should meet her boss. And brought me with her across the street to the Radio Station, where she worked. And we went in, and she sent me to her boss, Tom, who was just walking by. (In real life, I hope I put my shirt back on when we crossed the street, if this was going to be an interview, that I wasn't expecting). He was walking to his office, and I followed him. I guess Miss Hightower is his secretary, or coworker. She is the one who steered me his way, and they must have been looking for someone like me. (In real life, she really didn't know me, but went with a gut-feeling).

We are on our way, when just before going in his office, he wants to straighten the sitting area with chairs and there was quite a few, maybe about twenty. And, so, I started helping him, and then this big guy comes up behind me, and then Tom grabs him. (By the way in real life, Tom is an Inmate too). I think he had been drinking, and Tom seems to know him, or he is really sympathetic for him. And sits him down, to talk to him about his problems. And then there was a lady there, who wanted two of the folding chairs. And I helped her with that as well, while they are still talking. And she said, she needed something, and I was explaining a logical answer to her, and Tom overheard and said the last three words at the same time, to this lady. And I looked at him and he at me, and I said jinx. He smiled, maybe I got a job as an assistant. Because that was the end of the dream, we never made it into his office. (In real life, I did want to work at a Christian Radio Station). End

'PIERCE DREAM'

I had a dream with Pierce Brosner, when he is a little younger, we're doing a take in a scene. At a restaurant at the top of a building. Because when I looked out the windows, it is all blue sky.

We are talking in a booth, and the camera is behind me, shooting out. And he is on one side, and my previous girlfriend and I are on the other side. In the film she is playing my girlfriend. (Vicki).

In this dramatic role he plays a bad guy, and wants something we have. He is a spy and threatens us with a gun. But I had one under the table, and I fired. And I told Vicki to run and get away from him. And that's when I woke-up. (Now, in real life, it is really hard to imagine Pierce as a bad guy. A spy, yes. I did thoroughly enjoy him in the series 'Remington Steele'; and I also put him second favorite in the James Bond films). (Of course he didn't die, he was the star of the movie, but how it ends I don't know?) End

CHAPTER 28

'100-YEAR PLAY'

This dream was about a play that they reenacted in the 21st-century, about a serious trial that took place 100 years before. The unique thing was some of the people in the audience were from the 24th century. Behind the Auditorium there is a room, and in the room, there is what looks like a cable box with cable connections. To activate the box, you un-connect the wires in a certain way, and you have two minutes to hook-it back-up and go through this slit-window in the wall which is 1 foot high and 4 feet wide. (In real life there is a slit-window in our cell that is about 5 inches wide and 3 1/2 feet tall to let a little natural light come in). To go back to the 24th century. And if you want to stay in the 21st-century; in that two minutes you have; you climb in this little box until the flash goes off. If you are standing by the portal when the flash goes off on the outside of the box and the two minutes are up. You will be vaporized. I went to check out this live-play there, so I watched how they unhooked and re-hooked it back up. And went through the portal from the 24th to the 21st century. And went into the next room where this live play was going on. There was a mixture of colors and races they're watching the play. Which was a play about civil rights for blacks.

The stage was an outdoor scene, a building and train tracks in front of that. So, it was a small town, that focuses on the downtown courthouse. Then where the trial is going on, the room is like extended outward so you could see the trial close-up, like if you had binoculars, and you are looking through the window at the trial softly going on. It shows the people in the court room as spectators and the jury to the side and they were all black. There Must have been more spectators. I couldn't see the judge or who was on trial from my angle. (In real life, which I was on a jury trial for this woman who got second-degree murder, even though my input was to give this woman the benefit of the doubt, and more self-defense, than premeditated, and go with the lesser crime of manslaughter.) (The dictionary meaning of manslaughter is... 'The unlawful killing of a human being without expressed or implied malice').

(The second thing in real life, when you are on a trial, the jury is all mixed up with different races and nationalities, and male and female, and all non-bias—meaning not to be prejudice so much, but as to go by the rules of the law, and judicial system of government).

Now, the audience was intently watching the play, and everyone is relieved that this race issue of the blacks and whites should be eliminated by now. And that this is old news of past events, about civil rights, and to move on. And to even make light of it even more, by some of those people of the 24th Century came in the Auditorium, and one black guy stands up and says, 'Yea, let's change the channel to the Flintstones, they're on'. And the people started to laugh, then a white guy stands up and says, 'Yea, I think the Jetsons are on too, let's watch that', then more laughter. So, I witnessed that, and wanted to go forward in time, back to my own time period. So, I am heading for the time portal and another guy from the 24th century followed me back. And he got there first, and started unhooking the cables to start the process, but he forgot the order how to put it back properly. So, the warning sound went off about the end of the two minutes. So, I jumped into the safe box. And he is still playing with the cables. The light goes off like a flash cube, and he vaporized. Then I get out of the safe-box and hook-up the right cable connections. Then go through the slit back to my own time period. End

'MALL DREAM'

I was in a mall, at a toy store. It was pretty small, maybe 20'x 30', and I was lost to know what to buy. And there were no other customers in the store. So, I went to the cash register area looking for the clerk. But there wasn't any there. Even though, I could hear a little girl playing on the other side of the register block area. And there were some displays on the counter which blocked my view. I assume her mother would be there too. So, I'll try to get their attention, 'Excuse me, I was wondering if you could help me?' And there was no answer. So, I walked around the counter, and the little girl is playing on the floor with some toys. So, I looked around, and no one is in the mall. Except, these two people sitting close by. So, I went to them and asked, 'Excuse me, could one of you help me pick out gifts for my nieces, and family.' And I lowered my mask to ask them. They weren't wearing a COVID-19 mask? The older gentleman looked at the younger woman. I am thinking to myself, a couple, or her father, and his grandchild. Anyway, he nodded to her to go and help. She is pretty, and she followed me to the toy store entrance. (Then I woke up) End.

'GRASS-PARTY DREAM'

I was working at a job installing carpet and pad at a residence. And I needed my trash can and some supplies. And I went to my garage and Tim was there at 8 to 10 years old with his friend, and they were riding bicycles. I said, 'Hi', to them, and they were enjoying their day. I went back to my project. And Tim wanted to help me at home, and he got on the small rideable mower and mowed our grass, then he opens the fence up. And mowed everyone else's too, and far as I could see. Even along this little canal ditch that's a couple feet deep and curves around to the next block. He cut the grass up to the ditch in that whole strip. I came back to the garage for something. I was surprised and impressed at the same time. Then I left there and went back to the house, and a party was going on too. And Steph was there, and I said, Hi to her. I said, 'I can't stay, I'll just get a bite to eat, and take a few with me in this little box.' Steph had a little box too, but hers was almost empty. I put a few in, tasty, pastry cookies. And I said, 'thank you', and left; I guess I went back to work. Because that was the end of the dream. End

CHAPTER 29

'PRAISE & WORSHIP'

This is a praise and worship teaching. That got finally finished; Welcome brother's, "Praise the Lord". In (Ps. 150:6) "Everything that has breath, praise the Lord. Praise the Lord! "The last part is reiterated (which means repeated). The Word is making a point of importance. Also indicating that every living thing with breath should be praising the LORD. In a joyful exhortation to the Lord our God; for He is worthy of Praise, Honor, and Glory. (Amen). If we don't: The rocks would cry out. The mountains and firmament of the heavens will exalt His name. Jesus' Name is above every name. In whatever language, Hebrew (#3091): Yehowshuwa (yeh-ho-shoo'-ah); Spanish: Jes'us is (Hay-suse). God knows your heart and mind and you are to worship Him as you know Him. You are honoring the Son of God, as unto the Father-Spirit of All. And those who Worship Him, must Worship Him in Spirit and in Truth. (That is accomplished through the Holy Spirit). That worship can be done Spiritually standing, kneeling, lifting hands, silently, but, mainly from a joyful heart, anywhere. But, primarily in the House of God, as we assemble together with all the Saints worshiping God. He knows we are worshiping Him. When I am in a Spanish service, I can't always sing praises to Him, because of the language barrier, but that I yield myself to His Spirit. In reverence, and vocal tunes and melodies of praise to Him. There are three-points in this study; First, is the definition and meaning of praise and worship. Second, who God is that we pray too, and thirdly, to include the different characteristic names of God in the Old and New Testaments. And how we can call on those names today. So, 'Call to Me'…. As (Jeremiah 33:3) says, "Call to Me, and I will answer you and show you great and mighty things, which you do not know."(NKJV) To call for our deliverance, strength, our peace. Since He is the same yesterday, today, and forever. Let's start with what are the obvious definitions of Praise: Out of Webster's dictionary; #1 to glorify the attributes of God with compliments and applause to Him. (Clapping hands). For he is worthy of praise, honor, and glory. Even the southern kingdom, and region of Judea or Judah. The tribe of Judah. And the name Judah, which is an ancestor of Christ. The Hebrew word Judah: its root word means Celebrate or Praise. 'Praise the Lord'. Or Hallelujah in Hebrew. Webster's Dictionary— '…. used to express praise, joy, or thanks.' [Heb] means: Praise ye the Lord.

David said in (Psalm 34:1)" I will bless the Lord at all times; His praise shall continually be in my mouth." Other Hebrew definitions for praise (to make show); (to boast in God); (to be clamorous to God); I thought what is clamorous? First thing I thought was clang-together like cymbals. Which is true; in (Psalm 150:5) "Praise Him with loud cymbals; Praise Him with clashing cymbals!" (NKJV) But the actual definition to clamorous is (make an outcry—demand loudly). You can verbally cry out to Him, in expounding praise, or cry out your confession, cry out your heart to Him in adoration, or cry out in pain, like David did in (Psalm 55:22). "Cast your burden on the Lord, and He shall sustain you (uphold you); He shall never permit the righteous to be moved (Shaken or be wavered to fall or to slip)." (NKJV) Another Hebrew definition, is Rave, it is a little four-letter word, and is powerful in praise, and in its meaning. 'To be over-enthusiastically in Praise to Him.'… 'To be unrestrained in Praise. To be extremely enthusiastic.' That's what those four-letters mean. We are to be excited in church.

What is being enthusiastic?

Websters dictionary: (1. Absorbing possession of the mind by an interest, study, or pursuit; ardent (fervent, passionate, burning interest). Seems like every time I look up a word; I have to look up another word to the definition of the last word; but, what's nice about that is, that's what the word says about meditating in is Law Day and night. (Psalms 1:2) says: V2)" But his delight is in the law of the Lord, and in His law, he meditates day and night. "Pretty soon the Word becomes clearer and clearer.

Websters dictionary: (absorbing [to take in and make part of an existent whole] possession [a state of having, control, owned something] ...of the mind by an interest or study). We are being renewed by the Word of God. (Ephesians 4:23-24)

V23)" And be renewed in the spirit of your mind, V24) and that you put on the new man which was created according to God, in true righteousness and holiness. "(NKJV). As we are being enthusiastic for God. In our praise (II Cor. 4:16) "Therefore we do not lose heart. Even though our outward man is perishing, yet the inward man is being renewed day by day. "(KJV). (And (Romans 12:2) (NKJV). "And do not be conformed to this world, but be transformed by the renewing of your mind, that you may prove what is that good and acceptable and perfect will of God."

All this came out of giving God raving praise. (Also means to Celebrate) in Webster's dictionary: To Celebrate Him; (means a commemorative day or event with festivals; To make known with honor or praise, to Extol, [is praising highly] Wherever the Saints come together and Worship God, in the beautiness and holiness of that Sanctuary). Amen.

We are doing that here at CSP this special day, 1-9-21 Saturday morning. We assemble the Saints together in one mind and one accord, In Worship, but, originally this message was for the brothers prayer group, and or Church group called the Potter House Church; at CVSP— and then it was going to be for, Redemption Church Choir group practice at McFarland MCCF; And it ended up today at CSP. With my Cellie and I in Worship to God, and an instructive teaching. The Scripture says:

In (Matthew 18:20) NKJV

V20)" For where two or three are gathered together in My name, I am there in the midst of them."

Worship—The Hebrew definition for Worship is: (Prostrate; In homage to Royalty or God; bow down, crouch; fall down flat). That is what you are doing when you prostrate yourself. (On your face) to humbly beseech (is to ask urgently and humbly).

As (Heb. 4:16) says in God's word:

V16)" Let us therefore come boldly to the throne of grace, that we may obtain mercy and find grace to help in time of need. "[to do reverence (respect), make to stoop, to depress, kneel down.] You can kneel in your heart or mind or physically, or possibly all three. I remember only one time, outside falling down flat on my face into the carpet. That was after losing my first wife in divorce; and I cried out to God loudly from my broken heart. And when I quieted down. I heard that soft still voice from God from within and He said: 'Loren, you will get through this, and you will help others.'

(And the Lord, He did that for me.)

There was another time inside, we were prostrate on the ground. At Wasco Reception yard. In our prayer circle there was singing 'Amazing Grace.' And the alarm went off and we had to get down. I continued to sing, 'Amazing Grace,' who saved a sinner like me, And the group continued with me, giving God the glory and praise. That was about six years ago, in CDC put us in a humbling position, but we used it for God's glory. Real worship, is rooted in the word. Typically, the music style of faster beat, playing of music and singing is praise music, and a slower beat, with music and singing is worship. You can engage your mind, and heart, and body with all three. But it is easier when it is slower. To engage to plug-in yourself Spiritually. As the Spirit of God is working in the room. When I am standing, worshiping God; in my heart and mind, I am kneeling before His throne. In humble adoration. Here we are worshiping God in the assembly of the congregation; in one mind and one accord; in Spirit and in Truth; with all your mind, heart, strength, down into your soul and spirit. Imagine the throne room of God. The Son of God is at the right hand of God the Father in the Heavens. The Father has given the

Anointed One, the Christ. Jesus the Christ, the Son of the living God, all power and authority over heaven and earth. The Father has given His Son His own Universe.

In the Old Testament through the prophet Isaiah, the Lord is speaking as (Isaiah 41:4) ....'I, the Lord, am the first; And with the last I am He.' Then (Is. 43:11) "I, even I, am the Lord...." Also, in the O.T. (Is. 44:6) V6)" Thus says the Lord, the King of Israel, and his Redeemer, the Lord of hosts: I am the First and I am, the Last; besides Me there is no God....."God uses those same words in the New Testament in (John 11:25) "Jesus said to her, I am the resurrection and the life" ....and in (John 14:6) "Jesus said to him, "I am the way, the truth, and the life. No one comes to the Father except through Me. "He reiterates Himself; He is God and there is none beside Him. And in, (Revelations 1:8,11) V8) The Lord is speaking, "I am the Alpha and the Omega, the Beginning and the End," says the Lord, "who is and who was and who is to come, the Almighty." .... V11) saying, "I am the Alpha and the Omega, the First and the Last," .... In the beginning of the book of Revelations and the end of that book. God is still God; He is all and all.... (Rev.22:13) V13)" I am the Alpha and the Omega, the Beginning and the End, the First and the Last." And God is still the same, meaning, in (Hebrews 13:8) V8)" Jesus Christ is the same yesterday, today, and forever. "He is the Great "I AM" of the Old Testament and the New Testament.

John Zebedee's vision, in: (Revelations 4:2,3) V2) "Immediately I was in the Spirit; and behold, a throne set in heaven, and One sat on the throne. V3) And He who sat there was like a jasper and a sardius stone in appearance; and there was a rainbow around the throne, in appearance like an emerald. "In verse three it tells us that there is a rainbow around about the throne. I would imagine it has beautiful colors. Also in verse three, it says Jasper, (which is a variety of quartz, used for making ornaments.) If you saw a rock of quartz and cut it open in half, it would look like a bowl of diamonds stuck together. And light passing through the prisms of this multi-faceted rocks of colors. V3) .... a rainbow around the throne in appearance, like an emerald." (The prize, of gems. Green in color, also is a variety of beryl, yellow, red (ruby), there is a blue-green, and other multi-color stones.) Imagine God himself sitting on the throne. Not like the last time they saw the master….When He had His glorified body. That Spiritual body, who could appear, and disappear, and make solid like flesh and bone, like in the upper room. Or when He ascended into heaven, like: (Acts 1:9-11) V9)" Now when He had spoken these things, while they watched, He was taken up, and a cloud received Him out of their site. V10) And while they looked steadfastly toward heaven as He went up, behold, two men stood by them in white apparel, V11) who also said, "Men of Galilee, why do you stand gazing up into heaven? This same Jesus, who was taken up from you into heaven, will so come in like manner as you saw Him go into heaven."

In (I Cor. 15:44) tells us there is a natural body and a spiritual body. Verse 44, "It is sown a natural body, it is raised a spiritual body. There is a natural body, and there is a spiritual body." This is talking about the resurrection from the dead. Just as Jesus did.

He will be in his Deity Body who is Faithful and True. As (Revelation 19:11,12) declare. V11) "Now I saw heaven open, and behold, a white horse. And He who sat on him was called Faithful and True, and in righteousness He judges and makes war. V12) His eyes were like a flame of fire, and on His head were many crowns. He had a name written that no one knew except Himself."

There is a physical Kingdom of Heaven in the Spiritual sense. But there is also; we have the kingdom of God within us, by the Holy Spirit. When He comes in His deity body, it will be full of Power and Majesty, and full of Light: Beaming and shimmering, blazing beams of fiery light.

(Rev.22:5) In the throne room; "There shall be no night there: They need no lamp nor light of the sun, for the Lord God gives them light. And they shall reign forever and ever."

That is talking about the new Jerusalem, the Holy City. And in (Daniel 7:9,10):

In Daniel tells of the vision of the Ancient of Days and the Son of Man who comes to them. Then He was given dominion, and He passes His Righteous Judgment upon the Earth. V9)" I watched till thrones were put in place, and the Ancient of Days was seated; His garment was white as snow. And the hair of His head was like pure wool."

(When Christ Jesus comes and brings judgment up on the earth as the Son of Man, is twofold. He is fully Man and fully God, as the Father has given all power and authority to the Son of God.) V9)..." His throne was a fiery flame, its wheels a burning fire;... V10) A fiery stream issued and came forth from before Him. A thousand thousands ministered to Him; Ten thousand times ten thousand stood before Him. The court was seated, and the books were opened."

So, there is energy like the sun, and a river of living crystal clear water coming from the throne. There is a sea of glass like crystal. The 24 elders, and seven lamp stands with seven Spirits of God. And from the throne lightning and thunder and voices. And the four living creatures. There is activity in the throne room. let's read it together from its entirety. (Rev.4:4-9). Starting at V4)" Around the throne were twenty-four thrones, and on the thrones I saw twenty-four elders sitting, clothed in white robes; and they had crowns of gold on their heads. V5) And from the throne proceeded lightnings, thunderings, and voices. Seven lamps of fire were burning before the throne, which are the seven Spirits of God.

V6) Before the throne there was a sea of glass, like crystal. And in the midst of the throne, and around the throne, were four living creatures full of eyes in front and in back. V7) The first living creature was like a lion, the second living creature like a calf, the third living creature had a face like a man, and the fourth living creature was like a flying eagle. V8) The four living creatures, each having six wings, were full of eyes around and within. And they do not rest day or night, saying:

'Holy, holy, holy,
Lord God Almighty,
Who was and is and is to come!'"

V9)" Whenever the living creatures give glory and honor and thanks to Him who sits on the throne, who lives forever and ever, V10) the twenty-four elders fall down before Him who sits on the throne and worship Him who lives forever and ever."

And lastly God's Hebrew names and His character attributes. His personal name. Which was so sacred that they would not speak it. Or actually couldn't even pronounce it properly, without vowels.

He is on his throne. He is [Heb.] El Shaddai; (Eng.) meaning: God Almighty & [Heb.] Elohim [Eng] meaning: Eternal creator, or self-existent one. Which makes statements like this understandable. ".... before there was, I AM."

Let's go back to His personal name:

YHWH or LORD [Eng.] [Heb.] יהוה [YAH] (Ps.68:4)

English reads left to right and Hebrew is read right to left. It was hard to pronounce until the vowel-points were added. In (Ps.68:4) shows God's name is YAH, for short. After the vowel were added, YHWH became 'YAHWEH'.

(Ps.68:4)" Sing to God, sing praises to His name; Extol Him who rides on the clouds, by His name YAH, and rejoice before Him." 'YAH' is 'LORD', or 'YAHWEH' (It is synonymous) …. Yahweh is Hebrew or Jehovah (is the Jewish National Name of God.) It started as Yehovah— until the Jewish alphabet got a 'J' in it. There had been an evolution of writing and pronouncing God's name, (tomato-tomatoe) it is the same, it is synonymous. God is still God, He is the Great I AM. (Psalm 50:7) "I am God, your God!"

In (Is. 44:6) Speaking through the prophet, with the Holy Spirit. Saying V6)" Thus says the Lord, the King of Israel, and his Redeemer, the Lord of hosts I am the First and I am the Last; besides Me there is no God. "God revealed Himself to Moses as I am, and to the children of Israel. As God of Abraham, Isaac, and Jacob.

Let's look at it in its entirety: (Ex. 3:14,15) (NKJV) V14) And God said to Moses," I AM WHO I AM." And He said, "Thus you shall say to the children of Israel, 'I AM has sent me to you,'" V15) Moreover God said to Moses. "Thus you shall say to the children of Israel: 'The Lord God of your fathers, the God of Abraham, the God of Isaac, and the God of Jacob, has sent me to you. This is My name forever, and this is My memorial to all generations'.

He had certain names associated with their Israelite people, and to express His characteristics to us Gentiles too.

O.T. Jehovah—Lord God—or LORD. N.T. 'Jesus is Lord '. (I Cor. 12:3) Another Word [HEB] for LORD is Adonai or Adonai. # (3091) Jehoshua-(Joshua) Heb.- Eng.—Hebrew—# (2424) Jesus-Gk-Eng. Gk or Justus. Christ—Gk. Christos lit. Anointed One......

In (II Tim. 4:18) says...." The Lord will deliver me...." He is our deliverer, ... In (Habakkuk 3:19)...'The Lord God is my strength;...' When we are weak, He is strong. He is the One who upholds you and sustains you. He gives you strength.

He is Jehovah Rophe:(The Lord who heals).
He is Jehovah Shalom:(The Lord our peace).
He is Jehovah Jireh:(The Lord will provide).
He is Jehovah M'Kaddesh:(The Lord who sanctifies).
He is Jehovah Nissi:(The Lord our banner).
He is Jehovah Tsid-Kay-Noo:(The Lord our righteousness).

The one high and above us and around whom we rally in difficult times. He goes ahead of us in battle. So, we know which direction to travel. God sanctifies us through His blood that He shed on the Cross at Calvary.

(Hebrew 13:12) NKJV

"Therefore, Jesus also, that He might sanctify the people with His own blood, suffered outside the gate." And the book of Jeremiah points to the coming Jesus the Christ, the perfect Lamb of God. As we believe in Him by faith, He becomes our righteousness. By His Grace, He saves repentant sinners, and we become sons of God by His promises.

(Jeremiah 23:5-6)

V5)" Behold, the days are coming," says the Lord, "That I will raise to David a Branch of righteousness; A King shall reign and prosper, and execute judgment and righteousness in the earth."

V6)" In His days Judah will be saved, and Israel will dwell safely; Now this is His name by which He will be called: "THE LORD OUR RIGHTEOUSNESS." (Jehovah Tsid-Kay-Noo)'

Back to the throne room: Not only is there a rainbow of light in the throne room of God. In the Heavens, God also said in (Genesis 9:12-15) That He put a rainbow in the clouds as a reminder, not to curse the Earth with the flood of water. His covenant between God and the Earth and God, and every living thing, including man. Tell you what, let's write that out just as God's word shows us in (Gen. 9:12-15) (NKJV)

V12) And God said: "This is the sign of the covenant which I make between Me and you, and every living creature that is with you, for perpetual generations: V13) I set My rainbow in the cloud, and it shall be for the sign of the covenant between Me and the Earth. V14) It shall be, when I bring a cloud over the Earth, that the rainbow shall be seen in the cloud; V15) and I will remember My covenant which is between Me and you and 3 living creatures of all flesh; the waters shall never again become a flood to destroy all flesh."

So, in conclusion, God is good, (All the time). Let us praise Him in the morning. For His mercies are new every morning. Let us praise Him at noon and evening. In (Ps. 113:3) says; "From the rising of the sun to its going down The Lords name is to be praised."

'EXEC. BATH DREAM'

Dad, Carrie, and I are on this executive bathroom job, to lay some kind of floor. We came into the customers executive office, and my dad is talking to the boss. While I am climbing over a desk to get to the corner of the room, where the bathroom door is. Because it is so cluttered in that office. I don't know where my sister went or why she is there? (But, in real life my dad, who passed away and my sister were on my mind before bedtime). (A bath job is usually a one-man job; and could take 3 to 8 hours to install a vinyl bathroom, depending on what needs to be done, subfloors, coving, etc. The average time is about 5 1/2 hrs. for most).

This office looks like an old school lawyer's office. It's dark, with dark colored furniture. With a lot of books, all the way around. The desks are huge, with stuff all over it. Woodwork finished in everything, but it doesn't fit this guy? This is a water company. It is a treatment plant. These guys purify bottled water. (In real life I have a longtime friend; John, who works for the water company. And there was one time I did work for a treatment water company, but not the way I described it). Now, two of the employees came out and greeted us; and said, Hi, good morning. Both are wearing these striped lined shirts going up and down. And one cracks a joke, but I didn't get it?, And then they left.

And so we begin, the three of us in this little bathroom. The first thing is to remove the toilet. It was expensive, a French Do-bay (low-boy style). It was designed for women, but men could use it too. It was on and spritzing a little fountain. I reached in the back to turn the water off. It was a funny leaf-lever? And for some reason all the water ran out? Maybe, that's the one with a drain instead of a hole? (Which in real life doesn't make sense?) My dad wanted me to put more water in it. I'm thinking why? They're heavier than an actual standard toilet, and more awkward to try to carry it. (In real life we use a toilet dolly. Four small wheels on a plywood board about 1'x 2'large).

(FYI, it is a low boy style, and generally colored to the colors of the bathroom, and or the porcelain sink and tub. The dolly makes it easier to move and keeps it level. Because, when you move a toilet with water in it, if you rock it side to side, or back and forth, it will flush. What water is still in the inside neck of the toilet, and with extra water in there. It would make full inside with pressure on it, and one bump moving will flush it). Anyway, there was some noise, and I woke up. End

'AREA RUG DREAM'

I was on the carpet flooring job, at this lady 's house. I was all done for today's work, and I would be back later tomorrow, as I told her. But, before I left, there was two area rugs I rolled up. For some reason, they were wet? A little extra moisture came through the rug; it looks like they just had the carpets clean. Even though that was not my business. I was installing carpet somewhere else in the house. (But I do make and bind area rugs, for sale and deliver, and put in, which sometimes includes moving furniture). (This was just an extra service for the flooring business. And installing carpet is more what I do). (I used to do some hand binding of carpet, with staples and 1 1/4-inch-wide cotton binding cloth tape in whatever color, to match your carpet, and then latex glue, to hold the binding tape on the back after it had been stapled to the edge of the carpet. But later I just hired my friend Al, and coworker. To bind it with his binding sewing machine. With a polyester 1 inch fabric roll). (Either one I charged $1.50 a perimeter foot. Which was a good deal. But, to make it worth my while. I charge a minimum of $35 with pick-up and delivery. So, to make it worth the customer to buy it. The customers are getting at least 23 perimeter feet. In other words, two doorway mats and say a half circle rug in front of a fireplace, to protect your new carpet from Ambers). (Now, this is just leftover carpet from the carpet installed. And we do want you to save some, in case of a spill or burn, and you need some for patching, God forbid). (Oh, FYI, If we do need some carpet for a repair, store your extra scape pieces in a dark sealed trash bag, to persevere the freshness, so it won't be dried out). (For binding, if you have enough left over, it is only a suggestion if you wanted to put the extra carpet too practical use. And saving the life of the carpet). (By wiping your feet on the area rugs, instead of getting on your brand-new carpet?). (I don't do carpet cleaning, but I did my own with a 'Bissell carpet cleaner', and it worked pretty well. For private use. —Did you hear the joke about, Mr. Hoover and Mrs. Eureka getting together and making a little dirt-devil).

Then back to the dream, and before I left, she said, what about this dust that was on the table. So, I took care of that; sometimes we stir up the dust in the house. Our main goal is that the customer is happy and satisfied. Then she had me doing something with the two double front doors. Wiping them down or something? But the weird part was I took the doors off its hinges for some reason? (In real life I could clean them when they are on). Anyway, on the outside of the door was a rotating shade on a spindle, continually rotating. Weird? Anyway, I woke up. End

CHAPTER 30

'ANOINTING'

(This is an anointing message, and a message for the brethren, for the believers to check themselves as they are still in the faith, and in Christ Jesus).

We are starting with (I-John 2:1-2) NKJV.

V1)" My little children, these things I write to you, so that you may not sin. And if anyone sins, we have an Advocate with the Father, Jesus Christ the Righteous. V2) And He Himself is the propitiation for our sins, and not for ours only, but also for the whole world."

(Commentary NKJV)

(Propitiation brings about the merciful removal of guilt through divine forgiveness. In the Greek Old Testament [the Septuagint], the Greek term for propitiation was used for the sacrificial mercy seat on which the high priest placed the blood of Israelites' sacrifices [see Exodus 25:17-22; I-Chronicles 28:2].

This practice indicates that God's righteous wrath had to be appeased somehow. God sent His Son and satisfied His own wrath with Jesus' sacrifice on the Cross. Our sins made it necessary for Jesus to suffer the agonies of crucifixion, but God demonstrated His love and justice by providing His own Son, the sacrifice of Jesus' sinless life is so effective that it can supply forgiveness for the whole world [see II-Cor.5:14,15,19; Heb.2:9]. Christ death is sufficient for all, but efficient only for those who believe in Christ. Not everyone will be saved, but Jesus offer salvation to all [see Rev.22:17]). (End quote)

In (Rev. 22:17) "And the Spirit and the bride say, "Come!" And let him who hears say, "Come!" And let him who thirsts come. Whoever desires, let him take the water of life freely." (God offers Himself to everyone. He gives His gift of salvation, to all who repent of sin, and ask Jesus into their heart. His anointing from Jesus and His Father. The down payment of His Spirit in you. And if you have question? There is a test in the next verses, to know where you stand).

(I-John 2:3-11)

V3)" Now by this we know that we know Him, if we keep His commandments. V4) He who says, 'I know him', and does not keep His commandments, is a liar, and the truth is not in him, V5) but whoever keeps his word, truly the love of God is perfected in him. By this we know that we are in Him. V6) He who says he abides in Him ought himself also to walk just as He walked. V7) Brethren, I write no new commandment to you, but an old commandment which you have had from the beginning. The old commandment is the word which you heard from the beginning. V8) Again, a new commandment I write to you, which thing is true in Him and in you, because the darkness is passing away, and the true light is already shining. V9) He who says he is in the light, and hates his brother, is in darkness until now. V10) he who loves his brother abides in the light, and there is no cause for stumbling in Him. V11) But he who hates his brother is in darkness and walks in darkness, and does not know where he is going, because the darkness has blinded his eyes." (That is our signature as Christians; is to love one another unconditionally. Yes, one another, but also those who are not lovable. To even love our enemies, and pray for, and bless those who despitefully use you. To be peacemakers.)

(The Apostle John is writing by the inspiration of the Holy Spirit to the believers in Christ. To uplift and encourage all the brethren in whatever Spiritual stage they are in now, and to give warnings of this present world).

(I-John 2:12-17)

V12)" I write to you, little children, because your sins are forgiven you for His name's sake. V13) I write to you, father's because you have known Him who is from the beginning I write to you, young men, because you have overcome the wicked one. I write to you, little children, because you have known the Father. V14)" I have written to you fathers, because you have known Him who is from the beginning. I have written to you young men, because you are strong, and the word of God abides in you, and you have overcome the wicked one. V15) Do not love the world or the things in the world. If anyone loves the world, the love of the Father is not in Him. V16) For all that is in the world—the lust of the flesh, the lust of the eyes, and the pride of life—is not of the Father but is of the world. V17) And the world is passing away, and the lust of it; but he who does the will of God abides forever." (As we get closer to the time of the end of this age, and the last hour. John tells us to be aware of what's coming. And the different kind of people you will be in countering. Let's move on).

(I-John 2:18-29)

V18)" Little children, it is the last hour; and as you have heard that the Antichrist is coming, even now many antichrists have come, by which we know that it is the last hour. V19) They went out from us, but they were not of us; for if they had been of us, they would have continued with us; but they went out that they might be made manifest, that none of them were of us." (John is saying, that even some of the so-called brethren of the church body, will fall away because, they truly were not a part of us. For the true and faithful ones with the Anointing of God. That is given to us, when we believed, and keep walking in faith, keep receiving that infilling of the Holy Spirit. So, he can lead you into all truth. To show you the Way. And the Way, is Jesus. Amen). V20)" But you have an anointing from the Holy One, and you know all things. V21) I have not written to you because you do not know the truth, but because you know it, and that no lie is of the truth." (Now, John describes what and who the antichrist is, of them and of us). V22)" Who is a liar but he who denies that Jesus is the Christ? He is the antichrist who denies the Father and the Son. V23) Whoever denies the Son does not have the Father either; he who acknowledges the Son has the Father also." (So, as long as we are in Christ, and abiding in Him, and obeying His commandments and loving one another. Keep the faith, and His promises to us. We will abide in Him. And see Him and His coming). V24)" Therefore let that abide in you which you heard from the beginning. If what you heard from the beginning abides in you, you also will abide in the Son and in the Father. V25) And this is the promise that He has promised us—eternal life." V26)"These things I have written to you concerning those who try to deceive you. V27) But the anointing which you have received from Him abides in you, and you do not need that anyone teach you; but as the same anointing teaches you concerning all things, and is true, and is not a lie, and just as it has taught you, you will abide in Him. V28) And now, little children, abide in Him, that when He appears, we may have confidence and not be ashamed before Him at His coming. V29) If you know that He is righteous, you know that everyone who practices righteousness is born of Him."

(I- John 3:1)

"Behold what manner of love the Father has bestowed on us, that we should be called children of God!"

(Matt. 25:1-13) (This is the Parable of the Ten Virgins).

V1)" Then the kingdom of heaven shall be likened to ten virgins who took their lamps and went out to meet the bridegroom. V2) Now five of them were wise, and five were foolish. V3) Those who were foolish took their lamps and took no oil with them, V4) but the wise took oil in their vessels with their lamps. V5) But while the bridegroom was delayed, they all slumbered and slept. V6) And at midnight a cry was heard: 'Behold, the bridegroom is coming; go out to meet him! V7) Then all those virgins arose and trimmed their lamps. V8) And the foolish said to the wise, 'Give us some of your oil, for our lamps are going out.' V9) But the wise answered, saying, 'No, lest there should not be enough for us and you; but go rather to those who sell, and buy for yourselves.' V10) And while they went to buy, the bridegroom came, and those who were ready went in with him to the wedding; and the door was shut. V11) Afterward the other virgins came also, saying, 'Lord, Lord, open to us! 'V12) But he answered and said, 'Assuredly, I say to you, I do not know you.' V13) Watch therefore, for you know neither the day nor the hour in which the Son of Man is coming."

(Luke 8:15,25,28,29,39) KJV-JSM

Special Edition

[This is the last verse in the parable of the Sower. Where we want, the word of God to plant on good ground, Amen]. (Luke 8:15) KJV

V15)" But that on the good ground are they, which in an honest and good heart, having heard the word, keep it, and bring forth fruit, with patience."

[So, we need to hide God's word down into our hearts. That's the Holy Anointing of the Word, the Word of God is Spirit and Life].

[Now, this is the end of the story of the storm where Jesus is sleeping in the boat]. (With commentary's)

(Luke 8:25)

"And He said unto them, 'Where is your faith?' (Christ is the answer concerning all the storms of life.) And they being afraid wondered (the Disciples had accepted His Messiahship, but had a most inadequate view of the same), saying one to another, 'What manner of man is this!' (They evidently did not recognize all the implications, which His office carried with it.) ... for He commands even the winds and water, and they obey Him (proclaims His total control not only over demon spirits, and sickness, and death, but as well, the elements.) end quote.

That's Right! Where do we get our Faith?

(Rom.10:17) Tells us:

V17) "So then faith comes by hearing, and hearing by the word of God."
NKJV [Now, this is after the storm, and they arrive on the other side of
the sea of Galilee, and Jesus delivered a man of a legion of demons. As Jesus
first gets near this man he says]: (with commentary)

(Luke 8:28,29)

"When he saw Jesus (the spirit world of darkness is subservient to the
Lord Jesus Christ), he cried out (for fear), and fell down before Him (an
acknowledgment of Him as Lord and Master) ....

and with a loud voice said, What have I to do with You, Jesus, You Son
of God most High? (Even though most of mankind professes not to
know, demon spirits know Who Jesus is.) I beseech You, torment me not
(proclaims them knowing and realizing that Jesus has the power to do
with them whatsoever He desires; proper Faith in Christ and the Cross will
put us in the position of tormenting demons, instead of them tormenting
us.) V29) (For He had commanded the unclean spirit to come out of the
man.... (end quote)

[At The end of the story of the delivered man, he wanted to go with Jesus
and His disciples. And Jesus said to him in v39.]

V39)" Return to your own house, and show how great things God has
done unto you (constitutes a commission for this man, and for all Believers;
for all Believers, the Lord has done "great things"). And he went his way,
and published throughout the whole city how great things Jesus had done
unto him (doesn't tell us exactly which city, but does proclaim this man's
success; the day before, he was a demonic maniac, totally insane; twenty-
four hours later or less, he is an Evangelist for the Lord Jesus Christ). (end
quote)

[So, now let's recap, we need to watch and pray. Be ready in season or out,
be about My Father's business as Jesus said. Keep preaching, teaching,
and loving one another; Tell others what Jesus has done for you. Tell He

comes again descending on the clouds, continually praising His Name, and having plenty of His Anointing oil (Holy Spirit) in you at His coming.] (Amen)

'Baby / bro. Dream'

In the dream I was sitting at the table at our grandpa's home. And I hear a knock at the back screen door. It was my brother (Gary), and he was carrying a baby. And wanted to come in. I got up and opened the door. He comes in, and we both moved toward the kitchen. I was trying to figure out who's baby this is? As he is holding this tiny little baby girl. And I knew somehow that this is the second girl born. My grandchild, thinking of my daughter-in-law and son 's baby number two. But why is my brother holding her? So, then I reach for her, and he pulls back away. And he gets taller. (In real life my brother is a little taller than me and he is older, as an authority figure) (And the part where I can't touch her, is my temporary position, but God willing I will be out and hold my grandchildren).

Then the scene changes, that we are outside our grandpa 's home, and he is still holding her. So, I ask him, 'Is this your grandchild?' And he didn't say anything? And I (woke-up). (But, in real life we are expecting another grandchild, this will be number three of our two kids with my first wife). (Before the second one was born, and before my daughter-in-law got pregnant, I had a dream that she was going to have a baby). (And on 1-21-21, I had a dream of interacting with a cute little baby). So, today, 1-23-21, this is the third time of dreaming. As my Cellie says, 'It is conformation. Father, Son, Holy Ghost. 1,2,3, there is three.' (End)

'Android Dream'

We we're outside and I was talking to this couple about these talented boys, who rode horses in a show. These kids are about 12 to 13 years old; and all lined up and moved exactly alike. Looking at them, I'm not sure if they are real or not? They move like androids, and in unison, and spaced out exactly apart. And I yelled out to the boys, to say hi to our visitors. They did it, one right after the other. 'Hi, I'm Johnny,' 'Hi, I'm Jimmy,' 'Hi I'm Timmy,' 'Hi, I'm Tommy.' Then each said, 'do you want to see our chip?' And all turned at once to the back of their ear. Then right behind the fourth one, was a want to be fifth rider. Her name is Darla, and she is getting into a small car. She is only 10-12 years old. So, I called her over, and she came and sat on my knee. To talk to the couple. I gave her a huge hug, and said, 'I miss you'. She said, my name is Darla, and I want to be a cowgirl like the boys. And ride horses. (I woke up) (In Real life, I probably dreamt that, because my Bunkie said, he used to have an android-type-monkey. Which looks and acts real, blinks his eyes, and opens his mouth, and moves his hands. And he got to scare his older sister with it also. (End)

CHAPTER 31

'TESTI.'

This is a testimony of when I was saved back in my early 20s. I believed the word of God that was preached that night, on TV, I repented of my sins, and asked Jesus in my life and heart, by faith, and received His free gift of Salvation by the Holy Spirit and the Grace of God. Things went all right with my first wife and I, and we had two children. Then about 6 to 7 years after I was saved, we got divorced. And I started backsliding and got into some trouble; I repented (meaning I turned away from those things) and got straightened out. For about three years sober.

Then I remarried a second time for almost 19 years together. And I got a neck injury from work. I was using icepacks and alcohol for the nerve pain, like medicine for six months. And I tried chiropractors, three different masseuses, and even an acupuncturist, with no avail. Then finally, I had surgery on May 8, 2014. And I worked all the way up to the 7th of May.

Thanks be to God, the surgery was a success, and the doctor went through my throat and neck. With six screws and a titanium plate fusing three vertebrae 's together. But I got a custom to taking in all that alcohol for nerve pain. Now, the pain is gone. —But I didn't want to stop drinking then, I was an alcoholic. The afternoon and evening of the day before the altercation happened. I had consumed at least a quart of vodka and possibly beer too, that Friday night.

That early Saturday morning on August 16, 2014. Only four-months after the surgery. My wife came in my recovery room, and woke-me up, because I was yelling in my sleep a nightmare. She said, 'I have had-it, with you and you're drinking, and was railing on me as I am trying to get away from her and landed on the floor next to the bed. Unfortunately, that is where I kept my .45 gun in between the mattress. And in fear, in my humbled, duress-position on the floor, on my knees. Before I knew it, the gun was pulled out, and I fired behind me twice, not knowing where I shot? She was turning too, and no eyeglasses on and not in my right mind. I actually shot her three more times, and I don't know exactly where? And didn't remember shooting more times until two-days later in jail. So, I pleaded no-contest, and received 14 years @ 85% w/ GBI. Now, 7-years down in August and about to get out, in Faith by God's Grace. So, I thought at the time, but God had other plans. He wants me to learn more lessons. Besides my EPRD date was later, I was believing for a miracle. I know God can do it. But I also have to consider Isaiah 55:8, which says: "For My thoughts are not your thoughts, nor are your ways My ways," says the Lord.

Jesus Christ saved my soul back in my early 20s and gave me the Gift of eternal life in Him, through the Holy Spirit. I was born again—Spiritually. But, in prison He restored me, physically, mentally, psychologically, and Spiritually. I am a new person (creation) in Christ Jesus. I am free, in Him. Jesus restored my soul and gave me a second chance. He has forgiven me; my second wife has forgiven me; and I had to forgive myself. I Lost 50 pounds and gained half of it back in muscle with no more sleep apnea, no more nightmares, no more high-blood pressure, no more depression or negative or suicidal thoughts. Thank God for the rehabilitation and reconciliation that I received in prison, through God's grace and mercy. Now to restart my life again on the outside. Back to church, back to work, back to school, with book writing and publishing. Back to ministry and blessing other people. Worshiping God and giving glory to God our savior Jesus Christ our Lord. Amen. (End)

'Bob Dream'

I was over at a customer's house, doing handyman work. It was at an exclusive and expensive home. And I was going from one project to the other. I was in their kitchen/den area, and there was this rectangle basket on the TV, and inside held this rectangular tin pan. It was for holding something like a decoration. But it wasn't in there right now. You know, it wasn't the right season now. So, the customer was talking to someone about that, and the pan is sticking out. It looked tacky. So, I said, 'I can cut that down for you, and grabbed it, took it down on the ground and grabbed a few kitchen cutting devices, like a grater or can-opener, with cutting tools on them. And I was going to try to use that. (In real life, I would just get metals cutters to start with). Where I put it on the floor, was near two large refrigerators and they were both open. So, I closed both of the doors to them. They were open for some reason, and nobody bothered to close them. Then the customer comes over, and he says, 'Oh no, don't use that, I got something in the garage.' And I was heading for my truck to get my metal cutters outside. And, I got up, headed for the patio, to go to the side gate, to the front. When I almost went through this large pane glass. It was a floor to ceiling pane of glass. It was clear as glass. Oh yeah, it is glass. Anyway, I go to the right of that, where there is an outside smaller slider door. Which I just put a new lock on that slider. I am in the patio, and Bob comes in the front door, and he is checking out some of the projects that the customer talked about. (In real life Bob, who likes to be called Robert, was our designer / salesman at the last carpet store that I work for. Which is no longer in business, because the owner-operator / salesman has retired after 40 some -odd years.) So, I waved to him, and he is coming out to see me, and also checking out the slider-lock. He would be the one who gave me the referral for this customer. [We, (the carpet store and installers) probably laid some kind of flooring in their house or we are about to.] end.

'RUNAWAY DREAM'

I was at the top of this hill; it was about 4 feet to 5 feet wide sidewalk. With a lot of people walking on it. And I'm going down weaving in between people on my skateboard. (As you know, skateboards don't have brakes; sure, you can stand on the back and skid a while to break). But I was riding on my knees like I was pretending to be on a toboggan run in the snow. It's a wonder, I didn't have to yell out, 'get out my way!' That actually might have made it worse, and they would have got in my way. At the end of this sidewalk was a four-way cross street intersection. And an old school gas station on the corner. You know the kind that had service to fix your car, plus gas, oil, water, and air. And some of them had real grass on the corner where they would put up in their sign. Later, gas stations just had cement and painted green like grass. So, as I am approaching the corner, and I still had a good head of speed. I purposely hit the curb where the real grass was. The skateboard stopped, and I was catapulted to the grass 10 feet away and then rolled across the wet grass to a stop. (It was that or go off the curb and land into the street, into traffic). (woke up) (In real life I went down a steep hill, on my rollerblades at near 5 PM traffic. To go retrieve my work vehicle down at the auto-garage at the bottom of the hill. Because my second wife did not want to drive me. So, little by little, side to side, using my back heel-break. There we're two major steep hills, the first steeper than the second. So, all I have to do is get through the first hill. And I almost made it. A streetlight, and level ground separated the two hills. The light turned red, and I needed to stop, but also not to be in traffic. So, I am way to the right. The only problem was loose sand on the asphalt. And as I tried to stop, I slipped in the sand, and fell, and twisted my knee. So, I got up, light turned green and went across the street and stopped to assess my damages. I was going to keep going, when my neighbor Kim, shows up and gives me a ride as she sees me limping). (End)

CHAPTER 32

'TIM/PASS DREAM'

We are going down the road in a Camry car. And Tim, my son is smaller and not old enough to drive. But he is steering for some reason. I am on the outside window semi-steering and driving or what I don't know? We are coming down the street called Auburn and going to turn right at Maywood. But what I didn't know my son was working the gas pedal too and going too fast. And I'm trying to stop, or slow down for the curb. (In real life I can't do that if I am hanging out the window, besides my son never did this). And we are going down the street in a power slide. Breaking and gassing it, and turning, and we completely missed the turn. So, we came back to the intersection, and the passenger says, 'what just happened?' And I said, 'Tim, was having a little fun at our expense.' (Woke up)

'TRAIN DREAM'

I was in a train race down on the freeway. In the race we are cars, but later our cars turned in to a train. And we were doing so well we were going to pass the leader. So, they threw us off, and sent us around into a train yard, that wasn't going anywhere. It was stopped in many locations; changing; unloading; loading; fixing; etc. But, not going. And we almost got stuck. So, I went around with 5 Extra Rail Rd. cars for extra credit. The guy that was with me gained some train cars also, he was helping me as a team, and gained six or seven and went another way. Where we were going, the doors almost closed on us. And working my way back to the main line. (In Real life I don't really need that, I'm already here). Now, I am on my way back to those jumped tracks I came from. I told the guy I was racing with, 'not only are we going to catch up that little train. I am going to surpass your train in the dust.'

(woke up). (pee break).

(In real life the guy I teamed up with, is my Cellie. The train yard is all these buildings we have to move too, that aren't doing anything productive. The train race is the race of life. And when we get out, we will be stronger, wiser, better, because of what Christ Jesus has done for us on the inside. Not only inside prison but inside are being).

'LETTERS FROM HEAVEN DREAM'

Carrie, my sister and I our dropping off Nicole, my niece at the Lencioni house driveway, and Nicole is reading some mail. And all of a sudden Nicole yells out, ' Praise God, Praise God, Praise the Lord.' So, Carrie just backs out of the driveway and leaves, like she already knew what Nicole was expecting to receive. As we got down the street. There look like someone I knew from the neighborhood. I said, 'He looked high'. And she said, 'no that's not him, it just looks a little like him'. And we went down the road, when we got to Auburn, the car turned into a bicycle. And I took off into traffic to make a left, but I had dropped a piece of mail. So, I went back and picked it up, and jetted over to the right lane to turn right and mail the letter in the mailbox up the road on Oswell. Before the traffic catches up with me on the road. (End)

CHAPTER 33

'THE K OF G'

The title of the sermon is the Kingdom of God; as Jesus is teaching the people and the Pharisees present. Just prior to that, Jesus healed the 10 lepers. And only one stranger comes back and gives God glory for his healing; he is a Samaritan. *ref. v17 (The 'Nine' were indicative of most of Israel of that particular time, unthankful!) KJV—JSM *

* (Luke 17:19)

V19) "And He said unto him arise, go your way, (Jesus lifts people up): your faith has made you whole (proclaims the fact that not only was he healed, but saved as well; all of them showed Faith by asking Christ for healing, which they received; however, only one, It seems, was given eternal life because he glorify God).

Now, Jesus is talking to the Pharisees about the Kingdom of God. (Luke 17:20) *

V20)" And when He was demanded of the Pharisees, when the Kingdom of God should come (the Lord, in effect, answered that the Kingdom of God was at that moment in their midst, for He was the Kingdom of God)....He answered them and said, The Kingdom of God, cometh not with observation (the Jews claimed that when the Messiah came, He would overthrow Rome, etc.; Jesus is telling them that their "observations" are wrong): *V21)"Neither shall they say, Lo here! or, lo there! (He is saying that all these outward signs they were talking about are not Scriptural, and really have no bearing on the Kingdom of God.) for, behold, the Kingdom of God is within you (would have been better translated, "the Kingdom of God is within your midst," for the Kingdom is Jesus, but Israel would not recognize Him; the "born again" experience brings Christ into the heart, and thereby places the Kingdom of God within the person"). Meaning as the Scripture says: "For greater is He who is in you, then he who is in the world." Once we have realized our fallen state through the word of God, and the conviction of the Holy Spirit, that we are poor, blind, and naked before God. That there is 'none righteous, no not one'. 'We have all fallen short of the glory of God.' And it is only by God's grace I am saved. His mercy led me to repentance. In my early 20s, I came to know Jesus. But it was he who chose me. He chose me, and lifted me up out of darkness, into His wonderful light.

* (1-John 5:11,12)

V11)" And this is the record (the "record" is the Word of God, which is the story of the Cross), that God has given to us Eternal Life (the Life of God flowing into and literally becoming a part of the Believer), and this life is in His Son." (Christ is the Source, while the Cross is the means.) V12)" He who has the Son has Life (through the Cross); and he who has not the Son of God has not life. (This rules out all the fake luminaries of the world.) In the dictionary for luminaries, means: (a source of light; Esp: a celestial body) In other words famous people or persons of influence, that can lead people away from Christ, instead of toward Christ Jesus for Salvation. At the end of (I-John 5:20,21) And John the Apostles journey with Jesus. Tells us for a fact, that John was there and saw Jesus, the Son of God, and most of His miracles too. It is a historical fact. Jesus came from the Father. He had a mission to do here on the Earth. That was, 'Jesus Christ, and Him Crucified.' For our sins. To be the Sacrificial Lamb of God.

Let's here John's last words in his letter:(I-John 5:20-21) KJV (JSM)

V20)"And we know that the Son of God is come (presents that which is not simply a historical fact, but rather an abiding operation), and has given us an understanding, that we may know Him Who is true (the real "One" as opposed to spurious gods), and we are in Him Who is true, even in his Son Jesus Christ (by virtue of being "Baptized into His Death" [Rom. 6:3-5]). Let's explore what Romans has to say:

* V3)" Know you not, that so many of us as were baptized into Jesus Christ (plainly says that this Baptism is into Christ and not water [I Cor. 1:17; 12:13; Gal. 3:27; Eph. 4:5; Col. 2:11-13]) were baptized into His Death? (When Christ died on the Cross, in the Mind of God, we died with Him; in other words, He became our Substitute, and our identification with Him in His Death gives us all the benefits for which He died; the idea is that He did it all for us!)....* V4) Therefore we are buried with Him by baptism into death (not only did we die with Him, but we were buried with Him as well, which means that all the sin and transgression of the past were buried; when they put Him in the Tomb, they put all of our sins into that Tomb as well): that like as Christ was raised up from the dead by the Glory of the Father, even so we also should walk in Newness of Life (we died with Him, we were buried with Him, and His Resurrection was our Resurrection to a "Newness of Life"). * V5) For If we have been planted together (with Christ): in the likeness of His death (Paul proclaims the Cross as the instrument through which all Blessings come; consequently, the Cross must ever be the object of our Faith, which gives the Holy Spirit latitude to work within our lives), we shall be also in the likeness of His Resurrection (we can have the "likeness of His Resurrection," i.e., "live this Resurrection Life," only as long as we understand the "likeness of His Death," which refers to the Cross as the means by which all of this is done): Back to v20 of

1-John ch.5 this is the True God, and Eternal Life. (Jesus Christ is truly God, and Faith in Him guarantees" Eternal Life.") V21) Little children, keep yourselves from idols. Amen. (This does not refer here to the heathen worship of idol gods, but of the heretical substitutes for the Christian conception of God, or anything that pulls us away from Christ and the Cross.) (end quote)

Loren L. Johnson

Heretical or heresy in the Dictionary is referring to 'adherence to a religious opinion, contrary to church dogma. And dogma is the doctrine or body of doctrines formally proclaims by the Church. To reiterate, that anything that pulls us away from Faith in Christ, and His finished work on the Cross. To repent, and to get right with Jesus Christ our Lord. Repent, means 'to turn from sin', turn away from those things that can harm you, and turn toward our Savior. Do what the Word says to do and do the Father's will. Love one another, as Christ, also loved the Church. And gave Himself up for her.

'VISIONS & DREAMS'

Let's start this study in (Heb.) definition for vision. (Heb.) #2377 Chazown, Khaw-zone: from #2372 a sight (ment.). i. e. a dream, revelation, or oracle-vision (35x) vision or (2) Chazown almost always signifies a means of divine revelation. (When I was writing this about vision, the Holy Spirit impressed upon me with divine revelation to write my family, for character reference letters, at this particular time and juncture.) (2a) First, it refers to the means itself, to a prophetic "vision" by which divine messages are communicated: (2b) Second, this word represents the message received by prophetic "vision", "Where there is no vision, the people perish; but he that keepeth the law happy is he." KJV (Prov. 29:18)

This is 1 of 4 verses in this study in titled 'vision & dreams'.

This was originally my Bunkies (Bruce) message. He mostly got dreams through his life from God to start one project or another. From doing ministry in his church; plays, songs, etc. Two starting Alpha-Quest in 1989. For almost 25 years. Which is an outreach ministry, a vocal choir who sang, at churches, events, nursing homes, to witnessing on the street, and even Christmas caroling in their season.

Personally, hearing his story, he should not even be in here. But as—

(Gen. 50:20) says:

V20)" But as for you, you meant evil against me, but God meant it for good, in order to bring it about as it is this day, to save many people alive." The enemy meant evil for him, but God blessed him with a yard ministry called "Amazing Grace Ministries" (AGM). And he has blessed hundreds, in turn. So even when you think you're down. God is in your corner, to lift you up, remember that. In my Bunkies sermon to me, how he started the "family prayer meetings", came to him in a dream. He got the family together and read and discussed the Bible and fellowship with a meal, once a week for 10 years. They read the Bible three times through. I think that's amazing in itself. (To reiterate: "where there is no vision the people perish.")

Let's go to the next verse:

(Job 33:14-16)

V14)" For God may speak in one way, or in another, yet man does not perceive it. V15) In a dream, in a vision of the night, when Deep Sleep falls on men, while slumbering on their beds, V16) then he opens the ears of men, and seals their instruction." (So, God wants to commune with you, or communicate, and if He can't do it in His word or a Holy Spirit filled Believer. He sends you a message from Heaven in your dreams.)

Next, (Joel 2:28)

V28)" And it shall come to pass after -ward that I will pour out My Spirit on all flesh; you sons and your daughters shall prophecy, your old men shall dream dreams, your young men shall see visions." So, we see God's Spirit being poured out in these last days, to help, teach, and instruct us. To bless us with His Spirit, from the Father of lights.

And the last verse he had in this study was: (Jeremiah 23:28);

V28)" The prophet who has a dream, let him tell a dream. And he who has My word, let him speak My word faithfully. What is the chaff to the wheat?" says the lord. So, as God gives you a message or a revelation, to share that message and act on that in faith. I received messages obviously in my dreams and not all have special meaning to you, but again, it may. And His word, He gives me, I give to you. And the believers are the wheat, and the unbelievers are the chaff. End

'MACHINE DREAM'

I had a dream about a computer machine who was controlling people. And my brother and sister-in-law were doing these mental tasks, in this square room. Being monitored by a computer machine. (In real life my brother-in-law with my second marriage had talked about this reality, like the 'Matrix', and thought of it before the movie came out. And my Cellie and I talked about it too. About (AI) Artificial Intelligence. He mentioned about computers thinking for themselves. And talked about this experiment with these two large computers doing certain tasks. Then they had link them together, and they were talking to each other in their own computer language, they created on their own. And the people doing the test on these computers, saw what they were doing. And they pulled the plug on the idea, and literally had pulled the plug so they would stop. Too scary of scenario like 'Terminator' or 'I-Robot' premise.) So, back to the dream, I came into the room where my brother and sister-in-law were working. I was mad at the computer for doing this to my relatives and told the machine it was an A-hole. The computer didn't know what I was saying, because it is a slang word for something. The computer says to me, 'What is the meaning of the words you used?' And I said, 'The whole thing is A-1'; So, the computer says it back, ' A-Hole, means I'm A-1 ' . And, I said, 'Yes!' My relatives just Laughed. (woke-up) end.

CHAPTER 34

'LOL'

I was playing cards by myself called solitaire, or so I thought. And more than once, but actually several times the last card under the pile to the right, which is the thickest pile. And it always is an ace of clubs. And I shuffled each time really well. …. God is having fun with me. But I didn't know what yet? Now, when I am done shuffling this time. I am going to look in the deck before I start to make sure the ace of clubs is in the middle or the end of the deck. So, I won't lose again. So, here I go and put out all the cards, and the ace of clubs comes out early on top, and I put it up in its place. Now, I lose again, and looking why I lost mostly. The key cards that I needed for that game were on the bottom of the deck pile number seven to the right. And the last three cards I couldn't get too; you guessed it; the other three Aces. (LOL), I laughed out loud, pretty good. Now, that's when I knew God was messing with me. And who said, God doesn't have a sense of humor. End

'EDDIE DREAM'

(I was having a dream with my first ex-wife's husband. We got along pretty well. I remember playing basketball in his front driveway with he and his son, and my son and me. They were just a tad-bit better than we were. You know, as divorce goes; God hates divorce. He is in the reconciliation

187

business. He allowed it with Moses in the Old Testament, because of the people's hardness of heart. Once the individuals decide to divorce. It's imperative to have forgiveness for your spouse and the other person he or she is with. Not only will they get along better with you, for you forgiving their actions. But also, God will forgive you too. But, if you hold unforgiveness with your brother, then our Heavenly Father will not forgive you. Don't harbor ill feelings for one another. And I know it can be hard, but do it for the kids involved, if you have children with that spouse. And pay your child support, and don't look at your spouse, and the significant other with resentment, and that your children suffer for it. Do it for your children and think of it that way. Besides, being a legal thing to do. That's how I looked at it, where all benefited in the long run. A win-win situation. For my first ex-wife and I, for a big major of the time, we traded out child support, with me completely remodeling my ex-wife's new husband's home. And everyone felt good about it. Win-win.) Now, for the dream, which was like basketball, but in a big way. We were throwing balls into a roll-off dumpster for a basket, and we were about 30 to 40 feet away. Throwing as hard as we could to make it. I went first, and threw the basketball over hand with all my might and made it. Now, it was Eddies turn, and his was a soccer ball, which is a little lighter and smaller. (In real life, my two children played soccer for 8 to 9 years, and Eddie was their coach for a few of those years.) Eddie, threw it, and this was at night, and it went up into the night- sky and practically disappeared like driving a golf ball. And it came back like one too, floating backwards, and instead of going in the roll-off; it landed right next to it on a golf green. It hit and rolled like a golf ball. (In real life it would bounce and keep going; also, I probably dreamt that too, because Eddie and my son were avid golfers.)

Now, the third guy did it with the same kind of ball, but when it landed on the golf green it kept going, and the other end of the golf greens were three bowling pins and he knocked them down. (In real life, I used to bowl on occasion, and with my children.) End

'THE LONG HALL DREAM'

I was working in this house laying carpet throughout the home. A two-story rectangular house, with an upstairs hallway that ran 3/4 of the long way down the hall. The customer, just bought the home and wanted a few things in this house, like they had in their last one. For instance, they had these big "X" s inserted into the carpet, into their big rooms. (Our's as an Installer; 'Ours is not the question why?' We just do it. Maybe, "X" marks the spot?) But this time they only wanted it down the long hallway. Well, this is an older house, and it had a pretty much standard width hall. About 3 feet at its narrowest. That's going to be one odd looking "X", being long gated like that. I told the little old man who was buying it, kiddingly you will be going down the hall, and start following one of these lines and run into the wall? He just laughed, and said, 'maybe so'. End

CHAPTER 35

'INTRO TO TESTI.'

This is an intro to my testimony in chapter 31, on page 175. And done as if it in front of a congregation.

Good morning brothers let's pray. 'This is the Day the Lord has made, let us be glad, and rejoice in it. This is the Lords Day of the Sabbath rest. Bless the words that come out of my mouth, Amen.'

I've been working out all week, and today I can have physical rest. As do, we have our Spiritual rest in Him too. What Christ did on the Cross at Calvary. We can rest in Him, because He did it all for us, and His finished work. He saved us from our sins and redeemed us by His shed blood. By dying on the Cross for our sins, He was buried and on the third day He rose from the grave according to the Scriptures. Jesus paid the penalty for sin and death, so we didn't have too. He became our propitiation, or substitute as the perfect Lamb of God sacrifice. Because of the sin in the world since the time of Adams day. Then Christ Jesus came and changed all that.

God the Father sent His only begotten Son into the world, that by believing in Him by faith, we have Eternal Life. So, that we won't have unbelief, and that we would perish. And be eternally lost and separated from God our Father. God makes a Way, His Way. His Way is Jesus; there is no other way. What does, (John 14:6) say, of Who the Way is? V6) Jesus said to him, " I am the way, the truth, and the life. No one comes to the Father except through Me." NKJV

I came to him years ago, and I am going to share my testimony of where I was, how it went, and how I fell back into temptation and almost destruction. But God save me then, and he restored me now. (Go to Chapter 31, p175) … And after I read that; I sang "Amazing Grace",(1V,2V,4v, and Alleluia).

'AUDIT. DREAM'

My dad and I are on this huge nightclub auditorium job. We are laying carpet throughout this office/house. The house is in front and as you go to the back it turns into bigger and bigger rooms. My dad measured the job. Because it was so big, to make sure we got all the cuts needed for the job. (Including the salesman, to double check his work too. Even though an experienced salesman, still likes a little input on a big job, to all being on the same page sort-of-speak.) (In real life) We were laying one of the rooms and I ran across a big lump. And I pulled back the carpet. And a piece of pad from the old construction was there. And now, I'm looking at the floor supports. The floor only goes partway and drops-off. It needs beams in there with cross supports, and plywood flooring. Before we can lay carpet down. Then I looked further, and we are supposed to keep going into this auditorium area. When I went in there, I was shocked. My dad measured it without me. He knows how to measure, and all. And probably did a good job covering all the square feet in this huge place. (Then in real life, figure it up and convert it to square yards.) (Which is simply, 'L x W = sq. ft. Divided by 9 = and you get your square yardage. + 5% To 10% added in for fills and waste'.) (This is a formula, that's why double checking with actual 12-foot widths, and length cuts of carpet or essential to it coming out right.) (And I'm sure it took literally hours to figure this job. What didn't he figure? Really is not our job, and we are not ready for the carpet phase yet.) ….

I took him into the big room and told him to stand in a certain place. And I said, 'Isn't there anything strange about this picture?' And he said, 'No', I said; 'This whole room is 2 to 3 feet lower than everything else, from where we started or left off. Where, unfortunately the owner overheard me standing nearby. And she expected us to do the foundation and subfloors too. That I believe was not figured in the original contract or bid. And I needed to get on the phone with the boss and salesman, on the details of what was covered and what wasn't. But, until that happens, she is upset. I would be talking to the general contractor. And he is responsible for the subfloors, and why isn't it done yet? So, we can do our job of laying the floors down. But, until then she is still upset, thinking it is our fault, and threatens to sue us; meaning the carpet company we were contracting through. So, we are done for today, until we get this straightened out. As I was leaving through the Home/Business; it turned into a restaurant hallway. In the hallway, I get with this one couple, and greet them, and say, 'Hello' ; also this other woman I know who came up to me with her business card, and said, 'Call me soon'. This is the owner's best friend. I said to her, 'That woman out there, didn't even recognize me for being your friend too.' 'You know? when we met before.' The best friend says, 'I'll calm her down.' 'And will figure it out.' I said, 'OK', 'I'll talk to you later.' And I left, and thought I wasn't in that big of a hurry, to get back, and talk this over? But, when I got outside, I forgot to get in my vehicle, and I am running down the road, back to the office. (I woke up)

(Commentary of the Dream)

(In real life we are not responsible for building the floor up.) or making the foundation, being of wood or concrete. That is on the builder or the General Contractor doing the job. We are floor coverings, not floor builders. We do some subfloors, when the surface is not up to standards. To do a proper job. We install subfloors of plywood from 5 mm to 7 mm generally. Or 5/16 to 3/4 inch of plywood. Which would be best in that particular situation.)

Loren L. Johnson

'OVERCOME DREAM'

I am in front of this 'Big house', and it is about to slide down the hill. And now, I am on it, trying to get by it, as I am climbing to the side of it. There were men in their tree-cutting of limbs. It was vibrating and the support was giving away.

And then this huge stump was taken out. It looked prehistoric in size, the trees diameter base. Then it was being loaded on the back of this pick-up truck. And I got to the other side and my brother was there and was asking me how it was going, or what was it like? And I was getting something out of my truck.

And I saw something in there I didn't recognize, what it was? I thought it was a popper. (you know, you throw it down and it makes sparks and pops; Or a firework?) I gave it to my brother's friend Jim, that was with him. It changed to some balancing device, then changed again into some small live animal. (Then I woke- up)

(In real life, we watched a nature show with animals my new Bunkie and me. And we talked about bicycles, motorcycles, ATV, and having good balance before bed. And the house represents prison and a big obstacle to overcome, and little by little, it is done, or being done, I got on the other side, I am an Overcomer.) Amen. End

CHAPTER 36

'NAMES & LABELS'

Today, I was pondering, why I haven't done a sermon on alcohol spirits, and drugs yet? Not that I was a big drug addict. I had tried a couple of things in my youth, but alcohol has been with me since I was a teenager. And being acceptable by my dad, and my grandpa, and my father-in-law. Also, by society, and also my second wife; it was a common practice. Then when you abuse it, it becomes a problem. God didn't say we couldn't drink alcohol; He says not to excess, where it becomes a problem in fact, He would rather you be filled with the Holy Spirit of God instead. We are going to look at those Scriptures today. And the things of the past are of today as well. Things haven't changed, just different names and labels. All the demons that Jesus and His disciples cast out of people; do you think they are gone completely? No. These fallen Angels and evil spirits still influence men and women today. These beings are immortal. They can be with you a while, then leave, and come back seven times worse. Back in Jesus' day, they were more aware of controlling spirits. And cast them out. Today, the Believers have the Holy Spirit, and full possession would be impossible. But you could be influenced to believe a lie or do something destructive to someone or yourself. Let's look at (Luke 11:24). But you open the door for that. V24)" When an unclean spirit goes out of a man, he goes through dry places, seeking rest; and finding none, he says, 'I will return to my house (that's you) from which I came.' "There are defenses for evil spirits; using the authority of Jesus name; prayer; using the word of God; praise, love, joy, peace, that the Holy Spirit gives. (James 4:7), V7)" Therefore submit to God. Resist the devil and he will flee from you."

Why do you think they call alcohol or liquor, alcohol spirits? Because they are demon spirits. What is the symbol for medical, or physician, drugs/ medicine, etc.? It is a stick, with a snake wrapped around it. Who was the biggest, baddest, snake (serpent), of all? Devil or Satan, in the Garden of Eden. And (Lucifer) a name given to Satan, and 1/3 of the fallen Angels in Heaven to Earth. (Reference —Is. 14:12; Rev. 20:1-3; Rev. 12:7-9). The enemy is not people; it is spiritual wickedness in high places. (Ref. Eph. 6:12).

We overcome the enemy by believing the word of God about Jesus power, by His shed blood on the Cross at Calvary. And of your testimony as Christians, saved by His Amazing Grace. And Faith in Jesus Christ. (Ref. Rev. 12:11). V11)" And they overcame him (Devil) by the blood of the Lamb and by the word of their testimony, and they did not love their lives to the death. "He did it all for you.!!!

Have you ever wondered how many angels were fallen and their powers? In (Daniel 7:10) talks about the innumerable servants of God, these are possibly not all angels; but it does tell us the numbers could be high. In this verse says 'a thousand-Thousands (which is a million) ministers to Him; ten thousand times ten thousand (which is 100 million) stood before Him. And then when Jesus was betrayed by Judas, and there was a great multitude of soldiers and religious personnel there. And Jesus says in (Matt. 26:53), "Or do you think that I cannot now pray to my Father, and He will provide Me with more than 12 legions of Angels?" * Commentary Ref. NKJV p1538 'A legion in the Roman Army words about 6000 men. When one considers the power of one Angel, as seen in the Old Testament (see Ex.12:23; II Sam. 24:15-17; II Kings 19:35) The power of more than 72,000 Angels is beyond comprehension. Jesus had all of powers of Heaven at his disposal, yet he refused to use it. His Father's will was for Him to go to the Cross.

(End quote)

(Rev. 16:13,14)

V13)" And I saw three unclean spirits like frogs coming out of the mouth of the beast, and out of the mouth of the false prophet, V14) for they are spirits of demons, performing signs, which go out to the Kings." .... There are different kinds of spirits and names for each, and their function. There is the spirit of fear, ... (Ref. II Tim. 1:7); A spirit of I'll will (depression), (ref. Judges 9:23); A spirit of sickness and uncleanness (Ref. Luke 8:2) & (Luke 8:26-40). Then The story of Jesus casting out many demons out of a certain man who had them a long time. And they got permission to enter the herd of swine. In the spirit world, (which is invisible, but that doesn't mean it's not there) the spirits recognized Jesus as the Son of God. (Ref. Luke 8:28). The whole story is (Luke 8:26-40) but, In V30)" Jesus asked him, saying, 'what is your name? '"And he said, 'legion', because many demons had entered him. "(end quote)

(This verse shows that demons, angelic or not, can manifest themselves into spirits, and only to do harm. For this man was possessed. It controlled him.) They even knew the punishment that would befall them in the future, or even right then and there. In V31) "And they begged Him that He would not command them to go out into the abyss." (That would be in the bottomless pit.) ;(Ref. Rev. 9:1,11; 11:7; 17:8; 20:1,3). (Let me repeat they're immortal and they're out there to harm you. If you open yourself up to them, or try to draw near them; like séances, a Ouija boards, and abuse of drugs and alcohol.) To allow yourself to be tempted. God says he will not allow you to be tempted more than you are able to bear. ...

(I-Cor. 10:13)

V13)" No temptation has overtaken you except such as is common to man, but God is faithful, who will not allow you to be tempted beyond what you are able, but with the temptation will also make the way of escape, that you may be able to bear it. "(Ref. demon, NKJV p1810) ..., these demonic principalities and powers have continued their warfare against those who are His followers... (Rom.8:38-39; Eph.6:12). Yet after Christ returns, the devil and his angels will be defeated and thrown into the lake of fire and brimstone … (Matt.25:41; Rev.20:10). (End quote)

And since the Cross, where Jesus has the ultimate power and control over them. And He can use the enemy, (as you will), as a way to strengthen you by adversity or opposition of the enemy. (Just like weights are resistance in exercising.) In the end, God wants you to be an Overcomer, in this life. So, to prepare you for the next life in Heaven.

(Prov. 23:29-35) V29)" Who has woe? Who has sorrow? Who has contentions? Who has complaints? Who has wounds without cause? Who has redness of eyes? V30) Those who linger long at the wine. V31) Do not look on the wine when it is red, when it sparkles in the cup, when it swirls around smoothly; V32) At the last it bites like a serpent, and stings like a viper. V33) Your eyes will see strange things, and your heart will utter perverse things. V34) Yes, you will be like one who lies down in the midst of the sea, or like one who lies at the top of the mast, saying: …. V35) They have struck me, but I was not hurt; they have beaten me, but I did not feel it. When shall I awake, that I may seek another drink?" (That person is an Alcoholic)—I know, cause those things happen to me. Not all the time, but enough. That I didn't learn my lesson, soon enough. There were consequences to my actions. (Did you take note of verse 31,32, &33.) V31–Red wine-That's dark, & is real strong, and … 'when it sparkles in the cup', (which is Champagne) and those bubbles to get you high faster. — But, the next line, 'When it swirls around smoothly; 'I'm not sure how the spirit world works exactly, but those could be spirits. (That swirling is also in Hard Liquor).

And V32–Representing the effects as unto a serpent biting you like a snake. And stings like a viper. (Which is a poisonous snake). And if you drink enough, or take drugs to excess, it is like that snake, it is poisonous, and it will kill you. Then in V33– (You we'll see double vision as getting drunk, and you would see hallucinations, depending on what drug you took. Drugs of old, like LSD, do that to you. Drugs of today, I have heard testimonies of people in prison, because of 'Meth'. They saw witches who were coming after them. The meth user used a machete on a person who he thinks is a witch. And after he is arrested and not under the influence of this drug. He finds out it is his best friend.)

It wasn't much different for me. The 1 quart of vodka and possible beer that Friday night, and my high-blood pressure went through the roof. I blacked-out memory, and the spirits took-over. And the end of V33— (The spirits get you agitated, argumentative, and angry. And you start cussing vulgar profanities.) V33) ...., 'and your heart will utter perverse things.' (Which normally I don't do that anymore. But I yelled at my wife one or two days prior, and swore loudly, which I regret.) (Ref. Matt. 12:34) for v33. (In the beginning, I felt guilty, and was upset with myself more about yelling at my wife, then shooting her. Because I was more conscious of my bad behavior. That morning consciously, I was barely there. But, at the first year down at CVSP; The reality of what I did hit me. Then it was a repentful-remorse as I cried. And I am extremely sorry for both. She did not deserve that at all. Thank God, I have reconciled with the Lord, and with her and myself.)

(Prov. 20:1) "Wine is a mocker, strong drink is a brawler, and whoever is led astray by it is not wise." (Mocker: is one who ridicules or treats with contempt.) or (mimics in sport or for fun.) (Brawler: a noisy quarrel, or a rumpus, a scraper, basically get into a fight.) (I think of a brawler, as one who is in the barroom fight.) (Led astray: meaning you just derailed or wandered off from the Spirit led path, and not abiding in Christ as we should.) (Led: meaning the temptation is there, dangled in our face. And the more we choose that lifestyle, the less the Spirit works in our life. And as the proverbs are there to teach us, even with a rebuke, saying it is not wise.) He didn't forbid drinking alcohol, he plainly tells us, do not do to excess. (my physical father (dad) use to tell me that, he said, 'you could over do anything, drink too much milk for instance'; It doesn't sound bad, but there would be a point when it is too much.)— (In Swedish, he says, 'No Hoen' (which means without restrain; don't overdo it.) And the Word would rather have us filled with the Holy Spirit. Because ... (Ref. I- John 4:4) "Greater is He who is in me, then he who is in the world."

199

(In Eph. 5:18) KJV. Says: "Do not be drunk with wine, where in is excess; but be filled with the Spirit." If the enemy can convince you otherwise, which is contrary to the word of God. He has already got more than a foothold in your life. The door is open. And if you let it continue, it could become a strong hold, and harder to break. And if continues, it can bring death. You need to repent, of that you were doing, and turn back to God and his word. His word is true, and it is there for you, to protect you, and guide you, through these difficult times. (If you don't know you are in the wrong or walking in disobedience and sin?) That's why we as Christians are instructed to pray continually. To be in the word, night and day. And to fellowship with the Saints in the assembly, to come and worship God together. This will help you., to recognize you're wrong. To be accountable to each other, confessing wrong to each other. Praying for each other, loving on each other, putting your brother in higher esteem than yourself.

David of the Bible was a great man and king, but he too is human, and we do still live in this tent of the flesh. David did or didn't know he was doing wrong consciously. But when his advisor told him he was sinning, with adultery and murder. What did he do next? He went out and repented with a humbled heart. He wept bitterly for his sin unto the lord, just as Peter did of his three denials of even knowing Jesus. Peter didn't even know it, until the cock road three times.

Let's look at the past and present again; Potion's, Chemicals, Sorcery, Magicians, aren't much different then modern-day medicine. (Just different names & labels) And gadgets(dict.) (a mechanical device) makes you appear better than you are. What was a peg-leg, is now prosthetics. Let's define some of these words; a potion of old, would be used by a witch; or sorceress. When I look up potion in the dictionary it means: (a mixture of liquids as liquor or medicine). (end quote) So, for today, that same word is used for alcohol and drugs. A chemical is similar to a potion, but more of a process. In the (dict.) it is: (1: of relating to, used in, or produced by chemistry ⌐reactions) end quote. In other words, mixing chemicals together to make a potion. Chemical potions of yesteryears could cure you or harm you. So, are the ones of today. (The use of chemistry and synthetics which means: 'produced artificially esp. by chemical means: also, not genuine', end quote). Small amounts of chemicals or drugs can be a medicine. But larger amounts will kill you. Take for instance, blood thinners for your heart to work better. It is made with components of rat poison in a small dose. But of course, if you had a large dose, you would be sick and largely, you could die.

I had heard cigarettes have about 100 to 120 chemicals in those coffin nails. And you are inhaling them. I know, I used to smoke. And to better myself, I was using more straight tobacco brands. But they're both bad for you.

Let's take the next word, sorcery, In the (dict.) is: (the use of magic or witchcraft). Sorcery and witchcraft are of the devil and we Christians are to avoid it. And personally, I don't believe there's any good witches or white magic, it is not recommendable at all. What does a magician do? In the (dict.) (a person skilled in magic). What is magic? In the (dict.) ['1 the use of means as charms or spells, believed to have supernatural power over natural forces; 2 an extraordinary power of influence seemingly from a supernatural force, and as used by magicians; 3 sleight of hand'. end quote]

What else does a magician do? (He is an illusionist, and makes you think or see something that isn't real. Or is not there. He makes you believe a lie.) I recall the magicians of the Old Testament, when Moses was talking to Pharaoh. And pharaohs magicians cast down serpents or snakes. But Moses was prepared and threw down his staff— which turned into a bigger snake and ate the magicians' snakes. Magicians are no match, for God. (Ref. Ex.4:1-4; Ex.7:11-12)

Because, TV and movies, magic is more acceptable. So is homosexuality; but according to the word of God it is not acceptable. (Ref. I-Cor. 6:9:11) V9)" Do you not know that the unrighteous will not inherit the kingdom of God? Do not be deceived. Neither fornicators, nor idolaters, nor adulterers, nor homosexuals, nor sodomites, V10) nor thieves, nor covetous, nor drunkards, nor revilers, nor extortioners will inherit the kingdom of God."- I know, I use to be in these categories, especially drunkard.

V11)" And such were some of you. But you were washed, (washed in the word of God) but you were sanctified, (you were made Holy—set-apart). But you were justified (by the blood of Jesus) in the name of the Lord Jesus (and Faith in the Son of God for Salvation) and by the Spirit of our God." (And by the Holy Spirit, we were born-again). The other reference to magic.

(Acts 19:19,20) V19)" Also, many of those who had practiced magic brought their books together and burned them in the sight of all. And they counted up the value of them, and it totaled 50,000 pieces of silver. V20) So the word of the Lord grew mightily and prevailed." (Ref. NKJV commentary v19);'These books were filled with formulas, spells, and Astro logical forecast. The volumes were expensive, 50,000 pieces of silver would have taken 10 laborers 20 years to earn. Burning the books indicated real repentance on the part of those who had practiced magic.

'(Ref.) to sorcery and the works of the flesh, are in (Gal. 5:19-21). What are potions and chemicals the sorceress' used, that they are made up of? Plants, herbs, things of nature mixed to a certain concoction. Isn't that what makes modern medicine? We have taken it one step further—and chemically synthesized it. We still use plants in herbs. You can use them for good or for bad. (Wildflowers-poppies make Heroin) Take aloe vera cactus plant for instance, it can be used for healing, of minor cuts. And marijuana can also be used as numbing, or pain relief, for certain people with cancer or disease, for a medicine of good. Or you can use it strictly to get high every day for no reason. I did the same thing with alcohol. I like the effects from it. It was calming, it was comforting. But it was a false comfort. And, as you use any drug or alcohol, you build up a tolerance to the thing (drug). Pretty soon, you have so much in you, it controls you. Let's go back to (Eph. 5:18) KJV

V18)" Do not be drunk with wine, wherein excess: ... (This is not talking about one or two drinks which isn't much. Even though the law states if you have two drinks, it is excess, and you are drunk to them, and will be arrested.) (And today, I heard it is about $10,000 worth of legal fees, for Drunk Driving.) This verse is talking about excess, (continually or habitually) (another way to say it, it is practicing sin.) Back to the end of the verse. ..." but be filled with the Spirit." The Holy Spirit is our goal. What is in part, being filled with the Holy Spirit mean? What does (Gal. 5:22,23) say? (KJV)...V22)" But the Fruit of the Spirit is love, joy, peace, longsuffering, gentleness, goodness, Faith, V23) Meekness, temperance: against such there is no Law." This is all Spiritual; (no Law—no flesh). This is what we need to be filled with, and I can have true comfort, from the original Comforter. Who is there to help me, not to harm me.

In the (NKJV) says it a little differently but the outcome is the same.... V22) ...." love, joy, peace, longsuffering, kindness, goodness, faithfulness, V23) gentleness, self-control. Against such there is no law." Also (NKJV) (Eph. 5:18) V18)" And do not be drunk with wine, in which is dissipation; (which means, expend wastefully) but be filled with the Spirit." This applies to alcohol, but it can also be applied to marijuana. What happens when you use or smoke a lot of marijuana to excess? You get loaded or high, and you want to do nothing. (Dissipation: expend wastefully). In other words, you are allowing yourself to be tempted, and indulge in a practice, that is contrary to the Word of God. End

'SHOPPING MALL DREAM'

Carrie, my sister and I, were at the mall. She had her shopping to do, and I guess I had mine too. But my new girlfriend was there, she had spiked hair, a brunette with highlights. A pretty faced woman with an average build. Who is new to me, and we have only dated a couple of times. I guess we met at the mall and had lunch and shopped. And she is getting ready to leave. She gets up and comes over and kisses me. I should have given her a regular kiss, but I forgot and started to give her my tongue. She stopped quicker and left. I said, I can do better. She comes back and we do a regular kiss. (woke-up) End

'BLUE BALLS DREAM'

Then, I was with this little boy, we are being tested for our sinuses. And a special procedure to fix it or heal it. This computer analyzes' what we need, then it administered these floating blue balls— light blue and dark blue. And it knows how many you need for the cure. For there were just a few blue balls went up my nose. Then the little boy, who has taken the test with me. 32 blue balls in both colors went up his nose? (woke-up)

Commentary on that dream: (In real life, I did have trouble with my sinuses back in my youth and my early twenties. In the dream, the boy was a representation of me in the past. And then me as I am older and have had little trouble with my sinuses.) (Since the day, shortly after I was saved and born again. I was on a job laying carpet on Flower Street. A motel manager or owner, or both. Came to me; I was working in the back room. We were talking about the Lord. And I told him I was a recent believer of Jesus Christ my Savior and Lord. He asked about the condition I am in, congestion—sneezing, pressure, runny nose, etc. He said, 'Jesus, can heal that'. I said, 'OK'. He said, 'do you want to be healed?' I said, 'yes'. The doctors call it chronic sinusitis. He prayed over me and laid his hands on me. I accepted it and received the blessing from God by Faith. Faith, in the Son of God, the Creator, for healing, and it was done. And for decades, I have had no trouble with my sinuses. Then he said, 'do you want the gift of tongues as well?' 'I am not sure what that is?' I said, 'yes, if that is more of God, then I want it.' He said, 'OK'...he started praying over me. I said, 'what do I do?' He said, 'start praising God, and give Him glory for your gifts'. I started praising the Lord....and all of a sudden, the Holy Spirit was speaking to God in an un- known tongue through me. But I didn't know what I was saying?)

In (I-Cor. 14:1,2) probably explains it the best.

V1)" Pursue Love, and desire spiritual gifts, but especially that you may prophesy. V2) For he who speaks in a tongue does not speak to men but to God, for no one understands him; however, in the spirit he speaks mysteries." End

CHAPTER 37

'JOHN'S READING'

A reading out of the Gospel of John, (John 15: 1-11).

V1)" I am the true vine, and My Father is the vinedresser. V2) Every branch in Me that does not bear fruit He takes away; and every branch that bears fruit He prunes, that it may bear more fruit. V3) You are already clean because of the word which I have spoken to you. V4) Abide in Me, and I in you. As the branch cannot bear fruit of itself, unless it abides in the vine, neither can you, unless you abide in Me." V5)" I am the vine, you are the branches. He who abides in Me, and I in him, bears much fruit; for without Me you can do nothing. V6) If anyone does not abide in Me, he is cast out as a branch and is withered; and they gather them and throw them into the fire, and they are burned. V7) If you abide in Me, and My words abide in you, you will ask what you desire, and it shall be done for you. V8) By this My Father is glorified, that you bear much fruit; so you will be My disciples. V9) As the Father loved Me, I also have loved you; abide in My love. V10) If you keep My commandments, you will abide in My love, just as I have kept in My Father's commandments and abide in His love. V11) These things I have spoken to you, that My joy may remain in you, and that your joy may be full." (end quote NKJV)

We are in Christ, to be obedient to Him; we are abiding in Him. To be in Christ Love, and His Words abide in you. …. v7… 'you will ask what you desire, and if shall be done for you.' v8...'By this My Father is glorified, that you bear much fruit; so you will be My disciples.' Jesus is the True Vine, and we are the branches. He is being the main source of our nutrients. Like a grape vine or a tree. So, without Him, we can do nothing. As we continue to abide in Him; as He too abides in the Father. The Father is the Vinedresser. He desires for His servants to become friends, as we get to know Him. As we produce fruit in our lives through the Holy Spirit, being used and productive as His Spiritual children. His Love, His Joy, and His Peace is Spiritual. And is lasting, and is more profound, unlike what the world provides.

God's command to us, is that we love one another as the Son of God loved us. His Love was so great. He laid down His life for us on the Cross. To save us from the penalty of sin. Jesus paid it once, and for all.

Jesus laid down His life for His friends. He calls us friends. All He asks us to do, is what He says. You didn't choose Jesus, He chose you, to become His disciple and friend.

On a personal note, don't we do things for our earthly friends; how much more benefit would it be to interact with God as His friend.

So, His Greatest Commandment to us is that we love one another.

That sounds like a win-win situation, don't you think?

(This study reminds me of the song) 'What a friend we have in Jesus'.

End

'WINE DREAM'

This was a dream about a pick-up and delivery. The first part of the dream, I was traveling down Niles Street at night going west. I was almost to Mount Vernon Avenue. There were a few convenient stores down that way, except they were closed. It wasn't because it was late, it had to do with being under the Covid-restrictions for so long.

(In real life this would be a test, and temptation to drink again, but, in real life and this dream, God will strengthen me, not to indulge; but as a servant and sober, to deliver this for an event that was important.)

I must have found the place, because the dream jumps to where the event is taking place, on top of a building. (In real life, in my subconscious, even though I've never been there. They have an event in Bakersfield, which is a party on top of a building. I think it was a fundraiser or something.) ... I guess, I brought a few, what looks like champagne bottles. It looks like a primitive way to get to the top of this high-flat commercial building by a ladder too.

And there is a lady about to go up the ladder, and I am joking with her and said, 'oh no, we use a catapult now to get you upstairs. I had given the lady the bottles, minutes before, but I didn't know she was going to use a ladder. (She just laughed at my catapult joke, but I thought she took me serious for a moment, because she looked around.)

So, I said, 'let me take those bottles, obviously you can't climb a ladder and carry bottles in your hands? ... Will figure a way to get that up to you, maybe a box & rope?'

Then I headed, to what seem like a wake. It is very somber. There are people all around me. There was a table to check in. I bypassed signing in, it was a Catholic church; then there was holy water there and I passed by that too. (In real life, I was a participating Roman Catholic for four years, I went to church with my first wife; I didn't grow up going to any church. Until I got saved in the first couple of years in our marriage. I consider myself back then A born-again Christian Catholic. I was saved by confession of sin, believe in Jesus Christ and Him crucified and His finished work on the Cross by Faith. Nothing I earned or work for, to receive His gift of Salvation; it was by His Amazing Grace that I was saved.... I prayed a heartfelt prayer to God, when I listen to God 's word on TV, and believed the word of God, said by the preacher. All was well, and after 4 years, the

Lord told me, I needed to leave the Catholic church. I resisted at first but did leave. I got too comfortable in my Spiritual walk. God wants you to grow, into the image of His Son. Besides, in the past I've brought questions up to the Monsignor about Salvation? I quoted to him: (Eph. 2:8-9)

V8)" For by grace you have been saved through faith, and that not of yourselves; it is the gift of God, V9) not of works, lest anyone should boast." (And he said, 'Oh, no that's too easy. It is by works.')

(In real life I am not practicing religious behavior anymore like when I was a Catholic.) (Just to comment on what he said, I believe that Salvation is as Ephesians 2:8,9, says, but after being saved by Grace and through Faith; then you through the Holy Spirit do good works as He produces the Fruit of the Spirit in your life. Which the first fruit is Love. Being loving, to one another is most important, and not just those who would love you back. Now, Catholic's are Christians too, and they do believe in the Son of God. And there will be some saved, even those who believe on His name. God 's got the criteria on who goes and who doesn't go to Heaven.

In (1-John 3:23) tell us with 2-Commandments, one is ....'that we should believe on the name of His Son Jesus Christ.... & 2nd...and love one another, as He gave us commandment.' (back to dream).

Then my stepmom stops me, and says, 'Oh, did you see Gikko's (a nickname for my stepbrother) new house? And I didn't have the heart to tell her. I tried to go over last night. But I was 30 minutes late. It was 9 PM. And he said, 'Don't bother', So I said, 'goodbye', and (I am waking up in my cell). End

'HOUSEBOAT DREAM'

I'm on this houseboat, and literally it was a big box, like two double-wide trailers. A square box floating in an inlet-slip. Which had a walled concrete block sides about as wide as a driveway where the water could come in and out.

I was kidding around with the one sister; she was on the back porch relaxing. And she said something about her sister and in the front. And I said, 'I am going to tell her what you said' She said, 'you better not'. And I walked off, as she is still yelling at me. I wasn't going to tell her sister, but I was getting up anyway to walk to the front to see the progress, of the front steps of concrete, rocks, and metal, etc.

There was a utility truck there doing some work. And needed his truck, and he is in the driveway area, and it is underwater. But there is a high spot where it could sit. He needs his truck so much, for tools-supplies and materials to carry. He just brought the whole thing. When he backed out, when he was done, the truck turned into a Van. I guess they're more buoyant and all the doors were duck taped shut, and windows closed. And then another smaller truck that operated like a beach-buggy, with the big balloon flap tires. He was floating and had come in behind the van that just pulled into deeper water and started pushing him away. All these vehicles had a construction label on their doors. And they were all painted a deep dark-green color like some work trucks in Bakersfield. I guess this wasn't their first rodeo. He pushed the van which is floating all the way over to the street. This was a small lake, and as he pushed the van toward the city and building, to the street. He got to the low water where it ended at the street, like a beach. No sidewalks or anything. He just started it up and drove off. (woke-up) End

CHAPTER 38

'RECOVERY DREAM'

I was recuperating in my parents' home, supposedly but not the one I grew-up in. It was a single level, big, modern, and open. My stepmom was resting in a recliner chair. (Which in real life I never seen her do.) There were all kinds of people in the house, guests coming by, and visitors for me, signing-in on top of the dresser-drawers. (That's another thing, my stepmom wouldn't be resting in a chair, when there are guests in the house, unless she was sick, or something.)

I just got up, I guess, I just had surgery. I was resting in my old back room behind the kitchen to the back of the house. And there were these young vinyl layers, making a pattern, using felt paper, in the kitchen and dining room. To cut out the vinyl, before you lay it. I was heading back to bed. (In real life, I would be the one laying the vinyl. And I didn't recognize these young men either.)

(There was one time I surprise my dad when he was out of town. He came back and I laid some luxury-modular vinyl tile in a pattern. In his entry-hallway, kitchen, and breakfast nook.) (back to dream)

And one of the two installers asked me, 'who are you'? I said, I guess I'm one of the ones who used to live here. Meaning I am older, and I moved out. But came back to recover in my parents' house. (In real life, just before

211

going to prison, I lived almost 19 years in a big 2 1/2 story 4000 square-foot home. And completely remodeled it, inside and out, and the yard too. But didn't dream of it once. Because it was never mine; With my second wife, she always referred to it as her house. So, in my subconscious, I was just a guest, a worker, doing a job.); back to dream.

The vinyl-layer asked me, 'what did you have done?', I said, as I looked down; down at my feet. Foot-surgery, plus these grey knobs (external prosthetics that were dangling on my feet?) As I get back into bed, I see people visiting me by signing-in, but I didn't talk to them actually. They talked up front with my dad in the entry-living room area. My parents wanted me to have a book for them to sign, so I could write them back, and then thank them for coming by and for the acknowledgment. Then I went back to bed. (And woke-up)

(In real life, I was recuperating after a neck/spine surgery for four months before coming into prison, and off and on wearing a neck brace.)

(And I was in a back room, my office/extra master bedroom and didn't get any visitors. The signing in the dream, probably represented recently, my relatives and friends wrote some nice things about me, as character reference letters sent to, and I heard would be hand delivered to the Governor.)

(But I give most of the credit to God for answering my prayer. And releasing me early with a Governors pardon.) (Just to note, when this was written and fast forwarding to now; I didn't get the pardon but, I did get into a fast-track program called MCRP and received 5+months off my sentence.) End

'PRINCIPLES'

I had read some principles, to live for God's glory, and this isn't all of what— Pastor, John Mac Arthur had to say about this topic of living in the grey areas. He and his leader-ship staff at 'Grace Community Church' had some edifying topics.

Here is part of one chapter:

(1-Corinthians 10:23) Paul explains that..." All things are lawful, but not all things are profitable.":

(I was talking to someone today at our lunch break time, from PIA, and he has been in multiple times, on drug related crimes. And I said to him; 'For me, it is no m'as (more), 'I am done with alcohol.' I said, 'Besides that, it lowers your inhibitions to choose rightly.' (I did things I am ashamed of. I don't want that shame or guilt anymore. I was trying to communicate to him, drugs and alcohol, is something to stay away from). (If it keeps bringing you into prison. I know the facts on recidivism. It is three out of every four inmates will reoffend. That's a lot, 75% of 100%.) (2016)

He was trying to convince me, maybe not alcohol, but you could smoke marijuana, they're making that legal. I said, 'legal or not, it is not for me.' (Will this activity produce Spiritual benefit? Questions to ask yourself, is this...). *p18 Something that is profitable is useful, helpful, or advantageous; and that which edifies builds up spiritually. So based on this verse, believers should ask themselves, will doing this activity enhance my spiritual life and the spiritual lives of others? Will it cultivate godliness in me and in them? Will it build up spiritually?" If not, then is it really a wise choice? ... When it comes to the gray areas of life, we should begin by p19 asking if the choice we are about to make is spiritually profitable, both for ourselves and for those around us. "(end quote)

(The name of this book, is called: 'Right thinking in the world gone wrong') *p19 #2

The enslavement principle: Will this activity lead to spiritual bondage? (The cross reference he gives for 1-Corinthians 10:23, is first Corinthians 6:12) ....'All things are lawful for me, but I will not be brought under the power of any. 'Paul was meaning, not to be mastered by, or controlled by addictions or compulsions. In other words, taking it too far, where it, that activity controls you. Prayer is key, in speaking God's word, as authority over that situation.) (For instance, and we covered some of this already in chapter 36, with names and labels. Like in:(Ephesians 5:18) KJV "Do not be drunk with wine where in is excess; but be filled with the Spirit.")

#3. The Exposure Principle:

Will this activity expose my mind or body to defilement?

Speaking specifically of sexual immorality, Paul commanded the Corinthians to avoid anything that might defile them. "Do you not know that your body is a temple of the Holy Spirit who is in you, whom you have from God, and that you are not your own? For you have been bought with a price: therefore, glorify God in your body" ... (1-Cor. 6:19-20).

Elsewhere, he told the Ephesians to reprove and avoid the sensual deeds that characterize the wicked, *p20)" For it is disgraceful even to speak of the things which are done by them in secret"(Eph. 5:12). Instead, believers are to dwell on those things that are true, honorable, right, pure, lovely, excellent, praiseworthy, and a good report... (Philippians 4:8) ref.

So, ask yourself if the decision you are about to make will expose you to the sinful, lewd, and the debauched elements of the fallen society. If it will, then stay away from it. In Romans 12:1–2 Paul wrote,

"I urge you, brethren, by the mercies of God, to present your bodies a living and holy sacrifice; acceptable to God, which is your spiritual service of worship. And do not be conformed to this world but be transformed by the renewing of your mind so that you may prove what the will of God is, that which is good and acceptable and perfect." How you choose to use your body, along with what you choose to put in your mind, should always reflect your concern to honor Jesus Christ (cf. Romans 6:12-13). Thus, anything that defiles your body or pollutes your mind ought to be avoided. (end quote)

(Now I 'll give you a couple more examples from this book.)

#5. The Evangelism Principle:

*p21. Will this activity further the cause of the gospel?

As those seeking to live out the Great Commission (Matthew 28:18-20), Christians should always consider how their actions will affect their witness to a watching world... Paul wrote, "Give no offense either to Jews or to Greeks or to the Church of God; just as I also please all men in all things, not seeking my own profit but the profit of the many, that they may be saved."

(1-Corinthians 10:32-33) end quote

.... Thus, he was willing to set his freedom aside for the sake of the gospel... (1- Corinthians 9:19-23). Whether or not you are aware of it, what you allow or disallow in your behavior affects your witness for Christ. It is an issue of testimony—what your life says about God—to the friends, relatives, coworkers, neighbors, or even strangers who might be watching you. Your testimony either tells the truth about God, or it tells a lie. The choices you make in the gray areas should reflect your concern not to bring offense to God's reputation but to bring Him praise instead. (end quote)

#6. The Ethnics Principle:

(I am going to just touch on this, but the main point is to have a clear conscience before God, now, and at His coming.)

*p21 quote. Will this activity violate my conscience? ... "He who doubts is condemned if he eats, because his eating is not from faith; and whatever is not from faith is sin..." (Romans 14:23). We sin if we act in any way that goes contrary to the convictions of our own faith and good conscience. (end quote)

......If you are not sure about it, don't do it. It is hard to overstate the value of a clear conscience, and it is definitely worth keeping your conscience clear so that your relationship with God will not be hindered. (cf. Psalm 66:18). (end quote) *p22. If you will keep yourself in prayer and the study of God's Word, you will rightly inform your conscience so you can "walk as children of light... trying to learn what is pleasing to the Lord."

Ephesians 5:8-10).

#7. The Exaltation Principle:

Will this activity bring glory to God?

quote...." Whether, then, you eat or drink or whatever you do, do to the glory of God"(1-Corinthians 10:31). We were created to glorify God and worship Him forever. As those who have been transformed be His grace and transferred into His kingdom, pleasing Him in both our highest aim and our greatest delight (II- Cor. 5:9). Our hearts cry is to glorify our Lord and Savior with our lives. So, when it comes to the gray areas, think about your decision, will God be glorified, praise, and exalted?

(end quote). End

'SEQUOIA DREAM'

I fell off this one giant pillow to the next in this dream. It was a soft landing to the next. But we are still really high off the ground. We're outside and supposed to be tree cutters or trimmers. And I am on my descent down to the ground. But we are in a literal forest full of these Giant Sequoias, 100 to 200 feet high. And I am not scared, but I started to be, when I was sliding off this parachute. And I realized that there is still another 50 to 75 feet to the ground. But falling— slipping—jumping from this high is fatal. And I was with someone else, but I couldn't see him. (In real life could represent talking on our bunk's but can't see each other.) (And the giant pillow or parachute represents me fluffing my big pillow just before bedtime.) As I looked up there was like a narrator telling me how small I am in this huge forest. And this section that we were in, cutting trees to clear an area. Maybe he's the guy on the ground guiding me. The other thing I was thinking, being on this pillow, when I slide off; Do I have spikes on my boots? And a strap to grab the tree? (In real life, I just started working in PIA — (prison industry authority) and got some boots, a size bigger 12 W; someone said, 'If they're new and hard they'll rub more. If super tight.' So, I got bigger ones, and use more socks. And the strap was on my mind, I was looking at guitar-straps in the package-catalog.) The guy on the ground mentioned two-references of how small I was in this forest; one was I am a spaghetti noodle in a huge bowl of spaghetti. (Well in real life, we had spaghetti for dinner.). And second reference was that I am a basketball in the court of a valley. (In real life my Bunky was watching a basketball game on TV.) (Then I woke up) End.

CHAPTER 39

'RESTAURANT DREAM'

This was the pre-opening of my restaurant, or just showing some guests around. Who happened to be my Stepmother (Josephine), and her neighbor, my first Mother-In-Law, came together to look around. My Mother-In-Law (Socorro), and I go to the entrance coming in, and I said, 'I would have these writings over the doors in the entrance. I hope I can fit it all in there. (In real life my mother-in-law would be proud of me, not only for starting a restaurant, but the reading and writing part too. She actually was my seventh-grade reading teacher as well. She wrote one time on a paper of mine. 'You have better potential; you just need to apply yourself'; she also would be proud of what kind of reading and writing too. The Bible school that I am in, which is called Harvest Bible University, but it's not about me. It's about Jesus Christ and Him Crucified. The Son of God is the Savior of the world, dying on the Cross for the worlds sin. And God the Father raising Him up on the third day from the grave, according to the Scriptures. He is in His Kingdom at the right hand of God the Father.) ref. (1-Cor. 15:3-4) ;(Acts 20:21) ;(John 3:16) ;(Romans 10:9-13) ;(Rev. 3:20) ;(Eph. 2:8-9) ;(Acts 2:38). — Believe in the Lord Jesus Christ and be saved.

Now, we are going to the back patio area. I'm still talking to my mother-in-law, and my stepmom heads off checking out the scenery of the mountains to the back and to one side. I was telling her there is supposed to be a small train you could ride and look through the port windows at the scenery.

(In real life my stepmom and my mother-in-law have both passed on to the next life.)

Then we are experiencing rumbling and dirty-dark gray smoke is coming out of the ground. She said, 'what is it?' I said, 'it is methane gas'. (But, in real life, methane gas wouldn't be dark gray, but clear and colorless). I was thinking the end of the world, but I wasn't scared. Because of my Faith in Jesus. That there is an Afterlife. There is a Heaven, and there is a resurrection from the dead. I am secure in knowing that. And I was trying to tell her that too. To re-affirm her beliefs of what she has already heard, About the end of days in the Bible. [In real life, I believe that Jesus Christ will return soon for His 'Bride' (the church) and the 'rapture will happen first'… (Meaning that the dead in Christ will rise first and those who still remain will be caught up in the air and be forever with the Lord.) (As the Holy Spirit in the Saints will be taken home.)]

(Then Jesus Christ will officially come the second time and He will pronounce judgment upon the Earth, and the spiritual realm.) ref. (I-Thess. 4:13-18; Daniel 7:9-14) (Woke-up). End

'CARPET GLUE DREAM'

I was working on one end of the house finishing up a master bedroom. With a commercial looking, real pretty, soft, short cut pile with a pattern to it. The rest of the house had some kind of Berber low-pile loop, with a pattern material. And apparently, we left our tools and some supplies in one of the back rooms somewhere, as to continue for the next day. (Most of the time we pick up everything and start fresh the next day). Anyway, this family is living there, during this remodel and replacement of carpeting. It isn't a new home, but fairly new-modern. A large one-story house, with large rooms.

And they have small kids who evidently found our stuff. We usually put it in a closet out of the way. The kids used our glue on the face of the carpet. It's a latex-glue that we use on the edge of the loop carpet (Berber), so it won't unravel. We'll the next day when I was finished in the Master bedroom, I came out, to leave for the day, and couldn't go through the back. So, I headed to the front of the house where all the carpet was completed already. I looked in the living room, and about 5'x 7'area had glue all over it. And I cringed, because I knew that dried glue isn't going to come off the face of the carpet easily. In fact, if we use a solvent to clean it off. The carpet would be damaged and the nap puffed-up or fluffed-up. Also, the back of the carpet which holds it together would break down or be jeopardized. The best solution would be to take out a big section of carpet 12 feet wide by the length of the cut in the direction the carpet is going, plus the pattern match. So, the customer was there, a husband and wife and some older teenage boys. Hu, we're helping to put back the furniture in the completed rooms. The customer asked me about, 'I need some more brackets'.... for something, and I took a few to match them up for ordering purposes. Then she said, 'the small bed frame isn't here'? I'm thinking to myself, 'I didn't bring it with me, with the carpet.' (But in real life we don't do brackets or bedframes). (But the Interior Designer could get certain things at their request, but most of the time, and the last company I worked for before coming in, could do paint, wallpaper, and blinds, and things like that.) (Back to Dream)

Anyway, I left to the outside of the house, and it is full of stuff scattered from inside the house, plus toys-play-areas, two 5-wheels—RVs, cars and etc. I'm saying to myself again, 'I need to leave through the front, and I guess I had a four-wheel-drive Jeep. (But, in real life, I've never owned a Jeep, but a lot of trucks and vans.) I took off and I almost got hit by a big monster of a vehicle tearing up the road. It was under construction. So, I'm riding on this tore-up Road, and even make a jump in the jeep with all the debris. And I end up in the mountains. And get to this new undeveloped area. Also, while under construction there is a lookout area on foot that you can go to and check out on the progress as it is completed. So, I get out and walk there. There are lots of people there. I recognize one person, then he turned into the Salesman and Designer for the job I was working on. Robert (Bob) is his name, and I proceeded talking about what happened to the living room carpet. More than likely, he would have to order another piece. The only bad part would be a dye-lot color match problem, for it would be two completely different runs of carpet made weeks apart. I told him that the customer doesn't know yet, but they will. That glue dries clear, but when dirt touches it; it will collect dirt like contact glue. He wanted to talk about the sites. He said, 'there is a tower out there, but no one 's there'. I said, 'some companies out there like PG&E, plans five years in advance in new areas. But it is still undeveloped land, and no one is there for a while. So, now we left that area, and I was riding some kind of cart. And Bob was pushing me along. And I think his wife was there too. And his daughter wanted my watch. It was a work watch, I said, 'If you need a watch for school or something, go ahead.' It had some glue on it. I said, 'you could clean the glue off with soap and water. And bring it back when you're done'. She saw the glue and said, 'Oh, that's OK, I don't need it now.' (And I woke up)

(In real life, I don't even know Bob's daughter or even know he has one.)

'R&R DREAM'

I was inside my dad's house first, where I grew up mostly. Showing people to the different rooms where they would be spending a few nights. There was a party or a reunion going on. As people are getting settled. I was using some kind of lifts for their luggage or furniture moving around. (In real life I do have a dolly for moving furniture or appliances, with wheels on it. Four; it uses a strap to go around the object, and uses a fulcrum lift with a short pipe for leverage.) I was in the house, and now I find myself in the backyard working on the fence, and the lifts are out there. The only thing is it is not my appliance lifts; it is these giant U-shaped steel bars going up 5 to 6 feet high and weighs 500 to 1000 pounds. (My appliance lifts only weigh about 20 lb.) (And there on large, easy rolling wheels.) I'm working on the corner of the fence, and I am actually on the fence, putting in a post for some reason. And I guess I used these lifts to get myself on the fence, instead of using a ladder. ....

(Which in real life doesn't make sense using or standing on the fence to put a post in.)

For as heavy as these things are, they move around pretty easy. When I was getting on the fence using these things; I pushed off them to jump on the fence. And when I did that, the runaway-rollers took-off down the backyard. And when it got to the grape stake-fence at the neighbors, it went on through like nothing. Two, 1 foot width slits of the fence were missing, and it was picking up speed through the neighbor's yard too, like it was going downhill, to the next yard. (In real life the yard is level.) I felt so helpless, I couldn't help stopping it. When it hit the 3rd yard over through that fence, it stopped. They have this heavy-duty gazebo-patio cover and crashed into that. Good thing, the pool was next. I went back inside, and ask dad, 'Do you have homeowners' insurance?'

(Woke-up) End.

CHAPTER 40

'MARY STUDY'

This is a study of Mary; the one who lives in Bethany, and has a brother Lazarus, and a sister Martha.

We are using the three gospel messages to get a clear picture of what this woman was doing, and how she was honoring God's only Begotten Son. (John 12:1-8; Mark 14:3-9; Matthew 26:6-13); Where Mary is anointing Jesus from head to foot.

This was a climactic time both before this event, and after.

Before, this event happened, Jesus had just raised Lazarus from the dead, after being in the tomb four days. It was a climactic display of God 's power and for His Glory. To show the Pharisees of the last, signs and wonders, so they would believe in Jesus, as the Christ or Messiah (The Anointed One). The one who they were waiting for as the Scriptures foretold. In the book of Moses, the Prophets, and the Psalms. In (John 11:43) KJV; As Jesus calls for Lazarus from the grave; ... "He cried with a loud voice, 'Lazarus, come forth.' "In V44) "And he who was dead came forth, bound hand and foot with graveclothes: and his face was bound about with a napkin. Jesus said unto them, Loose him, and let him go." (JSM) (comm.) (refers, as is obvious, to this burial shroud being taken off his body; Lazarus had been called up from Paradise where he had been for the past four days; one can only surmise as to what happened when the Voice of Jesus rang out in that place concerning Lazarus.)

From that event, there were many there that believed in Jesus. There were many there, comforting the sisters of Lazarus, and some from the Synagogue (The Jewish congregation place for Worship).

In V45)" Then many of the Jews which came to Mary, and had seen the things which Jesus did, believed on Him." V46)" But some of them went their ways to the Pharisees, and told them what things Jesus had done. V47) Then gathered the Chief Priests and the Pharisees a Council, and said, What do we? for this Man does many Miracles."

Just as it was prophesied by: (Isaiah 61:1-3) V1)" The Spirit of the Lord God is upon Me, Because the Lord has anointed Me to preach good tidings to the poor; He has sent Me to heal the brokenhearted, To proclaim liberty to the captives, and the opening of the prison to those who are bound; V2) To proclaim the acceptable year of the Lord, and the day of vengeance of our God; to comfort all who mourn, V3) To console those who mourn in Zion (Jerusalem), to give them beauty for ashes, the oil of Joy for mourning, the garment of praise for the spirit of heaviness; that they may be called trees of righteousness, the planting of the Lord, that He may be glorified."

(John 11:53) KJV

So, after the religious leader's council, in v53) then decided what they were going to do. The first climactic thing... V53) 'Then from that day forth they took counsel together for to put him to death.'

(John-Chapter 12:1:8) (JSM) (KJV) V1)" Then Jesus six days before the Passover came to Bethany (represents the closing days of His Ministry and Work), where Lazarus was which had been dead, whom He raised from the dead. ...V2) There they made Him a supper (probably in the house of Simon the Leper [Mat.26:6; Mk.14:3]); and Martha served: but Lazarus was one of them who sat at the table with Him ...(possibly Simon the Leper was there as well! if so, there would have been seated at the table two transcendent proofs of the Power of Jesus to save not only from the semblance of death as was Simon the Leper, but from the reality of death by the Resurrection of Lazarus).

V3) Then took Mary a pound of ointment of spikenard, very costly (probably worth about $10,000 in 2003 currency), and anointed the Feet of Jesus, and wiped His Feet with her hair… 'In the other gospels she broke open an alabaster box of ointment and poured it on Jesus' head' -(Mark 14:3; Matt. 26:7): and the house was filled with the odour of the ointment (it was testimony to His coming Resurrection, and she knew she would have no other opportunity; incidentally, Mary was not found at the empty Tomb; she was too spiritually intelligent to be there). (end quote)

In (Matt. 26:7,12), this shows the point of Mary's Faith and her believeth that Jesus was about to die on the Cross at Calvary, and be buried, and three days later rise from the grave as Jesus foretold; ref. (Matt. 20:17-19).

She believed and acted on it.

(Matt. 26:7b) …. and poured it on His head, as He sat at meat (anointing Him while He was alive, proved that she believed in His Resurrection; seemingly, she was the only one who did; there was only one anointing). (end quote)

Normally the Anointing was done after death, and preparation to subsequent burial.

Jesus says in (Matt. 26:12)" For in that she has poured this ointment on My body, she did it for My burial." 'Before I get to honoring this woman for her faith; and what Jesus says about this woman. The second climactic event, or should I say last straw, with Judas Iscariot.'

Let's continue in John's Gospel reading (John 12: 4-8).

V4)" Then said one of His Disciples, Judas Iscariot, Simon's son, which should betray Him (was not Simon the Leper in whose house this supper was prepared), V5) Why was not this ointment sold for three hundred pence, and given to the poor? (Reynolds said, "sinful motive often hides itself under the mask of reverence for another virtue.) V6) This he said, not that he cared for the poor (this was not his real reason); but because he was a thief, and had the bag, and bear what was put there in (had the ointment been sold and the money given to Christ, Judas would have stolen it; unfortunately, most of the money presently given for that which is supposed to be the Work of God is "stolen", i.e., "used for the wrong purpose"). V7) Then said Jesus, Let her alone (Jesus places His Seal of approval on what she is doing): against the day of My burying has she kept this (indicating she had this ointment for quite some time). V8) For the poor always you have with you (presents that which is regrettable, but true!); but Me you have not always (Jesus would not be with them in the flesh very much longer)". (end quote)

In (Matt. 26: 14-16); Talks about Judas' betrayal of Jesus, and that last-correction Jesus gave Judas about the ointment, just before this.

V14)" Then one of the twelve, called Judas Iscariot went unto the Chief Priests, V15) And said unto them, What will you give me, and I will deliver Him unto you? And they covenanted with him for thirty pieces of silver (this was the price of a slave [Ex. 21:32]; as well, it was prophesied hundreds of years before, that Jesus would be sold for thirty pieces of silver [Zech. 11:13]). ....V16) And from that time he sought opportunity to betray Him."

Now, in (Mark 14:4) Judas wasn't the only one taken by the fact, that she was wasting the ointment. But he took the lead. V4)" And there were some who had indignation within themselves, and said, Why was this waste of the ointment made?" In V5b) ...." And they murmured against her" (no case of murmuring has ever been justified or sanctioned by God in Scripture regardless of how right the cause; and to make matters worse, this cause wasn't right). V6)" And Jesus said, Let her alone; why trouble ye her? she has wrought a good work on Me" (even though they didn't understand it, her action showed her faith in His Resurrection). V7)" For you have the poor with you always, and whensoever you will you may do them good (the two, Himself and the poor, are equivalent in His sight [Mat. 25:40-45]): but Me you have not always" (speaking of His present position, which was soon to change). .... V9)" Verily I say unto you, Wheresoever this Gospel shall be preached throughout the whole world, this also that she has done shall be spoken of for a memorial of her" (this act is connected with her and will never be forgotten).

As opposed to the other women, and the other Mary, Mary Magdalene. The woman who came there that early morning just before dawn to anoint Jesus with spices and ointments. Because they thought he was still dead. This was Sunday morning the first day of the week. There were some days of waiting before they could even go to the grave site for religious observants. But also, they must have not known, that it was supposed to be sealed, and Roman guards posted not to enter. And then they didn't know how they were going to solve the dilemma of moving a huge round stone, to the entrance of the sepulchre (cave burial hole or entombment). They had some faith of just being there, but not of the Resurrection. Because He is risen!!! There was no need of any ointment. Even Tho, Mary Magdalene became the first woman Evangelist when she did finally believe. When she looked into the grave hole, and saw He wasn't there, she assumed someone had stolen Him. And she was weeping and crying. Until there was a man whom she thought might be the gardener. But, when Jesus spoke to her, that all changed. In (John 20:26-18) KJV V16)" Jesus said unto her, Mary. She turned herself, and said unto him, Rabboni; (which is to say, Master.") V17)" Jesus said unto her, Touch Me not; for I am not yet ascended to My Father: but go to My brethren, and say unto them, I ascend unto My Father, and your Father; and to My God, and your God." V18)"Mary Magdalene came and told the Disciples that she had seen the Lord, and that He had spoken these things unto her." End

'TRANS. DREAM'

This dream is about where these two prisoners are being transported in a four-seater convertible car. There is one officer in plain clothes, and one-woman trainee with him, and also in plain clothes. They were in the car and went into the building, and they came out to get in the car, in the parking garage. It is like I am watching a movie, I'm not one of the four characters in my dream. So, they were about to get in the car, and there was a scuffle. The two inmates jumped on the male officer and one got away. The other was pounding on the man officer on his back, on the ground. The lady trainee just watched. The two were wrestling around like they were connected or something, because he couldn't get away. The two prisoners handcuffed only in the front. Then the first Inmate who supposedly got away. Tries to steal a car, and it ends up, upside down in the parking garage. You see it doesn't pay to try to run away; besides they would find you. (And in real life, this wouldn't have happened anyway. They chain your feet and hands together, and they are both handcuffed. And you ride in a bus or a van, and they carry guns in case you run, or someone helps you. And the lady officer, wouldn't have done nothing, but would have got involved, regardless of if she is new). (Woke-up) End

'VINYL JOB DREAM'

I was on a vinyl flooring job out of town. And when I get to the job, and went to the owner and I wasn't sure what area I was supposed to do first or at all? Thinking I had something to do with the yards? Then lay the living room. He's talking to me about my son got paint on the vinyl floor. And I said, 'you can get that off with a little charcoal lighter fluid, (distilled petroleum) which is the main ingredient in paint- thinner.' There was some plants and a cat in the way. (In real life, when I go to work at PIA in the morning, there are Wildcats they're looking for breakfast from us.) Anyway, I'm still not sure where the vinyl is supposed to go? And the man questions me; 'are you sure you're from the company I bought it from?' I wasn't wearing one of their company shirts that day. I was contracting the job out and wearing my own. (In real life I still wore their company shirt when they buy the material through their particular retailer). So, we go back outside, I think I forgot something, yeah, my work order; I didn't bring it in with me? I went out and I started to go to a truck; Then I realized I have my van today. I was all confused. (In real life, I'm not that way.) But I didn't want the customer to know that and made an excuse for going toward the truck. 'I used to have one like that'; (not really). (In real life, when I woke up, I was trying to figure out what God was trying to tell me in this dream?)

And it was revealed to me, that the work order represented the Bible. It is the instruction manual for life. To read it every day and know it, meditate on it. And the work order, tells me everything I need to know, and I am fully prepared, before I leave town to the job. End

CHAPTER 41

'LUSY DREAM'

I was at Lucy's house/office in my town of Bakersfield, and I went to go visit her. I brought her some kind of wall hanging that I made. She knew I had been in prison and like the story about me working in the PIA cookie factory, where we package cookies, bread, almonds, in plastic, and package the lunches with peanut butter and jelly, bread, pretzels, or sunflower seeds, and 2-cookies. Or a cheese block & three 2-cracker packets, and sunflower seeds. I sat in a big fluffy one-person seat with her in her living room. And gave her a hug. I said, 'I appreciate her giving laughter to the world; (For it brings medicine to those who need it.) Her staff was there too, doing things for her. Then she said, 'she had visited the space shuttle while she was temporarily in Kern County and Bakersfield, from I assume LA somewhere. (In real life, I never met her or the other Actors I have had in my dreams. I do pray for a lot of people, including actors and actresses, family, friends, Inmates, Presidents, Governor 's, etc. Also, I don't think she ever stayed in Bakersfield, or went to the space shuttle? But she could have? The reason I had it in my subconscious; One of the companies I worked for, we laid some flooring for Annette Funicellio. She had a home in LA somewhere and also was married to someone in Shafter California. Who owned a Quarter-Horse Ranch. This home had a picture of her in the hallway, at Edwards Air Force Base, with the Space Shuttle.)

(In real life too, I had just talked to my daughter on the phone that same evening about the PIA-job and if she ever saw the one episode with Lucial Ball in the Candy Factory, and how I explained, while that was me at first.) (Woke up) End.

'LOVE STUDY'

This is a study about loving and obeying God and loving others. A study of what to do, and what not to do. If you would like to see Heaven, and be with our Creator? Salvation isn't so much about doing but believing in Jesus the Christ and His finished work on the Cross by Faith. It is about repenting of sin and receiving Jesus Christ into your heart by the Holy Spirit of God. (Eph. 2:8-9). V8)" For by grace you have been saved through faith, and that not of yourselves; it is the gift of God, …. (Salvation is a gift) (you must come humbly and asked for it.) …V9) not of works, lest anyone should boast."

In verse 10) of Eph. 2:10. God wants us to do good works after we are Born again, and love one another, as God has commanded. V10)" For we are His workmanship, created in Christ Jesus for good works, which God prepared beforehand that we should walk in them." NKJV

We are owned by God after being saved. He purchased us with His own blood shed on the Cross at Calvary. And as verse 10 says… in Christ Jesus…, so we have to be abiding in Christ. He is the true vine and God the Father is the vinedresser. We are the branches, and we cannot do anything without Him. God the Father, and in Christ Jesus, through the Holy Spirit wants us to yield ourselves and produce Fruit in our lives. The Fruit of the Spirit is in (Galatians 5:22-23), V22)" But the fruit of the Spirit is love, joy, peace, long-suffering, kindness, goodness, faithfulness, V23) gentleness, self-control. Against such there is no law. "NKJV Because of what we do for Christ now, it should be for His glory.

Or we are not our own, (Gal. 2:20-21) says V20)" I have been crucified with Christ; it is no longer I who live, but Christ lives in me; and the life which I now live in the flesh I live by faith in the Son of God, who loved me and gave Himself for me." V21)" I do not set aside the grace of God; for if righteousness comes through the law, then Christ died in vain." NKJV

Let us begin with the first of seven passages for this study.

(Matt. 22:37-40) #1 V37) Jesus said to him," 'You shall love the Lord your God with all your heart, with all your soul, and with all your mind.' V38) This is the first and great commandment, V39) And the second is like it; 'You shall love your neighbor as yourself.' V40) On these two commandments hang all the Law and the Prophets." NKJV. Love God with your whole being and love your neighbor as yourself. OK, who is this neighbor we are supposed to love? Let's go to (Luke 10:30-37). #2 V30) Then Jesus answered and said: "A certain man went down from Jerusalem to Jericho, and fell among thieves, who stripped him of his clothing, wounded him, and departed, leaving him half dead. V31) Now by chance a certain priest came down that road. And when he saw him, he passed by on the other side. V32) Likewise a Levite, when he arrived at the place, came and looked, and passed by on the other side. V33) But a certain Samaritan, as he journeyed, came where he was. And when he saw him, he had compassion. V34) So he went to him and bandaged his wounds, pouring on oil and wine; and he set him on his own animal, brought him to an inn, and took care of him." V35)" On the next day, when he departed, he took out two Denarii, gave them to the innkeeper, and said to him, 'Take care of him; and whatever more you spend, when I come again, I will repay you.' V36) So which of these three do you think was neighbor to him who fell among the thieves? V37) And he said, 'He who showed mercy on him.' Then Jesus said to him, 'Go and do likewise.'"

And Jesus says in like manner, about loving people, having mercy, and compassion. Let's go to:

(Matt. 25:31-40) #3 V31)" When the Son of Man comes in His glory, and all the holy angels with Him, then He will sit on the throne of His glory. V32) All the nations will be gathered before Him, and He will separate them one from another, as a shepherd divides His sheep from the goats.

V33) And He will set the sheep on His right hand, but the goats on the left. V34) Then the King will say to those on His right hand, 'Come, you blessed of My Father, inherit the kingdom prepared for you from the foundation of the world : V35) for I was hungry and you gave Me food; I was thirsty and you gave Me drink; I was a stranger and you took Me in; V36) I was naked and you clothed Me ; I was sick and you visited Me; I was in prison and you came to Me.'"

(This will be at Jesus' second coming, and Judgment to all the Gentile nations of the world.)

Their response in ... V37)" Then the righteous will answer Him, saying, 'Lord, when did we see You hungry and feed You, or thirsty and give You drink? V38) When did we see You a stranger and take You in, or naked and clothe You? V39) Or when did we see You sick, or in prison, and come to You?' V40) And the King will answer and say to them, 'Assuredly, I say to you, in as much as you did it to one of the least of these My brethren, you did it to Me.' (This second coming is foretold in Daniel's night vision, in (Dan. 7:13-14), * NKJV ref. com. V13- (where is mentioned ....'the "Son of Man" ....'the perfect representation of humanity' ...and in His coming the Perfect Son of God as well. .... 'Jewish and Christian expositors have identified this individual as the Messiah. Jesus Himself used this name to emphasize His humanity as the incarnate Son of God'.)

(Dan.7:13-14) V13)" I was watching in the night visions, and behold, One like the Son of Man, coming with the clouds of heaven! He came to the Ancient of Days, and they brought Him near before Him." V14)" Then to Him was given dominion and glory and a kingdom, that all peoples, nations, and languages should serve Him. His dominion is an everlasting dominion, which shall not pass away, and His kingdom the one which shall not be destroyed."

Let's go on to the 4th passage:

(John 15: 7-11) V7)" If you abide in Me, and My words abide in you, you will ask what you desire, and it shall be done for you. V8) By this My Father is glorified, that you bear much fruit; so you will be My disciples.

V9)'As the Father loved Me, I also have loved you; abide in My love. V10) If you keep My commandments, you will abide in My love, just as I have kept My Father's commandments and abide in His love. V11) These things I have spoken to you, that My joy may remain in you, and that your joy may be full."

(Ok, let's re-cap a bit; Love God with your whole mind, heart, and soul; Love your neighbor or stranger as if he was your family, out of love and compassion for others. Visit the sick in hospitals, and in homes, even nursing homes; feed the hungry and give drink to the thirsty; care for the poor and the down trotted. Love those who can't pay you back. Visit the ones in prison, and care for the homeless; Keep abiding in Christ, and His words abide in you. Bear much fruit. Keep His commandments, and abide in His love, and retain the joy, for it will be full.) (John 15: 12-17);

#5 V12)" This is My commandment, that you love one another as I have loved you. V13) Greater love has no one than this, than to lay down one's life for his friends. V14) You are My friends if you do whatever I command you. V15) No longer do I call you servants, for a servant does not know what his master is doing; but I have called you friends, for all things that I heard from My Father I have made known to you. V16) You did not choose Me, but I chose you and appointed you that you should go and bear fruit, and that your fruit should remain, that whatever you ask the Father in My name He may give you. V17) These things I command you, that you love one another."

(So, He commanded us to love one another as He has loved us. He lay down His life for His friends. We need to do the same for Him. To be that living sacrifice, transformed by the renewing of our minds. And not to conform to this world …Be that living sacrifice, holy and sanctified for God's use. To serve God and behave like a Christian should.)

(Romans 12: 1-21) V1)" I beseech you therefore, brethren, by the mercies of God, that you present your bodies a living sacrifice, holy, acceptable to God, which is your reasonable service. V2) And do not be conformed to this world, but be transformed by the renewing of your mind, that you may prove what is that good and acceptable and perfect will of God. V3) For I say, through the grace given to me, to everyone who is among you, not to think of himself more highly than he ought to think, but to think soberly, as God has dealt to each one a measure of faith. V4) For as we have many members in one body, but all the members do not have the same function, V5) so we, being many, are one body in Christ, and individually members of one another. V6) Having then gifts differing according to the grace that is given to us, let us use them: if prophecy, let us prophesy in proportion to our faith; or ministry, let us use it in our ministering; he who teaches, in teaching; V8) he who exhorts, in exhortation; he who gives, with liberality; he who leads, with diligence; he who shows mercy, with cheerfulness.

V9) Let love be without hypocrisy. Abhor what is evil. Cling to what is good. V10) Be kindly affectionate to one another with brotherly love, in honor giving preference to one another; V11) not lagging in diligence, fervent in spirit, serving the Lord; V12) rejoicing in hope, patient in tribulation, continuing steadfastly in prayer; V13) distributing to the needs of the saints, given to hospitality. V14) Bless those who persecute you; bless and do not curse. V15) Rejoice with those who rejoice, and weep with those who weep. V16) Be of the same mind toward one another. Do not set your mind on high things, but associate with the humble. Do not be wise in your own opinion. V17) Repay no one evil for evil. Have regard for good things in the sight of all men. V18) If it is possible, as much as depends on you, live peaceably with all men. V19) Beloved, do not avenge yourselves, but rather give place to wrath; for it is written, "Vengeance is Mine, I will repay," says the Lord. V20) Therefore, 'If your enemy is hungry, feed him; If he is thirsty, give him a drink; For in so doing you will heap coals of fire on his head.' V21) Do not be overcome by evil, but overcome evil with good."

As you can see from the last 21-verses, there is a lot to think about and apply. Let's move on to the last passage: # 7.

Most Christians are familiar with this passage and needs to be read and understood from time to time. It puts me in my place, and what is important. What love is, and what it isn't.

(I- Corinthians 13: 1-13); V1)" Though I speak with the tongues of men and of angels, but have not love, I have become sounding brass or a clanging cymbal. V2) And though I have the gift of prophecy, and understand all mysteries and all knowledge, and though I have all faith, so that I could remove mountains, but have not love, I am nothing. V3) And though I bestow all my goods to feed the poor, and though I give my body to be burned, but have not love, profits me nothing. V4) Love suffers long and is kind; love does not envy; love does not parade itself, is not puffed up; V5) does not behave rudely, does not seek its own, is not provoked, thinks no evil; V6) does not rejoice in iniquity, but rejoices in the truth; V7) bears all things, believes all things, hopes all things, endures all things. V8) Love never fails. But whether there are prophecies, they will fail; whether there are tongues, they will cease; whether there is knowledge, it will vanish away. V9) For we know in part and we prophesy in part. V10) But when that which is perfect has come, then that which is in part will be done away. V11) When I was a child, I spoke as a child, I understood as a child, I thought as a child; but when I became a man, I put away childish things. V12) For now we see in a mirror, dimly, but then face to face. Now I know in part, but then I shall know just as I also am known. V13) And now abide faith, hope, love, these three; but the greatest of these is love."

To conclude this study with a few other verses; to make us think, reflect, examine, and make corrections where needed. Jesus said in (Matt. 7:21); "Not everyone who says to Me, 'Lord, Lord,' shall enter the kingdom of heaven, but he who does the will of My Father in Heaven."

In (Matt. 12:46-50). V46)" While He was still talking to the multitudes, behold, His mother and brothers stood outside, seeking to speak with Him. V47) Then one said to Him (Jesus), 'Look, Your mother and Your brothers are standing outside, seeking to speak with You.' V48) But He answered and said to the one who told Him, 'Who is My mother and who are My brothers?' V49) And He stretched out His hand toward His disciples and said, 'Here are My mother and My brothers! V50) For whoever does the will of My Father in heaven is My brother and sister and mother.'"

Then we have (Matt. 6:19-21,33). V19)" Do not lay up for yourselves treasures on earth, where moth and rust destroy and where thieves break in and steal; V20) but lay up for yourselves treasures in heaven, where neither moth nor rust destroys and where thieves do not break in and steal. V21) For where your treasure is, there your heart will be also." V33)" But seek first the kingdom of God and His righteousness, and all these things shall be added to you."

And lastly, (1-John 2:15-17). V15)" Do not love the world or the things in the world. If anyone loves the world, the love of the Father is not in him. V16) For all that is in the world—the lust of the flesh, the lust of the eyes, and the pride of life—is not of the Father but is of the world. V17) And the world is passing away, and the lust of it; but he who does the will of God abides forever." End

'A WIFE'S DREAM'

My second wife at the time, and this is maybe 10 years ago or more, she had a dream of the Sun coming close to the Earth, the brightness coming closer and closer, but no heat, and as it arrived, she wasn't harmed. End (Jesus is the light of the world) — ref. (John 12:46); (John 9:5); (This dream is probably not about the Sun, but the other Son; The Son of God coming to Earth.) 'His Second Coming'.

(John 12:46); V46)" I have come as a light into the world, that whoever believes in Me should not abide in darkness. "But in reality, the Earth is going to be destroyed with fire and the elements melt and fall from the sky. And then a new heaven and earth.

(Rev.21:23); V23)" The city had no need of the sun or of the moon to shine in it, for the glory of God illuminated it. The Lamb is its light."

Pastor John MacArthur says it best in his book, 'Right thinking in a world gone wrong.' P148);

"The earth we inhabit is not a permanent planet. It is, frankly, a disposable planet – it is going to have a very short life... when God's purposes for it are fulfilled, He will destroy it with fire and create a new earth. (II- Peter 3:7-13; Rev. 21:1)."

(II-Peter 3:7-13); V7)" But the heavens and the earth which are now preserved by the same word, are reserved for fire until the day of judgment and perdition of ungodly men. V8) But, beloved, do not forget this one thing, that with the Lord one day is as a thousand years, and a thousand years as one day. V9) The Lord is not slack concerning His promise, as some count slackness, but is longsuffering toward us, not willing that any should perish but that all should come to repentance." V10)" But the day of the Lord will come as a thief in the night, in which the heavens will pass away with a great noise, and the elements will melt with fervent heat; both the earth and the works that are in it will be burned up. V11) Therefore, since all these things will be dissolved, what manner of persons ought you to be in holy conduct and godliness, V12) ... looking for and hastening the coming of the day of God, because of which the heavens will be dissolved, being on fire, and the elements will melt with fervent heat? V13) Nevertheless we, according to His promise, look for new heavens and a new earth in which righteousness dwells."

(Using that much heat to exercise God's goal, it is possible He could use the sun to accomplish that? Or just speak it done, or both; then put it back in its placement. There is no limit to what God can do.)

(Revelation 21:1); V1)" Now I saw a new heaven and a new earth, for the first heaven and the first earth had passed away. Also there was no more sea."

There is another couple of pages probably answers a few questions of the future events of this world. In that same book, on page 155,156. Ref.#5 'We must rest in God's Sovereign Purposes': It is not a cop-out entrust God with the global destiny of our planet. To be sure, God's sovereignty never excuses man to be lazy or irresponsible. But knowing that He is in control should guard Christians from the doomsday mentality that characterizes the global warming movement. After all, whether the ice caps are melted melting or not, God specifically promised that He would not flood the earth again (Genesis 9:11). God has already revealed to us how this world is going to end – with Christ's return (I- Thessalonians 4:13; 5:3) and reign (Rev. 20:1-6), followed by the creation of a new earth (II- Peter 3:10; Rev. 21: 1-7).

During the Great Tribulation, God Himself will do much worse to this planet than mankind ever could. There will be famine (Revelation 6:5-6), pestilence (6:7-8), cosmic disasters (6:12-17), vegetation that is burned up (8:7), sea life that is destroyed (8:8-9), waters that are contaminated (8:10-11), demonic "locusts" (9:1-12), deadly plagues (9:13-21), terrible sores (16:2), seas and rivers that are turned to blood (16:3), scorching heat (16:8-9), darkness and pain (16:10-11), drought (16:12-16), and total devastation (16:17-21). After these divine judgments, Christ will come and establish His Kingdom by force (19:11-21). A thousand years later (20:1-6), as the millennial kingdom transitions to the eternal state, God will ultimately destroy this world with fire (20:9; cf. II-Peter 3:10-12) and create a new heaven and earth (21:1; cf. II-Peter 3:13). In spite of societies best attempts to cool down the planet, the Bible tells us how the world is going to end. It is going to get hot, but not because of carbon emissions. When God 's divine fury is finally poured out on the world, no amount of environmental protection will be able to stop it. Our Lord's words about anxiety, though specifically with regard to physical provision, serve as an appropriate reminder for those Christians who have allowed environmental fears to distract them from their God given mission. Who of you by being worried can add a single hour to his life? … Do not worry then, saying, "What will we eat?" or "What will we drink?" or "What will we wear for clothing?" For the Gentiles eagerly seek all these things; for your heavenly Father knows that you need all these things. But seek first His kingdom and His righteousness, and all these things will be added to you. So do not worry about tomorrow; for tomorrow will care for itself. Each day has enough trouble of its own (Matthew 6:27, 31-34).

In that same context, Jesus notes that the birds of the air and the lilies of the field need not worry, because God is taking care of them (verses 26–29).

Just as the Creator oversees the animals and plants He has made (such that they need not worry about their future), He will also take care of those who give first priority to His kingdom purposes. (End quote).

CHAPTER 42

'LITTLE STORY'

This is a little story, about the pencil-picture I drew through our little slit-window, at CSP. 3BO5-144.

One day it rained, and I drew that in a long with fences, buildings, road, etc. Even though it was the next day, and it was dry when I drew it. And then the next day, there was a little weed that had grown overnight 5 to 6 inches in height. Then we were back to Sunshine, being springtime and unpredictable weather. And by the end of the day the weed withered. (That part reminded me of Jonah in the desert in front of the city of Nineveh.)

(Jonah 4:6);

V6)" And the Lord God prepared a plant and made it come up over Jonah, that it might be shade for his head to deliver him from his misery. So Jonah was very grateful for the plant. (Obviously the plant was a lot larger, but the same idea.) V7) But as morning dawned the next day God prepared a worm, and it so damaged the plant that it withered. V8) And it happened, when the sun arose, that God prepared a vehement east wind; and the sun beat on Jonah 's head, So that he grew faint. Then he wished death for himself, and said, 'It is better for me to die than to live.' V9) Then God said to Jonah, "Is it right for you to be angry about the plant? "(as a question) And he said, "It is right, for me to be angry, even to death!" V10) But the Lord said, "You have had pity on the plant for which you have not labored, nor made it grow," which came up in a night and perished in a night. (God was showing Jonah an example about mercy). V11) And should I not pity Nineveh, that great city, in which are more than one hundred and twenty thousand persons who cannot discern between their right hand and their left—and much livestock?"

(A couple of things come to mind and mind you this is the end of the story of Nineveh.)

In the beginning, Jonah was told by God to preach repentance to the people of Nineveh, and they had a 40-day time. To react. And as the story goes, he tried to run away from God, like anyone could do that? Really? But he tries. God brought him back to Nineveh, and he did preach to the people; and the king and his nobles, which made a decree to all the people. In V7)" Let neither man nor beast, herd nor flock, taste anything; do not let them eat, or drink water. (Fast) V8) But let man and beast be covered with sackcloth, and cry mightily to God; Yes, let everyone turn from his evil way and from the violence that is in his hands. V9) Who can tell if God will turn and relent, (show mercy, lessen His anger) and turn away from His fierce anger, so that we may not perish?" (God will have mercy on whom He wishes.)

(Romans 9:15) For He says to Moses, "I will have mercy on whomever I will have mercy, and I will have compassion on whomever I will have compassion."

The people repented, and God relented in the destruction of the city at that time. End

'HOPE IN GOD'

There is a chapter in the John MacArthur book, that has five reasons you can hope in God, which corresponds with the title of this series of books; 'All My Hope', that God the Holy Spirit helped me write. It's because of His Word which strengthens my Faith, which in turn gives me more hope.

p.200 of 'Right thinking in a World gone wrong'.: ref.#1

'You can Hope in God because His Person: of Who He is'

(God is trustworthy; God is wise, God is righteous, and God is unchanging).

'First, believers can hope in God 's promises because He is absolutely trustworthy – His Word can be trusted because He can be trusted.

God's personality backs up the reliability of everything He says... God's reputation does not contradict His promises. Thus, we can be confident that every assurance He makes will come to pass exactly as foretold down to the smallest detail.'

(God's trustworthiness is in His three attributes: God is wise; God is righteous, and God is unchanging.)

Ref. quote: 1. God is wise. Believers can hope in God because He is perfectly wise. Psalms 147:5 notes that His understanding is infinite. And Paul, in Romans 11:33–34, exclaimed, "Oh, the depth of the riches both of the wisdom and knowledge of God!" How unsearchable are His judgments and unfathomable His ways!" God needs no additional advice or help because He already possesses infinite understanding. He knows every situation, circumstance, and possibility in complete detail. He is never surprised or caught off guard. As Christians, we can place our confidence in God 's decisions because He knows exactly what He is doing. Our response to God's perfect wisdom, then, must be to trust in Him rather than in ourselves or anything else. Even Solomon, the wisest of men, advised, "Trust in the Lord with all your heart and do not lean on your own understanding" …. (Proverbs 3:5).

Ref. quote: 2. God is righteous. God's perfect righteousness also allows us to hope in him completely. The Bible is clear; God is absolutely holy, without sin, and morally perfect in every way (Daniel 9:14; 1- John 1:5). In fact, God 's Holiness is a motivation for our own righteous living. Peter, quoting from Leviticus, urged his readers, "Like the Holy One who called you, be holy yourselves also in all your behavior; because it is written; "You shall be holy for I am holy" …. (1-Peter 1:15-16). So how does God 's righteousness fit in with His trustworthiness? The answer is simple: Because lying is contrary to God 's perfect Character (Proverbs 6:16-17; 12:22; cf, John 8:44), His righteousness does not allow Him to have any part in it. Perhaps more to the point, God cannot lie because God cannot sin. His righteousness means that He will never act in any way that compromises or contradicts His perfect holiness. Unlike a crooked politician who says one thing but means another, our holy God always means exactly what He says. He can be trusted because He is pure and breaking His word would violate His Character (see John 17:17). Ref. quote 3. God is unchanging.

Not only is God perfectly wise and perfectly righteous, but His character never changes. Psalm 102:26–27, contrasting God with His created works, says, "Even they will perish, but you endure; and all of them will wear out like a garment; like clothing. You will change them and they will be changed. But You are the same and Your years will not come to an end. "James 1:17 reiterates this point, nothing that in God there is no shifting of shadows. Hebrews 13:8 says, "Jesus Christ is the same yesterday and today and forever. "Whereas people are always changing, God remains constant. His character never changes.

Gods' immutable nature means that He will not suddenly change His mind about promises He has made. He won't arbitrarily decide that Salvation is no longer found in Christ or that eternal life is no longer available. We can trust Him because He is still the same as He has always been and will always be. We can cling tightly to His Word because an unchanging promises.

God's person – specifically, His wisdom, righteousness, and unchanging nature – allows us to trust Him because of Who He is. His words are certain because His character is certain. On the other hand, for Him to violate His Word would be to contradict Himself Yet that is not possible, For "it is impossible for God to lie "(Hebrews 6:18). End quote

(I'm not going to rewrite his whole book, read Pastor John MacArthur's book for yourself.) The other four Hopes are: Ref. #2 His Power: 'You Can Hope In God Because He Is In Control'. #3 His Plan: 'You Can Hope In God Because He Knows Exactly What He's Doing'. #4 His Past Record: 'You Can Hope In God Because He's Been Faithful Before'.

#5 His Parental Care: 'You Can Hope In God Because He Loves You'.

Ref. quote: We began this chapter by noting that this world is filled with false hopes and half-truths. From Television ads to Junk mail to electronic spam, our lives are inundated with empty promises... (end quote).

(But God's Word is True and Faithful). (Revelation 3:14) …. These things say the Amen, the Faithful and True witness….and

(Rev. 21:5); V5)" Then He who sat on the throne said, "Behold, I make all things new." And He said to me, "Write, for these words are true and faithful.". (end)

'OCEAN DREAM'

I was working at a customer's home, who was very rich. I was there as a practically live-in servant; I was there so much. (In real life, there are jobs where we work for weeks, and even a month sometimes, but rarely. But we are practically like family at the end). I was there, even cooking something, and I was walking around the house. They had guests in the front of the house. And in the back, in a, —what looks like a circle pool. With a short-board floating devices and little motors on them. And they were racing around and around in the pool. Then the guests went in the back of the pool toward a dock. The owner lady was asking me about renting boats and the cost, to take their friends out. I gave some answer to the question. But, instead of boats, they keep walking down the beach. So, I walked with them, and the Sea seemed to be more massive, and turbulent. And off in the distance was title-waves, and stone pillars, and large waves and rocks. It looked massive and strong; and I turned and stopped. Looked over there at it. (meaning the sea scene). It is like one of the 7- wonders of the world. (In real life, not really, but impressive). And a large wave that was far off, came close, and ended at our feet. So, we went into the cave to get out from it. And it was a restaurant, and the owner lady was asking me, how much money she had? I said, 'I don't know?' I wasn't her husband. She said, 'I didn't bring my purse to pay for her guests' that was still with us. But it was a rhetorical question, her picture was up on the wall, because her family owned it.

End

CHAPTER 43

'HE IS RISEN'

This is an Easter service sermon, especially made for whoever would like to attend. The dayroom 3BO5 @CSP, since our Chapel services are pretty scarce, and numbers low. This way, with permission of the CO's. To have an informal gathering. Starting with an opening prayer, and blessing for the gathering in Jesus' name, and requesting for the Holy Spirit's presence. Amen.

Welcome church, Happy Easter!!!

Thank you for being here today. Before we can talk about Jesus Christ raising from the dead this glorious Easter Sunday morning, and the title for this is: 'He Is Risen'

We are going to look at some Scriptures that Jesus foretells His death. Starting in:

(Mark 9:30-32) (Jesus had just healed and delivered a demon possessed boy) .... V30)" Then they departed from there and passed through Galilee, and He did not want anyone to know it. (There are always throngs of people, to be healed or ministered too. But Jesus had something Important to discuss with His disciple's) V31) For He taught His disciples and said to them, "The Son of Man is being betrayed into the hands of men, and they will kill Him. And after He is killed, He will rise the third day. V32) But

251

they did not understand this saying, and we're afraid to ask Him." (Jesus is preparing His disciples for what is coming).

(Matt. 17:22-23); Says about the same thing; This is after staying in Galilee a while, and this could be the same message that Mark wrote. But sometimes Jesus reiterates, or repeats Himself, when something Important is happening or going to happen, especially when the disciples didn't quite understand it the first time. ... (Matthew 17:22-23).

V22)" Now while they were staying in Galilee, ... (at the north-western part of the Sea of Galilee, is like their headquarters, Simon and his brother Andrew. James and John's fishing business with their father Zebedee). (Eventho they left all to follow Jesus, they are still in that region to begin Ministry). Jesus said to them, "the son of man is about to be betrayed... (The Son of Man is Jesus' title He gave Himself, that as the perfect specimen of Humanity). (And is about to be betrayed—we all know He is talking about Judas Iscariot) into the hands of men, (And those men were the religious leaders of the day, the Pharisees and Sadducees). (Do you know why they are called Sadducees? because their Sad—U—See...they don't believe in the Resurrection or Angels; only the 'Torra'— The 5-books of the Law. Genesis thru Deuteronomy). ...V23) And they will kill Him, and the third day He will be raised up." And they were exceedingly sorrowful. (The disciples were sad, for two reasons, their teacher, master, friend, whom they love (except the one traitor) is about to die, and at first, they thought their troubles were over about the long-awaited Messiah come to set up His kingdom and remove the oppression of the Roman empire on them. Eventho, Jesus teaches them that His Kingdom is not of this world; this world is passing away, but His Word is forever).

Luke 9:43-45 version is similar to Mark's version.

Jesus had just healed the boy who was demon possessed. The one that the disciples couldn't cast out. In another passage Jesus explains that they couldn't do it, because that type only came out with prayer and fasting. So, in verse 43) "And they were all amazed at the majesty of God. But while everyone marveled at and all the things which Jesus did, He said to His disciples,... V44)"Let these words sink down into your ears, for the Son of Man is about to be betrayed into the hands of men, V45) But they did not understand this saying and it was hidden from them so that they did not perceive it; (How is that, that they did not perceive it? Because Jesus is always speaking words given to Him from the Father; they are Spiritual Words of Life. So, they are Spiritually discerned too). ....And they were afraid to ask Him about this saying."

(The disciples understood some, but still needed more to learn, and confused of how the suffering fits into God 's plan.)....

God's plan was before the foundation of the world, that the Father of all things would send His only Begotten Son to this world, as the Lamb of God who takes away the sins of the world. The Ultimate Sacrifice, to pay the penalty for sin and death. With His shed blood on the Cross. The Cross was ever the goal of our Savior and Lord. Because of His Grace, His Love, and His Mercy. He came the first time to this world, born of a virgin birth. He came to seek and save that which was lost. (He is Risen and will come back again for His Bride (the Church) and to set things right, to judge the living and the dead.) ....

Now, Let's go to the Empty Tomb in: (Matthew 28:1-8);

V1)" Now after the Sabbath, as the first day of the week began to dawn, Mary Magdalene and the other Mary came to see the tomb. V2) And behold, there was a great earthquake; for an angel of the Lord descended from heaven, and came and rolled back the stone from the door, and sat on it. V3) His countenance was like lightning, and his clothing as white as snow. V4) And the guards shook for fear of him, and became like dead men. V5) But the angel answered and said to the women. "Do not be afraid, for I know that you seek Jesus who was crucified. V6 He is not here; for He is risen, as He said. (He said it in Matthew 17:23 also) Come, see the place where the Lord lay. (Then angels were in the tomb) V7) And go quickly and tell His disciples that He is risen from the dead, and indeed He is going before you into Galilee; there you will see Him. Behold, I have told you. V8) So they went out quickly from the tomb with fear and great joy, and ran to bring His disciples word."

In Marks Gospel Chapter 16: 1-7. That is the same angel or another in the tomb. Says again the same thing. In Matthew's version the angel says, 'Come see the place where the Lord lay.' (So, Mary went in more than once?) In John's Gospel, when Mary Magdalene; she looks in and sees two angels one at the foot and the other at the head where Jesus had laid. (Just like the cherubim angels on each side of the mercy seat on top of the ark of the covenant).

Let's here Mark's Gospel 16:1-7.

V1)" Now when the Sabbath was past, (which is Saturday, and no work, and limitations on travel for the Sabbath. And other reasons had passed for religious rituals —being clean, not going there any sooner, for supposed touching the dead would make you unclean, also the Sabbath day rest on Saturday). But, He is Risen!! (It's a mood point). Mark 16:1 'Mary Magdalene, Mary the mother of James, and Salome bought spices'...(As we know Mary Magdalene; Jesus delivered 7-demons from her, and she became a devout follower; Mary the mother of James, could be Mary — Jesus' Mother and James as His earthly half-brother. Or the Apostle James (of Alphaeus) and if his mother's name was Mary?) ...'and Salome', ...who was the wife of Zebedee and the mother of James and John the Apostles.

Also Ref. Matt. 27:56; And at the Cross, 'Mary Magdalene, Mary the mother of James and Jose's, (Mary the mother of Jesus and His half-brother) ...'and the mother of Zebedee's sons '(Salome). In Luke 24:10 on Resurrection Sunday, 'It was Mary Magdalene, Joanna, Mary the mother of James, and the other women with them, who told these things to the apostles.' The first Evangelists spreading the Good News of Jesus' Resurrection. In John 19:25, the women present at the Cross is Jesus' mother and her sister, (and some scholars think Salome could be Mary's sister and if so, James and John would be Jesus first cousins.) And another Mary is mentioned, the wife of Clopas. So, there was a group of women there and Apostle John, V26-27. (Mark 16:1-7); Were still in V1) ....'that they might come and anoint Him.' (This tells of their unbelief; they wouldn't need the spices if He is Risen. Which He did). V2)" Very early in the morning, on the first day of the week, they came to the tomb when the sun had risen. V3) And they said among themselves, 'Who will roll away the stone from the door of the tomb for us?' (They had some faith for being there and had a job to do, not knowing how it was going to get accomplished.) (They also must not have known it was guarded by Roman soldiers and the tomb was sealed. [Probably with wax as a seal and possible signet ring or emblem, as of authority.] But that was all gone. V4) But when they looked up, they saw that the stone had been rolled away for it was very large. (Multiple-of hundreds of pounds.) (Probably about 3-4 feet in height or diameter; the entrance of the tomb is short, and you have to stoop over to enter). V5) And entering the tomb, they saw a young man clothed in a long white Robe sitting on the right side; and they were alarmed." V6) But he said to them, "Do not be alarmed. You seek Jesus of Nazareth, who was crucified. He is risen! He is not here. (I'm a little excited, "hallelujah", which means Praise the Lord.) …. See the place where they laid Him. V7) But go, tell His disciples —and Peter — (They mentioned Peter, they wanted him included and that he is forgiven, after the denial of the lord 3x.) …that He is going before you into Galilee; there you will see Him, as He said to you." ….So, these women were the first Evangelists, telling the Good News, that Jesus is Risen!!! ; From His Death, Burial, and Resurrection according to the Scriptures. This Easter Sunday remembering He is alive, and on His Throne. And He is coming back soon. And we as Christians, should be about My Fathers business, as Jesus puts it. Until He returns. And for those who don't know the Lord. It is: …'repentance toward God, and faith toward our Lord Jesus Christ.' (Acts 20:21).

In closing with a blessing on all that is here. (Numbers 6:24-26);

"The Lord Bless you and keep you;
The Lord make His face shine
upon you,
And be gracious to you;
The Lord lift up His countenance
upon you,
And give you peace." Amen.
(Peace be with you, be well, and go with God.)

Today is the day of Salvation, if you would like to receive Jesus Christ into your heart by the Holy Spirit. Say this prayer out loud if you really mean it and believe it in your heart.

'Dear God, I am a lost sinner and ask You to save my soul and cleanse me from all sin. I do accept Jesus Christ into my heart and do believe He died on the Cross to purchase my redemption by His shed blood. And I confess with my mouth the Lord Jesus and believe in my heart that God has raised Him from the dead. I have called upon your Name and believe right now I am saved. In Jesus Name, Amen.'

'PISMO DREAM'

I had a dream with my first wife. We were going on vacation to Pismo Beach California. But, the young neighborhood girl, who had some business to do, who had a little baby. And she wanted us to watch her while she is gone. I think my wife didn't mind; she loves children. Her and I have two lovely children together. Then we got divorced. She remarried and had three more lovely children. She is also a pediatric nurse and is around children at her work. So, we brought the baby for the weekend to Pismo Beach, and we still had a good time there. (Now, in real life that hasn't happened) (and another reason I was thinking about a baby, and a young mother—my daughter-in-law and son are going to have a baby soon) (In March 2021, we had our 2nd grand child with them). End

'N.L.S.—SONG'

V1. You unravel me with a melody; You surround me with a song; Of deliverance from my Enemies: Till all my fears are gone.

Chorus:

(I'm no longer a slave to fear I am a child of God) (2x)

V2. From my mother's womb; You have chosen me; Love has called my name; I've been born again, into a family, Your blood flows through my veins.

(Back to Chorus)

Bridge:

You split the sea, So I could walk right through it.
My fears were drowned in perfect love.
You rescued me, and I will stand and sing,
I am a child of God,
I am a child of God. End

CHAPTER 44

'BANK DREAM'

I had a dream with my co-flooring installation worker and me. After work one day, we were at the bank to make some transactions. Old money, into new bills. The Benjamin Franklin $100 bills with the bigger face on it, and the water marks to help identify it better. And the rest; 50s, 20s, tens, fives, and ones. Also, receipts coming out of the teller's window too. And we were putting them back into a machine, or a slot and it comes out with a new receipt. And I was in one lane or line, and he was next to me in his line. I heard his teller say to him, 'You are done'; and he would say, 'No, I don't have the right receipt yet?' And the bank is full of people, and papers, receipts, everywhere on the floor. I dropped one of my receipts, and couldn't find it on the floor, but I know I can find it. It had writing on the back so it would stand out easier. And while I was down on the floor, there were a bunch of cats running around. I was playing with some of the young frisky cats. And not sure we got all our receipts. (then I woke up)

(In real life, when I would go to the PIA job, just outside the gate going in would be a numerous amount of cats, young and old, and I heard kittens that weren't far away.)

(As far as the money exchange, it was a gradual thing, not one day. And there never was a receipt exchange. And Al, my co-worker and I had different banks; So, we weren't in the same bank together at the same time. Some apprentices, yes.) End

'GIVE THANKS'

This is a song, that came to me this morning, from the Holy Spirit. It is an obvious song, that we should be grateful for the things God has done for us. And that He sent His only begotten Son to this world to redeem us from sin and death. Thank you, Father, for sending your Son to die on the Cross, and become the propitiation; the substitute for our guilt, shame, and sin. Through repentance toward God, and faith toward Jesus Christ our Lord. We may be born again into the Spiritual family of God. We may have life, and more abundantly. We can receive the gift of eternal life from God. And as children of the most high God. We are beloved of Him. So, give thanks to God who loves you. When we acknowledge our weakness, He is strong in us. ...

#38. 'Give Thanks'

Give Thanks with a grateful heart! Give Thanks to the Holy One, Give Thanks because He's giv'in

Jesus Christ, His Son. And now let the weak say, "I am strong "Let the poor say, "I am rich,

Because of what the Lord has done for us." Give Thanks; give thanks.

'HOTEL DREAM'

We were at a big Hotel, with cars lined up. And while we were there, the Hotel provided a Motorhome for the bigger families. I'm thinking, I've got dibbs on driving it, since I have years of experience with them.

The Hotel seems to be full, bustling with people. We get checked in, and at dinner time, a large crowd of people sat down to eat. No spacing, or masks required. But our family was still working on some details.

On one side of the restaurant was a stairway leading to the garage. I thought they were bringing to us the RV and having it ready for after dinner.

But it had to do with Gary, my brother. He was bringing his truck around. And on the other side of the restaurant. We were moving my old twin-bed, and my brother wanted to use it. It was fairly new and in good condition. (In real life none of this happened, except the part about having an RV experience.)

Back to the dream, this is a kind of odd thing to be moving now, and my niece was there Jamie, helping Gary, her dad. And I'm pretty sure her sister probably is close by. Her name is Amiee. This was all during dinner, and all the people didn't seem bothered by the moving around at all.

(Woke up)

CHAPTER 45

'THE P.P.'

There was another interesting book I read called 'The Pilgrims Progress', by originally John Bunyan's, his theme for the book, but this is by Alan Vermilye who updated it into a readable modern-day version classic John Bunyan's Pilgrim's Progress. The writer, Alan uses the most brilliant of allegories to express the Story-Adventure. It is very interesting, a dream about a pilgrim, who read a book and changed his life, and started him on a faith journey. His name was Christian.

It's a good read for all Christians, and makes you think, and reflect. Of a course of where I am on my journey or race? To the heavenly kingdom? It takes you on a Spiritual journey of a believer in Christ Jesus our Lord from our first conviction until the moment we enter Heaven.

In one section in the book on their journey, Christian was walking with a man named Hopeful. And they were discussing backsliding. Christian was going to tell Hopeful his thoughts on a man called Ignorance and people like him. He posed the question, just before that to answer. *(Ref. p208-114) *The question was: Do you think they grasp the seriousness of their sinful condition and experience godly fear? *p209. I would say that sometimes people like Ignorance might experience conviction of sin followed by the fear of God. Being Spiritually blind, they do not understand that such convictions are for their good, so they desperately try to suppress them while at the same time convincing themselves that their hearts are good. Hopeful nodded. "I agree with your opinion, for the fear of God is a good motivator: at the beginning of a pilgrimage to encourage people to do the right thing. ""Without a doubt, this is what happens but only when the fear of God is right and true, said Christian." For God's Word says, "The fear of the Lord is the beginning of wisdom." (Ps.111:10). "How-would you Identify a fear of God that is right and true?" Hopeful asked. "I would say that you could identify it in three ways, Christian said." First, it begins with a serious concern for our sin that helps us see the need for a Savior. Then, it motivates us to quickly turn to Christ as our only Hope for Salvation. And finally, it instills and maintains in us a great reverence for God, His Word, and His ways. This reverence keeps us mindful of God 's presence so that we would be careful in turning our affections to the right or the left or to do anything that may dishonor God, break its peace, grieve the Spirit, or give Gods enemies a reason to speak scornfully of Him and His kingdom. "... (Hopeful asked Christian why do they suppress their fear?) *(p210) Christian said, "Well, I can think of four ways." "For one, they think their fear is from the devil when actually it's the work of God, so they resist the fear less they be defeated. Also, they think their fear will undermine their faith when, unfortunately for these poor misled souls, they have no faith to begin with, so they harden their hearts against it. Some even presume they should have no fear, and so despite their convictions, they brazenly ignore them. Still others see fear as making them weak and less sure of themselves rather than spiritually strong and pious, so they resist the fear in an effort to appear self-righteous."

Hopeful lifted his hands. "I confess to knowing something of this myself because before I knew the truth, I used to be just as bad. "(I can relate to some degree in these statements too.) (Now, the two of them jumped on another topic.)

*(p211) "Well then, said Christian, about 10 years ago, did you know a man named Temporary who lived near Vanity Fair? At one time, he was determined to become a pilgrim and was very passionate about religion back then. ""Know him!" Hopeful exclaimed. "Yes, I most certainly did.

He lived in Graceless, a town that lies not more than 2 miles away from Honesty, and he lived next door to a man named Turnback. ""Yes, and he actually lived under the same roof with Turnback, "said Christian". Well, at one time, his life was very much awakened spiritually, and I believe he received some conviction of his sins to the point where he became overwhelmed with the consequences that were due, for them. ""I believe you're right," Hopeful said. "My house was not more than three miles from Temporary's, and he would often come to me weeping over his sin. Honestly, I felt sorry for the man, but I was not all together without hope for him. However, as you know, not everyone who cries, 'Lord, Lord!' Is a true believer. " Christian nodded, "He told me once that he was determined to go on a pilgrimage just as we are now. But before long, he became friends with a man named Save-self, and after that, he began to treat me like a stranger and distant himself from me. ""Since we're talking about Temporary," said Hopeful, "Let's see if we can figure out the reason for his sudden backsliding, as well as others like him." Christian thought this was an excellent idea, "Yes, but this time you be the one to begin! "*(p211) …Hopeful thought for a moment. "Well, in my opinion, there are four reasons for backsliding." *(p212) "First, even though the consciences of such people have been temporarily awakened spiritually, their minds are not yet changed. Therefore, when the power of guilt wears off so does their desire to pursue holiness, and then they return to their former sinful ways. We see this illustrated in a sick dog that vomits what he has eaten. He does not vomit because he has a free mind, if it can be said that a dog has a free mind, but rather because his stomach is upset. But once he is no longer sick and his stomach feels better, the desire for what he was vomited returns, and he licks it all up. And so that which is written is true: 'The dog returns to his own vomit.' (II-Peter 2:22). "This is like the person who initially is enthusiastic for Heaven but only because their fear and shame were strong, and they sensed the torments of Hell. But as their fear and shame diminish, so does their desire to pursue holiness. Then, overtime, when their fear and shame are gone, and their desire for heaven and happiness die, they return to their former sinful way of life."

"The second reason for backsliding is that people have unreasonable fears that overwhelm, as when they begin to fear man more than God, as is written; 'For the fear of man will prove to be a snare.' (Prov. 29:25). So even though they appear to be enthusiastic for heaven so long as the flames of hell are real to them, when that tear has passed, they begin to have second thoughts. They begin to think that it's wise not to run the risk of losing everything -or bring themselves into unavoidable and unnecessary troubles – And so they return to their worldly ways again."

"The third reason for backsliding is their convictions that arise in a time of weakness then become a crutch in times when they feel confident and strong. *(p213) In their pride and arrogance, they view religion as base and contemptible. Therefore, when they've lost their sense and fear of the torments of Hell and the wrath to come, they return to their former sinful ways again."

"The final reason for backsliding is they dislike feeling guilty and ashamed and prefer not to think about their wrath and judgment before it happens. Though perhaps if they could see it, and then look to Christ, it might encourage them to flee to safety with the Righteous. But as I hinted before, they suppress their conviction and ignore any thoughts of guilt, shame, and the wrath of God. As soon as they are rid of those feelings, they gladly harden their hearts and choose ways that will harden them even more. "Christian nodded.

"You're pretty close to the heart of the matter, which, at the root, is a backslider's inability to truly change their mind and will. They are like a criminal that stands scared and trembling before the judge. He appears to repent with all his heart, but motivation is his fear of the noose, not any true remorse for his crime. This is evident once he's set free and returns to a life of the very and dishonesty. However, if his mind and heart were truly changed, he would live differently. ""Now that I've shared with you my thoughts regarding backsliding, please share with me your thoughts on the progression of sin that causes people like Temporary to begin to backslide. ""Gladly, set Christian as he started to list his reasons one at a time."

"First, they stop thinking about anything that reminds them of God, death, and the judgment to come and instead, focus on thoughts that produce pleasure and comfort. ""They give up and pretense of acting like a Christian in their personal life by neglecting prayer, giving into temptation, and not feeling any grief over sin." *(p214) "Then they avoid the company of joyful, vibrant, and mature Christians that are sharing personal testimonies and asking questions. ""From there, they become less enthusiastic about church attendance and no longer listen to preaching or the public reading of God 's Word or participate in corporate Worship. ""To justify their actions, they start to nitpick and look for faults in the lives of other Christians. Their evil intent is to discredit religion and to provide an excuse for avoiding church. ""Then they begin to find friendship and belonging by surrounding themselves with sinful, immoral, and godless people, who just lead them further into sin. ""Eventually, they give into immoral and ungodly conversations in their personal lives, hoping to discover others with whom they can relate and find encouragement as well as who will not put them down. ""Emboldened and unrestrained by godly influences, they now begin to sin more openly and excuse and rationalize their sins. ""And then, with their hearts now hardened, they reveal themselves for what they truly are worse off than they were before they professed faith in Christ. Unless A miracle of grace prevents it, they will eternally perish in their own deceptions. "Reference (Luke 11:24-26).

(That was me, I was worse off, regardless of the circumstances, good or bad, the results were 7x as bad. But thank God I've repented in prison, and have been walking the straight and narrow, sober-free and Praising the Lord Jesus in Worship Services for delivering me from those evil spirits. It woke me up spiritually, that Jesus is the Answer for everything. Now, it is like (Phil. 3:10) says, … "That I may know Him and the power of His resurrection… "; He has given me new life, and a second chance to redeem myself. Even though, it's not so much me anymore, but Christ in me. 'Greater is He who is in me than he who is in the world.' '…. which is Christ in you, the hope of glory.' (Col. 1:27). And the part of the dog returning to his own vomit, is a gross analogy, but it is true. It is also found in the book of Proverbs 26:11. The vomit represents sin, or whatever that thing or things have entangled you with. (The alcohol was gradual, then it was out of control. Six-months before surgery, more and more as a pain medicine with ice packs every day after work. Then surgery, and I am cured from my neck nerve pain. And now I'm back to begin a full-blown Alcoholic. No, more nerve pain. And I was supposed to be off work a year and wear my neck brace 3 to 4 months, and I did wear it. I also came into prison in the middle of the fourth month. I changed my diet to fruits and vegetable smoothies. That would have been great, but I was still drinking Vodka, cold-straight, with mixers of orange juice, soda, or Gatorade.) (So, those good smoothies, just made me sicker. You can't do both. You have to change.) (Matt. 6:24). V24)" No one can serve two masters; or either he will hate the one and love the other, or else he will be loyal to the one and despise the other. You cannot serve God and mammon."

(This is referring to money or riches; but the principal is the same, anything we put before God; so, any god, or addiction, etc. Where you serve it, and not let it master you.) But, with God, He can give you the strength to Overcome those obstacles in your life. So, you can master them in Christ, Amen; then you will be an Overcomer. Amen. End

'KNOWING GOD'

There was another book that I had read, that interest me and apparently from part of the title, should be: 'The Highest Priority in Life', and of course the title is:

'Knowing God'

And on the back cover from: (Phil. 3:10) "That I may know Him.... *(p6) "But let him who glories glory in this, that he understands and knows Me, that I am the Lord." (Jeremiah 9:24). *(p7) Though we can never fully know God because His mind is so much higher than ours; He does reveal Himself little by little to those who seek Him. "And you will see Me and find Me, when you search for Me with all your heart. " (Jeremiah 29:13). (So, we can find God if we diligently search for Him.) *(p7) Even understanding Him a little is the most excellent treasure of life. (Knowing God is like a treasure, instead of the things of this world.) (That's why (p5) makes so much sense, in the completed verses of (Jeremiah

9:23-24). *(p5). V23)" Thus says the LORD: 'Let not the wise man glory in his wisdom. Let not the mighty man glory in his might. Nor let the rich man glory in his riches; …. V24) But let him who glories glory in this, that he understands and knows Me, That I am the LORD, exercising lovingkindness, judgment, and righteousness in the earth. For in these I delight; says the LORD."

(I want my Children and Grand Children to know God too.) (On p4— King David wants to pass on a little godly advice to his son Solomon.) *p4)" As for you, my son Solomon, knows the God of your father, and serve Him with a loyal heart and with a willing mind; for the LORD searches all hearts and understands all the intent of the thoughts. If you seek Him, He will be found by you; But if you forsake Him, He will cast you off forever. "(I- Chronicles 28:9).

(Let's even go back to p3) where the Gospel of John, defines knowing Jesus Christ synonymous with Eternal life.) *(p3) "And this is eternal life, that they may know You, the only true God, and Jesus Christ whom You have sent. "(John 17:3). (And on p9 gives a good point; that before we came to the Lord and became born again into a Spiritual Family. He was that light, that beaming light of Hope. As we walked in darkness before Christ.)

*(p9) Before God shined the knowledge of the Lord into our hearts, we as others, had dark harden hearts. We walked in darkness, fulfilling our natural wicked desire.

Ref. (Romans 3:10,23); That's because: "There is none righteous, no, no one… for all have sinned and fall short of the glory of God… "(And for me, even after knowing God and going into a backslidden state. Where Grace had to abound for a time, for my foolish, sinful, Pride, and wayward way.) … (Then repenting in prison and turning back toward my Savior and Lord Jesus Christ.) (Just because we are under grace, and everything is lawful for us, but not everything is beneficial.) (So, should we sin, that grace may abound? God forbids!)—Ref. (Rom.6:1-15). Back to p9.

*(p9)" For it is the God who commanded light to shine out of darkness, who has shone in our hearts to give the light of the knowledge of the glory of God in the face of Jesus Christ. "(II-Cor. 4:6).

And pg. 10,11)

*(p10,11)" I am the light of the world. He who follows Me shall not walk in darkness but have the light of life. "(John 8:12) ...And in conclusion to this segment, and one of Bob's chapters on p13) and 14), Paul says it best, through the Holy Spirit of God; in (Phil. 3:8-10). V8)" Yet indeed I also count all things loss for the excellence of the knowledge of Christ Jesus my Lord, for whom I have suffered the loss of all things, and count them as rubbish, that I may gain Christ V9) ... and be found in Him, not having my own righteousness, which is from the law, but that which is through faith in Christ, the righteousness which is from God by faith; V10) that I may know Him and the power of His resurrection, and the fellowship of His sufferings, being conformed to His death,.....'" End

'ROCK REMODEL DREAM'

I dreamt about remodeling a garage full of Rock-Boulders, they were in the attic of this two-story garage. The rocks were big-chunks of rust -gray color jagged-rock; and apparently, I was taking those rocks out and putting them in the driveway to build it up, for some reason? (In real life you wouldn't be able to drive on it?) (And to add, the only Real Rock to build on as it's Foundation is Jesus).

So, I began to remove the pieces, one by one, to take them from the inside to the outside. First one was kind-of-long, so I used a sledgehammer on it, and broke it in half. I removed it by taking it out and placed the first one down in the corner of the driveway.

But, when I removed the first half, the other half almost fell out. So, when I was walking back, and the rock fell out. And fell about 6 to 7 feet down. But it was like in the movies. One rock fell and started a chain reaction and others fell. Then an avalanche. As I am backing up backwards, and almost get crushed by these rocks. And I jumped with a backflip right out of the room as it all fell. (Then I woke up).

(The meaning, I had just written that day, about dark and light. From our old man to our new man, in Christ. That we are a new creation in Christ Jesus. (II-Corinthians 5:17) reference… behold all things become new (In our inter-man). That garage is my buddy John's in the dream. On the outside, and he didn't put a lot of lights in, so it seems dark like a cave with rocks above you. And since it is a two-story, no skylights either. There is just one fog style window in there). End

CHAPTER 46

'Ship Dream'

I was on a ship, in this dream, and I was in a play. And I played one of the good guys, the Christians, the righteous men by Faith in Jesus Christ. And His Righteousness, not mine. By His finished work on the Cross and shed blood, as an atonement for the whole world's sin.

And off in the distance I saw the other crew in the play; they all stuck together in their separate groups, just like us Christians in our group.

And to play the part, they are actually we're bad guys. Including this witch, and I despise them so. It was a play with this French-whip-swords.

And I ran up to the one witch, and her back was turned. I could have cut her in half for real, but I didn't. She turns and says, 'You had your chance', and I said, 'That's OK, I'm just practicing'. She says, 'I thought this was a ship?' I said, 'It is, it is the Hotel-Princess.' It did look like a big hotel inside, with walkovers, which we were on. And open areas for a show. I said, "I didn't cut you in half, because, The Word of God says, 'Vengeance is Mine says the LORD.'" (In real life, I dreamt this dream, because I was watching my Bunky's TV – Hell's kitchen, and it is in a big Hotel in Las Vegas. The thin sword is from watching modern family, and the righteous part was something I had just read. And the last, is Scripture from the Word of God in the Bible, straight from the Lord.) End

'EVENT DREAM'

There was some kind of an event, that we were going to, and I was driving. A family event, or wedding. Or something we're all dressed up for. And I was driving my mother-in-law's car, and apparently two small boys too. Maybe my nephews through my first marriage. We we're in a parking lot downtown and we needed to get going; we're already running a little late. This is a crowded parking lot, in the mid-west of Bakersfield, off of California Avenue, one of our business sections. I'm driving them out of the parking space, and now my mother-in-law and I are on bicycles still trying to leave and go to the event. I'm riding on the grass, so she could ride on the sidewalk, it would be easier for her. And now we take a shortcut through a building. A walk-way entrance with glass on both sides, and glass commercial doors. So, we entered and picked up the bikes, so not to ride inside. And walk through about 50 feet. Then continued on the other side, we are in the car again, with the kids. And some kind of present to take with us. (It looked like a basket full of black and white, with red penguin poppers?)

My bicycle in the walk through the hallway turned into a chair, and I slid it. (In real life I was at PIA food packing plant a couple of days ago, and there was one chair, which prisoners don't see much of, in certain prisons, just cement or wooden benches to sit on. Anyway, this chair was in my way, and I pushed it and slid it under the packaging rollers to the shipping area.) (The other thing, I don't know what the whole penguin popper thing is all about. It is a gift.) (And my mother-in-law and I never rode bicycles together. My dad, yes, and kids yes, rollerblades.) The gift is just like our Salvation from the Lord, it is a Gift.

And it is accomplished by …. repentance toward God, and Faith toward our Lord Jesus Christ (Acts 20:21), is how to obtain it. Confess your sins and believe in Him for Eternal life. Receive that living water, and the bread of life. He will change your life for the better. (Romans 3:23) says: V23)" …for all have sinned and fall short of the glory of God, …" And (Romans 6:23) says: V23)" For the wages of sin is death, but the gift of God is eternal life through Jesus Christ our Lord. "And (Romans 5:8) says:

V8)" But God demonstrates His own love toward us, in that while we were still sinners, Christ died for us. "And (Romans 10:9) says: V9) "That if you confess with your mouth the lord Jesus and believe in your heart that God has raised Him from the dead, you will be saved. "And in (Romans 10:10) says: "For with the heart man believes unto righteousness; and with the mouth confession is made unto Salvation."

(I-John 5:11) says: V11)" And this is the Testimony, that God hath given to us eternal life, and this life is in His Son. "Then (I-John 5:12) says: V12)" He that has the Son has life, and he who doesn't have the Son of God, doesn't have life. "(Probably the last thing I could say about that dream, was regardless of what event it was. The world will be going along as usual. In the last days, people will be getting married, and events will happen. We do not know the day, nor the hour, of Christ return, and only the Father knows the day and hour. – The day of the Lord. Jesus Christ is coming again to receive His Bride, the Church. Then the living and the dead, after the Rapture there will be a righteous judgment upon the Earth and the people of the Earth.)

(Boast not in Tomorrow for you do not know what it will bring? Today has troubles enough in it. For today is the day of Salvation. Wait not, to see the flames of Hell, then it will be too late). End

'FLOWER DREAM'

I had I dream of working in a restaurant, and I was wearing a black and white uniform. But I wasn't getting paid, I think? I was helping my new girlfriend out. In the dream, - that's me-and I knew what position she worked, but I don't know by observing it. For one, we are just setting-up and getting ready to open. I had just given her a single flower, and then she left for a moment. I went to go look for her in the entrance. But she stepped out into the mall area.

The flower she left at the desk. It wasn't a traditional red rose, like everyone does. This was a small purple daisy. It was hand-picked, and wrapped in paper and plastic like a rose would be. (Which some women knew about me, I would give them my attention, and give them flowers, candy, and jewelry.) (Well, I must not have had much money then, but I am sure I put my heart into it.) (This must be spring or summer, because we opened some double doors for some fresh air. It also makes sense that we are in a mall restaurant, because it is so narrow.)

(I'm sure my good-looking blonde girlfriend will be right back. She probably had to run an errand before the restaurant opened for lunch.) (Then I woke up). End

CHAPTER 47

'ABIDING'

There was an interesting article with Gloria Copeland in the: …. "Believer's Voice of Victory ".

It was talking about how important it is to be abiding in the True Vine, communing with Jesus everyday – anytime, through the Holy Spirit of God. To have overcoming victory in our lives. She started off very simple: *ref. Magazine quote: "There are two approaches to living the Christian life. One is to follow a set of rules: to focus on religious do's and don'ts and endeavor to live by them. That's called legalism, and it's hard. It's a recipe for frustration and failure.

The other approach is to simply stay in living contact with Jesus, and to focus on cultivating union with Him, that's much easier than legalism and it works a whole lot better. It's a recipe for joy and victory because it's the God-appointed method of living the Christian Life. As believers, we're divinely designed to live in union with Jesus! We've been made one spirit with Him through the new birth (I-Corinthians 6:17). He's living on the inside of us through the agency of the Holy Spirit. Our inner man has been re-created in His likeness and we've become partakers of His divine nature (II-Peter 1:4).

Talk about having it made! We don't need a bunch of religious rules to follow. We have within us the Good Shepherd who said, 'My sheep hear my voice... and they follow me' (John 10:27). We don't have to struggle to keep a long list of law's, we're one with Christ Himself. We just have to choose to walk in that oneness. The choosing is our part of the program. As much as Jesus loves us and desires to be involved in our lives, He won't make our choices for us. He won't just barge in on us and take over. That's not His style. Jesus isn't a dominator like the devil is. He waits for us to give place to Him. He operates according to the principle in (James 4:8): 'Draw nigh to God, and He will draw nigh to you.' (KJV) 'But, I don't know how to draw nigh to God,' someone might say. It's simple, you just turn your heart and mind toward Him in an attitude of faith and obedience. You just acknowledge His Lordship and His presence and begin to fellowship with Him by faith." (End quote)

(That's most of the first page; of course, there is more good stuff. She gives you five-key points to get you started.)

p5) #1 Through The new birth you have been united to Jesus. *ref. (I- Cor. 6:17).

#2. Maintaining living contact with Jesus enables you to walk in that oneness and produce the fruit of it. (John 15:4).

#3. If you don't stay in contact with Jesus, you will shrivel up Spiritually and become a victim of the world instead of a victor over it. (John 15:6).

#4. What you do with God's Word has everything to do with your abiding in Jesus. (John 15:7).

#5. When you make abiding in Jesus your top priority, you can tap into heavens resources. (Matt.6:33).

(End quote)

'MATTHEW DREAM'

There was this guy in the dream who was delivering a vacation trailer up north. Partly by faith, he had only a $100 —for the trip for gas and food and a place to park. From California, through Oregon and on to Washington state. (You could park in a Walmart parking area overnight if you knew where to go at no charge) (A camping spot for the night wouldn't run you over $100, but you would need all of that for gas, especially pulling something in real life). (It would be better to get a large cup of coffee and drive straight through in real life). (Spending one night in Oregon at a RV camp; and the next day go on up to Washington, is what my second wife and I did visiting her relatives in Oregon and Washington state).

This person who was driving, I thought it was me. But I only saw him from the back, he was tall with a good build, blondish-brown hair. (And for me, I have a few more years—of gray hair too on him).

Then I saw him, it was Matthew McConaughey. He was delivering this trailer to his girlfriend in Washington. So, one night he spent in Oregon and the next day, he delivered this long trailer, up there with his pick-up truck. He phoned her, and later he was going to do the paperwork with her, of all the title and stuff. But some man comes up to him, and they were both standing near the railway.

Matthew's girlfriend walks up and kisses him. She also was young, and tall, with long blonde-hair. She was light complected. And he said to her, 'I'll get with you later. 'Here are the papers, as he is looking over at the man. Then changes his mind, because of the man's presence, and says, 'I'm going to hang onto these for a couple of weeks and send it to you.' The man had just said something to him about where he was staying at, the previous night?

Matthew was trying to explain to this man. 'That is the way it is. One day you stay here and then there. One day you own a trailer and next you don't.' (woke-up) End.

Loren L. Johnson

'FORGIVENESS'

There is another article in the same magazine from 'Believers Voice of Victory,' by Kenneth Copeland. There is important information in it where forgiveness is tied to Faith, Love, Worship, Prayer, and being forgiven by God. ref. p26* The title of it is 'Keep the power flowing '(Then starts off with a question). *Quote: 'Did you know there is one place where Faith won't work? It's true. Even though Faith in God has the power to move mountains. Even though all things are possible to them who believe, and faith in God 's WORD will work in any nation, in any economy, and in any circumstances, there is one place where it will not work. Faith won't work in an unforgiving heart. Jesus made this clear in the Gospels. Although there are other hindrances to Faith, he repeatedly put unforgiveness at the top of the list.' 'When teaching on the prayer of Faith in Mark 11, for instance, he said: '"Have faith in God. For verily I say unto you, That whosoever shall say unto this mountain, Be thou removed and be thou cast into the sea; and shall not doubt in his heart, but shall believe that those things which he saith shall come to pass; he shall have whatsoever he saith. "KJV

"Therefore I say unto, What things so ever ye desire, when ye pray, believe that ye receive them, and ye shall have them: And when ye stand praying, forgive, if ye have ought against any; that your Father also which is in Heaven may forgive you your Trespasses "(v22-25). KJV

(End quote)

(Kenneth went on talking about a vision he had with Jesus and a plate of cookies.) It was a lesson on belief, receiving from God… Thanking Him for it, and lastly… 'I forgive if I have aught against any.'

(He goes on to explain the meaning)

'That this teaching was a spiritual principle or law, like the law of gravity in the natural. "Faith… worketh by love "(Galatians 5:6) and refusing to forgive is unloving. Therefore, holding onto unforgiveness short – circuits our Faith.' (End quote)

(Just like Gloria's message, Kenneth has five key points he wants you to know starting with):

*Quote #1. According to Jesus, to receive what we believe for when we pray, if we have anything against anyone, we must forgive them. (Mark 11:25).

#2. Forgiveness is an act of love, and apart from love faith won't work. (Gal. 5:6).

#3. Love is our New Testament Commandment. (John 13:34).

#4. You have the power to forgive anyone anytime of anything because you are born of God who is Love. (I-John 4:16).

#5. You don't have to be afraid to forgive those who've done you wrong; you can just love them. (I-John 4:18). (End quote)

CHAPTER 48

'COMM.—FORG.'

(This is a follow up for the end of chapter 47; for this is the commentary for forgiveness).

And this is a testimony of what the Lord showed me. Being in prison and going through unpleasant situation's that brought me back to dealing with my 2nd wife on a daily basis. I didn't have a name to call it, or how to fix it then at home. It was clouded by the sin of being right in my own eyes, and the alcohol to excess. It would have been better taking the ibuprofen until I didn't need it anymore, then becoming an Alcoholic. For my nerve damaged neck, and my vertebrae's out of joint. Before and after surgery.

Let's go to the first part of May 2021, where for days, I have been inquiring to the COs here and inmates about moving to an empty cell; Where not to bother anyone or offend anyone by my snoring. And out of the three buildings available 03,04,05. None have openings as of today. So, today when I was at PIA food packing, a brother in the Lord gave me a Scripture to read, (Matthew 7:12) 'The golden rule ', "Therefore, whatever you want men to do to you, do also to them, for this is the Law and the Prophets."

So, I was thinking if I was in his shoes; & I have been, with my last Cellie, but it didn't keep me up. Between my earplugs and my Christian radio in the headphones I had no trouble. Actually, it was not that bad, and frankly

I was use to it. My second ex-wife snores loudly. But my present Cellie is a light sleeper, I think. It has been bothering him, and wearing on him, for a little while now. I asked my Cellie if I snored? he downplayed it so much, like it was nothing. Also, he would go to sleep first too, so he didn't hear me if I did. He could sleep very easily. You could be talking to him, and the next minute, he's sleeping.

My present Cellie has not been so pleasant to me. He barely tolerates me. A dislike to a hate at times, unforgiving, unloving, grumpy, sharp or short with me. He resents me, with some envy and jealousy for I received my packages, and canteen, and got my stimulus sent to me in a check and was deposited in my Inmate account and his wasn't. And the canteen he did have was in someone else's name and that bag got lost for him, when trans-packing from building to building and yard to yard. I feel the tension in the air, how the resentment is so thick. He is mad at me, while holding it in. He has contempt for me and doesn't talk to me. I also don't have the same enthusiasm about sports as he does. I offer him food all the time, at first, he took a few things like chicken on the bone, but lately nothing. His heart was hard for me. He would serve me to be fair, and it was right to do. And for him and I to share responsibilities to the cell, as cleaning, and we did agree on that. So, I don't want to see him suffer on my account anymore. I need to get away from him. And ask for his forgiveness for causing him so many sleepless nights. I cannot help it, if I snore. Once I found out that I did, I thought it wasn't too bad, what others said about me as far as being loud or not. But cell living does amplify the problem. The concrete ceiling, walls, and floor, and it's close proximity.

So, I did try to concentrate on sleeping on my side, making sure my nose was clear, and I even lost 10 pounds from 200 to 190 pounds, and then asked him if it made a difference? Do you know, if it helped at all? Well, by this time, he was not talking to me, like he's mad at me, and just ignores me. It was a legitimate question.

Days later, he did answer me, when I asked him again. And he said, 'It is about the same.' What the Lord showed me by this experience. Of what this looks like, and how it started, and what it is? It is the results of unforgiveness. What does the word tell us about that?

In (Matthew 18:21-22). V21)" Then Peter came to Him and said, "Lord, how often shall my brother sin against me, and I forgive him? Up to seven times?" V22)" Jesus said to him, "I do not say to you, up to seven times, but up to seventy times seven."

(Which is 490 times; it wasn't an exact number, but more rhetorical, meaning: continually). To keep peace in the cell, with no anxiety or frustration, and no strife or tension. I will leave and have been for a few weeks now trying. In three buildings, so far, no luck of getting in with someone yet, but I will by God's grace amen. This is how it starts, as resentment that is unresolved, and needs to be forgiven for that thing. The snoring continued, because I can't control it. The resentment keeps building as days pass by, plus irritability on my bunkies behalf, because of lack of sleep. Which just adds more tension and strife, and pressure on me too.

And now I could tell something was bothering him in the beginning it was pretty obvious; so, I said to him, 'If I have done something to offend you, I am sorry.' And I was sorry; but I can't correct that thing and I think he knew it too. So, his response was, 'No, there's nothing wrong.' And I asked about him not speaking to me? And his response was that he didn't talk much, only for needed communication. It affected me talking, interacting with him, or trying to give him something was like pulling teeth, useful things but mostly food. But each time or day that goes by, his heart got a little harder, which could also affect his prayer life. The reason I know this, it is because my second wife reacted in a very similar way. So, when it was happening in the cell, it brought me all the way back to my wife and I in our conflict, and not forgiving each other daily. And to resolve those disputes, or arguments, at least by bedtime.

If you are upset and your anger is flared up. Pray to God, for a solution, and expect to see the answer to the problem. The Scripture says, In (Eph.

4:26–27) "Be angry, and do not sin; do not let the sun go down on your wrath, nor give place to the devil."

Even though God 's mercies are new every morning. Is yours and your spouse's forgotten in the morning? And not to bring it up again anymore? Or is it still unresolved? God wants you to forgive each other. So, He can forgive you, any trespasses, debts, or sins. We walk by faith, and not by sight. We walk in the light of the word of God and do what it says. If we walk by the Spirit of God, we will not fulfill the lust of the flesh. That our walk can be blameless, at the coming of our Lord. We are already righteous in God 's site, by faith in Jesus Christ for Salvation, He sent the Son of God and His obedience and love to willingly go to the Cross, for our redemption. And redeemed by His precious blood shed for our sins. He atoned the sins of the world and fulfilled the law. That He has Victory over sin and death. That we walk in the grace of His accomplishments. But we need to walk worthy of His Grace. So, forgiveness is a big lesson.

(Mark 11:25-26).

V25)" And whenever you stand praying, if you have anything against anyone, forgive him, that your Father in Heaven may also forgive you your trespasses.

V26) But if you do not forgive, neither will your Father in Heaven forgive your trespasses."

If we sin, we can act on: (I-John 1:9). V9)" If we confess our sins, He is faithful and just to forgive us our sins and cleanse us from all unrighteousness."

Since we are still this tent (body)of the flesh. But greater is He who is in me, then he who is in the world. We die to self and die to flesh. That the Spirit have victory in us, and we can be called Overcomers.

And we will fall short in this world; but that is part of the learning process. Get back up, dust the dirt off, confess the wrong. And be better next time. Hopefully not to keep repeating the same mistakes over and over. It took me a few times with the alcohol abuse. But, now in Christ, I can, and will be an Overcomer. In Him, abiding in Him, Overcoming Power from within, by the Holy Spirit of God, Amen. End

'MT. TOP DREAM'

At first, I was walking in the valley, singing in an amusement park. There are people all around me; and I am walking along singing, I have music inside my earphones. (In real life I had my headphones on listening to Christian music on Spirit Radio 88.9).

Now I'm on the side of the mountain, and hip-hop rap comes on. And someone changed the channel. Someone yells from the bottom of the hill, and says, 'It's satellite music, I said, 'I know ', Then he said, 'Be careful of the people in front of you. Like they were going to push me down the mountain? I just went around them.

And at the top of the mountain. Was a DJ playing the music. He is an older gentleman. He says, 'I got you. 'I'll be still playing your songs, and he showed me it, it was a gold record album. He had a turntable for my music, I said, 'Wow, old school.' (In real life, my second wife bought a commercial turntable for us to listen to our old albums). Then he asked me about one of the songs music or lyrics. I said, 'I don't know? ', I worked it out. The machine looks like an old cash register, and while it's playing, he is using a wrench on it. (In real life the machines in the PIA food packing plant, needs wrenches on it from time to time). Then, these golf balls came rolling out of it. (I guess because we are in an Amusement Park?) He says, play with these, and I'll play your music. End

'ROCKY RD. DREAM'

Dad and I were in the old Rambler station wagon, with his girlfriend and her daughter. We were at a cabin to spend some time on vacation. But, for some reason, my dad and his girlfriend didn't get along. And dad and I left down the road. The road was made of large rocks, yet we were driving over them. (In real life, this is during a possible Trans Pak to another building). And I looked over at my dad, who was 30 years plus younger at least, and I said, 'What happened?' And he just kept driving and didn't say anything. (In real life my dad passed away while I was inside, so he won't be talking to me again in this life, but he and I have the hope and faith of the next life; to talk again, God willing.)

I was frustrated and I wanted to know what was going on. We were headed for a man named Jean E. Sr. who was my dad 's boss at the time and mine. This cabin could have been a trade out for a carpet repair job. End

CHAPTER 49

'ASSEM.STONE'

This is in support for AB292(stone) 'Access to programming Act', a form letter, and then you add your part.

Assembly member stone:

I write in support of your AB292 (stone) bill, known as the access to programming act. This bill will remove barriers to accessing programs such as long waiting list, frequent transfers, and inflexible work schedules that conflict with program availability, while also ensuring that programming continues during lockdowns. This bill also creates a path for people who have their 'VIO' determinate removed to earn half time.

I support this bill because… Access to programming, is one-way Inmates can move one step closer to home: besides getting an education, and or a trade for the outside. Learning classes, GED (your equivalent high school diploma), or other merited classes. To help engage a person's mind, and to move in a positive direction. Especially, with the rehabilitative classes. I took a lot of them when I first came into the prison system in 2015 and 16. But, there wasn't any milestone credits back then.

I took them to get well, to learn where I went wrong, and correct my pattern of bad behavior, to confess my miss behaviors, and be willing to change, your mind and attitude to positive, with spiritual freedom, and to show my relatives, I am working on myself, for the better.

God has set me free, through Spiritual and Educational Programs like 12-Step Celebrate Recovery. We need these kinds of programs made available to Inmates. Not only for time off, but for Hope and for Deliverance.

Thank you for your time and consideration. Sincerely, Loren Johnson (End).

'2-MIC'S DREAM'

This dream starts off in a bar, with a country singer on stage; he was giving me advice if I went up and perform with him. I was there with my sister and her friend of the same approximate age. The country singer said to me, to come up there with him, and if I am nervous, don't show it. In front of him was two mics', to sing from, as the band is ready to play. (In real life I did like country music, but I love Christian music more.) (In real life, the only true country bar in town is the Buck Owens Crystal Palace, and I do have a sister and she does have her long-standing girlfriend from high school.) (And in real life, it could be Buck Owens son Buddy Allen, whom I haven't met. But I have seen and heard Buck Owens and Georges Jones, and Clint Black in person in Bakersfield. (And as a teenager, at The Buck Owens Bakersfield Country Club Golf Celebrate Classic, I met a lot of Celebrities. To raise money for cancer research. I got an autograph from Tennessee Ernie Ford who is a country singer too.)

Now, I'm going up to use one of the two mics, and show my sister and her friend I can. But one was turned down, so I had them turn it up the same as the other.

(In real life when I was at a private prison in McFarland, California, called GSMCCF. I was in the worship team for three years and part of the last year, the lead singer (Ernie)was also the choir Director who actually did an excellent job at his work. Anyway, he would turn down my microphone a little, because I had a strong lower voice, and he didn't want me to overpower his. But, toward the end of our time there. He let me adjust it to what I needed. He delegated others to lead songs, and he said I blended in nicely with the rest of the group. That we sounded nice together. That is because of prayer, and the Holy Spirit helping us perform.) End

'2-CR. CARD DREAM'

This dream is about a woman and I walking around this rectangle Atrium area at a Commercial Office Complex before dinner. I needed to make reservations at this exclusive restaurant, that was on multiple floors. There was window seating to those patrons who are blessed to see the trees and the plants and the ponds below.

I went up to make reservations and to see if I have enough money to cover the dinner with cash? I had just got out, and I didn't have my two-credit cards, American Express and Visa. (In real life, they went into foreclosure do to nonpayment. And after seven years you can start over, so I was told.)

Now, the woman and I went down the street, while waiting for dinner. And we, or I cut a limb off a tree for some odd reason. And took it with us a while. Then the dream changed, and we came to a house, even though we need another? The people in the house were remodeling from a mobile home, to building their own house, little by little. (In real life I do need a new home.)

They had big lights in each room. Two- 4-burners gas stoves, and a dishwasher. (In real life there is no gas-dishwasher that I know of.) This house was small, with a simple design. And practically everything in the same room. (In real life, that is like a motorhome, which my second wife and I had for about five years.) (In real life, when I remodeled a room in our house, I would set-up these two-big spotlights so I could work and see what I was doing.) (We had bought a new four-burner electric stove for the house with a double-oven, and in the Motorhome, it was a three-burner gas stove.)

These people we talked to were retiring... (In real life, like us.)

Now, it jumps back to the restaurant, outside there, where there are fountain pools to look at. And again, for some unknown reason, we waited through the water there that was about 3 to 4 feet deep, and it had a diagonal current. By the time we got to the other side, I figured a better way to tread water and she didn't. (You could say in real life, the struggles, as going against the currents of life, but learning to adapt to your environment, like the apostle Paul; to be content in all circumstances, amen.) (But, in real life there was a time on vacation my second wife and I were on a Wave Runner and was about to go out into the main part of Shaver Lake. But she had no balance whatsoever, and we dumped it before we got to go out into the deep.

At a 1/2 mph. turning slightly to our relatives on the shore. And away we went. Her life-jacket rode-up on her and she was having trouble to adjust. So, I said to relax, and I'll pull you from behind to shore and I did, with the help of the Wave Runner putting us in at idle speed.)

(More on the interpretation of this two-credit card dream. I was about to go onto the next chapter. When the Holy Spirit gave me the answer to why I cut the limb off in my dream? There was a book given to me a few days ago by a past Cellie of mind. Because he knew I have been writing books for years now and including dreams in them. So, the answer was in Sigmund Freud book; 'The interpretation of dreams.' At first, I didn't read it, and didn't think I would find much in this over 100-year-old book, coming from a secular and psychologists' viewpoint. But I did find something, and in the third chapter, called 'A dream is the fulfillment of a wish.' And also in that chapter, on page 149, in his reference at the bottom, In KJV (Isaiah 29:8): 'It shall even be as when an Hungry man dreameth, and behold, he eateth; but he awaketh, and his soul is empty: or as when a thirsty man dreameth, and behold, he drinketh; but he awaketh, and behold, he is faint, and his soul hath appetite.'

In most of the chapter gives at least a half a dozen persons who have similar dreams of wishes, including his children. In all these dreams, including mine, was a dream fulfillment that didn't happen in real life for some reason. Plans change, or put off for another time, so what you wish for didn't happen in real life. You had to experience it in your dreams to make it happen.

In the verse with (Is. 29:8). The man was physically thirsty and hungry. And he satisfied himself in his dream. But when he awakened, he was still thirsty and hungry. I had trimmed the trees and bushes and cut the grass at my second wife and I's nice home. And there was one limb on our big pine tree that my wife planted when it was in a test tube size. The limb I was going to cut, was about 10 inches in diameter, with a lot of branches. I cut through it about 1/3 of the way through and stopped. I had just cleaned up the side of the house, from the last limb mess. So, I put it on hold for another time. Well, that never happened, and that was about seven years now since I have been down. I think about it from time to time, that I wished, I had cut that branch, and it wouldn't be on my mind now.)

And the verses in Isaiah chapter 29 speak of woe to Jerusalem, but even more to those nations who would fight against her. For He who said He is coming, He is going to come. (Rev. 22:12-17). V12)" And behold, I am coming quickly, and My reward is with Me, to give to everyone according to his work. V13) I am the Alpha and the Omega, the Beginning and the End, the First and the Last. V14) Blessed are those who do His commandments, that they may have the right to the tree of life, and may enter through the gate into the city. V15) But outside are dogs and sorcerers and sexually immoral and murderers and idolaters, and whoever loves and practices a lie. V16) I, Jesus, have sent My angel to testify to you these things in the churches. I am the Root and the Offspring of David, the bright and Morning Star. V17) And the Spirit and the bride say, "Come!" And let him who thirsts come. Whoever desires, let him take the water of life freely. " (NKJV)

(Jesus is that living water; Believe in Him; Trust in Him. Repentance toward God, and Faith in the Lord Jesus Christ.) pp. ref. (John 8:37-39) and (Acts 20:21). End

CHAPTER 50

'YACHT DREAM'

I was on top of this big boat. And it had a single seat hot tub on it with a hard cover. And steam was coming out the back. The water was hot, and it was cold outside, but I wanted to use it. But I had work to do downstairs. There was a toilet I had to install first. And I was preparing this one fixture to be put in, except I was only doing one side with the bolts and was going to do the other in the bathroom. (In real life you would put together what you could in a comfortable place and space, and your nuts, bolts, washers, wax ring, water supply hose, etc. In the bathroom and build your toilet outside the bathroom, [and use a toilet dolly]; like some like to do it in place, because of the weight of handling the pieces, instead of the whole thing put together.) …

Now, there is some lady in there watching TV, a football game is on. She is not using the bathroom but watching the game in private. So, I turned on the TV in this living room area, which had a remote handy. It had a monitor on the remote. I turned the power on and was going to get the game on what she was watching so I could go in there and finish installing the toilet. But I was flipping through the channels, and with this fancy remote. I couldn't figure out how to get the channel? One had this game and the remote had another. Then it went split screen, and I was about to tell the person to come out and put it on out here when I… (Woke up).

(In real life, recently I was watching the transformers on TV in the dayroom. And wanted to turn up the volume. Because it is usually no sound on it. But there were three or four of us watching it from our benches. The remote was there, and I was pushing the volume-up, but nothing was happening. So, I handed it off to someone else, and he had the same results. So, then finally I tried one more time. There was a second volume on the remote. And I got it turned up.) End

'MANSION DREAM'

I was in this Big Mansion, and through the window, I saw what I thought was my sister, but it wasn't. And she was hugging some of our relatives, like my aunt or my ex-wife. I wanted to be there and couldn't see well through the glass. So, I went outside and went toward them. And it was dark outside, but beyond them in the distance, the light was on. She walked away and they're walking through me, but didn't stop, only touched hands. But I thought she was going to introduce me? So, I continued and went to the light in the backyard. Then I could see how big the estate was. Huge. And I was looking for the back gate to get back in. And there was a mound of dirt I had to get over. I looked down, it was about a 12" drop down to a walking bridge. And two people were on it, a man and a boy. So, I knew I had better go farther down to a safer way to the walking bridge. To go back inside again, as I close my eyes, and I wasn't scared as dirt was falling, as I moved lower, and then ...... (I woke up). End

'FUTURE CAR DREAM'

I was with my first ex-wife, and we were about to get on the freeway. The 178 curve at Golden State Highway, but I stopped halfway up? I was so excited, I had to show her right now. This, what look like a toy. Was a prototype car of the future with a molded body called Sacarr. She was only relatively impressed.

Then the dream jumps later that day, we were at some function, and about to leave this house. And I had to show her again this new invention. I had a business suitcase and opened it up and showed her the model again. This is it, Sacarr, then I started talking about how great it was. And she says, 'Isn't this the one Tim opened up at mom and dads?' I said, 'That was another car, with windows and doors that opened. That one's nice too. But, completely different.' (Tim is our son, and it was about a Christmas or birthday only in the dream.) This is the car I showed you earlier today. She thought it was a birthday or Christmas present for our son when we went shopping earlier that day. (I woke up)

(In real life, being with my first wife and first child, would put the timeframe in the early part of the 1980s. But this event didn't happen. But the future car probably came from the movies I had watched in the past, that was in my subconscious or memories.) (Like in future time-period movies, with Michael J. Fox, Sylvester Stallion, Arnold S., Tom Cruz, Shawn Claud Van dam, Will Smith, all made future car movies). End

CHAPTER 51

'CLINT DREAM'

This was a dream with Clint Howard, but I don't remember the details except he was the one I was to pray for now. Not his brother, his brother is a famous actor and Director. But Clint had his own show too, as a child star in 'Gentle Ben.' A boy and his bear. I actually am old enough to recall, and I watched it too. I like the show. And his brother Ron Howard is nice enough to put him in all his movies that he directs when he can. End

'LOBBY DREAM'

I was repairing the carpet in a lobby of a Hotel-Restaurant. A busy hallway to other businesses, restrooms and waiting area. The restaurant was closing, or just relocating their reservation podium. A man came over and removed the podium. He was probably from management, and he left a square hole about 6 inches each way. The floor is made of plywood, and the podium was just toenailed in. (Meaning some small finish nails were put in diagonally through the base into the wooden floor.) Then he left some carpet and pad scraps from the original installation. And he walked away. So, I started to put in the pad scrap first. But, needed to remove the tack strip around it and clean it up first. As I was working, I was kidding around, and talking out loud to myself or whoever was walking by.

Pretending, as a joke if anyone was listening, I said, "Hey! Who stole the podium? If it is not nail down around here, people walk off with anything, oh yeah, it was nailed down here, and it is still gone." In the dream, I don't think I impressed anyone walking by. I just continued to work, but I don't see my Toolbox and Carpet-Iron to have the tools to put them back together as one piece again. Basically, what we call a patch-job. To make it look as invisible as possible. (Woke up). End

'TWO-STORY DREAM'

My dad and I are on a two-story old house job, and he and I were measuring for carpeting. The house was just in a storm or some disaster. One room is all settled and being the lowest sunken room. It had one to one and a half feet of water still in it. (In real life, especially in the wintertime, we would get a certain amount of Insurance Jobs, through the different retailers who sold the carpet and other flooring needs to the customers.) Also:

(In real life, my second wife and I had a 2 1/2 story house, with a sunken living room, (which means the floor is 6 inches lower than the main floor or the rest of the downstairs living area.) ....it was close to what I was dreaming, but a completely different home; and the disaster was me before coming to prison unfortunately.) End

CHAPTER 52

'KELSEY II DREAM'

This dream, Kelsey and I are at some Industrial area. For about one minute, we were chasing bad guys. Kelsey cuts over going after one of them in the bushes. 'I got you!' he says, he said some other line in his unique voice that he has.

And now Kelsey was doing some surveying, and spray painting the ground with numbers. Then he went to this main aisle-way walking really slow and careful. And I checked out what he wrote in paint. And I could hardly read it. One said 35 and the other three or eight. I'm not sure? So, I start to yell to him, to ask him if he wanted me to re-paint, it a little more readable. The paint was too close together, but something was going on to my left, and the same direction Kelsey was pointing. I started to get his attention a few times by yelling out his name. It seemed like we were close friends and working together on some project. So, each time I yelled out, I got a little closer so he could hear me. He originally was about 50 feet away. I ended up going all the way to where he was, and asked, 'Do you want me to go over those paint markers? I could barely read it.' He looks at me and says, 'No, (pause) Oh, yes go ahead". But, instead of me fixing that. I just kept walking with him straight in his direction.

We saw some things set-up and running. But it was dark, and no one was around. As we walked closer, it was movie cameras, 5 to 6 of them lined up next to each other running. Then some other movie equipment running as well. And we are walking right into it and realized it and ducked down.

Then there is a sound machine that's recording something on a screen. Meanwhile, I'm thinking the movie studio company is going to have to edit that out of the picture. I'm thinking, I hope they don't charge us for it, or fine us? Anyway, I slid underneath the rays of this machine that was going on. And he was also looking for a way out of this room too. Feeling a little embarrassed walking into it. When I slid to the other side, I ended up in a department store, with the lights on. And people all around. I started walking down the hallway, thinking, "What in the world, what am I doing here?" (And I woke up.)

(And realized, I'm dreaming, but at 4:45 AM went back to sleep, back where I left off walking in the hallway, but was more enclosed in the inter-rooms.) ...In titled: 'Robert Dream'. ....

'ROBERT DREAM'

I walked in this hallway to these different sets. Movie sets of different scenes were happening in each set. Stairs here, doors there, oops? You don't want to go down those narrow-tunneled stairs. (I guess in real life I dreamt this other dream before I got to the hallway dream). I just escaped, the gas station scene and killing this long snake and he was dead, but the person turned into a snake inside. So, I got into my truck and got out of there as soon as possible, and others jumped on too, they wanted out of there also. (In real life I was watching Spider-Man, and he was fighting a human lizard). And now I am walking again, still leaving, but I can choose of two movie sets. One old -time Cowboy Western and one more modern as I was leaving. I saw one of my favorite actors, from the star of 'Wild, Wild, West,'...the original with Robert Conrad. He was doing a regular part of a man helping some people in the Old West. In the 19th century, setting. (Then I woke up). End

'GBOYH DREAM'

I was at this Tournament, and there were different levels, for the game, and physically. I climbed this block wall to the next level. And men were talking and sitting all around me. I jumped up and lost my balance, and I went over the edge, but I did it in a way that I'll land on my feet. (Like a cat). And I did it and went around and climbed it again. I had a case with me. A small – rectangular case. What could that be? I was going to enter a game of pool. (At the top of the block wall) (With a breakdown pool stick). It was a professional billiard pool game tournament. (In real life, I use to own a pool table, actually two of them, at different points of my adolescence.)

(Also falling off the wall, remind me of GBOYH – 'Get back on your horse.' Or keep trying, keep moving forward, endurance, determination, don't give up. Amen). End

CHAPTER 53

'GIRLFRIEND DREAM'

I had a girlfriend, and she had a little boy, and we were walking into the house. And she was singing with a beautiful voice, "Peace be still", and one part when she went up a whole octave higher. I started singing with her a little softer, I wasn't that familiar with the song. (In real life, typically I have a tenor to bass voice.) I said, 'you really hit that one, and even went up another octave; she said, something in her own way. About we got this, and we will take it one step at a time. (Meaning our relationship and not responding about the singing.) Then I helped carry her boy over as I said something like, 'we are flying over the gorge of this area.' (In real life, I had my headphones on with my Christian music.) end.

'GIRLFRIEND DREAM II'

(This is in reverse order of knowing...her.) This dream is where I just met her as I was standing there in this medical or health food store to buy something or waiting for something. And there was a weight scale up on the counter. And there was a boy asking about it? What is that? I said, 'to weigh you, 'Do you want to know how much you weigh?' 'Yes', he answered. I looked to his mother as she nods yes. I picked him up and put him on the scale. He didn't weigh much, as I put him down and his mother asks, 'can I use your calculator?' And I said, 'yes', 'but you have to clear it first.' She starts to use it standing up all bent over. I said, 'have a seat,' and said it again. The second time I put my hand on the small of her back. But she preferred to stand. And I woke up, but I knew she was the one from my last dream as my girlfriend. So, this was our first meet. (In real life, at PIA packing plant, at CSP, we had a scale on the counter to weigh boxes). End

'GIANT DREAM'

I had a dream of doing a job with a utility room that had a drain in it. Then I find myself walking down the street. And was in a dispute, in an argument over something. Except one was a regular man, and the other a giant, like 40–50 feet tall. And it was getting dark. And I couldn't see him that well. No streetlights, and the police was trying to hear them out, each one's story. I stayed a minute and went down to a house, and there was a 4-foot-high chain-link fence and teenage girls in the yard. And they two were young police officers for the future. One was wearing a badge, and another on her shirt; It said, 'Little Lieutenant.' About a half a dozen of them. Then I went into the yard, and I knew the parents. They were all working on a construction pool project together for the girls, because they were all swimmers too, and making a special lap pool. (I woke up). …. (In real life, after PIA, I was waiting for the shower, and on the State-Movie was an Indian family (from India). About this one girl and she was a great soccer player, and she had a lot of teenage girlfriends. So, in my dream I made them swimmers instead, and potential police officers.) (Also in real life, the COs are all around us and they are police officers keeping the peace.) (The Giant in my dream could be the C.O. or Correctional Officer up in the tower.) (Or it could be that part in the first Transformer movie, where these machine robot like men Giants, are in the dark in the kid's backyard hiding from his parents.) (Which I saw a few times, being it was a State-movie too.)

CHAPTER 54

'FISHING DREAM'

This fishing dream is also during war time. There we were a bunch of guys on a lake with boats along the shore. We were fishing and trolling around. We had our gear, and our bait, and poles. There were two groups of us. We partnered up, but we hadn't caught anything yet. And, wasn't deterred, but was going to pray – through and continue on.

Nearby there was the enemy who actually wanted and tried to take our boats out with these bombs that they dropped from a hot-air balloon, and it splashed into the water and was propelled coming our way. Like a magnet type, looking for metal, with a timer and so many seconds, and 'Boom'! And just before it got to us, it went off, and the water went up 10 feet high in a circle of about 15 foot in diameter. And there was another 5 to 10 feet away from that. And we continued on like nothing happened. And prayed some more. Thank God. And then threw our lines out once again. (And then I woke up.) .....

(Interpret Fishing Dream)

(Since today we went out of the Institution to the eye doctor. There was a group of men, one in a bus and the other in an SUV-car of CO's). And there was prayer and guidance that I asked for from God. I was praying for the men, (The Inmates and COs for Salvation & or Sanctification in Jesus name, amen.)

There was a brief quiet time, and the COs were outside. When The guy in front of me, I wanted to talk to and ask him if he is at Christian? And does he know Jesus as his Savior and Lord. But he didn't respond, in fact, didn't respond at all.

I took it as the enemy hardened his heart and wasn't going to give me the satisfaction of even a nibble of fishing. So, with some more prayers asking for God 's Will to be done and asking God to guide me who you want me to talk to about your Son Jesus Christ. And express your Word and my Testimony of how I came to know you too. And in the waiting room upstairs in an office. There was a man who didn't know Jesus as Lord and Savior yet. But I first told him, 'God loves you'. That God sent His Son Jesus Christ to die on the Cross for our sins. And told him (John 3:16) NKJV

V16)" For God so loved the world that He gave His only begotten Son, that whoever believes in Him should not perish but have everlasting life."

(And my Testimony, coming to the Lord in my 20s. How I was drinking alcohol, and then I got into some trouble, and I was convicted by the Holy Spirit of the wrong that I was doing. That night as I was watching TBN on TV, as I was flipping through the channels. I prayed the sinner's prayer and repented of my sins, believe the Word of God and accepted Jesus in my heart by Faith. That's it).

He didn't say much, but that's OK, as the word says, preach the word, in season and out of season.

Paul seeds, Apollos waters, but God gives the increase. I had invited him many times, and places for Christian English and Spanish services on the yard. And the next day gave him a gospel track for him to read and respond when the Holy Spirit was ready with him, amen. End

'Store Dream'

We were around the back of this building, my dad and I and one of my dogs. [I think it was China. —. (That's her greyhound's name.) She had what they call a China eye, one brown and one the other blue.] In real life: She died just prior to me coming into prison. She was my favorite. She was a very sweet and loyal dog. When I was sick in bed or recuperating as I was for my neck surgery. She was right there for me. I would take her and her sister for walks over at my dad's house, a block and a half away. Then they would play in his backyard. Stay a while and then take them home.) ....

We were in my pick-up truck; we were done inside the store building. But the dog was gone, she must've jumped out of the pick-up. So, I left my dad in the truck, and I ran down around the corner of the building and found her running around. She came and we headed back to the truck. We came around the corner and now the truck was gone and my dad inside. I thought oh, I left my keys in the ignition. And my dad was looking for me. But he didn't come back. (In real life my dad passed away on 11-7-20; He was 98 years old and my best friend.)

There were some people in the back of the store. The parking lot was empty where we were. And at night, it probably was closing now. I asked one young man; can I use your cell phone? And he said, 'No! (pause) ha, ha, yes', and then he says, 'sure, it's right here.' It was huge and complicated; The last phone I had was a flip phone that I dialed 911 in 2014. (I woke up)

'The Flood Dream'

In the dream, I was a baby, and I was on my mother's shoulders. And we survived 'The Flood' in the town. We were right next to it when the Dam broke. We were riding the waves, and my mother was body surfing. And she steered us to the left to the shore, and we were saved. Then years later the dream jumps forward where I was talking to these men who had these old 35 mm cameras. They had film in them and then, they didn't. And I wanted to take some pictures; (I was an amateur photographer in real life.) (Also now, today everyone's a photographer with their cell phones, pictures, videos, etc. ... But I used to carry a Camera everywhere I went. And took unique pictures.) (Also In real life, that's before the cell phone had cameras in them. Then when flip phones did have cameras or Internet capable, I didn't use it, too expensive.) So, he says, 'you can use them and take your pictures and bring it back, but you need to get film in the camera first.' So, I left there and went to the convenience store on the corner, it looks like a liquor store. (In real life, back in the day, they also sold 35 mm, and 110 mm and did developing. 100 speed film – for standing still pictures; 200 speed for walking; 400 speed for running; and 800 speed for absorbing light and quick motion like fireworks, 1600 speed, for long-term light absorbing time shots, where it is set up on a tripod, because the shutter will be open for a period of time at night.) .... But it was closed, and there was policeman all around, but I didn't do anything wrong. Except the two cameras he wanted me to borrow, they were stolen that morning. And very expensive relics because they were cameras that survive the flood. (In real life the flood with my mom, the men, the two cameras, the policeman, the liquor store with film never happened.) (In real life the last two cameras I had, was an automatic digital camera and a nice 35 mm.) So, I just headed for my vehicle which in the dream was one of my old vans. And apparently it also had carpet or vinyl material in the back sticking out, and I noticed the van back doors needed to be bungeed closed before I go. (In real life this could mean; It was said by me that I was the disaster, my wife who is 10 years older than me, symbolize my mother, who was scolding me with a tongue lashing, and me being a small child on the ground on my knees bent over.) End

CHAPTER 55

'DUCKS DREAM'

(The first dream was about getting my ducks in a row. First things first and so on. Get ready, prepared beforehand like it's going to happen.) The actual dream had me standing with these wooden quarter inch flat pictures, and in the shape of a duck. And setting them in little teacup saucers. And lining them up in a straight line, and you will—put my ducks in a row.

[The second dream – was about Education, housing, jobs. Working on one old house, buying low, and selling high. And at the same time doing something else (meaning a new job) in small steps(increments) or saving something gradually.] In the dream, I was using these small boards from one house to the other as an example.

(In this dream, was about that I should write down some goals, things that I actually will be doing, when I get out, God willing all goes well according to the Father's will, through the Lord Jesus, and done in the Holy Spirit amen.) End

'FREEWAY DREAM'

I was dreaming of driving down the road by my grandparents' home. A familiar street that leads straight into Valley Plaza Mall (which is our large mall in Bakersfield). The road was under construction, the side that I was on, or I should say we were on. My second wife and I are in our Toyota Camry car. It was always like new; we hardly drove it. Well, that day we were traveling on a torn-up road under construction, retrofit of an expanding highway. Like a two lane to a 4 Lane Highway, one lane at a time. Well, the new cement lane was done to the right of us. So, I came in at a slight angle and jumped up to the new cement lane. It was just asphalt before that. Everything was running fine for quite a while and then the nice road ended. And instead of pointing south, we are pointed north. The road was wide and deep. It was dirt now, and the more we traveled on this road, it was going downhill into the earth, and I didn't see an exit. I said to her, 'We need to get off this road and get over to the exit'. (In real life, my wife and I on vacation, up near Carson City. I took a wrong exit, because of two exit names (a, & b) and loops. Then we got off the freeway onto the shoulder in the dirt, and back to the turn off, back to the loop exit, on the highway we needed to travel on, in the class 'A' motorhome.) dream…

But, instead of going up to the road, we had to go down this dirt hill or embankment first to go up again. The car is gone and two of us are on foot, down this dirt hill. We made it, and a door to go through, I was on the right and her on the left, and she tripped on something and fell to the ground. My wife, nicely dressed in black-slacks and a pretty blouse. Her hair and make-up were flawless. She landed on the dirt with rich soil. Real dark. But, when she stood up, remarkably she wasn't that dirty; and she had a good attitude, she was cheerful, and we were going to carry on, but the dream ended. End ….

(Interpret of this dream)

(First of all, in real life, it is a 2 Lane Rd. in a residential neighborhood, and probably will never be a cement highway.) (The first part of 'the rough road' was about arguments and compromise, mostly on my part for two years. So, the road was a little bumpy. 'Then the cement road was good', we had a pretty good life together with adventures and recreation for about 8 to 9 years.)

('Then the road went wide and deep into the Earth,' like you are putting in an underpass, and you can't back up.) (But, instead of 'going down that deep road', there was another to the left except it was steep and all dirt, and we had to get out and walk down the dirt hill and go through a doorway at the bottom.)

(As far as 'pointing South first, and then North.' At one time my wife wanted to go to Houston Texas, which is South, and then she wanted to go to Idaho, which is North of us.) ... (The dirt hill we went down was the years we both were recuperating, mentally, physically, emotionally, and Spiritually. Her on the outside and me on the inside, in prison).

(Then, 'the door' represented getting through and having victory over and getting past this part of our lives. She and I had to heal, to forgive each other our shortcomings, and be well of all the things mentioned above. And when I talked to her, five-years to the day of coming incarcerated. She got closure with me and wished me a happy life, and I wished her the same.)

('The falling down' represented her being the victim in the beginning and when 'she stood,' no dirt stuck to her, she was clean, with a good attitude to start her life again in the fullest. And also, a new life for me too, as we walk into this brightly lighted room.) End

'ROBERT DI NERO DREAM'

We were at this exclusive Restaurant-Hotel-Casino, and I was with his family. Not as family, but as a friend or observer. Robert was explaining to his family how nice it would be staying here and explaining all the amenities it had. He said to his wife that if you want to play the slots in here you can. Because you are part of the hotel package. They were eating at this one indoor restaurant. And I noticed a man standing in the aisle way just staring out. I figured he was security there. And this other man was making noises with his mouth. Real annoying, and then I went back sitting down by myself, but I could hear Robert's voice. And then he said, 'Wait till we get to go to Shaver Lake and then, I'll explain about the water and sand dunes and the home on the beach you could stay.' He is explaining in that comic-voice like in the movie, 'Meet the Focker's'. It was so funny. When I woke up, ... laughing!

But before that I was at this big home next to some sand dunes and there was grass in the yard. I had a lawnmower and was cutting the grass. It was tall only in some areas. It seemed to be that I had been at this beach area before and looked around again. No, similarity and kept moving.

(In real life Shaver Lake is in the mountains, and the sand dunes are for the Pacific Ocean, which was a separate vacation trip). End

CHAPTER 56

'DISC. / ST./ BAP.'

This was a discipleship class number two and on the study of baptism, (recapping).

Last week we did the study using the study pamphlet from a Baptist Church on the outside. But we are going to discuss again the definition of 'The baptism with the Holy Spirit and what water baptism is about; out of the Expositor's New Testament, with (JSM)(KJV)p1117'

*Quote: Now that you are saved, you should ask the Lord to baptize you with the Holy Spirit (Acts 2:4).

While it is certainly true that the Holy Spirit came into your heart and life the moment of your Salvation, still, he now wishes to endue you with power from on high. Consequently, Jesus told all of His followers immediately before His Ascension, that they should "wait for the Promise of the Father (Acts1:4). He was speaking of being "Baptized with the Holy Spirit." (Acts 1:5). You must understand that there is a great difference in being "born of the Spirit" than being…" Baptized with the Spirit." They are two different works altogether. To be "Born of the Spirit" is that which took place at your conversion, as the Holy Spirit brought you to Christ and performed the work of regeneration within your heart and life. To be "Baptized with the Spirit" is in order that you may have power with God

(Acts 1:8). Every believer should ask the Lord to fill them with the Holy Spirit and expect to receive (Luke 11:13). (End quote)

V13)" If you then, being evil, know how to give good gifts unto your children: how much more shall your Heavenly Father give the Holy Spirit to them who ask Him? "KJV (He will give you the Holy Spirit to those who ask Him.) …. Testimony:

I asked to be Baptized in the Holy Spirit. Weeks or months after I was saved in my early 20s at my conversion when I repented of my sins, believing the Word of God that evening on TV by a preacher-about forgiveness of sins, and Faith in Jesus Christ for Salvation by the Grace of God. Meaning His gift of eternal life for me. Receiving the down payment of the Holy Spirit, as a guarantee. Christ redeemed me by His shed blood on the Cross at Calvary. His sacrifice for the sins of the world, 'Once for all.'

When I came into prison, I repented again for similar sins and more; excessive alcohol drinking, confusion, pride, lust, perverted-thinking, depression, suicide, unbelief, sickness. But this time I got on my knees and ask God to forgive my bad behavior. Not for salvation again – but a right relationship with God again. As sin separates you from Him. As you draw near unto Him, He will draw near onto you. Especially with a contrite heart. You be real with Him, honest and true in your heart, and He will respond to you.

I was doing a carpet job on the outside at this motel across from the Hospital in Bakersfield. And the manager came in as I was working in the back room. He said something to me about if I had a cold or something? I said, I had what the doctor calls, 'chronic sinusitis.' About every 3 to 4 months, I was sick with this virus, that usually went into a bacterial lung infection. So, I would be on antibiotics for at least two weeks sometimes a little more. Penicillin, Ampicillin, or Amoxicillin. He is a Christian and asked if I wanted to be healed …. I said, 'Yes, I hate being sick.' So, he prayed for me, and I believed God would heal me. And He did, I never had it again. I have been sick, but not like that anymore.

'Thanks be to God—Amen! 'Then he says, 'Do you want to receive the baptism of the Holy Ghost?' And I being a new Christian, asked, 'what is that?' He said, 'it is more of God in you.' So, I said, 'I am all for that, more of God.' He said, 'you will receive the gift of tongues,' I said, 'what is that?' 'What do I do to get it?' He said, 'just praise God, and thank Him for your gifts. Just keep praising God.' I did it, and all of a sudden, my lips were moving without me doing it. And making strange sounds. Later I found out that is the gift of unknown tongues. Spoke of in the Scriptures, ... (I-Corinthians 14: 1,2). V1)" Pursue love, and desire spiritual gifts, but especially that you may prophesy. V2) For he who speaks in a in a tongue does not speak to men but to God, for no one understands him; however in the spirit he speaks mysteries, "NKJV

This is speaking of the unknown tongue or language to God. Verse 1 says: 'Pursue love'. As the climax to first Corinthians 13:1-13, about Love. V13)" And now abide faith, hope, love, these three; but the greatest of these is love. "NKJV

Love is the most important thing. Love saves you. It's as simple as that, and that's true, Love is God, and God saves you. God is a Spirit. He also manifested Himself through His Son Jesus Christ while He was here on earth. (John 1:14) "And the Word became flesh and dwelt among us, and beheld His glory, the glory as of the only begotten of the Father, full of grace and truth. "Then in (Titus 2:13) says Jesus is God......" looking for the blessed hope and glorious appearing of our great God and Savior Jesus Christ,"

Let's get back to (I-Cor. 14:1) ... 'desire spiritual gifts'; it's ok to ask for gifts from our 'Spiritual Heavenly Father. The rest of the verse, 'but especially that you may prophesy. (There are 2-definition's prophesy in the dictionary, (#1 is to speak or utter by divine inspiration.) (As I am now, speak God's Word of Truth) & (#2 is one who predicts or foretells future events.) Which I am not doing. And verse two of (I-Cor.14:2), "For he who speaks in a tongue does not speak to men but to God, "(So, it is not a language that any man, or any language on earth could understand, but God can.) To finish the verse, 'for no one understands him; however in the spirit he speaks mysteries," Before I read the definition of the Sign of being filled with the Spirit.

(On pg. 1118) JSM-N.T. Greek translation.

The Holy Spirit gave me Revelation in September 2020. Here's the answer: I got that, deposit or down payment of the Holy Spirit, at Salvation – by the grace of God, through faith in Jesus Christ. And using a car as a metaphor for Salvation with the Holy Spirit –God put a down payment on your car. (You own it.) And you didn't pay for it or work for it; it was a gift to you. (Jesus did it for you). You have that gift, that car, it is yours, God is with you, (in the car.) God is in you. God will never leave you, nor forsake you. Now, when you are baptized in the Holy Spirit —He pours or infills you with more of Himself, the Holy Spirit (Ghost). And when it happens there is evidence of speaking in tongues… Now, you have gas to put in your car. That's what gives you power, to go. The Holy Spirit empowers you, if you will let Him.

Still there is a will of Choice. (The ultimate goal is we decrease, and He increases in our lives, Amen). Then continuing that infilling when you come to church. As you are praising Him in worship; you're asking Him to bless you (He infills you.'). And when you hear the word of God in faith, receiving spirit in life. ('He infills you'). Which 'God willing,' we will get into after fully explaining baptism.

#3) The Importance of the 'Word of God.'

Let's read (JSM) of what the Baptism with the Holy Spirit is all about. *(JSM)(KJV)(pg.1118):

Once one is Baptized with the Holy Spirit, many things will transpire in our heart and life. In other words, there will be many tell-tale signs that we have been filled. However, the initial physical evidence that one has been baptized with the Holy Spirit, is that they will speak with other Tongues as the Spirit of God gives the utterance (Acts 2:4; 10:45-46; 19:1-7).

There is nothing in the Bible which suggests that this awesome indwelling power of the Holy Spirit has been declared unavailable in our day. We know there are literally millions of committed, fruitful, effective Christians, who give all the credit for their effectiveness to the experience of having been baptized with the Holy Spirit, with the evidence of Speaking with other tongues. In fact, for you to be what you ought to be in Christ, the Baptism with the Holy Spirit is an absolute necessity.

Jesus died on Calvary that men may be saved. The great Salvation process includes the Holy Spirit taking up abode (or residence) within our hearts and lives. Every Christian needs Him desperately. And to be sure, His full potential cannot be realized, unless we go on and be baptized with the Holy Spirit which as stated, will always be accompanied by the speaking with other tongues as the Spirit of God gives the utterance – (Acts 2:4).

He is our 'Helper', and as well, "guides us into all truth" (John 16:7-15). End quote

'Water Baptism'

What is the significance of Water Baptism? Haven't we, by confessing Christ with our mouths, done everything the Bible tells us to do to insure Salvation? Is there any reason we should go further in proving the fact of our conversion? In truth, there are several reasons for water baptism. First of all, Jesus set the example for us by being baptized in water. He did it to "fulfill all righteousness" (Matthew 3:13-15). Water Baptism signifies (a type-symbol) the Death, Burial, and Resurrection of the Lord Jesus Christ. Hence, when He was Baptized in water, this signified that which He would do in order to Secure our Salvation. We likewise are to be Baptized in water, as a public proclamation of our submission to God, and acceptance of the Lord Jesus Christ, as our Savior. Water Baptism does not save us, or contribute anything toward our salvation, but is rather a sign that we have already been saved, which we wish to declare to the entirety of the world. In fact, Water Baptism is the great symbol (something that stands for something else) that one has given his heart and life to Jesus Christ.

As well, it typifies (#2 to produce a copy) our death to the old life, with all that was ugly and ungodly being burned, and us being resurrected into a new life in Christ Jesus. That's the reason that water Baptism is by immersion (to rise, come forth) (out of the water, being fully submerged). It signifies the old man being buried, and the new man being raised in newness of life (Romans 6:14). End quote *

(p1119) *

'The will of God for your life'

Now that you have become a Child of God, the Lord has a perfect Will for your life. In other words, you are very important in the Kingdom of God, and the Lord will treat you accordingly. In as much as you have given your heart and life to Him, He will now open up the Kingdom of God to you, and your place in that kingdom (John 3:3). In fact, one of the great works of the Holy Spirit in your heart and life, is to bring about "the Will of God" for you (Romans 8:27).

In other words, the idea is that your will be swallowed up in the Will of God, which is the most wonderful, fulfilling life there could ever be. If you will allow the Holy Spirit to have His Way within your life, He will bring about the Will of God, and help you to walk in that Will, doing what the Lord wants you to do. *(p1120) Actually, the Lord has a perfect Will for every Believer and that means you. What He has for you, cannot be done by anyone else. So, you are to seek the Will of God, and you will find beautifully and wondrously, the Holy Spirit making Jesus more and more real in your heart and bringing you to the place in which God desires that you be. Isn't that wonderful to have such help, and above all, to have such leading and guidance (John 16:13-15). End quote *

(John 16: 13-15) NKJV Says:

V13)" However, when He, the Spirit of truth, has come, He will guide you into all truth; for He will not speak on His own authority, but whatever He hears He will speak; and He will tell you things to come. V14) He will glorify Me, for He will take of what is Mine and declare it to you. V15)

All things that the Father has are Mine. Therefore I said that He will take of Mine and declare it to you. " End

'DEVELOPERS DREAM'

I was in the Mountains, maybe not so high up, but in the foothills anyway. And the main guy who is spearheading this project of a house-track in the foothills, but spread out a bit, wanted me to give the pitch to this group of people who would back, or finance, help, architect, design and layout of this project. I told them, that they were the innovators, the pioneers, for this project not us. As I looked around, most homes I could see were two-story – large, massive vacation homes.

But, I said, 'we need something smaller and more affordable.' There was an old model T-Ford that someone, or a group came up in. They wanted a country-drive in the foothills and to get the full experience. The front wheel had fallen off, and I grabbed the frame and lifted it and said, 'put that back on.' I showed confidence. I could do anything, and it showed. [In real life, 'I can do all things through Christ who strengthens me.' Philippians (Phil. 4:13).] ....

The investors were impressed and was considering the project to go through. The dream jumps to that street again that my second wife and I were on (Castro Lane) in the freeway dream. But we were stopped on the west side of the street near the elementary school. We were in a bus. My dad called me on my cell phone, to tell me that the estimated time I said he would take to finish that grass entrance porch job, was right on, exactly 1 hour. I said, 'I'm near your house,' and I stuck my head out the window on the right side of the bus, to see if I could see the roof, to the other street. I could hear kids playing, and I know I was close. But it wasn't close enough. (In real life, that house I was looking for was not my dad's house, but my grandfathers.) End

Loren L. Johnson

'TRI—DREAM'

The first dream was at my sisters and her husband. There was an entrance to this room that was curved and a hallway, with this curved bar there. And the whole bar area was about 5 to 6 feet long, and it was suspended from the ceiling for some reason? And they had me look at the carpet in the hallway for replacement. And I looked up and the bar is about 1 to 2 feet off the ground, it looked like it had good supporting legs with rubber bumpers on them. – – Then the dream jumps to an outside campus or parking lot with a main building, and parking all around like our Valley Plaza Mall in Bakersfield. I was on the east side and wanting to go to the northside. I got on this lawn – mower/hovercraft, which was a square flat vehicle. — And last jump of the dream back inside to an office setting with a main hall. It seemed like we were underground and low ceilings. The office had multiple-rooms, and the main hall had Secretary Desks everywhere. And people all around. The floors looked like commercial carpet, covering a series of drains. The floor looked like a crisscross pattern of storm drains. All covered in carpet. And water was turned on flooding these low areas. It looked like a canal system, like Venice Italy. Except this, you walk over the canals. I asked them, 'what is this all about?' Then I said, 'I don't want to know?' There is a distinct place to walk in an aisle way. Being that everything was covered in carpet. I said to the office staff, 'you know this might be a problem in the near future. Where the carpet will mildew or rot, – etc.' End

CHAPTER 57

'KATHY DREAM'

I was dreaming, I was at this house – which was being used as an official White House business. I was on the floor with an inanimate object, that looked like a Lego truck. I went to touch the top, and it moved. And then I tried again, and the same thing happened. So, I was following it as it was going all by itself? Then on the way back in the room, it turned into a plastic, wooden, metal-boy, and when I talked to him, he was a smart, sweet, innocent, little boy, but he wasn't real. He was a puppet; And when we came back around, I was resting and thinking. I told the commissioner and advisor of this department. I said, 'I saw there was two, no – three things about this kid I like. He is a good kid, and kind, and lastly, I hate for anything bad to happen to this little kid. As he (the puppet) is being brought around to examine him. He is melting or breaking down in degeneration. He can't take the atmosphere. This was like a Sci-FYI movie, there was a few men in suits walking around me, and a lady; she was introduced to me as Madam Secretary. She looked like Kathy Bates. (In real life, it reminded me of the parts of that futuristic movie (AI) with Jude Law, and it had an android boy in it. But Kathy Bates was not in that movie.) End

'ELVIS DREAM'

We were on this assembly line, putting together something. And we were talking, and we do it to pass the time. (In real life when I was in prison working in the kitchen at SAT-F or McFarland we talked among ourselves on the serving line to pass the time.) Someone said something about his mother, but when it got down to the end of the line. This guy says, 'no one talks bad about my mother.' This guy was Elvis Presley; and in the break room as he is a young – good looking strapping man of about 18–20 years old. He says, 'Love Saves You'. 'It's as simple as that.' And that's true, Love is God, and God saves you. End

'ARNOLD DREAM'

'It's okay to cry. It's okay to fall-apart.' 'Sometimes it's the only-way to heal a broken heart.' There was a policeman, in the Police Headquarters where Arnold Schwarzenegger and I were. We were playing around with someone else a game. Killing time, until we had to go out and fight crime. And he, this police officer was singing this song with lyrics above. And I was coming around one way of this aisleway, and Arnold the other, and the other guy in the middle. It was like a game of Tag – but not. Then I came around this wall, and in the other room was this officer singing. A nice looking – middle-aged man with dark hair. He's singing with real conviction and passion. And he was showing me the lyrics on the counter as I walked up to him. (In real life, just before bed, I was working on copying lyrics to songs for church yard service.) (Also In real life, I went to sleep with my headphones on playing Christian music, on the radio-Channel 88.9 Spirit Radio out of Visalia—Bakersfield —100.1 FM.) (And that song was playing when I woke up to use the restroom. 'It's OK to fall apart', I'm guessing that was the title, I found out. That the Lord, through the Holy Spirit is talking to me about that song. And then woke-me up so I could write this down. I haven't grieved properly yet for the loss of my dad. There is no privacy in prison. And cried very little, prison is not the best place to cry. And yet it is the best place to cry and get healed. You just do it with a lot of men surrounding you that care. The song repeated at the end of the dream.)

'It's okay to cry. It's okay to fall apart.' 'Sometimes it's the only-way to heal a broken heart.' End

CHAPTER 58

'ANTHONY DREAM'

This was an Old English setting in this small fishing town. Anthony had riddles to a secret message and supposed hidden treasures. The two Investigators was on the case gathering clues. My partner Sherlock Holmes gathered most of the leads, but I jumped into a trunk and got the last clue. It was where the answer was to be found. On the back of this old whiskey bottle. And more on the location of where it was. But when I gave them the clue, the secret was made known. But it wasn't a treasure map or treasure. Just a message in wait, to another friend, hoping he will follow the same clues as we did to the conclusion. The funny part of this dream was like watching a movie, with the modern Sherlock Holmes and Watson movie Wit. And a very smart advisor as Anthony Hopkins, he pulled one over on the 'Duo'. A trick as you will and escaped one time, only to be found again for more information. Anthony had told them you need to set-up some kind of contraption and keep them busy, because each had to hold each of the two ends. While Anthony said, 'when you use a beam of car lights to shine through it, you get the next clue. And Anthony offered to turn on the light in what looked like an old model T-Ford. At the turn of the 1900s – Anthony, was still in custody and temporarily under arrest. It was a rogue (a dishonest trick from that person). He got in the car and said, 'well, got to go, see ya boys.' And drove off in the old car. Anthony was caught, and later that evening snuck out again. And I made chase. Sherlock and I were going fishing on the morrow. I was running in my socks, and it was cold on my feet. But caught him again, and found out the end, which I explained in the beginning. (And I woke up). End

'TIRE-MECHANIC DREAM'

I was working as a tire mechanic, at a tire shop. It wasn't really what I do, but I could learn. I knew some, by watching how they do it. It was a nice sunny day, downtown in a not too busy street in the old part of town. (There was a tire shop in real life I took most of my tires and brakes work in Bakersfield). The boss wanted a couple of guys to go across the street, and get some supply's or something? And to help with this outdoor sign that we bring out each day, and at closing bring it back in. The sign has a round cement bottom to it, so it won't blow over in the wind. And to stand up properly. Well, this guy and I went across the street but at different times, and I don't know where he went. I am new, I'm watching to learn, I was waiting for him, and I had something in my hand when I went back across the street. Now, I see the other guy, and he's trying to bring the sign across the street by himself. He could see me, why didn't he call out? And where did he go earlier? So, he is rolling the cement bottom to the other side of the street. And gets 3/4 of the way and trips in the street. I think the sign makes it, but he falls. I'm not sure if a car was coming or not? I dropped everything and ran out to help him. Then the boss shows up. I told you to help him with the sign. …. I would have if he didn't disappear and wanted to do it on his own. He didn't ask for help. I was willing to help. But the responsibility was on me because the boss had told me; So, I told him, 'I forgot, I'm sorry, I messed up.' 'And I'm sorry that guy didn't want to work with me.'

(In real life I am a team player, but there is always room for improvement.) End

'AL DREAM'

Al and I are on a laminate wood job together. He was there before, he laid the first laminate wood job for them, in this customers house. In their kitchen, and they liked it so well, they wanted to continue the same product into the dining room and the den area.

(In real life, it is true, you can continue that product on easily without harm. The Dye-Lot (color) is consistent. With the tongue and groove still on one of the ends and is not damaged. You can keep going with that product, or you could change the color, or their direction, or even make a custom border system.)

I am working in one room, and he is in the other. He's already ahead of me. (In real life, that was true; I was always catching up to him, he seemed to do all flooring, effortlessly.)

He was talking to the customers son, as he is interested in watching us lay flooring. The kid was young like five or six, like Al's grandson, but of course his grandson is older now as time moves on.) I woke-up.

End.

CHAPTER 59

'WORD-WISE VS FOOL'

This was the discipleship number three study. But was changed to the Importance of God's Word, and a study mostly in the book of proverbs. I sent study number three to my sister, so through the Word of God she could increase her Faith in Christ. The word says in: (Romans 10:17)" So then faith comes by hearing, and hearing by the word of God."

And I told her to share it with my ex-wife, so she could grow too. I also sent about 16-verses for her to read, I said, "one at a time, and meditate on it, study it. "Since, my 2nd ex-wife doesn't want any more communication, and wants to move on. My sister is neutral for us and can pass information either way if she wants too. My ex-wife is a spiritual woman, but not a godly woman. There is a big difference. (I'll get into that in a minute). (I am giving a Bible study or teaching at Corcoran State Prison, with what little access we did have in the Chapel, and limited on number of people attending, mainly because of the Covid-19's virus.)

Today we're going to combine the word of God study with the wisdom study in number 12 through the discipleship study put out by the Hopewell Baptist Church in Napa, Ca. With permission, and sent through Bible tracks, Inc.

This is a responsible tool (showing the track) to get out the gospel message. And who ever didn't receive one of these tracks on our first study of Salvation, will get one today. To pray over and pass it on. Someone you know who isn't saved yet; but can be if they understand properly the gospel message given to them. 'Christ and Him Crucified.'… 'Repentance toward God, and Faith towards Jesus Christ.'

(I-Corinthians 1:23-25); V23)" But we preach Christ crucified, to the Jews a stumbling block and to the Greeks foolishness, V24) but to those who are called, both Jews and Greeks, Christ the power of God and the wisdom of God. V25) Because the foolishness of God is wiser than men, and the weakness of God is stronger than men."

And the other verse: (Acts 20:21) says: ….'repentance toward God and faith toward our Lord Jesus Christ.' ……—That is the gospel in a nutshell for short. But that may be too blunt a message today, and maybe not. They need someone like you to take them through it step-by-step. And these tracks, give you the process to do that. Read them, pray for someone to give it too. It may even fit that person perfectly – the testimony behind it, that is. Pray that the Holy Spirit, will give you the right words to say. Mostly, being the word of God, I hope. It's all about Him; His death, burial, and resurrection. We didn't do anything, He did it all for us. Tell someone how you believed in Jesus Christ by Faith, repented and received Him in your heart. And how He has changed your life. I know He has changed my life for the better. There were bumps in the road. It just made me stronger. He made my car into a Hummer. Remember using the metaphor of four weeks ago, of the car as our gift of Salvation from the Holy Spirit. I am going to give you some wisdom I learned the hard way, by what this study calls the reproofs of life. (Proverbs 15:31) says: V31)" The ear that hear the rebukes of life Will abide among the wise." (Meaning): That's the goal, someone hears (listens)and acts on it. And avoids the pitfalls of life and becomes wise. And if you don't, (the difficulties which occur because you have violated one of Gods principles.) I think everyone here, including myself can easily understand that verse, since we are all in prison.

Testimonial: My first wife was the girl next door. At 14 and 15 years old going together. All through high school. She went to a Catholic school, and I went to a public school. She went to the traditions of her family in the Christian Roman Catholic church. And I hadn't grown up in a church or with a mother. She died when I was 7 years old, with Lupus. And even when we got married 5 years later, at 19 and 20 years old. I wasn't saved yet. So, I have some excuse. But my advice to you single men, is pray to God for a godly woman. Who can be your Spiritual Help Mate, who is on the same page as you Spiritually, maturity, and goal oriented. Praying for God 's will in your lives. And Christ in the center of your marriage. So, my first ex-wife is more of the religious type, and my second is spiritual type. I was saved two years into my first marriage. Our marriage date was blessed, 3-7s: 7 – 7–79. Then we had two beautiful children. And I went to her church, for 4-years. I didn't know much about anything Spiritual wise, just what I got off of TV and radio. Then the Lord said to me, and I am PP-(paraphrasing) [It's enough, I want you to leave the Catholic Church (or Catholic Faith as some call it)]. It was hard at first, but I did. And it did disrupt our family a bit, and I was comfortable there. But Jesus is not a religion or religiousness based about Him. The Son of God is real and is sitting at God the Father 's right hand in glory, in the heavens. And they sent the Holy Spirit here to live in the hearts of believers like you. Through the Holy Spirit, He will reveal all truth to you. As a second advice, pray for a godly church to attend when you get out. Amen.

(Testimony)

I was driving down the road, praying (basically talking to God); Now that I am out of the Catholic Church, I asked the Lord, where do you want me to go? I was heading downtown, South on Union Avenue, just past the RxR crossing at Sumner St. coming to that funny 5-way street intersection at 21st. And Golden-State Hwy./Union Avenue. Then I heard that small still voice say to me turn right. I'm thinking to myself, do I turn right on Golden State Highway or turn right on 21st? So, I turn right on 21st and then I heard it again. Turn right, so I turn right. Now I am heading for a big semi-round building, that cars are parked at. There was no sign out front, (newly painted white). I know what that building used to be in Bakersfield. It was 'Strong Bow Stadium', (a boxing ring).

I went inside to check it out, and found out what this place is? There were people at the entrance welcoming me. I said, 'what is this place?' They said, 'this is Victory Outreach Church'.

Wow, I got my prayer answered. Not a religious church, or a traditional church, (It would be Lutheran for me as a Scandinavian.) Not even a church you feel comfortable in, but one you can grow in. One that preaches the whole word of God and believes the gifts of the Spirit of God. And Outreach to the Community and the World. With the Gospel of Jesus Christ, in missions.

My first wife and I went through marital counseling, and we were together married almost 10 years until she had an affair with a coworker at the hospital where she work. And then divorce me. This is bump number #1–. (Now, I started drinking again, smoking, and having sex with, or sexual encounters of women of all ages. I called myself the marrying man, but nobody wanted me.)

Just because those things happened, doesn't give me the right to start racking up sin, so God's Grace can cover it. It is not about feelings and the flesh. It is about faith in the word of God. And what it says that we should do.

The reproofs of life; right after the divorce and falling apart, emotionally, psychologically, and anxiety. I went about it all wrong, being worldly, not seeking counsel, not casting my cares on the Lord and trusting Him. Not praying first. But, last in desperation. I got down on my face in the carpet, in the dining room at apartment number 12. He heard my broken heart, as I cried, 'Why Lord?' 'What am I going to do?' 'I don't know how to handle this?' And the Lord spoke to me, He said, 'Loren; You are going to get through this, and you will help other people.' That had to do for now, His promise got me through it, and He will get me through this prison thing too. Amen.

Nearing the end of the two years, after the divorce. I got engaged for a minute. With an expensive engagement ring, and she gave it back to me.

I got comforted from the wrong person, and it cost me bump #2. When I got straightened out, no more alcohol or cigarettes. And I started attending a Celebrate Recovery Class in a church setting. And went to Counseling for three years and was going to a nondenominational Christian church. Thanks be to God, life was good. Reconciliation is the key. With God, and with the people I harmed while under the influence.

Three years went by, But I was lonely, and working all the time. (Working for a living laying flooring, carpet, vinyl, wood; trading material and labor for child support in General Construction; and trading material and labor for rent by Construction also). So, I prayed to God for a Spiritual woman. Thinking spiritual and godly are the same thing. (A Godly woman is using the word of God as her guide, praying, going to church and be a part of what God wants her to do; to use God's gifts, given to her to help build up the body of Christ; working hand-in-hand with her husband, as two-become one flesh in Christ. If Christ is it in the center of your marriage, there should be no reason for harm).

I'm not saying you won't have disagreements, but you can work them out in love and forgiveness. That you want to work on it for Christ's sake, and the sake of your sanctified marriage.

(Then I met a Spiritual woman, who believed in Jesus as the Son of God. But was lacking in her prayer life, to Jesus our Mediator to the Father through the Holy Spirit. She didn't use the word of God, the Bible as her inspiration and guide for life. She even though the Bible was obsolete and wasn't needed anymore. She had hints of palm reading, prophetic knowledge and future events like divination. She could predict some events to come, when someone was about to die, or someone whom they will marry.) And Christ Jesus wasn't in the center of our marriage. My 2nd ex-wife: I got what I prayed for. But be careful what you pray for, be specific. Big difference: I compromised Gods principles for her. It was wrong. Three wrongs don't make a right. I learned the hard way.

#1. She got me to start drinking again after three years sober.

#2. I stop going to church, which was at least two times a week with two services.

#3. And then, I tried to prove her wrong with her New Age Book; that I read to compare with the Bible.

At the time I didn't see wrong in it, but now God corrected me when I was in Wasco Reception Prison: (He reminded me of being single minded to the word of God again.) When I said, 'I didn't see any wrong in it?' Reminds me of the (Prov. 12:15) says: "The way of a fool is right in his own eyes: But he that hearkeneth unto counsel is wise. "(KJV) I didn't see it, I was blinded by her beauty, and thought it was OK. But it wasn't. I was one of those wish-washy Christian's picking and choosing what I wanted to believe. You have to believe the whole word of God.

Now, I've prayed, and have hope of a third wife. Third time is a charm. My first one religious, my second one spiritual, my third one God willing, Godly. Enough of this, let's get back into the study of wisdom and the word. Which is mostly in the book of proverbs.

Now discipleship study number 12 is called 'Wise vs Fool'. They start off with a question?

Quote: 'What is the number one objective in the Christian life?' And three probable answers: Is it to win souls? Is it to pray? Is it to learn the Bible? (What do you think?) … (none of these, but there all good answers). —

(Prov. 4:7) says: "Wisdom is the principal thing; therefore get wisdom. And with all thy getting get understanding. "A Christian's main objective is to Get Wisdom! Wisdom is the perfection of common sense. It is to know oneself, one's God, one's neighbor, and properly be able to relate to each. Wisdom is the ability to tap God's mind. There are three basic characters in life that you will meet as you read Proverbs. They are the wise, simple, and fool.

Who you spend time with and who you listen to will determine what you become. – Starting with, WISE— Why do I need Wisdom? Wisdom is seeing things from God 's viewpoint. Without wisdom, your effectiveness for God will not be great. You will incur "reproofs of life" unnecessarily. (Bumps in the road). Many trials people face is self-inflicted. Every Christian need's wisdom. We need it in soul winning, in business, in overcoming Temptations, in friendships, in making decisions, and in child rearing. A Christian without wisdom is like a desert without sand, and ocean without water, a bird without wings, and a church without a Bible. (I-Kings 3) gives the account of a young man who would soon become king of a great nation. He dreamt one night that God would grant him any request he asked for. In the dream, he did not ask for riches, long life, or the lives of his enemies – he asked for wisdom! God granted him his wisdom! His name was Solomon. He is, to this day, known as the wisest man in the world. People traveled great distances to have their questions answered by him. People are drawn to someone who has the answers. People in this world need you to be wise.

(What are some results of wisdom?) (Proverbs 2:9) KJV (Understanding) V9)" Then shalt thou understand righteousness, and judgment, and equity; yea, every good path." (When God's finished with you, you will have understanding). You have: 'Deliverance from Evil People'. — (Prov. 2:12) says: "To deliver the from the way of the evil man, from the man that speaketh froward (In the NKJV is perverse)-(A man speaking evil things, lying, deceit, etc.)things;"

There was a co-worker like that at PIA for a time. He would speak loud and boisterous, always talking, and easily would argue and blame others. And even lie, to make one superior. He would get loud and angry. We will call him John Smith, or the contentious spirit behind it. He flustered me, getting me upset, and even though I would apologize, or say to myself I forgive you for your rude, loud, obnoxious, behavior, cussing and accusing, of wrong. Saying to me: (I am too slow, or I don't do it to his satisfaction, etc.) Another coworker and I both corrected this man – (being that he is supposed to be Christian), and sometimes, he accepted his wrong, and changed his ways for a few hours, half day, maybe a day. And then back to the same old disruptive spirit. A strive spirit. (I'm calling it what it really is.) Since it wasn't getting any better, and I needed to get away from this angry man. (Because, I thought of the wisdom of proverbs, and remembered down in my heart this verse.) (Prov. 22:24-25) NKJV "Make no friendship with an angry man, and with a furious man do not go, lest you learn his ways and set a snare for your soul."

I went to the lead-man of the group, and asked if I could move positions. He said yes, and this was a two-fer for me. Because my left shoulder was inflamed in bursitis, being a catcher (That is a person who catches appox. 100 lunch boxes a minute and fills 55 in a case, taking turns with the guy in front of you or in back). So, I moved to the bread-line packing. Problem solved. (The funny part about this move, the person I was going to work with on the breadline; we introduced each other, and I thought he said my name is Davin; he said, No, it is Devil.) (I thought here we go again, but that wasn't the case).

When the Lord saw that I got out of that situation, He was pleased. The reason I know this, is because the way I responded to him later. And the fact that I reconciled with him, the best I could do. Apologized again with gifts of food. And he did the same, after he went through some things. He ended up leaving PIA, and getting away from the top floor, and any 2-5's hateful spirits. And of course, the climax, of the fight with his Cellie in building number five, which is where I am too.

After all that, his demeanor changed completely. Then I knew another Proverb would complete the reconciliation. (Proverbs 16:7) says: "When a man's ways please the Lord, he makes even his enemies to be a peace with him." On Friday the 13th; he, (my Cellie) and I had a spread together. In peace, and prayer of thanksgiving to God.

And I blessed him (my enemy from work) on his way out soon, out of prison, he is short to the house. With prayer and food. Back to finishing the list of benefits to wisdom:

—— You'll receive Happiness—

(Proverbs 3:13) says: "Happy is the man that findeth wisdom, and the man that getteth understanding."—

—You will get Long Life and Riches— (Proverbs 3:16) says: "Length of days is in her right hand; and in her left-hand riches and honor." (The Bible refers to Wisdom as a she). —It will help you Not to Stumble—

(Proverbs 3:23) says: "Then shalt thou walk in thy way safely and thy foot shall not stumble."

—You will have Lack of Fear—

(Proverbs 3:24) says: "When thou liest down, thou shalt not be afraid: yea, thou sleep shall be sweet."

--You will be Promoted in Promotion--

(Proverbs 4:8) says: "Exalt her, and she shall promote thee: she shall bring thee honor when thou dosest embrace her." (Exalt wisdom and understanding and wisdom (she) will exalt you). .....

—A Grace Crown of Glory—

(Proverbs 5:9) says: "She shall give to thine head an ornament of grace: a crown of glory shall she deliver to thee."

—You will receive Riches and Honor-

(Proverbs 8:18) says:

"Riches and honor are with me; yea, durable (enduring) riches and righteousness."

—Glad Parents—

(Proverbs 10:1) says:

"The proverbs of Solomon. A wise son maketh a glad father: but a foolish son is the heaviness of his mother."

—A Leader's Favor—

(Proverbs 14:28) says:

"In the multitude of people is the king's honour: but in the want of people is the destruction of the prince."

—Gets more accomplished with less effort—

(Ecclesiastes 10:10) says:

"If the iron be blunt, (not sharp) and he do not whet (put the iron to a course whetstone, with water or without) the edges, then must he put to more strength: but wisdom is profitable to direct. "….

In the NKJV says it this way:

V10)" If the ax is dull, and does not sharpen the edge, then he must use more strength; but wisdom brings success. "(So, the wisdom is to have your sword or ax sharp, to use less effort and bring about more success. For instance. I do a lot of writing, so a pencil sharpener and eraser are a wise investment, to make my job easier.)

—How to recognize a wise person—

—He will hear— (listen's more than speak)— (Proverbs 1:5) says:

"A wise man will hear and will increase learning; and a man of understanding shall attain unto wise counsels:" (So, if you hang around wise people, you too will become wise also).

(When I was young, I wanted to play tennis better, so I played tennis with Ron, a guy from across the street, because he was a way better player then I.)

—He is a Hard Worker—

(Proverbs 10:5) says:

"He that gathereth in summer is a wise son: but he that sleepeth in harvest is a son that causeth shame. "(kind-a-like an ant-colony that find food in the summer and stores up for the winter).

— There are those who Receives Commands—

(Proverbs 10:8) says:

"The wise in heart will receive commandments: but a prating (means foolish lips) fool (dict.1,2,a person who lacks sense or judgment; joke, to spend time idly or aimlessly) shall fall (means thrust down or ruined)."

(The wise man is the one who does the will of God. Who does the word of God.) (What a man thinks, he is; what we speak can have a prophetic outcome in our lives. We are supposed to have the mind of Christ. And we are to speak God 's word.) Two verses come to mine.

(II Corinthians 9:6) & (Galatians 6:7); 'Sowing Seeds of Life'— 'Speaking Words of Life' (NKJV)

V6)" But this I say: He who sows sparingly will also reach sparingly, and he who sows bountifully will also reap bountifully. "(Let's read on two verse nine).

V7)" So let each one give as he purposes in his heart, not grudgingly or of necessity; for God loves a cheerful giver. V8) And God is able to make all grace abound toward you, that you, always having all sufficiency in all things, may have an abundance for every good work...... [The Lord provides that good work for you to do; He speaks of that in (Eph. 2:10).] Could I have someone read that. .... V10)" For we are His workmanship, created in Christ Jesus for good works, which God prepared beforehand that we should walk in them. "] ......cont. V9) As it is written: He has dispersed abroad; He has given to the poor; His righteousness endures forever."

(This sowing and reaping law doesn't just work for giving money to the poor. It is also our time and energy).

V9–says: … (giving to the poor across the Oceans, to feed, clothe, shelter, bring medicine, Spiritual guidance, to the orphan, to the widow, to the oppressed people in foreign lands.)

(This is the right thing to do. Amen.) (The second verse is about the outcome of what we say and do?)

(Gal. 6:7-10): V7)" Do not be deceived, God is not mocked; for whatever a man sows, that he will also reap. "V8– (explains another aspect of the sowing & reaping law)

V8)" For he who sows to his flesh will of the flesh reap corruption, but he who sows to the Spirit will of the Spirit reap everlasting life. V9) And let us not grow weary while doing good, for in due season we shall reap if we do not lose heart. V10) Therefore, as we have opportunity, let us do good to all, especially to those who are of the household of faith (Us, His Church people)." (Love your brother first, then also love your neighbor, in word and deed. Love is an action word. Not passive.)

(In closing for today, with some of the 16 verses I sent to my sister about the importance of the Word of God. Write these down and go over them later in your cell.)

(John 8:51; 14:24; 17:17) ;(Acts 13:48) ;(I-Cor. 12:8) ;(Eph. 5:26); (Phil. 2:16) ;(Col. 3:16) ;(Luke 8:21); (Rom. 10:17); and next, could I have someone read Hebrew's 4:12:

V12)" For the word of God is living and powerful, and sharper than any two-edged sword, piercing even to the division of soul and spirit, and of joints and marrow, and is a discerner of the thoughts and intents of the heart. "(The Word is Living and Powerful.) How about Hebrew's 11:3; V3)" By faith we understand that the worlds were framed by the word of God, so that the things which are seen were not made of things which are visible."

Could I have someone read; (I-John 2:14); V14)" I have written to you, fathers, because you have known Him who is from the beginning. I have written to you, young men, because you are strong, and the word of God abides in you, and you have overcome the wicked one."

(God wants His Word to abide in you.) (The Word of God is Spirit and Life)! Jesus' very Name is called 'The Word of God'. (Revelations 19:13) says: "He was clothed with a robe dipped in blood, and His name is called The Word of God."

(John 1:1) says: "In the beginning was the Word, and the Word was with God, and the Word was God. " [The Word (the Son of God) was with the Father at creation] ...V2) (He was in the beginning with God.)(I asked what else did the word do?)

(John 1:14) says: "And the Word became flesh and dwelt among us, and we beheld His glory, the glory as of the only begotten of the Father, full of grace and truth."

Are very Faith is increased by the Word of God. (Romans 10:17); "So then faith comes by hearing, and hearing by the word of God. "(Now that we've heard it, we need to be doing it). (Luke 8:21) says: "But He answered and said to them 'My mother and my brothers are these who hear the word of God and do it.'" A cross verse for that is (James 1:22)" But be doers of the word, and not hears only, deceiving yourselves." The ending verse for today is also in (James 1:5): "If any of you lack wisdom, let him ask of God, who gives to all liberally (or abundantly, or generously) and without reproach, (or disgrace or discredit or disapproval) and it will be given to him."

That is God's promise to you. The only condition is to ask in Faith. In V6) says with no doubting. Amen. Faith is what pleases God. V6)" But without faith it is impossible to please Him, for he who comes to God must believe that He is, and that He is a rewarder of those who diligently seek Him. " End

'PART II (W VS F)'

Hello brothers, back again for the part-two of the wise vs fool study; plus, the importance of the Word of God. We left off-on, how to recognize a wise person? starting with:

—This Person-Lays up Knowledge—

(Proverbs 10:14) says:

"Wise men lay-up knowledge: but the mouth of the foolish is near destruction."

—One who —Controls lips—

(Proverbs 10:19) says:

"In the multitude of words there wanteth not sin: but he that refraineth his lips is wise."

(there is a cross verse that comes to mind). —— (James 1:19).

—He who is—Humble—

(Proverbs 11:2) says:

"When pride cometh, then cometh shame but with the lowly is wisdom."

—He has—Leadership Qualities—

(Proverbs 11:29) says:

"He that troubleth his own house shall inherit the wind: and the fool shall be servant to the wise of heart."

—He will—Win Souls—

(Proverbs 11:30) says:

"The fruit of the righteous is a tree of life; and he that winneth souls is wise. " End quote

I have cross verses to the first part of this proverb, and what came to mind is (Ps.1:1-3) NKJV but, also of the importance of meditating on the whole word of God, and not just the New Testament.

V1)" Blessed is the man Who walks not in the counsel of the ungodly, nor stands in the path of sinners, nor sits in the seat of the scornful; V2) But his delight is in the law of the Lord, And in His law he meditates day and night. V3) He shall be like a tree Planted by the rivers of water, that brings forth its fruit in its season, whose leaf also shall not wither; And whatever he does shall prosper. "(In these verses, plus (Ps.1:4-6); and (Prov.1:20-33) show a grand contrast between the way of righteousness, and the way of the wicked.) a contrast to choose wisely:

(Proverbs 1:20-33) NKJV

V20)" Wisdom calls aloud outside; She raises her voice in the open square. V21) She cries out in the chief concourses, (main gathering areas, where people come together) At The openings of the gates in the city She speaks her words: V22) 'How Long, use simple ones, will you love simplicity?' For scorners delight in their scorning, and fools hate knowledge. V23) Turn at my rebuke; Surely, I will pour out my spirit on you; I will make my words known to you. V24) Because I have called and you refused, I have stretched out my hand and no one regarded, V25) Because you disdained all my counsel, and would have none of my rebuke, V26) I also will laugh at your calamity; I will mock when your terror comes, V27) When your terror comes like a storm, and your destruction comes like a whirlwind, When distress and anguish come upon you. V28) Then they will call on me, but I will not answer; They will seek me diligently, but they will not find me. V29) Because they hated knowledge and did not choose the fear of the Lord, V30) They would have none of my counsel and despised my every rebuke. V31) Therefore they shall eat the fruit of their own way and be filled to the full with their own fancies." V32)" For the turning away of the simple will slay them, V33) But whoever listens to me will dwell safely, and will be secure, without fear of evil. " (next one).

quote: —Listens to Counsel—

(Proverbs 12:15) says:

"The way of a fool is right in his own eyes; but he that hearkeneth unto counsel is wise."

(Note, this is a good one, you can't know everything, it's good to learn.)

—Controls the Tongue—

(Proverbs 12:18) says:

"There is that speaketh like the piercings of a sword: but the tongue of the wise is health."

—Listens to his parents—

(Proverbs 13:1) says:

"A wise son heareth his father's instruction: but a scorner heareth not rebuke. "end quote

(I was a little rebellious in my teenage years, that stressed my dad out a little, but for the most part I did what he told me to do.

We worked together off and on for some 10 to 20 years in the floor covering business.)

quote: —Well Informed—

(Proverbs 13:10) says:

"Only by pride cometh contention: but with the well advised is wisdom."

—Is Constructive—

(Proverbs 14:1) says:

"Every wise woman buildeth her house: but the foolish plucketh it down with her hands."

—Understanding—

(Proverbs 14:8) says:

"The wisdom of the prudent (wise) is to understand his way; but the folly of fools is deceit (deception,trickery,lie)."

—Gives Knowledge—

(Proverbs 15:7) says:

"The lips of the wise disperse knowledge: but the heart of the foolish doeth not so."

—He can take a chewing out—

(Proverbs 17:10) says:

"A reproof (correction) entereth more into a wise man than a hundred stripes into a fool."

End quote— (Note)

(It sounds like this foolish man, just doesn't get it. He possibly was corrected 100 times. You will understand why this person does what he does, when we get to the section of 'What a fool act like?' We can also learn what not to do, as well as what to do. Amen.)

(So, their closing statement is: The wise person seeks to pinpoint and practice God's principles. Amen).

(Next title)

'Characteristics of the Simple'

(Proverbs 14:15) says:

"The simple believeth every word: but the prudent (wise) man looketh well to his going (He considers well his steps)." Simple means "unpleated" or "inexperienced." This is the young person who has not gotten acquainted with life's dangers.

This also applies to the new Christian. (A simple person's ear are open to the tempter's whispers.)

(The simple is easily swayed and is the target of schemes and cults.) (The wise man knows God 's commands and the simple man does not. He needs teaching. The entire book of Proverbs was written to the simple so he could avoid all the unnecessary traps of life.) (End of quote)

(I can contest to the fact I was simple many years. And even now, I am still barely learning. But it is getting easier. Thank God. They give examples of people in the Bible who were simple:)

Eve, in the garden of Eden, was simple when she believed the serpent. Jacob's daughter, Dinah was simple when she desired to meet the heathen girls around her.

(Proverbs 7:7) says: "And behold among the simple ones, I discerned among the youths, a young man void of understanding." The youth in this story falls into immorality because he was not warned in advance against it's dangers. Since the simple believe every word, it is easy for them to believe anything they read and hear. They are prime prospects to listen to gossip. There is no sin in being a simple Christian — but it is a sin to stay simple.

The only area in a Christian is to be simple in is, "simple concerning evil. "The simple person needs to get into God's word quickly.

Notice God's promise in (Psalm 19:7) which says: "The law of the Lord is perfect, converting the soul: the testimony of the Lord is sure, making wise the simple."

(Simple—That Doesn't know God's principles yet: God is making you wise)

—Characteristics of the fool—

The foolish is without aim. He is opposed to those who walk uprightly. He lacks character and feels he needs no counsel. He is easily offended, impulsive, and makes quick decisions.

—All are born foolish—

(Proverbs 22:15) says: "Foolishness is bound in the heart of a child: but the rod of correction shall drive it far from him." End quote

(We should correct our children when they are small, if you don't, they keep getting their way, they can control you, not only that, but those tantrums as small children, can get pretty nasty or dangerous as teenagers.) ….

—Has no control over their mouth— (Proverbs 9:13) says: "A foolish woman is clamorous (noisy shouting); she is simple, and knoweth nothing."

(Proverbs 12:23) says: "A prudent (wise) man concealeth knowledge: but the heart of fools proclaimeth foolishness."

(Proverbs 18:6-7) says: "A fool's lips enter into contention (One who brings strive, contest or argue with someone; striking blows physically or with words / flattery), and his mouth calleth for strokes (Blows to fight). A fool's mouth is his destruction, and his lips are the snare of his soul."

—Someone who has a temper and argues—

(Proverbs 12:16) says: "A fool's wrath is presently known: But a prudent man covereth shame."

(Proverbs 14:16-17) says: "A wise man feareth, and departeth from evil: but the fool rageth (rage is one step greater then anger, it is… 'violent and uncontrolled anger), and is confident he that is soon angry dealeth foolishly: and a man of wicked devises is hated."

—Someone who …Has Pride—

(Proverbs 14:3) says: "In the mouth of the foolish is a rod of pride: (A symbol of Authority in haughty-pride) But the lips of the wise shall preserve them."

—Characteristics of a fool—

Is a person Deceitful – who (rationalizes); dict.#4 (to find plausible but untrue reasons for their conduct).

(Proverbs 14:8) says: "The wisdom of the prudent is to understand his way: but the folly of fools is deceit."

—A person who Slanders and Lies—

(Proverbs 10:18) says: "He that hideth hatred with lying lips, and he that uttereth a slander, is a fool."

—A person who practices Sins—

(Proverbs 10:23) says: "It is as sport to a fool to do mischief: but a man of understanding hath wisdom."

(Proverbs 14:9) says: "Fools make a mock at sin: but among the righteous there is favor."

—Sees no need for Counsel—

(He feels he is always right)

(Proverbs 12:15) says:

"The way of a fool is right in his own eyes: but he that hearkeneth unto counsel is wise."

—No desire to Learn God's Word—

(Proverbs 23:9) says: "Speak not in the ears of a fool: for he will despise the wisdom of thy words."

—Becomes Grief to Parents—

(Proverbs 17:25) says: "A foolish son is a grief to his father, and bitterness to her that bare him."

—Does Right when forced— (Proverbs 26:3) says: "A whip for the horse, a bridle for the ass, and a rod (correction stick) for the fool's back."

—Who doesn't learn and repeats the same folly—

(Proverbs 26:11) says: "As a dog returneth to his vomit so a fool returneth to his folly."

—Hard to change—

(Proverbs 27:22) says: "Though thou shouldest bray (the characteristic harsh cry of a donkey) a fool in a mortar among wheat with a pestle, yea will not his foolishness depart from him." (In the NKJV explains it, a little simpler to read and understand).

(Proverbs 27:22) NKJV "Though you grind a fool in a mortar with a pestle along with crushed grain, (It's saying you correct a fool, and he is in his lowest state of punishment, broken down to a powder by a pestle, (which is a long-gated handle of stone for crushing.)...Yet his foolishness will not depart from him."(So, he continues in his folly).

-Does not like to be told what to do-

(Proverbs 15:5) says: "A fool despiseth his father's instruction. But he that regardeth reproof (correction) is prudent."

—Undependable—

(Proverbs 26:6) says: "He that sendeth a message by the hand of a fool cutteth of the feet, and drinketh damage. "(This means you wouldn't send a message to someone, by a fool because you are not certain it will get there?)

—Quick to give opinion—

(Proverbs 29:11) says: "A fool uttereth all his mind: But a wise man keepeth it in till afterward."

(Proverbs 29:20) says: "Seest thou man that is hasty (having excessive-eager-quick) in his words? There is more hope of a fool than of him." (It means a man who is excessive and quick with his words is even worse than a fool; so 'don't blurt out everything you know quickly without restraint' of wisdom and knowledge).

(My first mother-in-law told me that in quotations; when I was young and she used to be my 7th grade teacher and next-door neighbor; I'm better now, but not perfect.)

The Bible mentions many fools. The following Characters showed some characteristics of foolishness in their lives, the Prodigal son, Cain, Lot, Samson, and Absalom. You will not find anyone in the Bible who was a fool who ever changed, A fool likes the limelight. He likes to have positions and titles. A fool does not like to work his way up the ladder of success, so he tries to take shortcuts.

—A fool Ignores and Defies God's principles—(Warning)

—Do not associate with a fool—

(Proverbs 14:7) says: "Go from the presence of a foolish man, when thou perceivest not in him the lips of knowledge."

—Do not agree with a fool— (Proverbs 26:4) says: "Answer not a fool according to his folly, lest thou also be like unto him."

—Do not Honor a fool—

(Proverbs 26:1) says: "As snow in summer, and as rain in harvest, so honor is not seemly for a fool."

—Do not seek a fool's counsel—

(Proverbs 24:7) says: "Wisdom is too high for a fool: He openeth not his mouth in the gate."

—Do not trust a fool to Relay a message—

(Proverbs 26:6) says: "He that sendeth a message by the hand of a fool cutteth off the feet, and drinketh damage." (NKJV drinks violence)

—Do not argue with a fool—

(Proverbs 29:9) says: "If a wise man contendeth with a foolish man, whether he rage (violent and uncontrolled anger) or laugh, (also uncontrolled laugher, where the wise man tells the foolish man truth, and it goes in one ear and out the other as he laugh's continually.) …. There is no rest."

—Let's Review—

—How to get Wisdom—

(There are three sources of wisdom)

: #1 —Wise People—

(Proverbs 13:20) says: "He that walketh with wise men shall be wise; but a companion of fools shall be destroyed."

#2 —Reproofs of Life—

(Proverbs 15:31) says: "The ear that heareth the reproof of life abideth among the wise."

(Difficulties which occur because you have violated one of God's principles.)

#3 —Word of God—

(Proverbs 19:7) says: "All the brethren of the poor do have him: How much more do his friends go far from him? He pursueth them with words, yet they are wanting to him."

—Guidelines for seeking wisdom—

—Fear God—

(Proverbs 9:10) says: "The fear of the Lord is the beginning of wisdom: and the knowledge of the holy is understanding."

Have a deep respect for God, his reputation, and His name. Meditate on His greatness and awesomeness.

—Listen—

(Proverbs 2:2) says: "So that thou incline thine ear unto wisdom, and apply thine heart to understanding;"

(Proverbs 8:6) says: "Hear; for I will speak of excellent things; and the opening of my lips shall be right things."

(Proverbs 9:9) says: "Give instruction to a wise man, and he will be yet wiser; teach a just man, and he will increase in learning."

God has given us two ears and only one mouth. Maybe He wanted us to listen twice as much as we talk.

—Ask Questions—

(Proverbs 2:3) says: "Yea, if thou criest after knowledge, and liftest up thy voice for understanding;"

(Luke 2:46) says: "And it came to pass, that after three days they found him in the temple, sitting in the midst of the doctors, both hearing them, and asking them questions." Jesus asked questions of the wise men of his day. When Abraham Lincoln was with someone who knew a subject well, he would ask so many questions that they felt drained afterwards.

—READ—

(Proverbs 2:4) says: "If thou seekest her as silver, and searchest for her as for hid treasures;" (We ought to read the Bible daily, do not read the Bible just for information, but pinpoint exact commands, promises, and principles for your life. Also, you need to schedule times of reading great Christian Literature, The Christian classics as, "In His steps" and "Pilgrims Progress" are so helpful. Read biographies of great Christians.

Abe Lincoln once said, "My best friend is a man who gives me a book I ain't read!"

Leaders are Readers!

—Watch Daily—

(Proverbs 8:17) says: "I love them that love me; and those that seek me early shall find me."

(Proverbs 8:34a) says: "Blessed is the man that heareth me, watching daily at my gates."

Be observant. You can learn much about life by simply watching people.

—Walk with Wise men—

(Proverbs 13:20) says: "He that walketh with wise men shall be wise: but a companion of fools shall be destroyed. "Birds of a feather flock together. Wisdom rubs off! Schedule yourself around the wise by your presence, reading their books, hearing them speak in person or by tape. Someone said, "A year from now you will be the same as you are today except for the books you read and the people you meet."

—Pray for it—

(James 1:5) says: "If any of you lack wisdom, let him ask of God, that giveth to all men liberally, and upbraideth not; and it shall be given him. "(Make asking for wisdom your Constant Prayer)

—Proper Discipline of Children—

(Proverbs 29:15) says: "The rod and reproof give wisdom: but a child left to himself bringeth his mother to shame. "Consistent correction drives foolishness from a child. A parent can help his child become wise if he is consistent.

—Our Example—

Who never sinned? Who never fell into the devil's traps? Who knew how to handle every situation? Who did all things well? Jesus. He was full of wisdom. Read His life in the gospels. Let us hunger and thirst to be like Him and have the mind of Christ and the wisdom He has! End.

'FAM.BUS. DREAM'

My Dad, my brother and I are working on a carpet job on a very steep hill, and at the very top. They are inside putting down the padding, and I went out to cut the carpet. It was already pulled off the truck or van and was laying there ready by the place where you park. And when I rolled it to the middle of the street, getting ready to start making cuts. That I already wrote down on a piece of cardboard. (In real life, carpet has plastic bands around it or wrapped in plastic, or both for shipping and to keep it clean.) As I am rolling it, and it got away from me. And since it is wrapped up it didn't unroll, but it did roll down the street. (In real life we do cut the carpet in the street sometimes when it is clear. We put out traffic cones, and the asphalt is free of oil and dirt. We possibly pre-sweep if needed to keep clean. It is a last resort, to a driveway, inside the garage, or even the lawn. Most streets are very clean.) (In real life, to be safe we cut the carpet sideways on the street, but it can possibly block traffic on the other side too. Even though on the hill, in real life, you can use it to your advantage by using gravity in your favor. By unrolling it downhill and making all your cuts all at one time. It just takes a few seconds to unroll it, when it's planned or even unexpected.)

Back to the dream, I ran after it. It went almost down to the very end. But, rolled into these people's yard. I needed to get it back to the top of the hill and get my brother and the truck or van and get down here and pick it up as soon as possible. ASAP. In the dream, instead of knocking on the door and explaining the situation to these people, if they were even home. They had a motorhome out front just like the Class 'A' RV that my second wife and I had. A 34-foot Pace Arrow Vision with 2-slides.

(In real life, she had divorced me and had to sell it and moved away.)

My last vehicle that I had was a Ford Cargo-Van, and in the dream, I didn't see any truck or van. But I had the Ford key, and the motorhome chassis is a large Ford truck. So, my key fit the door and I started the RV.) (In real life that couldn't have happened, and it didn't; what I mean is the top-part of the Motorhome is made by Fleetwood, and the door is a little key. Not a Ford key.) Back to the dream, anyway, I'm borrowing it for a minute to go get my brother, so we could bring the Van down, and load it back-up as quickly as possible, and return the RV and finish the job. I went to the top, and got my brother, turned the RV around, and we both went down to get it. We got down there and the people were there and were outside toward the back yard. A father and his son. As my brother and I talked to

357

Loren L. Johnson

what I thought was the owner of the house. That is the father, but it was the son, as he is walking up. It is the sons house and RV; he is the owner.

Then my dad leaves the job looking for his sons and followed the vehicles down the hill. Because, we haven't told him what was going on. He showed up behind me. So, I was nervous and emotional, and I introduced them to the father and the son. And they were not upset, and the son's neighbor saw the whole thing. And they weren't concerned for me borrowing the RV for a minute. (Then I woke up)

(In real life, you don't take someone's vehicle unless you have their permission. I probably dreamt that because of some stories my bunkie shared with me.)

'The Interpretation of the dream'

[The first part of the three of us working on a job was normal. The second part, sometimes we do cut carpet in the street or parking lot, especially in commercial work is common. The three fears are having someone drive over the material (I can recall only 2x in 40 years they ran over our carpet), the rolling away of carpet and unrolling accidentally. And the third part of talking to the father and the son, was my subconscious coming out in this dream, about introducing Jesus, The Son of God and God the Father – the living Spirit of God, to my brother and my dad at different times.] Amen.

CHAPTER 60

'BANK DREAM'

We'll, apparently, I worked in a bank, in this dream. And we were closing for the day. And we were working on the ATM machine. It was open, but there was no money in it. It was already moved to the vault. We were waiting for something too. I think some of the other employees wanted to use the ATM machine too, but it was empty and won't be restocked till morning. I am outside, waiting with a beer-bottle, it was brown. I had finished it and ran to the parking area. To the parking lot trash-can. And I'm assuming I threw the bottle away. And I was walking back when a Deputy Sheriff was sitting on the hood of his car. And I looked over at him. I have nothing to hide; number one the beer is the non-alcoholic type; number two I work at the bank; number three we are about done working on the ATM machine and we're going home. End

(I woke up) …. went right back to sleep and I was dreaming I was on a carpet job.

'CARPET DREAM'

I was at a customer's home, and it was very large. And they were pretty well off. I had worked for them before. I was working in the front of the house in the living room. And I walked to the back, because there was a lot of talking and noise. They were cleaning and sanding of the old vinyl flooring. The dad and two-employees were working in this large room kitchen – dining combo room. One room almost square, about 21 feet wide and 24 feet deep.

I went to the dad of the home, and I said, 'what company did you go through? I probably knew them, and at one time work for them.' He didn't know. And he pointed to his wife who was outside by the side door. I went out, and told her, you know I could have done this job too. I do vinyl besides carpet; In just a few days, I could do your whole house, if it was empty. But, with dollies, skat-skates, sliders, and a hand-truck, it can be done too with furniture, just takes longer. But I'm glad you found someone else for your kitchen. Thinking to myself. The size of that room. I would have to hirer help with that roll, to get the material in place and glue it down. It would also be extremely large role with a 12-foot width. 2–21-foot cuts, plus pattern match. Generally, 3 inches to 36-inch pattern match. 21 feet +21 feet +3 feet equals 45'x 12 width = the square footage, then divided it by 9 and get your square yardage. Which is 60 sq. yds. of vinyl. And I'm sure it is of a heavy gage material, of more mils thick. — (A couple thousand pounds possible).

(In real life, the customer wouldn't be preparing their own floor by sanding. The flooring installers does that. Very rare we need to sand it, most of the time we chemically clean the floor of any dirt or wax. Then use what we can call an embossing leveler to fill in the old pattern material. It is a cement base product with a latex-additive for bonding to the old product and it gives bonding now for the new adhesive to glue down the new flooring. For health, and for the dust it makes, power sanding is out. But, scraping the floor with the topside of the scraper-blade. And we scratch the floor to make it more bondable to the leveler or adhesive, or we take up the old material down to the cement.

And if you have up to three floors down now, or it is loose or damaged. They have to come up and go back to the concrete. If you have a wood floor— We put down a high-density plywood flooring over the top of the old material and staple or nail it down. This is called an underlayment of 5 mm to 7 mm thick.

And to remove any excessive amount of moisture in the slab of cement before installing the new product. There are two or three different kinds of moisture testing devices to make sure there is not excessive amount of moisture in the slab. Also, by placing floor-fans to dry the water (the moisture) out of the slab, the cement leveler, and or the adhesive to a tack-able lay.)

The mother (customer) hired 2-helpers to prep the floor and clean the kitchen. End. (woke-up)

'PRAYER'

#1 I pray Heavenly Father for wisdom and knowledge and guidance for our current president. Pray for no more bombing at the Airport in Afghanistan, and safety of the remaining Afghan people and our military forces as they leave and comfort those family members of those who died at the Airport. In Jesus name amen.

#2 God bless the people of Harvest Bible University and New Hope Mission, God bless all the students. Pray that the new printer continues to work and print out all the booklets. I pray all went well with my homework. God bless all the teachers and staff. And Lord, watch over Pastor Cho, help him in his work, so he doesn't work too hard. He is an inspiration to me. In Jesus name amen.

#3 God bless Wednesday's message in the Chapel at 3 PM. And my testimony in Jesus' name, amen. End

CHAPTER 61

'LOOP DREAM'

We we're on the freeway in a big city with concrete around us, at an Interchange. We were heading one direction, and now we are heading another. We were in our 97' Toyota Camry, but they called it a 1998 Toyota Camry. In the fall time they get ready to sell next year 's model and clear-out last year's model.

We entered the loop and went around almost to the top and the car stopped. (Which in real life never happened, and our Toyota Camry was very dependable. Also, my wife researched that 1997 Camry to be the best car of the year by Consumer Reports.)

(But this is the second time I've dreamt about stopping on a loop. The first time was with my first wife in a previous chapter of writing. And I am assuming the second time was with my second wife, because of the year and model of car, for the time period.) (There was someone in the seat, but I didn't look over, it was like she wasn't there.) (No communication in real life or in the dream).

We get out, and I go for help. The freeway structure had some kind of narrow passageway with a storage area for Cal-trans people and their supplies, and a way down. I jumped into the supply area and men were close by and heard me, thinking I was going to take their stuff. But, instead, I told them, 'No, we are stranded at the top of the loop. Can you call for a tow truck?' Since they were right there below, I got in their truck, and they came up to us with their lights on, so we didn't get hit by other drivers making the loop. Until the tow truck driver showed up. (Then I woke up.)

(Dream II) Then I went right back to sleep and dreamt about, being on another loop somewhere else. The same place on the loop and the same narrow passage and remember telling the worker I was in this for the second time today. I've gone through this passage before. (In real life, I think God wanted me not to lose this dream and He repeated it. It wasn't about the loop or freeway; it is about what a loop does?

(A loop is the part on a freeway that allows you to change directions. That is the definition of repentance, in the Greek.)

(The first dream, I changed directions – or divorce with the first wife. Then the same, for the second wife. The third time was for me not to forget the dream and write it down.) (But, also the third time, is about the change I received in prison for the better. My repentance of my sins and behavior and faults; have changed direction into the will of God, amen.) End

'CPT. CLE. DREAM'

I was at this house doing some carpet installing. And other workers were there too. I was babysitting the house for the customer while they are gone. I was getting something out of my van, when another older van backs in the driveway. This lady gets out in a uniform, that says carpet cleaning. And a robot carpet cleaner. The Lady is auto controlling him. The customer didn't tell me they were coming and frankly they would be in my way. Plus, using any water for cleaning the old carpets up to my new carpet I'm laying would be a problem.

I use an electric-Iron to heat the plastic glue on a release papered back tape, with a nylon netting for strength. To put together the carpets, and if it is wet? The Ironed tape won't bond properly. They came up to the front door and there is a thick threshold one and a half to 2 inches high. And a 6 inch drop at least into the living room area. (In real life, the threshold is not an uncommon height, it was just shaped different than most.) (And the sunken living room are never coming in the front door for safety reasons; there's always an entrance hall or entry before the sunken living room.)

While, the Robot had a big-wheel and didn't want to jump the threshold to the next level, like it had a personality? It was supposedly being operated by the lady. I was coaching the robot to jump into the living room. (Which in real life, you would just program it to move forward regardless, it was taking your commands.) End Dream.

'QUES. & ANS.'

I had an unanswered question for a while. I had heard a number of preachers, when thanking God; they make a point to change or phrase it differently and made you know that they did. And I am wondering why? In this book, called 'Beware! The lies of Satan.' I was reading, by Frederick KC Price. Whom I've watched many times on the TBN Channel. Starting back to the 1980s when I was saved and born again. Listening to one of those preachers on TV – believing the Word of God, of Christ and Him Crucified. Believing Christ died for me and the whole world. He paid the penalty for sin and death with His own blood sacrifice. The Word revealed I was a sinner, and that there was no one righteous who ever lived except Jesus the Christ. That's why He was and is perfect. The perfect Lamb of God, who takes away the sins of the world. He fulfilled the law and the prophecies. And became our atoning Propitiation to appease the Holy Father. And that I needed a Savior. And I believed that Jesus the Christ was Him. That the Son of Man —Son of God, died, was buried, and on the third day, God the Father who is a Spirit, rose Jesus from the grave according to the Scriptures. It was about 1981, that I repented or turned away from my sinful behavior, and toward Jesus in Faith, and asking Him into my heart, by the power of the Holy Spirit. And now I am a born-again believer, with eternal life promise to me by the Word of God and the Holy Spirit which resides in me. By God's Amazing Grace. His Loving Mercy on me, lead me to repentance. So, I am Saved by the Grace of God through Faith. And nothing I did to work for it. Because it is a gift from God. God made that invitation to all who would believe. In (Romans 10:13) says: For "whoever calls on the name of the Lord shall be saved."

God 's love is eternal love, and He loved us that much, to send His only begotten Son to die on a Cross, so we could live, with life everlasting in Heaven. (John 3:16) tells us that. V16)" For God so loved the world that He gave His only begotten Son, that whoever believes in Him should not perish but have everlasting life."

Let's start in Chapter #6: in titled:

"Thank God for Everything no matter what". Chapter 6, starting on p.87, answers my question I had on why? (quote): The Apostle Paul tells us in Ephesians 5:20, giving thanks always for all things to God the Father in the name of our Lord Jesus Christ: On the surface, this verse would seem to say that we should thank God for everything that happens to us. But are we really supposed to always give thanks for all things to God, no matter how good or bad those things may be?

That is what some people would tell you. For many years, the idea of thanking God for everything, no matter what, was a very popular teaching in the Christian community. What stymied me when I first heard this teaching promulgated was that I would have to thank God for everything good thing and every bad thing that happened to me. It would mean that if I had a relative who was an alcoholic, unsaved, and was hit by a car and went to hell, I would have to thank God for that. It would mean that if some Christian who serve God and for all intents and purposes lived a godly life was stricken with Cancer at early age and died from it, I would have to thank God. That person was too young to die. Nevertheless, I would have to say, "Praise the Lord!" Thank you, Lord, that this person died of cancer."

I certainly am in agreement with the fact that if a person takes a positive attitude and thanks God for everything that happens to him, he will be the better for it mentally. However, it does not do credit to the Heavenly

Father, and it does not do credit to the Word of God, to take that attitude, even though you may be the better for it in terms of being able to handle the situation. In short, it is not what the Word of God tells us to do.

'Rendering What is Due'

Read Ephesians 5:20 one more time and allow me to point out something the Spirit of God revealed to me. ....," giving thanks always for all things to God the Father in the name of our Lord Jesus Christ.... Notice the words to God. It would be simple to give thanks for all things to the Heavenly Father in Jesus name, so why emphasize to God? Those two words are the key here.

In Matthew 22:15–21, we have an incident recorded that clarifies why to God is so important. "Then the Pharisees went and plotted how they might entangle Him [that is, Jesus] in His talk. And they sent to Him their disciples with the Herodians, saying, "Teacher, we know that You are true, and teach the way of God in truth; nor do you care about anyone, for you do not regard the person of men. Tell us, therefore, what do you think? Is it lawful to pay taxes to Caesar, or not? "But Jesus perceived their wickedness, and said, "Why do you test Me, you hypocrites? Show Me the tax money" So they brought Him a denarius. And He said to them, "Whose image and inscription is this?" They said to Him, "Caesar's". And He said to them, "Render therefore to Caesar the things that are Caesar's, and to God the things that are God's." Verse 21 alerts us to the fact that not everything is Caesars, and not everything is God's. It tells us that we should not give Caesar credit for what God has done. And second verse that directly connects with this Idea in Romans 13:7: Render therefore to all their due: taxes to whom taxes are due, customs to whom customs, fear to whom fear, honor to whom honor. Caesar, who is he really? What we are told to do in Matthew 22:21 and Romans 13:7 is to make a value judgment of all the things that happen to us. We are to evaluate those things, and determine whether or not those things are Caesars, and whether or not they are God's. If they are Caesars, we should give Caesar credit for them. If they are God's, we should give God credit for them. I am sure you realize that actually, there are only two person– ages, or two forces, we really have to contend with in our Christian walk —the forces of God, and the forces of Satan. We really do not have to deal with Caesar as such, yet I believe that in this story, Caesar really represents the powers of Satan, and we can Matthew 22:21 this way: "… render therefore to Satan the things that are Satan 's, and to God the things that are God."

……In 1-John 3:8, this is further elucidated:

"He who sins is of the devil, for the devil has sinned from the beginning. For this purpose, the Son of God was manifested, that He might destroy the works of the devil."

That means there must be such a person as the devil, even though certain religious groups say he does not exist. Not only that, but if Jesus was manifested to destroy the works of the devil, then the devil must have some works, as well. Otherwise, there would have been no works for Jesus to Destroy, and He would have wasted His time by coming into the earth realm. The word destroy here does not mean to obliterate or wipe out something. If it did, there would not be any more works of the devil. All you have to do it look around at all the mess in the world today to know that is not true.

In the original Greek, Destroy is the word 'Luo'. And it means "to loose or set free from". What that implies in the context of this verse is, because of sin, mankind was bound by satanic influence and was limited in the ability to move and act freely. Jesus came into the world to set men free. Once a person accepts Jesus as his personal Lord and Savior, the sin and the power of Satan that restricted his life is broken, and he is set free from it.

'The Devil's Works'

Now that we know the Devil has works, what kind of things would be classified as works of the devil? Since the Bible tells us there are works of the Devil, we can expect it will categorically list for us what those things are. That way, we will be able to tell whether something is a work of God or a work of the Devil, and not blame God for something the Devil did, or vice a versa.

In John 10: 1–10, Jesus gives us the modus operandi of both God and Devil:

"Most assuredly, I say to you, he who does not enter the sheepfold by the door, but climbs up some other way, the same is a thief and a robber. But he who enters by the door is the Shepherd of the sheep. To him the dookeeper opens, and the sheep hear his voice; and he calls his own sheep by name and leads them out. And when he brings out His own sheep, he goes before them; and the sheep follow Him, for they know His voice. Yet they will by no means follow a stranger, but will flee from him, for they do not know the voice of strangers."

Jesus used this illustration, but they did not understand the things which he spoke to them. Then Jesus said to them again, Most assuredly, I say to you, I am the door of the sheep. All who ever came before Me are thieves and robbers, but the sheep did not hear them. I am the door. If anyone enters by Me, he will be saved, and will go in and out and find pasture. The thief does not come except to steal, and to kill, and to destroy, I have come that they may have life, and that they may have it more abundantly. "I am the good Shepherd. The good shepherd gives His life for His sheep." Jesus says, "I am the good Shepherd." We can therefore consider ourselves to be the sheep.

The thief, who comes to steal the sheep is the devil, because the devil is the only person interested in stealing the sheep. He is the avowed foe and antagonist of God. In verse 10, Jesus says that He came so we might have life, and have it more abundantly. Abundant life does not include things being stolen from you. It does not include having things destroyed, or having you killed. Jesus says the thief is the one who comes for those purposes. Therefore, anything that steals, kills, or destroys is of the devil, and God does not have anything to do with it. Jesus uses a very loaded term when He says, "The thief does not come except to steal, and to kill, and to destroy."

A thief does not come to your front door, ring the doorbell, and say, "Good morning", I'm here to rob your house." He tries to be as unobtrusive as possible, in a place where he is not exposed, because if he is exposed, he is taking a chance of being caught.

Jesus says in Luke 12:39: "But know this, that if the master of the house had known what hour the Thief would come, he would have watched and not allowed his house to be broken into." The thief comes when you least expect him, when you are not looking for him. That means it is possible for the thief to steal, kill and destroy if you are not constantly on your guard. In the case of the Christian, on your guard means keeping watch with the Word of God and weighing everything accordingly. —Thank God for what God does—keep in mind what we have read about the works of God, the works of the devil, and rendering honor or blame to whom honor or blame is due and read Ephesians 5:20 once more. "Giving thanks always for all things to God the Father in the name of our Lord Jesus Christ. "As I said at the beginning to this chapter, the key words here are to God. And, as I said before, if you are going to thank God for every blessing and every calamity that befalls you, the words to God are unnecessary here. However, thanking God for every blessing and every calamity is not what this verse is telling us to do. Rather, it is telling us to give thanks to God for the things God does for us — for all things to God, or in other words, for all things that are God's. That also means that if we are going to give God thanks for everything, He does for us, we should not give him thanks for what the devil has done. We should not thank God that someone is sick, poor, dying, or dead.

First Thessalonians 5:18 is another scripture like Ephesians 5:20; and on the surface, it would seem to contradict what I have just said. Remember, though, that the Bible instructs us to be diligent to show ourselves approved unto God, rightly dividing the Word of truth. God is not the Author of confusion, and many times what may at first seem confusing or contradictory is not really that way once we look at it in detail, especially concerning the things of God. First Thessalonians 5:18 says this: "In everything give thanks; for this is the will of God in Christ Jesus for you. "When they read this verse, many people think, "You see! It does say to thank God for everything! "You may have thought the same thing yourself. However, that is not what this verse is saying at all. If you read this verse very Carefully, you will notice that it does not say, "for everything give thanks" – or, if you turn it around, "Give thanks for everything." It does not say for. It says, in everything give thanks. In other words, "give thanks in everything." We are supposed to give thanks in sickness, in poverty, in adversity. We are not supposed to give thanks for those things, but while those things are happening to us, we are to give thanks. If that is the case, what are we supposed to give thanks for while these things are happening to us? If we are sick, for example, we are supposed to give thanks that, according to I-Peter 2:24, with Christ's stripes we were healed, and we do not have to accept sickness. We are supposed to give thanks that He Himself took our infirmities and bore our sickness (Matthew 8:17). We are supposed to give thanks that the Lord Himself said, "For I am the Lord who heals you "(exodus 15:26).

Instead of thanking God for whatever calamity Satan throws against us, we should stand on the Word and thank God for the solution that He promises us in his word to deal with that challenge. In the face of situations that seem to tax us beyond human abilities, we can rely on God as our Source, because His word says in Philippians 4:13, "I can do all things through Christ who strengthens me." That means we can rise up in the middle of that situation, flex the neck, and cast them out of our circumstances! When a negative situation arises, I can say, "Praise God," and thank God right in the middle of it. I do not have to rely on myself, because the Bible says I have the Creator living in me, and that Jesus has been made unto me wisdom, knowledge, and sanctification through the Holy Spirit. I can do anything through Christ, so I can give thanks in any situation. I do not have to say, "Oh, I hope this doesn't happen". I have the Greater One inside me, and He has all the answers.

When the economic wolf is at the door, and the prices at the supermarket are going up faster than my paycheck, I can give thanks, because Philippians 4:19 says, "And my God shall supply all your needs according to His riches in glory by Christ Jesus." "Praise God that I can still go into the store and buy anything I need, because my Father is my source; not my pocketbook!" What about Temptations, trials, and tests? There is no way you can get around them, and no place where you will not be tempted, tried, or tested in this earth realm. You do not give thanks for the Temptations, trials, or tests. It is never nice when they happen. They do not feel good, and there is nothing in the temptation's, trials, or tests in themselves to be thankful for. However, you can give thanks that I-Corinthians 10:13 says, "No temptation [trial or test] has over taken you except such as is common to man; but God is faithful, who will not allow you to be tempted [tried or tested] beyond what you are able, but with the Temptation will also make the way of escape, that you may be able to bear it."

We can say, "Praise the Lord that I don't have to say in this thing ", push the eject button, and, in the name of Jesus, bail out of this trial. The latter part of that scripture should also prove without a shadow of a doubt that God is not the one who tests, tries, or tempts you. God knows human nature, and he knows we will always take the path of least resistance, so if he gives us an escape route, it defeats any purpose he may have in trying us. Therefore, it must be the Thief, the murderer, and the robber – Satan – who brings the Temptation, trial, or test. All God gives us is the way out.

Do we thank God for everything? No! We thank God for what God has done. We will have to have accurate knowledge of the Word, so we can know the mode of operation of the devil and the mode of operation of the Father. That way, we can give the devil his due, and give God credit for what He has done, and walk from there to Victory after Victory in Christ Jesus. Amen (end)

CHAPTER 62

'MULTI. —TRADE DREAM'

I am working in this house, which I believe is new. And there are a multiple of workers in the house, all doing their own various trades. And if they're – there, then I can't do my trade? (Which is pretty obvious in this book. I am a Flooring Contractor.) (And in a new house situation, I am one of the last people working on the inside, for finishing the home.) (And most of the time, the other tradesmen are all gone by that time. And it is my turn to beautify the home.) (In real life it is the general contractor who organizes the subcontractors to do their jobs, and in an orderly manner. That is, lining them up to get the job done. But, sometimes of time constraints or pressure of an Impatient buyer, or the project is taking way too long, and he needs it so for the financing, on the next project. And could be working on multiple homes at the same time, or whatever, we are all in there together.)

So, in the dream, we are talking, a group of us, in one of the bedrooms and the T shaped hallway. Which is shaped more like this: It looks more like a tree stump, with flaps or wings. But it is the main-hall, and the little niche is about a 4'x 4' area, where the two-bedroom doors are. The little lines are the doors, looking at it, as a top view. I was talking to the guys in general, and said, 'what do you need me to help you with? Because I can't do anything until you guys are gone.' I started to pick something up by the far wall. When they started talking about the cabinet guy. And some of the built-ins in the bedrooms. Built-in clothes cabinet with chest-a-drawers.

Going in the closet or on one of the walls opposite where the bed would be. It is all in the plans of the home. This is where all the guidelines of installation are, and if you have any questions, you will ask the General Contractor. It is better asking then; then to put something in the wrong place, and then having to move it again. Because the cabinets are tall, and boxy. They were wondering if they will fit. To make the door-jam, or to fit the cabinet around the corner in the hallway. (In real life, most standard bedroom doors are 30 inches in width – some 32". And if the door is off. And the door jamb-stop on each side, make it about 3/4 of an inch less, on a 30-inch door. The widest opening would be 29 1/4" wide. So, more than likely, they will open a window and take the screen-off and bring the cabinet through the window. Because most cabinets are pre-built at a cabinet shop, and then delivered to the house on a flat-bed trailer and stored in the garage, until ready for Installation.)

'CPT. FILLS-DREAM'

I was on a carpet job by myself with a lot of furniture. The main floor of the house and the basement. And I was working in areas where the furniture wasn't, like the end of a room, and the hallway. (But, in real life that is the opposite of how we do it. We empty out the whole room areas, make the main cuts for each room, then the balance of the roll is for the hallways and fills. For large rooms that are wider than 12 feet that is; since most carpet rolls are 12 feet wide.) I was going back and forth from the top floor to the basement, through a rectangle slit between floors, to save time going up and down the stairs. (The interpretation for this dream is, like in real life. I had a lot of work to do, writing and reading, but it wasn't getting done, because of distractions, some food and drink, but mostly TV watching. And the slits remind me of our windows in the cell, except we don't go through them.) End

'HOPE'

In this June edition 2021, of the magazine called 'Decision'. Put out by the Billy Graham Evangelistic Association. On the front cover has a huge U-turn sign on it. With it entitled: 'Revival always begins with Repentance'. [The word repent in the Greek means (to turn from or turn away) to turn from sin, in one direction, and turn the opposite direction toward Christ Jesus, our Lord and Savior.]

The article by Franklin Graham, is talking about 'Hope' in a testimony in his hometown. The title of the story is: 'Hope in an age of lawlessness'.

p4) quote: 'On April 28, my hometown of Boone, North Carolina, was shaken by a horrible tragedy that took the lives of two of our county Sheriff's Deputies, Sergeant Chris Ward, and K-9 Deputy Logan Fox, who were ambushed when they answered a call to check on residents. In the days following, we saw an incredible outpouring of sympathy and respect for our Law enforcement men and women. When the bodies of Sergeant Ward and Deputy Fox were transported from Winston-Salem back to Boone, law enforcement personnel from numerous counties and towns, along with first responders, escorted them in a procession that stretched for miles, Along the 88-mile route, hundreds of people lined the highway and overpasses, silently and tearfully expressing their support and love for the fallen heroes.

At a community wide memorial service, thousands gathered to pay their respects to the men who sacrificed their own lives to protect and guard others. I had the privilege of opening in prayer and sharing the Hope of the Gospel at the Service, which was attended by law enforcement from across the nation. All that respect reflected the America that I know and love, and it stands in stark contrast to the voices of anarchy that have recently fills our streets.

We've seen it play out on our screens as violent protests against law-enforcement have broken out in numerous American cities. Police stations and police cars have been burned; officers have been shamelessly heckled and have come under attack by throngs of angry protesters. Calls to defund the police which began with the George Floyd case, spread quickly into city councils, and even into the halls of Congress. An officer in Los Angeles was called a "murderer" and a "racist" at a simple traffic stop. A California college student was berated by his professor for expressing his support of the local police in the Bronx, New York city police officers were heckled and cursed while responding to a call for help. "Sadly, this is the result of years of elected officials de moralizing police officers and decriminalizing important behavior, said the local police union." "We will only be successful in reducing crime if the good people of the community lend us a hand by showing support for police."

That's why we at the Billy Graham Evangelistic Association are working to show our respect and gratitude for officers around this country who hold the line every day against every kind of evil and criminal behavior. This past month, we held appreciation dinners for law enforcement officers in the Portland, Oregon/Vancouver, Washington, area and in Seattle. We've also held appreciation dinners in Asheville and Charlotte, North Carolina. Across the nation, law-enforcement personnel are under intense pressure; in Seattle alone, more than 200 officers have left the police department in the past year. Our appreciation dinners are wonderful opportunities for us to express our support and provide encouragement to the men and women who keep us safe every day. At Samaritans Purse, we are welcoming law-enforcement officers and their spouses to participate in our operation Heal Our Patriots ministry in Alaska.

This is a program designed to strengthen the marriage of wounded military veterans, and we know that police on the Homefront deal with many of the stresses and trauma as do our soldiers who fight on foreign soil to protect our freedoms. The Bible says," For the mystery of lawlessness is already at work, " (II-Thessalonians 2:7).

Behind the ever-rising tide of violence, rage and anarchy is the evil one, the devil himself, spreading his wickedness in increasing intensity. The sheer brutality that has infected our culture is shocking, but not to our adversary who delights in it. God appointed civil authorities – including our law-enforcement – along with the godly influence of the church of the Lord Jesus Christ and the Supernatural ministry of the Holy Spirit, to restrain evil to a degree (Romans 13:1; II-Thess.2:7). One day — and I believe soon — "The lawless one will be revealed"

(II-Thess.2:8), and that is none other than the rise of the Antichrist in the Great Tribulation. "The coming of the lawless one is according to the working of Satan, with all power, signs, and lying wonders. "(II-Thess.2:9). I believe the Devil is called the lawless one because he has, openly rebelled against Almighty God and seeks to oppose Him at every turn, the enemy has no regard for the degrees, statutes and Commandments that God has laid down in Scripture. But as Martin Luther so famously said: "Though this world, with devils filled, should threaten to undo us, we will not fear, for God hath willed His truth to triumph through us. "God's word put it this way: "The Lord will consume [him] with the breath of His mouth and destroy [him] with the brightness of His coming" (II-Thessalonians 2:8).

Hi, look forward to that day, don't you? In the meantime, we live in a world stained by sin and its awful consequences. In fact, the Apostle John put it quite succinctly in his first pastoral epistles: "Whoever commits sin also commits lawlessness"

(I-John 3:4) How grateful we should all be that Christ appeared in order… "to take away our sins, "… (I-John 3:5). In the midst of the growing chaos and lawlessness that sin brings, the Billy Graham Evangelistic Association is faithfully proclaiming the transforming Gospel of the Lord Jesus Christ, this fall, we are planning to follow famous old "Route 66" across America 's heartland, from Chicagoland/Joliet, Illinois, to San Bernardino, Ca., stopping at various cities along the way. Please be in prayer for this and other festivals we have planned around the world. (End quote) 2021

BGEA Bible Version in the (NKJV).

CHAPTER 63

'Daycare Dream'

In the dream, I was at a daycare, bringing a rectangle fold-up table. And slid it into the room with the small kids. And I propped something against it so it wouldn't fall. There was a young boy who came up to me with blondish brown hair. He was some kid from the past. And then Timothy was there at 2–3 years old, also who was wearing big boy pants and he asked, 'if he could go to the bathroom?'

Then my first ex-wife shows up in a black pantsuit. It was very sharp looking, and she had short hair. And Karen her sister came in with her too, but clearly Brenda was dressed up. And Karen was in her casual clothes. (Usually, it was Karen who was all dressed up, working in an office setting). And I was putting little toy-men on the arm of Timothy my son at this time. (But, in real life, this didn't happen; it could have, but it didn't.) (And the reason I was dreaming about small children is because, today is my grandson 's fifth birthday). (Dec.2021). End

'Clint Dream'

Clint Eastwood and I were at the bottom of the hill. And he started walking, he had a mission, and some place to go. Before he left, we looked -upon the top of the hill. There was a lair or a hide-out of the bad guys. It was mostly a glass house with white walls. These two main bad-guys like in Clints movies. Are actually Elizabeth Taylor and Richard Burton. (And before bed, in real life, my Bunkie and I were talking about this older famous Actress, because she was on TV for something of the past.) Well, as Clint had his walk-on; it was next to this dirt canal. And from the hilltop, a 50-caliber machine gun went off, trying to shoot Clint. The dirt was all shot-up next to him. But it didn't hit him or bother him either. He even taunted them by jumping down to where they shot on the canal bank, and then jump back on the dirt road. (woke-up) End.

'FELLOWSHIP DREAM'

My friend from school, from elementary to high school and we were neighbors also; his name is John. We were going out to lunch with the grandkids. We had two of his kids, or one grandson was mine. And one was his. We were walking and talking about God; that he would handle the situation, whatever that was, as we were walking in the parking lot.

We got to the front door, went in and the next doorway the kids hung on to the door casing and wouldn't go through. And there was someone behind us. So, I pushed the two boys who were about five years old through the door and picked both of them up and set them down on the waiting bench-seat. We went in and got seated. I think it was a Basque Restaurant, but I am not sure. We sat down and you could see a lot of the kitchen staff, – no wall in between and two waitresses we're on their knees ready to serve someone. That opening where the kitchen staff was; kind-a-looked like it was also a fast-food window. (Which in real life, Basque Restaurants don't have that, plus they aren't on their knees waiting to serve us. And there is a wall in between the kitchen.) (And the reason I was dreaming this, I just talked to John, my friend on the outside, and we talked about grandkids, and that it was Zach's fifth birthday today.) End.

CHAPTER 64

'WALKING IN VICTORY'

God wants us to walk in the Spirit of God; In Victory, walking in the fruit of God, in His Spirit, which is love, joy, peace, patience, kindness, goodness, faithfulness, gentleness, and self-control. (Ref. To: Gal. 5:22-23). Walking in Faith, (which is His Word) as a spiritual man of God; he needs to be totally dependent on Christ and the Cross. His finished work on the Cross at Calvary. Die to self and live for God. So, the Holy Spirit can work in our lives with Power and accomplishment. And we still have this Tent to contend with; (this body); (Ref. To: II- Cor. 10:3-5). NKJV V3)" Though we walk in the flesh we do not war against the flesh. V4) For the weapons of our warfare are not carnal but mighty in God pulling down strongholds, V5) casting down arguments and every high thing that exalts itself against the knowledge of God, bringing every thought into captivity to the obedience of Christ. "(Ref. I-Thess. 5:16-18); Brothers, V16)"Rejoice always, V17) pray without ceasing, V18) in everything give thanks; for this is the will of God in Christ Jesus for you." (James 1:2-5) ; V2)"My brethren, count it all joy when you fall into various trials, V3) knowing that the testing of your faith produces patience (long-suffering, endurance, or perseverance). V4) But let patience have its perfect work, that you may be perfect and complete, lacking nothing. V5) If any of you lacks wisdom, let him ask of God, who gives to all liberally and without reproach, (or disapproval) and it will be given to him." And to fulfill the law of liberty which is love one another in Christ.....Ref.(Rom.8:1-11)

V1)"There is therefore now no condemnation to those who are in Christ Jesus, who do not walk according to the flesh, but according to the Spirit, V2) For the law of the Spirit of life in Christ Jesus has made me free from the law of sin and death. V3) For what the law could not do in that it was weak through the flesh, God did by sending His own Son in the likeness of sinful flesh, on account of sin: He condemned sin in the flesh, V4) that the righteous requirement of the law might be fulfilled in us who do not walk according to the flesh but according to the Spirit. V5) For those who live according to the flesh set their minds on the things of the flesh, but those who live according to the Spirit, the things of the Spirit. NKJV

Commentary: ('The Greek word rendered set their minds includes a person's will, thoughts, and emotions. It also includes assumptions, values, desires, and purposes, setting the mind on the things of the flesh or on the things of the Spirit, means being oriented to, or Governed by those things on which we focus'.... our attention on.) V6) For to be carnally minded is death, but to be spiritually minded is life and peace. V7) Because the carnal mind is enmity (has ill will; mutual hatred; animosity; is at odds) against God; for it is not subject to the law of God, nor indeed can be. V8) So then, those who are in the flesh cannot please God. V9) But you are not in the flesh but in the Spirit, if indeed the Spirit of God dwells in you. Now if anyone does not have the Spirit of Christ, he is not His. V10) And if Christ is in you, the body is dead because of sin, but the Spirit is life because of righteousness. (We are made Righteous by Faith in Christ Jesus and His finished work on the Cross. He who fulfilled the righteous requirement of the Law. (The Law of sin and death) ... 'He who knew no sin to be sin for us, that we might become the righteousness of God in Him.'.... (II-Cor.5:21) ...He who took it upon Himself the sins of us all, to Atone for sin and death; a debt we could never repay. His sacrifice to appease the Wrath of God. He did it Once, and for All, for the forgiveness of sins for all mankind. He is the second Adam. The first, brought the curse of sin and death, and the second, by one man, took it away, that man be Christ Jesus.

By the shedding of His own blood on the Cross made this possible.) V11) But if the Spirit of Him who raised Christ from the dead will also give life to your mortal bodies through His Spirit who dwells in you." (Let's keep going). V12)" Therefore, brethren, we are debtors—not to the flesh, to live according to the flesh. V13) For if you live according to the flesh you will die; but if by the Spirit you put to death the deeds of the body, you will live. V14) For as many as are led by the Spirit of God, these are sons of God. V15) For you did not receive the spirit of bondage again to fear, but you received the Spirit of adoption by whom we cry out, "Abba, Father. "V16) The Spirit Himself bears witness with our spirit that we are children of God, V17) and if children, then heirs—heirs of God and joint heirs with Christ, if indeed we suffer with Him, that we may also be glorified together. V18) For I consider that the sufferings of this present time are not worthy to be compared with the glory which shall be revealed in us. (The glorious and wonderful heaven, that awaits those who believe). (I Cor. 2:9) says: but as it is written: "Eye has not seen, nor ear heard, nor have entered into the heart of man the things which God has prepared for those who love Him." Ref. Comm. NKJV—V19) For the earnest expectation of the creation eagerly waits for the revealing of the sons of God." —Earnest expectation— (Literally means to watch with outstretched neck.)—Creation— (Is impatient to see the revelation of the sons of God.) That is us, who believes; The called; The Saints in Christ, and the Spirit of God who makes intercession for us with groanings which cannot be uttered, when we don't know how to pray.

(Romans 8:28–31): V28)" And we know that all things work together for the good to those who love God, to those who are the called (one whom are being changed from glory to glory into the Image of God's Son) according to His purpose. V29) For whom He foreknew, He also predestined to be conformed to the image of His Son, that He might be the firstborn (speaking of Jesus rising from the dead in His glorified body) among many brethren." (Then us, at the Rapture: In I-Thess. 4:13-18) He is coming: In V13)" But I do not want you to be ignorant, brethren, concerning those who have fallen asleep, less you sorrow as others who have no hope. V14) For if we believe that Jesus died and rose again, even so God will bring with Him those who sleep in Jesus (who died in Christ, in waiting). V15) For this we say to you by the word of the Lord, that we who are alive and remain until the coming of the lord will by no means precede (come before) those who are asleep. V16)

For the Lord Himself will descend from heaven with a shout, with the voice of an archangel, and with the trumpet of God. And the dead in Christ will rise first. V17) Then we who are alive and remain shall be caught up together with them in the clouds to meet the Lord in the air. And thus, we shall always be with the Lord. V18) Therefore comfort one another with these words. "(Rom.8:30-31); V30)" Moreover whom He predestined, these He also called; whom He called, these He also justified; and whom He justified, these He also glorified. V31) What then shall we say to these things? If God is for us, who can be against us? "And coming to a close, in (Jeremiah 29:11-14); V11)" For I know the thoughts that I think toward you, says the Lord, thoughts of peace and not of evil, to give you a future and a hope. V12) Then you will call upon Me and go and pray to Me, and I will listen to you. V13) And you will seek Me and find Me, when you search for Me with all your heart. V14) I will be found by you, says the Lord, and I will bring you back from your captivity;" ... (whatever addiction or compulsion, bad behavior, or habit He will bring you back from captivity).

In conclusion, God loves you. He died for you, He is sitting at the right hand of God the Father in heaven, making intercession for you. You are God's sons, His children. Walk therefore in the Spirit, and not into the lust of the flesh. God said, "Be holy, for I am holy." (I-Pet.1:16).

(And Ref. Eph. 5:8-14); As the Scripture teaches us: V8)" For you were once darkness, but now you are light in the Lord. Walk as children of light (for the fruit of the Spirit is in all goodness, righteousness, and truth), V10) finding out what is acceptable to the Lord. V11) And have no fellowship with the unfruitful works of darkness, but rather expose them. V12) For it is shameful even to speak of those things which are done by them in secret. V13) But all things that are exposed are made manifest by the light, for whatever makes manifest is light. V14) Therefore He says: 'Awake, you who sleep, A rise from the dead, And Christ will give you light.'"

'Walk in Wisdom'

V15)" See then that you walk circumspectly (meaning carefully), not as fools but as wise, V16) redeeming the time, because the days are evil. V17)

Therefore do not be unwise, but understand what the will of the Lord is. V18) And do not be drunk with wine, in which is dissipation (meaning expend wastefully); but be filled with the Spirit, V19) speaking to one another in psalms, hymns, and spiritual songs, and making melody in your heart to the Lord, V20) giving thanks always for all things to God the Father in the name of our Lord Jesus Christ, V21) submitting to one another in the fear of God." (And Gal.2:20-21); V20)" I have been crucified with Christ; it is no longer I who live, but Christ lives in me; and the life which I now live in the flesh I live by faith in the Son of God, who loved me and gave Himself for me. V21) I do not set aside the grace of God; for if righteousness comes through the law, then Christ died in vain. "He is coming soon church, prepare yourself (look up), for His arrival with great expectation. Stand firm in the faith you have in Him. Make sure that your conscience is clear. And you are wearing your righteous clothes of faith in Him, and the Cross of Christ. And for those who don't know Jesus, as Lord and Savior.... Come to Him now. Tomorrow may be too late. (John 3:16-17); V16)" For God so loved the world that He gave His only begotten Son, that whoever believes in Him should not perish but have everlasting life. V17) For God did not send His Son into the world to condemn the world, but that the world through Him might be saved."

(God Invites you now): With every eye closed, pray this prayer with me, and acknowledge your willingness to make a Faith step, of repentance (a change of mind or direction), toward God (And Faith toward our Lord Jesus Christ). Turn from sin and death, and turn to Jesus, the Author and Finisher of our Faith. Into life, and life more abundantly, into the Living water. PP (Ref.Acts20:21; Rom.6:23;Heb.12:2; John 10:10b;7:38)..... Now, raise your hand, (thank you) you are saying yes, to Jesus and your realization of the fact, the Scripture says in (Romans 3:10-12), V10)"There is none righteous, no, not one, V11) There is none who understands; There is none who seeks after God. V12) They have all turned aside; They have together become unprofitable; There is none who does good, no, not one. "And V23.... for all have sinned and fall short of the glory of God.... (Pray this Prayer, from your heart out loud to God) quote:(JSM/KJV p.1113,1114) *

"Dear God in Heaven, I come to you today as a lost sinner. I am asking You that you save my soul and cleanse me from all sin. I realize in my heart my need of salvation, which can only come through Jesus Christ. I am accepting Christ into my heart and what He did on the cross in order to purchase my redemption in obedience to your word, I confess with my mouth the Lord Jesus, and believe in my heart that God has raised Him from the dead. You have said in your Word which cannot lie, 'For whosoever shall call upon the name of the Lord shall be saved.' I have called upon Your name exactly as You have said, and I believe that right now, I am Saved In Jesus Name Amen." ......*

"If you have sincerely prayed these words, which I have written out for you, and believed in your heart upon the Lord Jesus Christ, you are at this moment saved, and your name is written down in the Lambs Book of Life. Congratulations!" end quote!

(Get yourself a Bible; get in a Bible based church; stay in the Word; let the Word teach you, and guide you, and let the Word wash over you, for the living water of the Word is Spirit and Life). (The Holy Spirit will guide you into all Truths).

* 'You are now a "new creation in Christ Jesus" (II-Cor. 5:17). As such, you have the Divine nature within your heart, which is the Nature of God, which means that the Holy Spirit actually now resides within your heart and life.

The entirety of your life is now going to be different. You have been cleansed from all sin and have embarked upon the greatest journey that one could ever undertake. A whole new world is about to open up to you.

You now have something to live for, and something to which you can look forward. Living for Jesus is the most exciting life that one could ever live, the most fulfilling, the most rewarding, the most wonderful. There is absolutely nothing in the world that can compare with this which you have just received, and which will never end.

.... But of course, Satan, the enemy of your soul, is not happy at all about you giving your heart to Christ Jesus; consequently, he will do everything he can to cause you problems, even attempt to get you to turn back. However, if you will heed carefully the following instructions that we will give, Satan will not be successful in pulling you back, and total victory will be yours.'

I am blessed reading this New Testament (Counselor's Edition). This is the Expositor's version, meaning this King James Version is being:(Modified by Jimmy Swaggart for Easier Reading.) Also, it has translations out of the original Greek to get a deeper understanding of the original text. And his explanation, and revelation that he received from the Holy Spirit. And now, you pray that the Holy Spirit will teach you what you need to know. Stay in the word. Victory is yours, in Christ Jesus. End.

CHAPTER 65

'DREAM W/ TIM'

Tim is all grown-up now in this dream, who is my son in real life. And he sent me to the movies. And afterwards, I met them outside walking to the car. And as I caught up with them. I gave Tim's new mother-in-law a hug. And Tim's wife, I asked how she was doing? – Then the dream changed – I was at this party – a celebration of some kind in the evening. We were eating, and received a biscuit – like cake, and part of some chocolate – dessert. And we were finished, I saved some for someone who wasn't there. A girlfriend of mine from the past. And I was almost at her door, and then I woke up. …

(In real life, this dream is four different events, it never happened this way, but similar in respect too, I had only met my daughter-in-law 's Mother two-times, once at their home, and the other, at their wedding. That was the celebration party and reception dinner. When I recall my daughter-in-law's mom, she is a real delight. Very personable, and charming. A lovely woman. And I'm sorry I wasn't there for my daughter-in-law and my son, when she passed away. As well, as my dad, to have been there for my daughter, grandkids, siblings, and the rest of my family. I am truly sorry I wasn't there the last 7+ years for them. End

Loren L. Johnson

'REALTOR DREAM'

I was one of three Realtors in this house talking – We all had the same idea and strategy. But when we all went and got into the car. I looked out the window and saw a well-known Realtor; and he was wearing a suit and tie, while cleaning the flower garden next-door. The scene— changed, and the three—became carpet layers with a job to do. And when we got there, the carpet was already delivered. We just had to work out a price and get started. Then the customers showed me their bathroom, and said the vinyl is defective and it is ripping. But the customers laid their own floor themselves over an uneven floor, and didn't fasten it down or even cut it in. And I told them, 'It is not the vinyl's problem, it is your installation that caused the damage to the flooring material.' (I woke up).

'ALEX DREAM'

I was put down in this arena-ring, and I have a spear in my hand. And maybe 50 feet in front of me, is two more gladiators with spears also. And I'm moving forward to take out my opponents. One on the left, I think it was a woman, and the one on the right a man. I was going to go left first then right. But changed it right to left. That sounds so sexist. But actually, I didn't want to fight regardless. If the gladiator was wonder-woman, I would have lost anyway. In the dream. So, I ended up stabbing both of them. And the big male gladiator was wounded and hadn't died yet. But, said to be of honor to die in battle. So, the male gladiator who was Alex Baldwin, said to me, 'run me through.' I picked up the spear and planted it under my foot on the end in the dirt. Just as he charged at me and the spear went through him, and he even pulled it almost all the way through. (In real life I was reading days prior, about O.T. times, and King David and his Mighty men of valor; also, how King Saul died; he was shot with an arrow and was dying and losing the battle. And he didn't want the enemy to torture him. So, he asked his Armor bearer to run-him-through, but he wouldn't. So, King Saul

390

leaned down on his sword. Also, I had dreamt that way, maybe because that's the way superman died pulling the spear through. Not to any disrespect to Alex Baldwin and the tragedy of that accident on the set of his movie. Alex was on my heart and mind to pray for, after seeing him in the news recently.) end.

CHAPTER 66

'CHER DREAM'

My first ex-wife, and I as teenagers, but of course we weren't married yet, but next-door neighbors. We were coming out of my dad's house through the garage door opening. There were some people in there like a party or something. But it was morning time? And my girlfriend comes out in her robe, and I was following her. She went over-around the corner where our trash cans were kept. I thought she wanted for her and I to make out around the corner of the house. But, when I went there, she was doing something to this car that was parked between the houses. She had the hood-up, and then Brenda looks over at me, and says, cover for me. And she is digging into the engine for something? She said, something about the spark plugs. Anyway, she had the air-cleaner off and a couple other parts laying on the ground. She didn't even have tools in her hand that I could see. Now, her mom comes out too, from the house in the garage, and she is in her robe also. And it is morning time, she has coffee in her hand and goes to the left toward the front door but was just in the front to relax and enjoy her coffee. The only thing is, when I turned the corner, I was going to stall her so she wouldn't see my girlfriend working on the car. But, when I looked at her again, it wasn't her mom, but Cher. Then, she headed past me, and I couldn't stall her any longer. And she sees my girlfriend working on the car, and says, 'What are you doing?' Then Cher says, 'This steering here is out of alignment. And this doesn't look right either'. But now the car is like a Jeep or a dune buggy in Mark's driveway next-door. More to

393

the right and the buggy is turned around the other direction. Now, my girlfriend is gone, but 3 to 4 other persons are in his driveway. As Cher is going on about the vehicle, two other people showed up from that time period of the mid-1970s. Tim and Kerry Ryan, and they are discussing, how to calm this situation here. (But in real life, none of this happened for real, except the part where Brenda and I made out on the side of the house, not at my house, but hers.) End

'Leonardo & Kate Dream'

I had a dream I was on a ship, on deck, and it is foggy out, it is really thick. And I was on the floor (the deck) on my knees and putting tape around in a square about 2"x2". And spray painting them a bright color like orange, about 2 feet apart, which is supposed to be for something to do with tennis. When I hear these two joyful young adults walking toward me, and I recognize Leonardo (Jack, from the Titanic movie right away), and I guess we were friends. But I didn't want him to see me working like this So, I put-up my collar and put my head down, and change my voice a little. He was asking me 'What are you doing?' I said, 'getting ready for tennis'…in a deeper voice. As they went along merrily in love with each other; happy and gay (merry and bright and lively). (woke up)

(In real life, as far as I know there is no tennis courts on cruise liner ships. If there were, the people sitting around the court at their tables having breakfast would be getting hit in the back of their heads all the time. Second, being extremely foggy weather would be a bad time to paint anything. And thirdly, I don't know Leonardo or Kate Winslow personally, but the movie, they did an awesome job together in the 'Titanic'. Oh, lastly, and the word gay I used for another happy word. Our generation has misused that word, as opposed to my dad's generation. But, still used today in a lot of old Christmas songs.) End.

'CAROL & NICOLE DREAM'

In this dream Carol Burnett, who was in her middle age, 40s to 50s. And Nicole my niece, was a young woman. (In real life, I always see her as a young woman all grown-up with a family, my sister's daughter.) And I was in this living room scene. It was an average 12-13 foot wide and maybe 15 to 20 feet long. With an extra-large fireplace at one end near the outside wall. And windows on each side, and a kitchen at the end with the lights out there. It was a calm, lovely day, of us sitting in some rocking chairs—talking. And I think there was a couch there too. I was standing and sweeping with a little broom on the hard floor. It looks like (VCT), we call it in the floor-business. (Vinyl composition tile.) 12"x 12"glue down, with pressure release glue.

Anyway, the floor I was sweeping had some dried crabgrass from the yard. I swept that up around the chairs and put it in the fireplace. It was huge, with large logs in it. As they were talking, Carol says to Nicole, 'Oh, so you are expecting a little child'. And she responded, 'Yes'. Now, Carol is up and about by the window, and I gave her a hug. I said, 'I love you, Carol.' And held her a minute. She says to me, 'If I wasn't married, you would be right in there'. (Then I woke-up)

(In real life, this didn't happen, the persons are real, but the situation didn't occur. Also, my niece wasn't pregnant when I dreamt this, but subconsciously one of the last times I saw her, she was pregnant. So, that is one of my last memories of her; for she lives back east now). End.

CHAPTER 67

'ABBEY DREAM'

This dream is with Abbey Carpet of Bakersfield employees, Sam, Bob, Al, and I. All working on a project together. It starts with me working outdoors on some kind-a platform or shelf in a chain-link enclosure. (In real life I was getting kind-of use to seeing chain-link enclosures.) Anyway, for the shelves, to wrap them with something strong and rough. Like rope, except it was chain. I guess it was for standing on, to make it a sturdy, non-slick surface to stand on. Anyway, the chain-links are small gauge, like in a chain-link from a swing set. The only thing is the chain-links weren't put together yet; you had to interlink the chain before you wrapped it. Well, one side had a loop and an opening on the other was closed. I wasn't sure how it all fits together. I was going to do a little section and see if I did it right. Then I thought, I'll just go inside and ask Al. Al, Sam, and Bob we're working on an inside project together. They were putting these giant size steel plates in for these wooden beams. The plate-steel had, 2 to 3 holes in each, for these large dowels (for fastening two pieces of wood, or a round rod) of wood to put together and make it strong. This seemed like this was for Sam, this project. I wanted to ask Al how to interlink those chains before I get started, so I don't mess it up. But as I got on the ground talking with Al as he is working on something there. I was just about to ask him, when the answer came to me.

(I know what he would say in real life; read the Instruction Manual.)

I was making a joke with them as they were fitting the plates into place on the beams with the dowels. And I said, 'It actually fits?', 'I'm surprised?', 'I mean, that's a good job, carry on.'

(In real life, we joked a lot at work together). (This was my last employment on the outside before coming into prison, it isn't there anymore.) End.

'BOOK MARKER'

This book marker inspired me, of God's love, and hope, and of His assurance, that God is with me. And I know in the Scriptures, that God 's grace is upon me. (II-Cor.12:9) says, V9) And He said to me, "My grace is sufficient for you, for My strength is made perfect in weakness. "It is from the 'Hand of Hope'; the Joyce Meyer Ministry —World Missions. The Book Marker says quote: *

Dear Friend,

We want you to know that we are thinking about you during this season in your life. His love will never fail you. (Hebrews 13:5b) For He Himself has said, "I will not in any way fail you nor give you up nor leave you without support. I will not in any degree leave you helpless nor forsake, nor let you down (relax My hold on you)! Assuredly not! (AMP) And We care about you! We realize that it is difficult when you are separated from your loved ones.

Suffering and hard times are never easy, but you can have the comfort of knowing that God is with you. He wants you to know today that you are precious in His sight, and He loves you very much. Don't let this time of trial separate you from the Love of God.

You are not alone. God's eyes are on you and His ears are open to your cry. Begin seeing yourself as God sees you – Loved, righteous, fearless, valuable, and determined.

Please be assured that we will be praying for you. Trust God that His grace will be sufficient to get you through until your time of deliverance comes. We are believing God 's very best for you.

God bless you, Joyce Meyer Ministries —PS "The eyes of the Lord are on the righteous, and His ears are attentive to their cry." (Ps.34:15) NIV. End.

'PRE—PRAYER'

In Joel Osteen's preaching message on TBN. He is the Senior Pastor of his Lakewood Church in Houston Texas. Where he starts off greeting his audience with a clean joke, and has everyone pray this prayer, every time he speaks from the word. And my bunkie and I would catch his 4 PM telecast and recite it too.

"This is my Bible, I am what it says I am, I have what it says I have, I can do what it says, I can do, today I will be taught the word of God. My mind is alert, my mind is receptive. I boldly confess, I will never be the same. In Jesus name. Amen. End.

'RENEW YOUR MIND'

This is a little excerpt out of Joel Osteen 's book, called— "Think better —live better." Let us start off in God 's word about what we are supposed to do. (Rom. 12:1-3); V1)" I beseech (I beg you) you therefore, brethren, by the mercies of God, that you present your bodies a living sacrifice, holy, acceptable to God, which is your reasonable service. V2) And do not be conformed to this world, but be transformed by the renewing of your mind, that you may prove what is that good and acceptable and perfect will of God. V3) For I say, through the grace given to me, to everyone who is among you, not to think of himself more highly than he ought to think, but to think soberly, as God has dealt to each one a measure of Faith." (This is the main point in verse two, about renewing your mind, and find the good and acceptable and perfect will of God for your life.) Amen.

Loren L. Johnson

The last words, of Pastor Joel Osteen's reprogramming your mind on page 23, chapter one, (quote): 'Start reprogramming your mind. All through the day, dwell on what your Creators says about you.' 'I am blessed. I am healthy. I'm talented. I'm valuable. My best days are still out in front of me. 'If you'll do this, I believe and declare, every virus is being cleared out, even right now strongholds are coming down. Wrong mind-sets that have held you back for years will no longer have any effect on you. As Joshua was promised, you will have good success and prosper in everything you do. '(end quote).

(II- Cor. 10:3-5) NKJV says:

V3)" For though we walk in the flesh, we do not war according to the flesh. V4) For the weapons of our warfare are not carnal but mighty in God for pulling down strongholds, V5) casting down arguments and every high thing that exalts itself against the knowledge of God, bringing every thought into captivity to the obedience of Christ," (We must be faithful to God till the end of our race.) (V6) says: V6)" and being ready to punish all disobedience when your obedience is fulfilled."

In Joel's book, in chapter 2 says, you need to get rid of labels that people put on you, or yourself, and stop believing and acting on those labels. You are limiting yourself from great potential that God wants, and knows you have.

Joel talked to a high school student who had a label put on her by her counselor who told her she was a 'C' student. The student asked Joel to pray for her final exam to get a 'C'. He asked her why you don't pray to God for 'A's. And she, replied, because my counselor said that's all I'm capable of. She defeated herself, by a label of some of someone else. In chapter 2 page 31, ask the question?

(quote): "Do you need to remove any labels? The label 'Divorced'— I'll never meet anyone new. (In this part, this person put the label on himself)....The label, 'Overweight'— I'll never get in shape. The label, 'Addicted'— I'll never break these bad habits....". end quote

(That's what I thought about my alcohol addiction, and worse, that I would die from it. And I would have, if God didn't allow the enemy to show me how wrong I was in my way of life at the time, and bring me into prison, to correct my way of thinking and in repentance. To get me back on track with God. He uses prison to restore my sanity. Because it was out of control.)

I got into His Word and got Wisdom. He is restoring me daily in His Word, by the Holy Spirit. God loves me enough to Chasten me to the right direction. (As Joel would put it, in another sermon, I bumped into my frame.) (Heb. 12:6) says: NKJV "For whom the lord loves He chastens, and scourges every son whom He receives. "Dear brother's & sister's, let us run the race of faith.

(Heb. 12:1-2) says: NKJV.

"There we also, since we are surrounded by so great a cloud of witnesses, let us lay aside every weight, and the sin which so easily ensnares us, and let us run with endurance the race that is set before us, looking unto Jesus, the Author and finisher of our faith, who for the joy that was set before Him endured the Cross, despising the shame, and has sat down at the right hand of the throne of God." In Joel's book, pages,...31, 32 : quote: "Whatever label you're wearing, you're going to become what that label says. You're giving that thought the power to shape & control how you live."

"This is why some people can't break an addiction. They're wearing the label, 'Addict'. The real battle is taking place in your mind. If you think you're an addict, you will live as an addict. You have to change the label. God says you are free. You are clean, you are healthy. You are whole. Don't go the next twenty years wearing the 'Addict' label. Put on some new labels today." Amen. (end quote)

We are supposed to have the mind of Christ. How do we do that? Jesus is the word. Get the word down into your heart so you won't sin against God. By doing what it says. The Word is Spirit and Life. He wants us walking in His Spirit, and He wants to give us life, and life more abundantly. Amen. —

Having the same mind with one another. Staying calm, and at peace with God and with men. And be humble and associating with humble people. To have one mind and one accord with each other. Let this mind be in you that is in Christ Jesus and set your mind on things above for the glory of God. (The battle is in the mind, and your flesh, is against your spirit.) (Take everything to the Cross, in Christ Jesus.) NKJV (Rom.8:6-8) V6)" For to be carnally minded is death, but to be Spiritually minded is life and peace. V7) Because the carnal mind is enmity against God; for it is not subject to the law of God; nor indeed can be. V8) So then, those who are in the flesh cannot please God. "….

Thank God He prays for us by the Holy Spirit when we don't know how to pray for ourselves or others. NKJV— (Rom. 8:27) says: V27)" Now He who searches the hearts knows what the mind of the Spirit is, because He makes intercession for the Saints according to the will of God. "(God, does give us His Armor if we will put it on in Faith, Amen.)

(Eph. 6:10-20) 'The Armor of God'

V10)" Finally, my brethren, be strong in the Lord and the power of His might. V11) Put on the whole armor of God, that you may be able to stand against the wiles of the devil. V12) For we do not wrestle against flesh and blood, but against principalities, against powers, against the rulers of the darkness of this age, against spiritual hosts of wickedness in heavenly places. V13) Therefore take up the whole armor of God, that you may be able to withstand in the evil day, and having done all, to stand. V14) Stand therefore, having girded your waist with truth, having put on the breastplate of righteousness, V15) and having shod your feet with the preparation of the gospel of peace; V16) above all, taking the shield of faith with which you will be able to quench all the fiery darts of the wicked one. V17) And take the helmet of salvation, and the sword of the Spirit, which is the word of God; V18) praying always with all prayer and supplication in the Spirit, being watchful to this and with all perseverance and supplication for all the saints — V19) And for me, that utterance may be given to me, that I may open my mouth boldly to make known the mystery of the gospel, V20) for which I am an ambassador in chains; that in it I may speak boldly, as I ought to speak."

So, in conclusion, God wants you to have a good positive outlook on yourself and get rid of all those labels that keep you down, bound, restricted, or holding you back. God is on your side; He is for you, not against you. I like the way Joel gave a couple examples on page 32-38. In the second chapter. Joel talked to a drug dealer who labeled himself, that he thought this is all I know how to do, and what I am good at. But Joel 's encouragement was, *pg.32; "If you can sell drugs, you can sell medical supplies. If you can sell drugs, you can sell stocks and bonds. Think about this to sell drugs you have to get the word out. That's advertising. You have to manage your inventory. That's administration. You have to care of your clients. That's customer service. Don't sell yourself short. Remove any labels that are holding you back."

*pg.34 "All God ask of you is to believe. When you believe, all things are possible. When you believe, doors will open that may never have been open otherwise."

*pg.35 The other example: "...was a young lady in the Scripture name Rahab. She was a prostitute. She had made a lot of poor choices in life. I'm sure many people had written her off and considered her a scourge on society. No doubt she wore the labels 'failure, outcast, not valuable, no future.' It's easy to think that God surely wouldn't have any different labels for her to wear; she had made too many mistakes. But God never gives up on us. " ....

*pg.36 "People labeled Rahab as 'Outcast, failure, not usable.' God labeled her as 'Chosen, restored, valuable, a masterpiece.'"

*pg.37 Even adds more, "I'm restored, redeemed, anointed, equipped, and empowered."

*pg.38 "God designed you precisely for the race he laid out for you."

*pg.35 "Get rid of the old labels" ... the washed-up label. Take off the failure, guilty, condemned labels and put on these new labels: redeemed, restored, forgiven, bright future, new beginning."

*pg.38 "You are a masterpiece of God in (Psalm 139:14) says: 'I will praise You, for I am fearfully and wonderfully made...'" (Thank you Lord for making me.) ...

*pg.72 God said in (Isaiah 26:3) "If you will keep your mind fixed on Me, I will keep you in perfect peace."

*pg.63 "Your Creator can see things in you that other people cannot see... God doesn't just see what you are, He sees what you can become."

(God still sees the eagle in you.) (Is. 40:31) NKJV "But those who wait on the Lord shall renew their strength; they shall mount up with wings like eagles, they shall run and not be weary, they shall walk and not faint."

*pg.181 "You are blessed, prosperous, redeemed, forgiven, talented, confident, strong, valuable — a masterpiece. " End.

CHAPTER 68

'BETRAYAL'

For my last chapter, and last dream/vision I had in the past between 1994 to 2001 I'm guessing. This is when I was home sleeping in my recliner. This dream was so vivid and long and I remembered so well. It was like watching a movie, and afterwords, I wrote it all down on paper.

There were four major stars in this dream then. Bruce Willis, Sybil Shepard, Ed Harris, and an actor named Pastorelli. I was in it, as the jail-keeper, at the Sheriff's Office in this little town. I was named Deputy Forest. (In real life, I could do an impression of Tom Hanks of his impression of the character Forrest Gump.) (And in real life, as in the last chapter, I am a supporter of law-enforcement.)

I was in the Kern County Sheriff's Search & Rescue for 4-years in the mid-to-late 1980's (1985-1989). After the divorce, I didn't have the heart for it anymore. But for 10-15 years, off and on when available I had taken tests in the Kern County Sheriff's Department, the Highway Patrol, and Correctional Officer. But wasn't picked. To many applicants, and only a very few openings. The closest I got was Correctional Officer. In the early 1990s when there was more of a demand for them. I did pass the written test, and would have passed the physical, because I was in good shape at the time, and I am again now, as I'm about to get out of prison. But the governing panel of 3 Leaders, two voted yes, and the third, didn't like the way I answered the hypothetical scenario question.)

The dream/vision I experienced, which I called its title: "Betrayal." Which I originally re- wrote around 2000. It was a murder mystery in a small coastal town up in Northern California. Where there are high cliffs and high Sand dunes to the top edge of the cliff.

I wrote it all down, and said, to myself. 'What now?' I originally wrote it down in a script form. And not a book. May be a little backwards now. I got that idea from a Mel Gibson's – four – series VHS tapes, which included a script for 'Lethal Weapon IV'. When I completed it on the computer and made copies.

I said to myself again, I need to send this to Bruce Willis, so he could use it in a future movie. So, I sent a letter to Haley, Idaho first, but no exact address, I figured they knew who they were. It was about the time when Demi Moore and Bruce Willis divorced.

In my letter to him, I was sad for them, that he and her split up. I told my second wife about what I was doing. She thought I was absurd. I wasn't absurd, I just went about it all wrong. She said, you need an agent, or his agent, and go through him or her. I got busy with my floor covering work. And the letter came back to me, and I forgot about it. But it is still a very interesting movie/dream. And now you and I can experience it together. The dream starts off in an aerial view of this little town, but more so on a certain restaurant — bar on the beach cliff, as we are also gazing into the ocean shot. It had a big sign on its roof, with the name Gilley's. (Which was a place that John Brackett [Bruce Willis] would hang out in the bar, and had a cocktail waitress to talk to, and other events happened there as well.)

Then the next scene is Bruce and Sybil's mansion on the cliff side next to the ocean also. A large expansive lot and home with a pool and a huge backyard for entertaining, and pool parties. The two of them have been married for quite some time, but their relationship was not the best. They were noted by their neighbors and friends to fight fairly regularly.

(In real life my second wife and I, after a few drinks would start arguing over the silliest thing. I didn't like arguing; she would say, 'we aren't arguing, we are having a deep discussion.')

Sybil Shepard's character name is Diana. (In real life, in my mind, I put them together, because of a series they once did together called 'Moonlighting'. They had a love – hate relationship. Which is similar to these characters played.) The next scene is them sleeping in bed together. And the reoccurring dream John has been dreaming lately. (In real life his character name was given for all those 'Die Hard' movies I watched. He made as Detective John McClain; It just seemed natural to call him John). (In the dream, he sees himself running down the beach, with this smokey white frame around the shot, as to show that it is in fact a dream he is dreaming. He is like running from something, but he doesn't know what, who, or why? And he heads for the cliffs to climb. As he struggles to make it to the top, with an urgency to get there.) He gets to the top, and there is a 4 to5 foot high white wooden fence there, with 1"x 10"slatted boards. He feels he needs to keep going and get away.

(In real life, I might have dreamt that because, in our backyard on both sides, left and right, the last owner painted the fence. So, I had the option of replacing it or repainting it again. And one side had dogs and we did too. Painting was the easier choice. Once you paint a fence, it is an ongoing maintenance of priming and painting this old wood fence that had 1"x 10"slatted dog-eared finish. Then I thought, since I decided to paint, I'll go ahead and paint the back fence too. The back fence is from another older neighborhood from the 1960s with those redwood grape-stake style fence 6 foot high, and the tops are cut pointy. Since it is raw wood, and with my airless paint-sprayer. I put on a coat of white primer. Before I put on the finish coat of beige paint. Well, while I was painting on the back fence white only of course on my side. The neighbor comes out and says, 'Stop painting my fence!' He said, 'I rebuilt this fence 6" in on my property.' But actually, it is the original fence of the 1960s. He just wanted me to leave the fence alone. Which legally is a common fence, and I can do what I want to do on my side. So, I only got halfway done. Now, I had a white primer fence on the left, and the raw fence on the right. I said to myself, 'I can't leave it like that.? 'So, he went in; I thought, at least finish it to the corner. But he comes back out and says, 'What are you doing? I told you to leave my fence alone!, Why don't you build your own fence?' So, by the time he got back outside, I got 3/4 of the way now. My second wife, before we got together, she had some issues with him also. So, I didn't want to make any more waves. So, I stopped and measured the back width of the yard. And 2 1/2 feet out from the old fence, I built a new 1"x 6"slat-cedar dogeared boards 6 foot high. And a fraction taller, so we don't have to look at his old fence. And it was a dual purpose, a two-fer, because that made way for reconciliation for us and him. He was happy that I built my own fence, and even gave us some persimmons from his tree as a peace-offering.) ......

(The dream continues): He then climbs over the fence and heads for the house, and there is someone spray painting their home. This person is wearing an all-white painter's jumpsuit with a mask and his head wrapped in a white scarf. John cautiously moves forward, and the painter is spraying the back of his home a bright white. And he doesn't know someone is walking up on him. Also, John does not know with all the white snow in the peripheral that he had in his dream, where he is? Or does he know this person? That is, he's focused on the Home and the painter. John gets almost up to the patio cover that goes around the house, where the painter is, and off to the left, is a fountain with a picture of Jesus at the top. The fountain is made out of lava-rock. (In real life when I was a kid, went swimming at one of the neighbor's house who had a lava rock theme with a dark-plaster finish in the pool which made the water look like the deep-blue Ocean.)

This picture was more of a modern-day Jesus rendering, of a dark brown – curly haired and beard. And more of an olive skin Mediterranean Nazarene. Then a blonde straight haired European looking Jesus. This man living there was a religious man, and was using this shrine for idol-worship, a form of godliness, but he was denying its power.

(But in real life, I believe Salvation is given as a gift from God through the working Power (regeneration) of the Holy Spirit, and the grace of God, through faith. Simply having repentance toward God and Faith toward our Lord Jesus Christ. (Acts 20:21b) is all you need for Salvation. Now, after being born again, because of our Savior, and His Spirit living in you, God will help you become more like His only begotten Son Jesus the Christ. As you surrender your life to Him. As He surrendered His life on the Cross for you. So, you may receive eternal life. That you will have your white wedding garment on in His righteousness, not yours.) ... (Back to the dream) ... [As this house painter is about to turn around, John wakes-up startled.] .... He has had this same dream all week. And his wife wakes-up too, and says, 'oh no, not again, that same dream?' He says, 'yeah, I don't know what's going on?'

So, they both start getting ready for the day. The wife gets, some coffee, and goes out with a book to their backyard to sunbathe and read her book, in her one-piece bathing suit by the pool. On a fold- down beach chair. John is also getting ready in their master bathroom before going, then back in the kitchen to get some more coffee, and say good-bye. He has already called his work, to see how his employees were doing earlier. John owns the lumberyard and the hardware store downtown.

Now, he's ready to go to work this mid- morning, and says goodbye to his wife, who he still loves. And even though they have had their spats in the past, they would find a way to reconcile with each other. Though, it was getting harder to do, as time went on. And there were temptations of the opposite sex for each one of them. As the fights and arguments in their relationship continued, so did their struggle to have a foundation of marriage to stay together.

The whole idea of continually forgiving each other was strained. Which brought on hardness of heart. Which escalated strife and discord. He went out to the backyard, as he sees her out there lying on the recliner as she is faced away from John. As he is telling her to have a nice day, and I'll be back about four to 5 o'clock. But she is not responding back to him. He says goodbye again, and nothing. So, he walks closer, and says, 'OK, what's bothering you now?' And to his shocking surprise, she has been shot, once in the heart and the other in the head. And since she just went out, he's thinking someone just entered the backyard, used a silencer on her, and killed her. That person dropped the gun and fled the yard, or did they?

So, he looks up, looks around to see if the killer is still close by. And he first hears bushes swishing and sees a glimpse of the bush's movement at the back gate, the only gate that is used to have access to the cliff area for maintenance and clearance for the property. But, because of the erosion, the cliff comes right up to the chain-link fence. Which is only 3 to 4 feet high, but the whole back fence and side, has bushes lined up against them 7-8 feet tall above them. So, John looks down at his wife again with compassion for her, and in discuss and anger for the person who killed her. He looks over at the gun, grabs it, and runs to the back gate, hoping to find the killer who just shot his wife. But instead find no one, looks over the chain-link gate, looks down, looks left, looks right, looks at the beach and just what he can see from the Cliffside of his property. Which was no one, not a person in sight, and no one below, in the Cliffs crevices. He was baffled, as he stood there a moment. He hears someone trying to get in the side gate. So, he heads for the other gate, with the gun in hand. The gate was pad-locked, but the persons on the other side cut it, and was about to enter.

(Only the gardener and his wife had the other keys to open it, and it's not gardening day.) John, not knowing who it was, raises the killer's gun toward the side gate, to the back yard entrance. The gate opens, and the Sheriff and two deputies behind him storm in the back yard. As they all look his direction and see him, and tell him, "Freeze, drop it!" And once John saw it was the Sheriff, he was relieved and dropped the gun, and said, "I'm glad you're here, but he's getting away, he must be on the beach somewhere?" And at the same time, they're telling him, "Get down, get down, get down, on your knees, hands behind your head." Now, after John gets down on his knees, and the deputy grabs one hand and cuffs it, then grabs the second, and locks it behind John 's back. The Sheriff, says, "Now what did you say John? the bad man went that way." (As he points toward the Ocean). "Yes," "I didn't shoot her," replied John. I I think he's down there, somewhere on the beach now. So, just for curiosity's sake, the Sheriff motions to the other deputy to go check it out.

The deputy goes to the back gate and sees nothing, as before, for miles both-ways, nothing. The deputy says to the Sheriff (which is played by Ed

Harris) there's no one in sight, or on the beach. Then John says, "maybe he's in the water?" The deputy turns again and looks, and then turns back and shakes his head 'no' to the Sheriff.

The Sheriff, knows John, and knows of his business, which has been established for many years in this town. He's also been called out to his loud pool parties that the neighbors had reported before in the past. And of his wife and him would get into it and yell loud enough to disturb the neighbors.

The Sheriff says to him, "This doesn't look too good for you John". As the Sheriff looks over at the lifeless body of his wife, (which is played by Sybil Shepard). We're here, right after you shoot your wife with the gun still in your hand, and you have the gall to say, "I didn't do it." "But, Sheriff, I didn't do it," John says. The Sheriff says, "Tell it to the judge." Take him back to the office, and lock him up, and get on the radio and call the corner to the one deputy. And tells the other deputy, cordon off the area with yellow-tape, and interview the neighbors, if they have anything add.

(So, in real life, as it happened to John Brackett; things, or events that happened to people are not always what they seem to be.) (Just like my second wife and I, didn't always see eye to eye on everything. And we got off track sometimes, but we never wanted to physically hurt one another. And we didn't for 19 years. But unfortunately, I was over medicated myself during a time I was in physical nerve pain from my neck injury. So, I had spine surgery going through the face of my throat, to put in a titanium plate and six titanium screws to stabilize my vertebrae's and stop the pinching pain. And thank God it was successful. But the end result I am an alcoholic [A recovering Alcoholic now as typing this, I have 9-years 4-months and 6-days sobriety thank God], and I was under the influence of at least a quart of 80 proof Vodka, and I was under duress, and depression. I hurt my wife, and didn't mean too, and wanted to take it back, as soon as I realize what I just did in a reactionary way. And then got my blood pressure so high, I blacked out memory and time and hurt her some more, thinking in the drunken-dream state I was in, was doing something merciful for her.) (I even asked to be on the local TV station, while incarcerated. They came to the Lerdo Prison Facility. The main thing I wanted to say to the people of Bakersfield; that this was not a hate crime, I love my wife. There was no premeditation, or planning, no malice or hate, no motive or real good reason for it.) (The 15-minute Interview; but they only use 10 seconds of me all choked up and made me look bad.) Is that their job? Mission accomplished. It was more of a reactionary, drunken state of not being able to control myself or my addictive behavior. It took prison, repenting to God in reconciliation, and the right relationship with Him again.

Then started the rehabilitation process through the 12-Steps Celebrate Recovery Program they offered freely. I was not forced or put there because of my crime. I wanted to be there in that class, to get well and show my friends and family, I can recover with God's help. Not on my own, amen. And there was no alternative motive back then in 2015–16, for milestone credits for less-time served. It was clearly to get well, to start a new fresh life again by the grace of God and His loving mercy.)

The next scene is John in jail, and him asking for his lawyer. Deputy Forest (Loren) as he is locking him in says, "yeah, yeah, you'll get your phone call alright." Then after a little time went by, one of his three closest friends and business partners, comes down to the Sheriff's office and tries to console John. (They had a city Corp. – meaning 4-businesses partnered up and got together.)

That is four-businesses down-town including John 's Hardware Store and his lumberyard behind it. One has a gift shop, and the owner is Mac; second is Fred, who runs his own clothing apparel shop. And the last one is an Art Gallery, with different artisans of glass, metal, and a painting. And the owners name is Frank (which is Pastorelli). And John was probably closer to Frank then the other two businessmen, because they are neighbors, and exchange greetings in the morning as they head-off to work. So, Frank comes down to the jail, and talks to John, and says, "I heard what happened, and they took you away." "What did you do?" John replied, "I didn't do anything." Frank says, "I saw the coroner down on our street. Is your wife, Ok?" "No," John replies, "someone shot her two times!" "Oh, I'm sorry John, what can I do to help?" replied Frank. John says, "get a hold of my lawyer ASAP." (John has a personal lawyer, besides his corporate lawyers.) John continues, "you know Bill, talk to him, and get him down here." " I need to clear myself of this mess," John replied. (Now before Bill shows up and they can figure out a strategy.)

The Sheriff comes in and says, "So, your innocent huh," and John speaks up and says, "Sheriff, why were you at my place this morning, anyway?" And he says, "because we got an anonymous tip this morning, that you and your wife were yelling at each other again in your backyard." "And, I wasn't surprised, so we checked it out. And there you were, gun in hand. And your wife dead in the lounge-chair, case closed, it's a done deal." "The only thing that baffles me, is that after questioning all your neighbors including you Frank. No one saw or heard anything. Is that right Frank?" (As he turns and looks his way.) ... "Yes, that's right, I was home this week doing some remodeling and didn't hear or see anyone, out of the ordinary." "Maybe it's one of the neighbors who still want to be invited to one of their parties," Frank added. So, the Sheriff walks away, and tells Forest, under his voice or breath. Not to speak too loudly, he says, "I want you to get a hold of the phone company records and backtrace that call. And let me know, as soon as you can, the ID on that caller. Then Forest replies, he said, "It might take some time depending on the type and source of the communication the person used, and the fact that their phone was blocked on the ID caller number, who called in."

Then Frank says, "Goodbye John, I'll call Bill for you, and get him down here." John says, "you're a good friend, thank you, I'll talk to you later." Now, Frank leaves the Sheriff's Office, and calls Bill on his cell phone, (a flip phone older dated back a few years ago). And tells him, "Hello Bill (the Lawyer), this is Frank, John's friend from the business group downtown. John needs your help now; Bill, he is at the sheriff's office in custody." Bill says, "what are the charges?" "The sheriff didn't say, but I would imagine, it would be first-degree murder. He shot his wife two times," Frank replied. Bill says, "All right then, I'll get there as soon as I can." (Frank hangs-up as he is driving downtown to Main Street. Which is only blocks away and sees his two other business partners in the street talking.)

(He goes and parks as close as he can to them.) Frank gets out, and they start their bantering, and saying, "I told you so, I knew something was going to happen like this," as Fred is talking to Mac, (and Frank is walking up on them hearing what they just said.) Frank sticks up for John and says, "I just talked to John at the Sheriff's Office; He said, 'he didn't do it.'" And Mac speaks up, "you believe that?" Frank says, "I don't know? I want to believe it." Then Mac replies, "you remember, you've seen them at their pool parties. One accusing the other of adultery."

(Flash Back)

(This is a scene in their backyard with a good 30–40 people having fun, and laughing, and talking, and splashing, in the pool. Drinking and making merry of the evening.)

Then a comment was made by John, "You should be a better tennis player by now, as much time as you've spent (money & time) in lessons!!" (As John shouts out, as he is standing near the pool, to his wife). (As everyone is still having a good time and overlooking their behavior and raised voices. But yet knowing there's something not right with them?) Then she (Diana his wife) responds with, "What about you and your friend, Jill, at Gilley's," (restaurant and bar), (with the same kind of tone.); end flash back.

Then Frank says, "Yea, your right Mac, there was a problem. But we have to be supportive to him regardless. He told me to take care of all his business affairs while he is in jail." (Even Tho we didn't hear him tell him that, but it could have been from a previous agreement they made, if something great, or sickness happened to one of them.) Then he said, "I have to get back to the Gallery," Frank replied. Fred says, "I got to go too. See ya, Mac, Frank." (They all dispersed).

Now, Bill showed up at the Sheriff's office. He's parking with a nice car, and walking in; (now, the next scene is him walking in the cell area.) John pop's up and says, "Oh, I'm glad to see you're here!" Bill replies, "whatever you've done, don't say anymore." John says, "I didn't do it, can you get me out of here? so I can prove my innocence." Bill says, "It doesn't look good for you, but we go back a long way. I'll talk to the judge, and see if there's bail at all? And I'll let you know. I'll even put up my house as collateral for you John, but don't you run. Don't scam me, or I will make them throw the book at you." John says, "thank you, you won't regret it." Bill looks over at Forrest (Deputy Sheriff) and says, "open this up, I want to talk to my client in private." (Forrest gets up and unlocks the door to the cell and Bill goes in, and they sit down together. Forest closes it, and locks it, and walks away and sits down where he was.) (The scene changes to John being in the cell a while in different positions as time moved on, hours, days, weeks?) The Sheriff comes in and says, "well John you made bail, the judge see something I don't?" (John gets out and walks to the hardware store. To see if his manager is running everything smoothly while he has been gone from work, and to get a ride home.)

(Being that it is a small town, everyone in town knows John was arrested for murder. He is getting looks from the town people, as he is walking along.) He enters the front of the store, and everyone stops and turns; then not to gawk with a stare, they all turn back and do what they were doing. The manager comes up to him, and says, "we are glad to see you. But we are also surprised to see you too?" John says, "I need to prove my innocence. How is everything been going?" "We are doing fine, business is still good," replies Tom the Manager. He said, "your friend Frank has been helping with the books while you've been in jail. He said it was all right with you, is that right?" "Ah, Ya, It's ok. There's no problem, thank you for your excellent service." "Is Frank here now?" John replied, and Tom says "No".

John says, "Who can you spare right now? so I can go back home and get my car." Tom says, Francine; (as he waved her over to them.) As she is walking toward them, he says, "can you give the boss a ride home?" She says, "yes, I'm parked down the street at the big parking lot, as you requested all the employees to do." John says, "good, I'll meet you there." She drops him off, and he says, "thanks," as he wave's good bye, at his home. Now, John is in front of his house, but without his keys to get in, because of the subsequent arrest unexpectedly. He didn't have away in yet. But he did have a hide-a-key under a rock in the garden. John gets in and gets his big set of keys in the dish by the door. Then goes back to take a shower and cleans up. Re-dresses himself and takes a drive, to think and figure out who set him up? He ends up over at Gilley's to think and get a drink. He says to the bartender, "A double bourbon, and a beer on the side." As he is sitting at the bar, Jill (his friend the waitress) comes over and says, "I'm sorry about your wife, you must be devastated." John says, "I am, and I didn't do it. But now, I have to figure out who did, before my trial date." John says, "thank you for being there all those times when my wife and I had arguments."

Then John leaves, and heads for Highway <1> to clear his head. And time to grieve some, as he thinks back. (Flashback) [Of the two of them together, happy sitting close next to each other, having some champagne, watching the sunset.]

Then he was awakened of this Day-Dream memory as someone is trying to pass or something and blows his horn. (Pushing John 's car toward the Cliffs edge.) (John is in a Mercedes convertible, and the other car is a large sedan with tinted windows.) John maneuvers not hitting an oncoming car, and crosses over the line and ends up spinning out of control in a dirt-gravel turn-out on the ocean side cliffs. Then that car is gone and keeps driving North up the coast. So, John gathers himself together and gets back on the road back to town. He's driving normal, and sees in his rearview mirror, a car coming pretty fast, and it looks like the same car that pushed him off the road. So, now he speeds up, and sees it is the car that was reckless. So, right then he gets on his cell phone and calls the Sheriff's office-dispatch. And they answer, "Sheriff's office how can I help you?" John says, "There's a maniac trying to run me off the road!!" What is your name? "John Brackett!!" He replied. "What is your location?", "going south on Highway one, just before town", he replied. Then he says, "can you patch me into the Sheriff?" "Yes, I can, he's on patrol right now", she replied. Now, the Sheriff (Ted) comes on the phone. "Yes, who is it?" John replies, "It's John Brackett!" Then Ted responds, "I thought you were supposed to stay out of trouble until the trial?" John responds, "look Sheriff, I didn't kill my wife; but now, someone is trying to kill me. He ran me off the road once." "Are you sure you didn't provoke that person?" "Yes, I'm sure! I didn't, and he's on my tail right now," John replied. Ted asks, "where are you right now?" "I am back in town heading for Gilley's."

John pulls into Gilley's parking lot, and John is still on the phone with the Sheriff. Ted says, "hang on I'm almost there." John says, "OK", and hangs up. He gets out of the car and goes inside. He knows they have a back terrace that leads to the beach. (In real life, some restaurants have access to the beach by a set of stairs, but in this dream, there were large sand dunes.) John runs through the restaurant and toward the Terrace. Jill, sees John comes in and says, "what's going on!?"He says, "someone is after me," then says, "go in the bar, you didn't see me!" As John heads for the patio, the person who was chasing him, comes in the restaurant. He (being Todd, the tennis coach for John's wife) see's John on the patio. John sees through the window who it is, and he's got a hate in his eyes for him. And he shows him he's got a gun. (Like a 38 special) Now, Jill, sees that too, and breaks away from John's site. And does go into the bar and calls the Sheriff's office.

Dispatch gets the distressing call about the man with a gun chasing John Brackett. Then, it was put out on the air for a code-3 lights and siren respond to Gilley's restaurant. (As Jill stays on the line and describes the gunman in more detail as follow up information is given to the officers.) (In real life the name of the restaurant-bar, was probably in my mind, because I like country music. And I heard there is such a place in Texas. Where Mickey Gilley— sings.)

(We also have such a place called the 'Crystal Palace,' in Bakersfield, California, which the founder is the Country Star, Buck Owens. It also has a stage for live music. That happens on Friday and Saturday nights before Buck Owens passed away. But his son continues the festive music on Friday and Saturday night. And keep the tradition going, also live on the radio 107.1 FM. Buddy Allen comes all the way from Arizona to entertain us.)

Now, the Sheriff was already in-route to Gilley's restaurant, and the Sheriff gets on the radio, and says to his deputies; "I am in the parking lot, and I want you guys to cordon off the area, let no one in or out, until we get a proper back up, and know who this gunman is? He may take hostages. Then Forrest gets on channel 2, from the Sheriff's office. He says, "Sheriff, this is Forrest", then the Sheriff answer's, "What is it, Forrest?" He says, "I have that Information you wanted. "Ted says, "What is it?" Forrest says, "I don't have the ID for the caller? But I do have the GPS of where the call came from, which Sir, could tell you one of the same." As Forrest gives the Chief the Information.

More Information comes over the Main Channel, dispatch says; The (RP)- (Reporting Party), (Which was Jill, also ID the gunman as Todd Bryant, tall, white, slender-build, 175 lbs., male, 6' 1", armed with a handgun, and extremely dangerous. He is wearing white shorts, striped shirt, and tennis shoes.)

(The scene changes to John jumping over the railing to the sand below; to get away from Todd who is chasing him. Todd is not far behind him, as John is hiding behind pillars and Sand dunes. Todd thinks he went down closer to the water or beach, but actually John got a little advantage on him. As Todd is looking down, for him he is talking to John, he knows he close, and he can hear him. He says, "John, why did you kill Diana? I love her! I know you don't love her, but I do. You could have just divorced her."

(Flash Back)

[It's Diana and Todd, doing lessons together on the court, being close and Intimate. Then them in a hotel room, having sexual relations, but not revealing too much, but gives the idea, that's what they did.] As Todd is speaking, and thinking of Diana, and takes his focus off killing John for the moment. John doesn't say anything, not to give his position away. John is on the hill above Todd. And John climbs to the top and jumps on Todd, grabbing the gun away from him as the two are tumbling down the hill. Now, the two are on the beach, John throws the gun in the Ocean. But not far enough that Todd can't find it. John tries to reason with Todd, "I didn't shoot Diana," as he says. Todd said, "yeah, like I'm goanna to believe that?" "I do love her, we just needed some marriage counseling," John replied. Todd went after John and they were fighting, "I don't believe you!" After some exchanging blows. Todd went for the gun, in the Ocean, and John headed down the beach.

Back in the Restaurant, the Sheriff is entering the entrance, and Jill runs to him, pointing to the patio. They both went that way. The Sheriff came in with his deputy and he's telling him, "Get all these people out of here for their safety's sake." Then the Sheriff goes out on the patio and sees them out in the open, and John runs away South down the beach. And Todd is in the ocean, trying to find the gun.

The Sheriff runs back inside, and goes toward the front door, and tells the deputy, "Get your back-up and get down there on the beach and arrest Todd. I'm going after John; I think I know where he's headed. There's an access to homes down the way." (The Sheriff leaves, but there is a plan in place.) Back to Todd in the Ocean, he finds the gun, and starts running down the beach. Being that Todd is in better shape and younger; Todd is gaining on John. He then fires the weapon, once, then twice. No, not close enough, Todd is thinking. Then John must be a quarter to a half mile down the beach when he sees his home up on the cliff. He's looking for a way up and doesn't see it, it is too steep with multi-crevices. (the crevices are eroded dirt and rock). He is also heading for those peninsulas of protruding rock formations that protrudes out from the Cliffs, trying not to be a target. Todd sees John heading for cover and shoots two-more times. Missing again but getting closer. So, instead of John climbing behind his house, he tries to go up, at the house next-door where there is better footing, and a partial set of wooden stairs, that hasn't been washed away from the elements and the Ocean.

John is climbing and making headway to the top, but that also exposes him to be in the open and Todd has two more bullets. Todd sees him, in Todd's pain and passion for Diana, he fires again. This time he wounds John in his side as a flesh wound. Then Todd sees he's hurt, and now has more of an advantage and starts climbing to get closer to finish him off, with his last shot. While John realizes this too. He makes a move towards the back gate, but it is locked. The white wooden fence is just low-enough for John to climb over. As John is climbing, Todd looks up and sees his revenge leaving, and raises his arm and fires his last shot. (He wasn't in a good position to fire as he was climbing but didn't have any more time.)

For John was almost over. When Todd fired his last shot and hits the wood near John 's face, as he turns away and it just misses him.

John is over the fence and sees a man spray painting the back of his home white. (Just like in the reoccurring dream, as he then glances back to the white fence with the big slats.) He starts walking forward and looks to his left and sees this lava fountain with the picture of Jesus. Then moves closer; he doesn't know if this is really his friend and neighbor, or is it a hired painter? Now, the painter realizes someone is walking up on him. And he turns around, and with a surprised look, says, "what are you doing here John?" (As the airless sprayer motor stops from knocking, and he cuts the power, so he can hear him.)

"I need you to call the Sheriff, Todd is after me with a gun, to kill me." Frank says, "OK, John, let me go inside and I'll get my phone." As John is standing there, he looks over at his property, since he has never been in Frank's backyard before. (As he moves a little closer) And notices something at the corner of the chain-link fence. Where his bushes are all lined up against John and Frank's property. There's a string through the fence which looks odd. (Then John remembers a [flashback] of the day his wife was shot and the bushes that moved to catch his attention as someone who was getting away. Or supposedly getting away.)

Then the scene in the house where you see Frank pick-up the cellphone, but not calling for help, but puts it in his left side pocket jacket, and grabs a gun in the drawer. And put the small stub nose .38 or .357 in his other pocket, getting ready for whatever. Maybe Plan 'B'. John was going to take a closer look at the string, and also notices he sees all the way to the pool area, through the fence. When Todd starts climbing over the fence. John stops, sees him, and runs into the house. Also, there is a scene of the deputies running down the beach and looking up at Todd climbing over the fence.

The two deputies are both out of breath, when they see Todd; they both look at each other, "go ahead," one of them says, and the other says, "no you go, I'll back you up." Then back to the house scene, where John is starting to be suspicious of Frank, and also remembers how he volunteered to help with John 's bookkeeping and accounting. So, John confronts Frank; like John knows the truth already but doesn't. He wants Frank to fess-up to the crime. John says to Frank, "why did you kill my wife?" John knows he had to be blunt with him, and he is fishing for the truth. John also knows, Todd is about to come in the back door. So, as John is conversing with Frank, and Todd hears him say, "why did you kill my wife, Frank?" He heard the whole thing. Todd stops and listens, from the kitchen. As the two of them talk in the living room. Also, since he is out of bullets. It literally stopped Todd in his tracks, but John needed something like that to throw Todd's attention to someone else. Not that John was wanting to throw his best friend under the bus, but to find out the truth. Frank, denies it at first, and says, "You heard me tell the Sheriff, I was home remodeling and didn't hear or see anything." John replies, "yeah, what about that string at the corner of the yard? That was there to shake the bushes, so I would think someone was getting away? Very clever Frank." Frank responds with, "you mean that's string that blew on our property's?

(Now, a flashback of Frank and a ball of string in his pocket. Slowly and carefully, stepping on the curb-footing, and grabbing the chain-link fence, slowly making his way from his property to John's back gate, at a very early time in the morning. Frank also knows John and Diana's Master Bedroom is on the South side facing his property, so no one is looking. He gets there and finds a good branch that moves easy. And conceals the string through the inside of the bushes so no one could see it in John's yard.) (Frank, knows Diana goes out in the morning every day and reads with her coffee, as he has been watching her, for some time.) (And this morning he waits for her to come out, and is watching the front of the house, to make sure John isn't gone yet either. Frank, has to time this, the best he can.) (Now, he makes the phone call with his blocked number, on his throw-away cell phone to the Sheriff's Office.) And reports a disturbance of them yelling in their back yard and disguises his voice and hangs-up. So, while the Sheriff is on the way. Frank sets up a stepladder where he can come and go. Then goes in the yard with his silencer gun and no prints on it. Walk's right-up to her and shoots her in the heart first, then second in the head. Then hurries back before John says good-bye and goes to work. He's back waiting. Frank hears the Sheriff drive-up. Plan 'A', if they come and want to talk to the both of them, it's not going to go well for John; Plan 'B', if Frank push John to pick-up the gun, it would probably seal the deal. And incriminate John in the process.) (It just so happens that John was leaving and saying good-bye to his wife at the same time the Sheriff was at his front door with his Deputies.)

(There was no answer, and they headed for the side gate. John was shocked and saw his wife lying there. Then heard and saw bushes moved and he grabbed the gun, as an instinct reaction, and investigated, but no one was there? Now, gun in hand, and the Sheriff coming in the side gate. It went just as has Frank planned it.) (Showing an outside scene where the Sheriff is at John's property looking for him and can't get in, so the deputy goes and gets the lock cutters to open the side gate.)

(Back to Frank's living room)

John is still fishing for information, and says, "I called the hardware store and asked about all your transactions you made it, didn't look good." (Even though he didn't call, he wanted to see how he would respond. And if John was wrong, he would always just apologize to his friend.)

Then Frank speaks-up, it looks like you know more then you should. John says, "what do you mean Frank, if you needed money, you could have just asked me for it?"

Frank says, "I got into deep, I needed a lot of money now. And I thought I was doing you a favor by getting rid of your wife." "And what, sending me to prison for years, that's your plan," John replied. "I'm sorry John. I've got a coke and gambling addiction problem." "I thought that was in your past and you were done with that," John replied. "I did too," Frank said. (Then Todd couldn't wait in the wings any longer.)

Todd comes in the living room where the two were talking with his gun in hand. "So, you're the one, you deserve to die, "Todd says. And fires, click – click – click. (Todd reacted in the heat of the moment and didn't know or did remember that he was out of bullets.) Then Frank pulls out his gun and fires at Todd in the chest and kills him, and down he goes. Then Frank says, "No, you do." John says, "now what are you going to do?" Frank said, "you always have to have a Plan 'B'. I was saving you from him, in self-defense, but unfortunately you were shot first by him. And I am the hero."

(The Sheriff, makes his way to Frank's house next after John's and not just for John, he has questions for Frank because that's the location of the GPS coordinates for the mystery caller.)

(Frank's living room, has a very Large Picture Window 8'x5'.)

(In real life, I had a window put in for my wife's aunt's room who was living with us a while. She could look out and see the pretty flowers we put in, and the birdfeeder close by; originally that was for my wife's mother who lived with us for time. Plus, to watch our three-greyhounds run in our big-backyard.) Frank raises his gun and is about to fire. When the Sheriff shoots Frank, and shoots through the window. It's deflected a bit, but hits Frank in the shoulder. Frank drops the gun, and John moves forward and pushes him out of the way and gets the gun.

John goes to the front door and opens it for the Sheriff. The Sheriff looks at John, and says, "Here, let me have that John, you have a bad habit of picking up guns that don't belong to you." John goes out with the Sheriff and a deputy goes in and handcuffs Frank. The Sheriff tells John, once we found out the location on the mystery caller, we needed more evidence, and motive for what Frank did. Starting with his withdrawal from your business downtown, and the shady people he was dealing with. John said, "I'm glad you finally believe me, and thank you for saving my life just now. He was about to shoot me. He shot Todd, in cold blood, and was going to call it self-defense. Then I was a loose end, and supposedly shot by Todd. And he was the hero.

(Frank was not shot that bad, that he needed an ambulance, they put him in the squad car, and was going to drive him down to the hospital, personally. John is looking at Frank in the car. Frank is looking out at John and says, I'm sorry John, but John couldn't hear him, but could read his lips and actions. So, John says, I forgive you. And they drive away down the street. The End

(Then camera pans shot from a helicopter from street level, to panning back of home and cliff side and the neighborhood, then the Ocean and at the same time running credits.)

'Cast'

John Brackett .... Bruce Willis
Diana Brackett.......... Sybil Shepherd
Ted (Sheriff)................ Ed Harris
Frank (Art shop) .... Robert Pastorelli
Forest (Deputy).........Loren Johnson
Bill (Lawyer)....................................
Fred (Clothes shop) ....
Mac (Gift shop) ....
Tom (Manager)..................................
Todd (Tennis coach) ....
Jill (Waitress)....................................
Francine (employee)..........................
Deputy One (younger).......................
Deputy Two (older)...........................
Dispatch voice (woman)....................

CLOSING THOUGHTS & SCRIPTURE

As I exit prison; now having been down 9-years and 85 days since the unfortunate drunken situation, where I committed a crime, and hurt my second wife, or ex-wife as I should say now. It was not planned or premeditated. I just reacted to her advancements to me, in my humbled-duress position on the floor, in fear as if getting scolded as a little child.

I remember the beginning and the end, but the rest is a blur, or no memory of what took place. I was not in my right mind at the time of the altercation. (Alcohol Abuse) ....

But, since what I have learned, is priceless. God has given me a second chance, to live right for Him. I plan to make the best of it, for the glory of God.

To walk by Faith; to take up my Cross daily; to deny myself; that Christ may live through me; by the power of the Holy Spirit, within me.

'Christian Liberty'

(Galatians 5:1); V1)" Stand fast therefore in the liberty by which Christ has made us free, and do not be entangled again with a yoke of bondage. " 'Stay out & don't come back'

*KJV-JSM. (Matthew 26:41) quote: V41)"Watch and pray, that you enter not into temptation (a warning of the temptation that was about to come upon them – the temptation to forsake Him.): the spirit (spirit of man) indeed is willing, but the flesh is weak (this battle can be won only by our faith being placed exclusively in Christ and His Cross, which then gives the Holy Spirit latitude to work within our lives) [Rom.6:3-14; 8:1-2,11]. End quote.

'Dead to sin, Alive to God' (Rom. 6:3-14) NKJV V3)" Or do you not know that as many of us as were baptized into Christ Jesus were baptized into His death? V4) Therefore we were buried with Him through baptism into death, that just as Christ was raised from the dead by the glory of the Father, even so we also should walk in newness of life." V5)" For if we have been united together in the likeness of His death, certainly we also shall be in the likeness of His resurrection, V6) knowing this, that our old man was crucified with Him, that the body of sin might be done away with, that we should no longer be slaves of sin. V7) For he who has died has been freed from sin. V8) Now if we died with Christ, we believe that we shall also live with Him, V9) knowing that Christ, having been raised from the dead, dies no more. Death no longer has dominion over Him. V10) For the death that He died, He died to sin once for all; but the life that He lives, He lives to God." V11)" Likewise you also, reckon yourselves to be dead indeed to sin, but alive to God in Christ Jesus our Lord. V12) Therefore do not let sin reign in your mortal body, that you should obey it in its lust. V13) And do not present your members as instruments of unrighteousness to sin, but present yourselves to God as being alive from the dead, and your members as instruments of righteousness to God. V14) For sin shall not have dominion over you, for you are not under law but under grace."

(Romans 8:1,2,11) NKJV V1)" There is therefore now no condemnation to those who are in Christ Jesus, who do not walk according to the flesh, but according to the Spirit. V2) For the law of the Spirit of life in Christ Jesus has made me free from the law of sin and death." V11)" But if the Spirit of Him who raised Jesus from the dead dwells in you, He who raised Christ from the dead will also give life to your mortal bodies through His Spirit who dwells in you."

'Glorify God in Body & Spirit'

(I-Cor. 6:12) NKJV

V12)" All things are lawful for me, but all things are not helpful. All things are lawful for me, but I will not be brought under the power of any."

* (I-Cor. 6:12) (KJV/ JSM)

V12)" All things are Lawful unto me (refers to the fact that Christianity is not a religion which consists of rules, etc.), but all things are not expedient (not profitable): all things are Lawful for me, but I will not be brought under the power of any (Grace does not give a license to sin, but rather liberty to live a Holy Life).

'Walk in Wisdom'

(Ephesians 5:15-21) NKJV

V15)" See then that you walk circumspectly, (means carefully) not as fools but as wise, V16) redeeming the time, because the days are evil. V17) Therefore do not be unwise, but understand what the will of the Lord is. V18) And do not be drunk with wine, in which is dissipation; (expend wastefully) but be filled with the Spirit, V19) speaking to one another in psalms and hymns and spiritual songs, singing and making melody in your heart to the Lord, V20) giving thanks always for all things to God the Father in the name of our Lord Jesus Christ, V21) submitting to one another in the fear of God."

* (Ephesians 5:15-21) (KJV/JSM)

V15)" See then that you walk circumspectly (carefully taking heed), not as fools (a person who doesn't avail himself of all Christ has to offer is a fool), but be as wise (draw close to the Lord), V16) Redeeming the time (take advantage of the opportunities that present themselves), because the days are evil. (The Cross must be our Foundation. Only then can we overcome the "evil," and carry out that which the Lord has called us to do.) V17) Wherefore be ye not unwise (time is precious because God has given us only a few short days to make choices that will bring Eternal consequences), but understanding what the will of the Lord is. (We can do this if we look exclusively to Christ and the Cross.) V18) And be not drunk with wine (speaks of being controlled by alcoholic beverage, which Paul desires to use as an example), wherein is excess; but be filled with the Spirit (being controlled by the Spirit constantly, moment by moment) ; V19) Speaking to yourselves in Psalms and Hymns and Spiritual Songs (refers to worship as it regards songs and singing), singing and making melody in your heart to the Lord (places the approval of the Holy Spirit on the same form of music and styles of worship as were begun in the Old Testament); V20) Giving thanks always for all things unto God and the

Father (all things which come from God) in the Name of our Lord Jesus Christ (proclaims in this Verse the Source of all Blessings, and the means by which these Blessings have come upon the human race as well); V21) Submitting yourselves one to another (this tells us that proper spiritual submission is always horizontal and never vertical as it refers to Believers, meaning that we submit one to another) in the fear of God (meaning that all vertical submission must be to God Alone, never to man)."

'Songs of Joy'

A song came to me in a Christian Spanish Worship Service, words came to me, and I started writing them down. The next day I asked one of the worship leaders what music chords he used. On that particular song. And in two days the song was done, and I wanted to share it with you today. And dedicate it to my Dad who passed away last year when this was written:

Lorenz G. Johnson

4-8-22 to 11-7-20

He was 98 years old.

(He was one of the last B-24 pilots of World War II. He was honored greatly at his funeral.)

(song cont.)

'I Am Free'

V1). I am free, oh-oh Lord, I am free, indeed oh-oh Lord, your all I need. Holy and Righteous are You Lord, You are King of all Creation.

Chorus: Glory to you Lord,
Glory to you Lord.

V2). Thank you, for Your Mercy, and Love.
There's nothing more I can say, except,
Thank you, for sending Your Dove.
And showing me Your Way.

Bridge:

Yes, Lord, I am free, oh-oh Lord,
Yes Lord, I am free, your all I need.
(2x)
If the Son shall set you free, you will be free indeed.

End:

Alleluia; Alleluia; Alleluia.

The End

'Comments of the book'

In a couple of lines, to a paragraph, what you thought of "All my Hope III "?

Was it entertaining? Did you get blessed? Was there something intriguing or insightful. In general, could you relate or have any revelations?

"Very helpful and insightful as well as entertaining. Even though we look at the world through different eyes, this book helped me realize we all are not that different after all. We may seem to go through different trials and tribulations but in the end, they are all similar."

Luis Martinez

2-19-22

This is a book of dreams and understanding of dreams. There are interpretation of dreams.

Real life experiences and interesting fiction in the dreams.

There are excerpts of my prison experience, in reading books, articles, magazines, and events, that I made note of in my life behind bars, '9 years and 85 days.'

Loren L Johnson

Printed in the United States
by Baker & Taylor Publisher Services